The Economic Philosophy of the Internet of Things

To properly understand the nature of the digital economy we need to investigate the phenomenon of a "ubiquitous computing system" (UCS). As defined by Robin Milner, this notion implies the following characteristics: (i) it will continually make decisions hitherto made by us; (ii) it will be vast, maybe 100 times today's systems; (iii) it must continually adapt, on-line, to new requirements; and (iv) individual UCSs will interact with one another. This book argues that neoclassical approaches to modelling economic behaviour based on optimal control by "representative-agents" are ill-suited to a world typified by concurrency, decentralized control, and interaction. To this end, it argues for the development of new, process-based approaches to analysis, modelling, and simulation.

The book provides the context—both philosophical and mathematical—for the construction and application of new, rigorous, and meaningful analytical tools. In terms of social theory, it adopts a Post-Cognitivist approach, the elements of which include the nature philosophy of Schelling, Marx's critique of political economy, Peircean Pragmatism, Whitehead's process philosophy, and Merleau-Ponty's phenomenology of the flesh, along with cognitive scientific notions of embodied cognition and neural Darwinism, as well as more questionable notions of artificial intelligence that are encompassed by the rubric of "perception-and-action-without-intelligence".

James Juniper is a lecturer at the University of Newcastle, NSW, Australia.

Routledge Studies in the Economics of Innovation

The Routledge Studies in the Economics of Innovation series is our home for comprehensive yet accessible texts on the current thinking in the field. These cutting-edge, upper-level scholarly studies and edited collections bring together robust theories from a wide range of individual disciplines and provide in-depth studies of existing and emerging approaches to innovation, and the implications of such for the global economy.

Automation, Innovation and Economic Crisis
Surviving the Fourth Industrial Revolution
Jon-Arild Johannessen

The Economic Philosophy of the Internet of Things
James Juniper

For more information about this series, please visit: www.routledge.com/ Routledge-Studies-in-the-Economics-of-Innovation/book-series/ECONINN

The Economic Philosophy of the Internet of Things

James Juniper

Routledge
Taylor & Francis Group

LONDON AND NEW YORK

First published 2018
by Routledge

2 Park Square, Milton Park, Abingdon, Oxfordshire OX14 4RN
52 Vanderbilt Avenue, New York, NY 10017

Routledge is an imprint of the Taylor & Francis Group, an informa business

First issued in paperback 2020

British Library Cataloguing-in-Publication Data
A catalogue record for this book is available from the British Library

Library of Congress Cataloging-in-Publication Data
A catalog record for this book has been requested

ISBN: 978-1-138-47817-6 (hbk)
ISBN: 978-0-367-58947-9 (pbk)

Typeset in Times New Roman
by Swales & Willis Ltd, Exeter, Devon, UK

Contents

Figures

Tables

Preface

It seems to be conventional, for an inter-disciplinary publication of this kind, to apologize in advance to disciplinary specialists for any offence that may be caused due to perceived lack of rigour, depth, or comprehensiveness in my treatment of technical material. Philosophers will be upset by the incompleteness of historical context and the fragmentary approach I may have taken with respect to extant traditions; mathematicians will be upset by the superficial treatment of lemmas, theorems, and corollaries; while computer scientists will be upset by the absence of coherence in the development of theoretical frameworks and languages of computation. Furthermore, I am first and foremost, a practising economist rather than a physicist or, for that matter, a sociologist.

Nevertheless, I have written this text because I believe that a work of this kind can fill a certain gap in the literature. It has been guided by social theory, but also by the notion that any research into the digital economy or Internet-of-Things should also be governed by an appreciation of theoretical developments in this particular field, especially research concerned with concepts of concurrency, interaction, hybridity, and decentralized control (to employ the terminology of Bruno Latour, the researcher must attend to the "networkiness of networks" while recognizing "both human and non-human actants").

In this regard, the text is probably close in spirit to Manuel De Landa's 2011 Deleuzean text, *Philosophy and Simulation: The Emergence of Synthetic Reason*. However, I have largely focused on semantic technology and cognitive computing rather than on simulation. And I have also chosen to distance myself from De Landa's more recent foray into Speculative Realism, for reasons that are acknowledged by Ray Brassier in Bryant et al. (2011)—namely, that 'Speculative Realism' is the umbrella term for a diverse range of philosophical frameworks that are more united by what they are opposed to, than by what they might share. Another proximate influence is Donald McKenzie's 2001 text on *Mechanizing Proof: Computing, Risk, and Trust*, which applies Actor-Network-Theory to the development of proof machines. I am sympathetic to the theory but prefer to remain within the discursive frame of political economy and philosophy rather than the sociology of science. MacKenzie (2006) seems to have moved along a similar path in his analysis of financial markets and high-frequency trading.

I should also take note of what has been excluded from my purview, primarily for reasons of brevity. For one thing, I have largely ignored the domain of computerized trading and exchange, which might seem a strange thing to do for an economist. Nevertheless, on one hand, I wanted to concentrate on issues relating to semantic technologies that are potentially of broader application than media of exchange; on the other hand, because in my view, enough material of dubious provenance has already been published on this set of themes (especially on Bitcoin, that promising new vehicle of speculative excess)! I have also avoided discussion of more concrete aspects of digital fabrication, instead, choosing to ponder over systems that support new product development, the conduct of large software engineering projects, and the application of process algebras to business process management. This is largely a reflection of the significant gaps in my knowledge about mechatronics, robotics, 3-D printing, and automated assembly.

For those of a more technical persuasion, I have provided a more formal guide to recent contributions in the sphere of theoretical computing. To this end, I have extended Meseguer's lucid 1997 survey of rewriting logic, drawing on applications of theory to practical examples of theoretical computing of relevance to semantic technology, ranging from the management of emergency services and search-and-rescue operations to the detection of digital network incursions. In the accompanying technical appendix, I have reviewed a selected sample of this research in more detail motivated by a desire to focus on formal research in semantic technology that is already being applied to economic, commercial, and industrial problems.

As explained in the Introduction, my philosophical commitments are Post-Cognitivist, and somewhat at odds with the Husserlian Phenomenological tradition. This research monograph on the nature of ubiquitous computing draws heavily on category and topos theory. I was introduced to category theory in the immediate aftermath of the dot-com boom, principally by Robert Rosen's (1985; 1991) abstract but highly intuitive inquiries into the nature of life and consciousness. From there, I quickly migrated to the classic text by Saunders Mac Lane (1998), Awodey's (2006) guide to the same, and eventually to Mac Lane and Moerdijk's (1992) text on Topos Theory. However, I soon found myself foundering in a miasma of divergent approaches to theoretical computing, process algebra, and the analysis of dynamic networks. In mid-2016, a visit to Stephen Lack, an active member of the Australian School of Category Theory, at Macquarie University, helped to put me onto the right track after he recommended that I pursue burgeoning research on the application of product and permutation categories, or PROPs, to transition systems and dynamic networks. During my study leave in the UK in June and July of 2017, I also visited Bob Coecke, in the Department of Computer Science at Oxford University. Bob, along with his co-author Aleks Kissinger, had just completed a major work on the application of string diagrams to the field of quantum mechanics and quantum computing and was applying similar techniques to the analysis of economic games and was kind enough to put up with a series of fairly naïve questions about string diagrams. I would also like to thank Jeffrey Johnson, of the Open University, for some fascinating discussions about hypernetwork theory and applied topology during my UK sojourn. Finally, I would like to thank Tony Atley for numerous conversations about category theory over the past half a decade, along with David Savage, from the University of Newcastle, NSW, for numerous discussions about Herbert Simon and contemporary developments in Behavioural Economics.

I would like to thank my partner, Jane Krippner, and her son Max, for putting up with weeks of grouchiness towards the end of this whole project, and for the occasional conversation about abstruse matters of philosophy or computational theory.

Bibliography

Awodey, Steve (2006). *Category Theory*. Oxford Logic Guides 49. Oxford: Oxford University Press.

Bryant, Levi, Graham Harman and Nick Srnicek (2011). *The Speculative Turn: Continental Materialism and Realism*. Melbourne, Australia: re.press.

Coecke, Bob and Aleks Kissinger (2017). *Picturing Quantum Processes: A First Course in Quantum Theory and Diagrammatic Reasoning*. Cambridge: Cambridge University Press.

DeLanda, Manuel (2011). *Philosophy and Simulation: The Emergence of Synthetic Reason*. London and New York: Continuum.

MacKenzie, Donald (2001). *Mechanizing Proof: Computing, Risk, and Trust*. Cambridge, MA: MIT Press.

MacKenzie, Donald (2006). *An Engine, Not a Camera: How Financial Models Shape Markets*. Cambridge, MA: MIT Press.

Mac Lane, Saunders (1998). *Categories for the Working Mathematician*. Graduate Texts in Mathematics 5 (2nd ed.). New York, NY: Springer-Verlag.

Mac Lane, Saunders and Ieke Moerdijk (1992). *Sheaves in Geometry and Logic: A First Introduction to Topos Theory*. New York, NY: Springer-Verlag.

Meseguer, José (1997). Research Directions in Rewriting Logic. In U. Berger, H. Schwichtenberg (eds), *Computational Logic: Proc. of the NATO Advanced Study Institute on Computational Logic held in Marktoberdorf, Germany, July 29–August 6, 1997*. Computer Science Laboratory, NATO ASI Series 165. Berlin: Springer, 347–398.

Rosen, R. (1985). *Anticipatory Systems*. Pergamon Press, Oxford.

Rosen, R. (1991). *Life Itself: A Comprehensive Inquiry into the Nature, Origin, and Fabrication of Life*. New York, NY: Columbia University Press.

Introduction
Post-Cognitivism and the digital economy

The aim of this Introduction to the text is to discuss computational aspects of the digital economy from a Post-Cognitivist, "digital humanities" perspective. In particular, it will investigate each of the elements which contribute to an understanding of those "neuroeconomic" aspects of the digital economy, which can be characterized by notions of enhanced communication and interaction, hybridity and decentralized control: attributes that are increasingly constituted on the basis of developments in artificial intelligence, machine-learning, and robotics. With the aim of enhancing our understanding of these computational developments and their limitations, certain views of cognitive scientists will be examined, which focus on the situated and embodied nature of cognition. This will be followed by a discussion of diagrammatic forms of reasoning, which sets the scene for a more extensive review of pertinent philosophical insights that can be associated with Post-Cognitivist research. In particular, the book examines the limitations of current AI systems before embarking on a detailed investigation of how these limitations could be overcome through the application of formal models of anticipatory behaviour and cognition.

An impressive body of literature has been generated at the interstices between cognitive science and the humanities, a significant portion of which has focused specifically on the relationship between the digital humanities and the sciences of artificial intelligence (for a review see the 2016 text edited by Vincent Müller, plus Franchi, 2006). One strand of this literature falls under the banner of Post-Cognitivism, which pursues the linkages between theories of embodied and active cognition (Lakoff, 1987; Lakoff and Núñez, 2000), the "New AI" of robotics engineer Rodney Brooks (1999), the neural Darwinism of Gerald Edelman (2006), the Neurophenomenology of Varela, Thompson and Rosch (1991; also see Rudrauf et al., 2003), and the *Naturphilosphie* tradition that stretches from Schelling, Peirce, and Bergson through to Whitehead and Merleau-Ponty, along with the Heideggerian scepticism of Hubert Dreyfus. Nevertheless, some of those consigned to this seemingly unified school of thought make strange bedfellows. Brooks, for example, is certainly closer in outlook and sentiment to Herbert Simon, than he is to Dreyfus! It is acknowledged that Simon expressed a disdain for philosophy in his anthropologically inspired pursuit of a universal epistemology (Franchi, 2011).[1]

For its part, the new and inter-disciplinary science of Neuroeconomics is situated at the heart of the adjunction between the cognitive sciences and the economic and organizational sciences. Research conducted in its name has served to overcome the pessimism of the early founders of neoclassical economics, such as Stanley Jevons, who doubted the capacity of any science to investigate the inner workings of the human mind. As Camerer, Loewenstein, and Prelec (2005: 10) argue:

> The study of the brain and nervous system *is* beginning to allow direct measurement of thoughts and feelings. These measurements are, in turn, challenging our understanding of the relation between mind and action, leading to new theoretical constructs and calling old ones into question.

Nevertheless, they point to two generic inadequacies of the "deliberative" approach to human decision-making. First, they observe that "much of the brain implements 'automatic' processes, which are faster than conscious deliberations and which occur with little or no awareness or feeling of effort" (Camerer et al., 2005: 11). Second, they note that "our behavior is strongly influenced by finely tuned affective (emotion) systems whose basic design is common to humans and many animals". Each of these two observations are captured in the quadripartite divisions of the diagram in Figure I.1.

Their interpretation of each of the four quadrants is as follows: **QI** captures the deliberative matters such as "whether you should 'refinance' your house"; **QII** involves controlled though affective behaviour like the process of Method acting; **QIII** essentially involves "working out 'what is on your plate'" by first decoding patterns, and then integrating them with stored representations; finally, **QIV** entails the pre-conscious fusion of information (conceived as sensory) with utility or dis-utility (emanating from the orbitofrontal cortex).

This Introduction is also situated in the region of intersection between disciplines in the Arts, Humanities and Social Sciences, on one hand (i.e. those such as Social Theory, Linguistics, Psychology and Economics) and, on the other hand, their calculative, logical, and algorithmic counterparts (i.e. disciplines such as Mathematics, Computer Science, and Engineering).

	COGNITIVE	AFFECTIVE
CONTROLLED	QI	QII
AUTOMATIC	QIII	QIV

Figure I.1 The Dimensions of Neural Functioning
Source: Camerer, Loewenstein and Prelec (2005)

In the field of linguistics, per se, we are witness to expanding efforts to understand natural language, through computational means and then engage in various processes of communication based on that understanding. Within the business community this region of overlap is increasingly portrayed as the domain of "semantic enterprise". For example, a recent public report by Price Waterhouse Coopers (2010) has argued that "the next generation of IT will be structured around unified information management, Enterprise-level, semantically aware search capabilities, and intelligent collaboration environments—all delivered through dynamic, personalized interfaces that are aware of context".

In this context, this Introduction will focus on two current research projects. One of these is the EU-funded CUBIST project, which had a total budget exceeding 4 million euros, and pursued the objective of developing semantic technologies for Business Intelligence (BI), largely in the form of conceptually based, though visual analytics. The resulting repertoire of applied techniques included Formal Concept Analysis (FCA), faceted navigation, and graph-based navigation for the purposes of qualitative data analysis, that was aimed at complementing existing approaches drawing on quantitative data analysis. The semantic technologies shared a graph-based data model that distinguished between subject, predicate, and object 'triples', thus affording a 'light-weight' approach to diagrammatic reasoning based on a hierarchy of types, relations, and various properties of relations.

The other research project is a more modest, on-going, EPSRC-funded project, funded for £400,000, supporting research by two Computer Science academics from Oxford University, Bob Coecke and S. G. Pulman. This project has the aim of developing a unified model of compositional and distributional semantics for natural languages. The researchers apply string diagrams, which began in the modern era, with efforts by Roland Penrose and Richard Feyneman, respectively, to develop a diagrammatic heuristics to inform the teaching and application of tensor calculus and the representation of Quantum Electrodynamics. Nevertheless, drawing on category theory, Joyal and Street (1988) developed rigorous foundations for string diagrams based on Symmetric Monoidal Categories (SMCs) (see Theorem 1.5 from Joyal and Street (1988), and Theorem 1.2 from Joyal and Street (1991), which establish coherence for planar monoidal categories).

Interestingly, both of these research projects share an interest in *diagrammatic aspects* of human reasoning and communication, but they would appear to have little in common beyond this shared concern. Therefore, I will briefly discuss research by Brady and Trimble (2000a, 2000b), which applies the string diagram formalism to Peirce's alpha and beta calculus, thus establishing a clear linkage between the techniques applied in each of the two projects.

In regard to the underlying theme of organizational decision-making, it should be emphasized that the conception at play here is one informed by the Dynamic Competency Theory of David Teece. For Teece, competencies are conceived as integrated clusters of skill and know-how that span a variety of product lines, and can even extend beyond individual firms, change more slowly than do products or services, thus serving as the only effective locus of competitive rivalry. On this view, the strategic role of dynamic capabilities is then to ensure the development, accumulation, combination, and protection of unique skills and capabilities, achieved through the coordination, renewal, and deployment of competencies, congruent with changes in the environment (Teece et al., 1997).

For Teece and his followers, *tacit knowledge* is seen to complement a formal or codifiable form of knowledge, but it can only be deployed or transmitted through face-to-face forms of collaborative learning-by-doing. Accordingly, tacit knowledge operates as the major barrier to replication on the part of rival firms. These tacit forms of knowledge become ever more critical as trade barriers are reduced and copyrights are strengthened, by virtue of their unique, non-imitable qualities and because their impact can be amplified by network economies, customer 'lock-in', and the consolidation of dominant technology and product standards (Teece, 2000). In what follows I will be emphasizing the importance of these tacit forms of inference to the cognitive function. I will also highlight resonances between Teece's conception of tacit knowledge, which he has taken from Michael Polanyi, and Alfred North Whitehead's notion of the visceral mode of perception.

Polanyi's (1965) notion of tacit inference describes the process as one that involves the isolation of a unified object (via *focal awareness*) against a background (*subsidiary awareness*) determined by a diffuse and almost subliminal perception. He suggests that this is also an irreversible process creating new qualities that are not explicitly present amongst the subsidiary elements. Polanyi cites the binocular perception of depth as a metaphorical example of a case where the whole is always greater than the parts, for when the perception of depth is reversed, each separate image arises without any apprehension of distance. He goes on to argue that tacit inference, while more obviously inherent in sporting activities, is no less important in playing chess or even in pure mathematical analysis. Tacit knowledge must be transmitted from master to apprentice through a process of learning by doing. Moreover, personal commitment is necessary for scientists to continue doggedly along a specific research trajectory even when evidence goes against them. Accordingly, Polanyi (1966) insists, in true liberal spirit, that financial support for scientific research should be determined by the scientific community itself, rather than by bureaucratic planners or cost-benefit analysts.

Embodied cognition

In what follows, I take up the naturalist programme of cognitive psychologists such as Eleanor Rosch, and her followers (who include Lakoff, Johnston, Chang, Feldmann and Ballard, and Narayan) who work for the Neural Theory of Language Project at the University of California. However, I focus mainly on what they have to say about formal and mathematical reasoning for reasons that should become clearer as my narrative proceeds. This group of researchers offer a wide variety of penetrating insights into the nature of human reasoning, yet they entirely avoid the question of its diagrammatic or iconic quality. This is surprising when we consider the motivation for this influential body of research.

The Naturalism of this school of cognitive science seems to mirror the pragmatic idealism advocated by W. V. Quine, who posited a simple isomorphism between the structure of the empirical and the forms of representation that are engendered by it, even while the latter, paradoxically, account for most of the characteristics of this very structure. Quine's conception seems to be predicated on a direct link holding between neuro-computability, on one hand, and a notion of cybernetics conceived as a scientific model of science's model-constructing capacity *in general*, on the other. Of this naturalism, Badiou (2004) complains, with some irony, that the Hegelian serpent of absolute knowledge is thus made to swallow its own tail.

In the case of Lakoff and Núñez (2000: 361), for example, we are offered insights into the linkage between "embodied image schemas" and mathematical propositions and structures. Here, they (Lakoff and Núñez (2000: 356–359)) follow the anti-foundationalism of Saunders Mac Lane, who cautioned that any "Grand Foundation" cannot explain choice between dominant mathematical structures (such as real numbers, Euclidean geometry etc.) and particular models of structure (such as rings, groups, linear spaces etc.) for "The real nature of these structures does not lie in their often artificial construction from set theory, but in their relation to simple mathematical ideas or to basic human activities". The human activities Mac Lane refers to include: counting (arithmetic, number theory), measuring (real numbers, calculus, real analysis), shaping (geometry, topology), forming (symmetry, group theory), estimating (probability, measure theory), moving (mechanics, calculus, dynamics), calculating (algebra, numerical analysis), proving (logic), puzzling (combinatorics, number theory), and grouping (set theory, combinatorics).

For Lakoff and Núñez, the schemas reflected in these mathematical processes of cognition encompass specific actions or embodied notions such as: "motion along a line" (characterized by concepts including source location, a moving trajectory, the ultimate goal or destination, the trajectory adopted, the direction, and the position at any one moment), the idea of categories as "object containers' (determining notions of collections, the size of such collections, and thus numbers and magnitudes, along with addition and subtraction), arithmetic as an "object construction' (relating parts to the wholes which they form, and notions of zero to the "lack of whole"), and the ubiquitous 'measuring stick' metaphor (conveying the notion that paths can be inscribed and thus numerically evaluated through the deployment of measuring sticks, of ever-diminishing length, that are placed end to end), which must then be supplemented by what the authors call the "Basic Metaphor of Infinity" (i.e. the notion that sequential processes that go on indefinitely are nevertheless conceptualized as having an end and ultimate result). Further refinements include Boole's metaphor (linking arithmetic to classes, restricting relevant entities to zeros and ones, incorporating the empty class and the universe whose values are, respectively, assigned the numbers zero and one, and conceiving of addition as union and multiplication as intersection), Cantor's metaphor of cardinality (assuming that sets *A* and *B* can be put into a one-to-one correspondence if and only if they have the same number of elements), and von Neumann's axiom of foundation (stipulating that, as "containers", sets cannot "contain" themselves). Lakoff and Núñez (2000: 48–52), go on to distinguish between two kinds of metaphors. First, there are *grounding metaphors*, which are both basic and directly grounded (e.g. in the description above, the ground metaphors are those of object collection, motion-along-a-line, the measuring stick metaphor, and arithmetic as an object construction). Second, there are *linking metaphors*, which lead to abstraction. Linking metaphors construct conceptual blends through a combination of, and correspondence between two or more cognitive structures (e.g. "number-points" on the line and motion along it). In addition, there are combinatorial groupings that integrate imagined groups into larger groups, and symbolic capacity, which associates physical symbols with conceptual entities.

Even though embodiment is seen to account for the stability, generalizability, and consistency of mathematics, as well as its receptivity to symbolization, itself, Lakoff and Núñez nonetheless stress that we can neither confirm nor disconfirm the objective existence of mathematical entities. In opposition to Radical Social Constructivists, therefore, they insist that mathematical propositions are neither arbitrary, nor purely contingent, nor for that matter, purely subjective. For them, the "truth" of statements implies that they simply accord with our embodied understandings of both situation and subject matter. In contrast to Wittgenstein, for whom, famously, "mathematics does not think!", Lakoff and Núñez argue (appropriately in my view) that mathematics does have 'ideas', which, nevertheless, should not be conceived as reducible to sets and formal logic, as required by the formalist school.

While Lakoff (1987) commends Varela for his research on relational biology and the phenomena of boundary-constitution, the implications for cognition of the latter's obviously metaphysical concerns are never really broached. In Varela's case, an early influence was the calculus of indications, whose author, Spencer Brown, conceiving of his calculus in Kabbalistic terms, insisted that the making of a distinction was equivalent to the selection of form, which implies the emergence of the marked or 'bounded' value as an 'entity'. Thus, the domain of interaction of the observer with the observed is specified through the mediation of a recursive loop insofar as the observer defines himself by specifying his own domain of interactions: first, s/he observes her/his own observation process; and second, describes her/his own descriptions, both of which are rooted in the 'closure' of the nervous system.

Eleanor Rosch, herself, comes close to such a mystical conception in her essays on mindfulness, when she urges cognitive psychologists to consider the implications for their science of non-dualistic modes of knowing the world. I'm not convinced, however, that J. J. Gibson's analysis of affordances (directly perceived properties of the environment relative to the animal) and effectivities (properties of animals enabling them to act on affordances) in perception, which she cites approvingly, come anywhere close to her own vision of expansive awareness. For example, Wells's (2002) Turing-machine formalization of the Gibsonian approach to Ecological Psychology, which is clearly based on affordances and effectivities and accommodates at least some of the relational aspects of what might be called the "ontology of everyday life", falls well short of any attempt to broach the issue of subjectivity and the emergence of consciousness.

For its part, Lakoff's (1987: 64–65) voluminous, and otherwise insightful, *Women, Fire and Dangerous Things*, only includes two brief references to subjectivity. The first of these references the seminal work of Bates and McWhinney on prototype theory insofar as the subject is conceived to be determined by the structural polarity between Agent and Topic, while the second discusses radial categories (where non-central cases are motivated by an implicit central principle). In this case, subjectivity is constituted in regard to both the *conjunction* of properties in subjects of simple active sentences and the *disjunction* of negated properties in case of passive sentences.

Apart from this refusal to engage in ontological enquiries into the nature of objecthood or subjecthood, and despite their emphasis on image schemas, Lakoff and Núñez do not investigate the diagrammatic aspects of mathematics (the focus of their text on Euler's famous theorem would seem to preclude such an orientation). Yet, as will be argued in the next section along Peircean lines, these diagrammatic aspects are central to human reasoning, which helps to explain their centrality to the concerns of both of the research projects discussed herein. Moreover, notions of human reasoning also play a central role in the economics of strategy, insofar as they provide insight into processes of collaborative learning and the formation of tacit knowledge.

Diagrammatic logic and human reasoning

The arguments made in this Introduction and in the text as a whole are grounded in the notion that both successful organizational approaches to semantic enterprise and improved ways of understanding the cognitive and linguistic aspects of human behaviour can be mutually informed by a diagrammatic approach to human thought and reasoning. The presumption is that, arising from their iconic generality, such diagrammatic approaches could provide the necessary integrative framework for trans-disciplinary research across the cultural divide between STEM and Arts, Humanities, and the Social Sciences. Nevertheless, each of the research projects mentioned above would seem to have pursued a markedly different conception of what it means to be 'diagrammatic', so that it is not immediately clear as to how they could be related. On one hand, CUBIST draws on the contributions that Charles Sanders Peirce has made to diagrammatic reasoning.[2] On the other hand, the EPSRC Project draws on string diagrams developed by category theorists and applied in diagrammatic representation of quantum phenomena.

Ernest Nagel explains that Peirce's ambition was "to construct a system of philosophy so comprehensive that for a long time to come achievements in all departments of research, in mathematics, in the natural sciences, in history, in sociology, would appear simply as details filling out its outline" (Keeler, 1995: 2; citing Buchler, 1939: xiii). For Pragmatism (Dipert, 2004), "the penultimate goal of thought is to have correct representations of the world, and these are ultimately grounded for the pragmatist in the goal of effective action in the world". From this perspective, Peirce (1906) always insisted that diagrammatic forms of reasoning should be privileged over other forms,

> Diagrammatic reasoning is the only really fertile reasoning. If logicians would only embrace this method, we should no longer see attempts to base their science on the fragile foundations of metaphysics or a psychology not based on logical theory; and there would soon be such an advance in logic that every science would feel the benefit of it.
>
> (Peirce, 1906)

Moreover, "a diagram has got to be either auditory or visual, the parts being separated in the one case in time, in the other in space" (1.418), and even "algebra is but a sort of diagram" (3.419). Nevertheless, Peirce also recognized the importance of symbols and contributed significantly to the development of symbolic logic. He recognized that the meaning of signs was obtained due to the structure of relations applying to the sign system as a whole, which reflected both a sign's degree of similarity to and a sign's dissimilarity to other signs. Moreover, for Peirce, "a sign is something which stands for another thing to a mind" (MS 380). In other words, "a sign is something, A, which denotes some fact or object, B, to some interpretant thought, C" (1.346). Understandably, then, a "sign does not function as a sign unless it be understood as a sign" (MS 599). As Keeler (1995) points out, for Peirce,

> Ontology can be viewed as examining one dimension of semeotic; its field of investigation is the structure of the world (elements and relations of existence). Epistemology examines a second dimension of semeotic; its field of investigation is the meaning of the world (our relations to the world through representations of its existential relations). Semeotic examines the third dimension, incorporating the first two dimensions in a field of investigation into the occurrence of meaning in the world (our experiential reliance on representations of the relations in the world, by which we continue to gain knowledge of it).

The most significant expression of Peirce's enthusiasm for diagrams can be seen in his work on Existential Graphs (EGs). As Mary Keeler (1995) observes, "[H]e [Peirce] produces his most intensive theoretical work, which includes the Existential Graphs, during the last 10 years of his life (40.000 pages, or nearly half of the whole collection [100,000 unpublished pages which are archived in the Houghton Library at Harvard])".[3]

Nevertheless, Birkoff attributes to Peirce the first formal definition of an algebraic lattice, while Gantner and Wille (1999) attribute to him the first formal definition of what we now call a concept graph, which is a type of algebraic lattice applied in Formal Concept Analysis.

As pointed out by both Ernst Nagel, and Mary Keeler in numerous of her papers, Peirce's work on EGs was motivated, above all, by his desire to both understand and improve upon scientific reasoning, in particular, and human reasoning, more universally. Keeler (1995: 5) observes that for Peirce, scientific progress can only be achieved through communicative means within a research community,

The real is that which, sooner or later, information and reasoning would finally result in, and which is therefore independent of the vagaries of me and you. Thus, the very origin of the conception of reality shows that this conception essentially involves the notion of a COMMUNITY, without definite limits, and capable of an indefinite increase of knowledge.

(W2:239)

In his own analysis of diagrammatic reasoning, Frederick Stjernfelt (2007) privileges Husserlian Phenomenological conceptions of the synthetic *a priori* along with Peircean notions of diagrammatical reasoning. He argues that,

A priori regularities hold, not because of the imposition on the world of some forms or faculties in the subject, but because of recurrent, stable structures of reality itself. And, for the same reason, the a priori does not, as in Kant, refer to anybody's 'judgment' but rather to the object of such judgments: propositions, and, in turn, to those states-of-affairs referred to by propositions. This has the consequence, now, that the a priori covers a much wider range of domains than Kant's notion, centered upon mathematics.

(Stjernfelt, 2007: 176)

As Barry Smith remarks—drawing on Michael Polanyi's notion of 'tacit inference' for corroboration—the knowledge of such *a priori* structures is more often than not implicit; and on being made explicit, what results generally, though not always, appears disappointingly trivial. Whitehead interprets the explicit knowledge of inferential processes as "perception in the mode of presentational immediacy", which is usually precise but trivial. In contrast, implicit knowledge or "perception in the mode of causal efficacy", which is visceral or embodied, is generally vague but important.

The philosophical contribution to Post-Cognitivism

This visceral quality of knowledge and experience looms large in Merleau-Ponty's critique of Phenomenology, especially in his last published work, *The Visible and the Invisible*, where he complains that Husserl's chosen method of Eidetic reduction, puts to one side "the question of Being" in accordance with a distinction he draws between the contingent and the necessary aspects of the known object. That is, for Husserl Phenomenology is a philosophy of (absolute) meaning, for which the "question of Being" merely concerns the intentional object. On one hand essence is ideal, being revealed in appearance. On one hand, congruent with this distinction between essence and appearance, on the other hand, nature, history, world and Being are also idealized.

Instead, Merleau-Ponty insists that this conceptual process of idealization must be surpassed by a better understanding of real experience, in recognition of the fact that our knowledge is guided by a fundamental principle of "perceptive faith" (that is, it is grounded in a more primordial form of contact with Being). Rather than engaging in an ill-feted search for the foundation of certainty that is external to the world, he argues that our knowledge of quantitative and qualitative relations, our sensations, and our representations are always firmly based on a prior experience of perceptive certainty.

In his method of eidetic variation, Husserl asks what things would remain the same if this or that element were taken away? Nevertheless, Merleau-Ponty insists that for us to arrive at this kind of questioning, there must initially be some kind of meaning that reveals itself: (a) in many appearances; albeit, (b) differing somewhat in different phenomena. For essence is not ground but mere expression and the coherence of our field of experience is not due to a Platonic domain of innate essences.

Merleau-Ponty insists that the "what" is the interior intelligibility, the connection, and the coherence of the "that". For, if it is the case that there is no necessity in the order of facts themselves, there will never be any necessity at all. Husserl's essence, then, is merely the expression of this interior connection of the facts. When essences are separated from facts, they become unintelligible insofar as they are separated from both their intelligibility and density of reality. Moreover, as Charles Sanders Peirce always insisted, the increasing objectivity of knowledge can also be explained by the enrichment of our access to Being, that results from our encounter with other scientists and philosophers.

In this search for the essential, Merleau-Ponty warns that a spurious choice is imposed on philosophy between two equally flawed extremes: for Idealism, to reach truth is to lose contact with the world (for supposedly, our mind imposes its own interiority onto the world); for Realism, to maintain contact with the world we never arrive at truth itself (for supposedly, the world imposes itself on a passive mind). Instead, Merleau-Ponty insists that it is simultaneously true that everything belongs to Being and is penetrated by the common reality of Being, but nevertheless, everything is a being in its own way, a "deflection" of Being—in much the same way that every visible thing is a contraction of the general visibility. He goes on to complain that, in general, Analytic thought is blind to the very context and structure in which things exist, thus projecting a false clarity.

Being is only intelligible because it has a structure which penetrates all particular beings, which are best conceived as structured deflections of Being in general. And while vision is an actualization of the visibility of Being, so too is speech an actualization of the intelligibility of Being. This coherence of structure constitutes both visibility and intelligibility. Furthermore, as essence cannot be primordial so too, the subject cannot be primordial. Perception is essentially reflective because we are "perceiving perceptibles", that is, as perceiving subjects we are inscribed by a structural form of reflexivity that pertains to all processes of interaction and enfolding in nature.

In conclusion, it would seem that, like Husserl, Merleau-Ponty also privileges tacit knowledge but, unlike Husserl, he emphasizes the fleshy and embodied character of knowledge over the abstractive powers of human perception and human reasoning, for it is through our flesh, as perceiving, that Nature, as perceptible, acquires a knowledge of itself.

Hubert Dreyfus holds to a similar philosophical position in championing Heidegger's critique of Husserlian Phenomenology. For the early Heidegger, Being is neither substance nor process but rather "that on the basis of which beings are already understood". Here, a pivotal role is played by his notion of 'comportment', viewed as *Dasein*'s mode of "being-in-the-world". Dreyfus argues that, on a mundane level, this understanding of being is a style of life manifest in the way that everyday practices are understood. The shared practices into which we are socialized provide us with a background understanding of what counts as things, what counts as human beings, and what it makes sense to do in relation to things and other people. It also escorts us into the domain of what Heidegger calls the clearing (*lichtung*), which both veils or limits and opens up: (i) with respect to what can show itself; and also, (ii) for what can be done.[4]

From an ontological perspective, the clearing is a mode of revelation, or enframing, whereas from an ontic perspective it concerns the manner in which our practices are so structured as to make beings show themselves merely as resources or 'tools' at our immediate disposal. On this view, the error of Western metaphysics has always been to conflate this clearing with some conception of a transcendental being, either in the form of the purely present ground of being, in the form of the being of beings, or conceived as the most perfect being.

From the perspective of Heidegger's middle-period works, Dreyfus observes that human beings in the West are now conceived as disclosers of a series of total worlds. In each of these worlds, practices are ranked in importance from the central through to the marginal. The later Heidegger subsequently introduces a more nuanced conception of local practices, which can be gathered together around such humble rituals as the sharing of a family meal or the partaking of a bottle of wine, in the very process creating temporary, self-enclosed, and localized worlds.

Husserl, too, recognized that practical activity is a crucial part of our relation to the world. Heidegger, however, always distanced himself from Husserl's emphasis on the concept of 'intentionality'. For Husserl, this term reflects the fact that mental states such as perceiving, believing, desiring, fearing and doubting are always directed towards something under some kind of description, irrespective of whether the given extra-mental object exists or not (Dreyfus, 1993: 2). Heidegger departs from this conception in observing that there is a more fundamental mode of intentionality, which does not involve any mental content at all. Moreover, the basic way that human beings are in the world does not involve intentionality at all. And it is this non-intentional way of being that must be recognized as the very condition of possibility for both the practical or non-mental, as well as the mental forms of intentionality.

Where for Husserl, phenomenology was the study of intentional structures after the bracketing of phenomenal reduction had taken place separating mind from world, Heidegger goes further. To highlight the nature of Heidegger's departure from the phenomenological tradition, Dreyfus falls back on a distinction introduced by John Searle between the logical and the phenomenological *conditions of satisfaction* associated with an intentional state. Searle goes on to argue that action, as a bodily motion caused by a mental state, must represent its own goal throughout the performance of an act. Moreover, the subject of the act must also experience the causal connection between the intention in action and the bodily movement. Dreyfus points out that, in contrast, Heidegger insists that intentionality *without* the experience of intentional content is characteristic of the unimpeded mode of our everyday activity. Moreover, intentionality is founded in *Dasein*'s transcendence so that transcendence cannot be explained in terms of intentionality (Dreyfus, 1993: 4; citing Heidegger, 2001).

Thus, on one hand Dreyfus rejects the notion that there must be a separable conscious component of perception and, on the other hand, the idea that experience represents its conditions of satisfaction, both in terms of the experience of 'acting' and the bodily movement that is effectuated. He argues that, for Heidegger, the experience of acting does not have to be correlated with that of my causing a bodily movement (similarly, perception does not have to involve an awareness of one's private visual experience or the associated causal role of an object in the world), nor must the experience of acting represent the goal of the action. Following the position of Merleau-Ponty, Dreyfus contends that, for the most part, the activity of everyday absorbed 'coping' is merely experienced as a steady flow of skilful activity with no self-referential experience of oneself as causing that activity. Only in the case of what Heidegger calls deliberative action does the experience of acting become an experience of the fact that one's intention causes one's movement. Examples of such coping include skilful activities such as playing tennis, habitual activities such as brushing one's teeth, unthinking activities such as rolling over in bed, and spontaneous activities such as fidgeting.

Heidegger uses the term 'comportment' to describe the non-conscious though involved activity of 'being-directed-towards' and the being to whom such comportments belong as '*Dasein*'. For Heidegger, the there-being of *Dasein* surpasses the Cartesian division between the immanent, inner world of the subject and the transcendent, outer world of the object. Both self and the world are brought together into a single entity structured by its being-in-the-world. Crucially, Heidegger insists that comportment provides the non-salient background for both on-going coping and deliberative, focused activity. In all our comportment towards beings—theoretical and practico-technical—a more fundamental understanding of being is already entailed. Comportment requires both background familiarity, which Heidegger calls 'ontological transcendence' and a practical circumspection, orientation, or grasping of circumstance associated with our various ways of setting-to-work, procuring, or performing (Heidegger, 2001: 405).

In the hands of Dreyfus, this Heideggerian conception of comportment serves as much to undermine crass forms of empiricism as it does idealist conceptions of transcendence. In particular, in his APA Pacific Division Presidential Address of 2005, it provides him with a weapon to attack naïve visions of 'thinking computers' that were promoted by members of the artificial intelligence community in the 1960s. In opposing over-optimistic and simplistic predictions that computers will soon possess the cognitive powers of human beings, Dreyfus points to the fact that computers are unable to comprehend the simple stories and fables understood by four-year-olds. He attributes this difficulty to what Marvin Minsky, head of MIT's AI Laboratory, has called the 'frame problem': knowing which facts are relevant to a given situation when certain features change. To grasp continuity-in-change computers need to have a conception of a range of typical situations that allows them to rank facts in order of relevance. A frame is then a description of a typical situation that a computer can deploy to ground its interpretation of this situation. Unfortunately, as Dreyfus points out, this merely transforms the problem into one of knowing which frame must be chosen to interpret any given situation. The computer must first know which facts are relevant so that it can then recognize the relevant frame. Dreyfus argues that we humans do not have to confront such difficulties because, unlike the computer, we are already actively engaged in the world. Moreover, the meaningful objects among which we live are not a *model* of the world stored in our mind; they are *the world itself.*

The AI domain of research seems to attract more than its fair share of crackpots, ignoramuses, and charlatans. For example, one team at the Technical University of Vienna advocate a psychoanalytic model of artificial intelligence (Dietrich et al., 2009). In accordance with this model the intelligent machine will be motivated by Physiological requirements that trigger Drive tension, expressed through Neuro-symbolization. The Erotic drives would then merge with their Thanatosian counterparts to ensure that the Thing content of the drive connects to Affect (still unconscious), which is then transported to pertinent Defence mechanisms. At this stage both Super-egoic and internalized Reality demands are initially weighed up and then either Repressed or converted to Secondary processes, at which stage they are connected to word representations. Reality demand has its origin in both the Environment and the Body, with each transformed into Neuro-Symbols, and then perceived as Thing-presentations activating Repressed content and Memory traces, which then merge to form Perceptual representation, before being connected to Affects while modes of Subjecthood are connected to Defence mechanisms. Affects may be pre-consciously or consciously Perceived, after which, these contents and associated Drive contents are passed on to the pre-conscious, the Super-Ego, the Decision-unit and attentive Outer Perception. In combination with Learned facts about Reality, the latter affect Reality Checking, informing the Decision unit, which leads then to a decision, with the help of Memorized Scenarios and Potential Action Plans, which in turn are influenced by Affects resulting from Inner Perception. The resulting Action Plan, in turn, will be decomposed into Motility Control, then Neuro-desymbolized (translated into physical signals) to control Actuators, the effect of which on body and environment is then detected by sensors.

The trouble with this application of psychoanalytic theory to AI is that it completely misconstrues the Freudian tradition that it supposedly espouses, by completely obfuscating Freud's key semiotic notions of symptom, condensation, and displacement. While adhering to the Freudian distinction between the 'word representative' and 'thing representative' of the drive, it assumes that it is the thing representative rather than the word representative of the drive, which undergoes repression, but how else could the processes of the unconscious, themselves, be structured like a language. For Freud, it is the word representative of the drive that undergoes repression and the affect is modified rather than being repressed (for example, repressed homosexual desire can be transformed into anger and hatred).

Another instance of misunderstanding carries over to the lack of any discussion about negation. Under the negating operation of the death drive, the object that has been expelled or negated, must first be re-found, for only in this way can the process of reality-testing be constituted, thus allowing for a distinction to be drawn between things that are hallucinated, remembered, or perceived! And Freud goes on to argue that the structural character of psychosis, neurosis, and perversion is determined in turn by different forms of negation—foreclosure, repression, and disavowal, respectively.

In the absence of this semiotic understanding, machinic intelligence would have to fall back on a limited, physicalist conception of semantics which conceives of communication in entropic terms as the transfer of information, within a psychotic, hallucinatory world entirely devoid of jokes, dreams, and poetic flights of imagination.

Freud, Lacan, and Post-Cognitivism

Fenichel (2016: 3–4) bears witness to the fact that Freud's notion of "Uncanny Belonging" has Schellingian origins. For Schelling, the unconscious is the static ground of existence and human freedom, and the dynamic source of both subjective experience and objective reality. Likewise, Freudian notions of subjectivity and the very structure of the unconscious, are inscribed by the altered temporality or "afterwards-ness" of repression (*Nachträglichkeit*). It should not come as a surprise then, that it is within a text that he describes as aesthetic—namely, "The Uncanny"—that Freud invokes Schelling; while observing that the uncanny convergence of fate and omnipotence, which as such, in turn, is the domain of freedom, can be most adequately addressed as feeling (Fenichel, 2016: 9).

For Freud (SE 1958: Vol. XVII: 224), "[u]nheimlich is the name for everything which ought to have remained . . . hidden and secret but has become visible". Likewise, for Lacan, the Uncanny is the key text explicated in his seminar on 'Anxiety' (Fenichel, 2016: 15; and fn. 19: 16).

> Thus heimlich is a word, the meaning of which develops towards an ambivalence, until it finally coincides with its opposite, unheimlich. Unheimlich is in some way or other a sub-species of heimlich.
>
> (Freud, SE 1958: Vol. XVII: 225)

Schelling speaks in very similar, dialectical terms about a kind of shuffling between one posited concept and its opposite.

> So the beginning of sin consists in man's going over from being to non-being, from truth to falsehood, from light into darkness, in order himself to become the creative basis and to rule over all things with the power of the center which he contains . . . In evil there is that contradiction which devours and always negates itself, which just while striving to become creature destroys the nexus of creation and, in its ambition to be everything, falls into non-being.
>
> (Schelling, 1936: 69)

In a recent blog, Matthew Segall (2015) insists:

> For Schelling, myth is not the way the human subject "reconciles itself with itself" or "achieves self-present mastery", as Bryant puts it. Myth is precisely the opposite: it is another way of speaking of the subject's inability to achieve complete self-mastery, of the *cision* at the generative root of subjectivity. Myth is the human imagination's way of coming to terms with the soul's creative becoming (i.e. with its lack of substantial being). Myth is soul-making. Humans do not invent myth; rather, argues Schelling, it is myth that invented (and continues to reinvent) humanity.

McGrath (2011) interrogates Žižek's claim that Schelling can be "fruitfully read" via Lacan, which is predicated, he suggests, on identifying an isomorphism between the neo-Kabbalistic notion of the contraction of being and the interdiction of the Father contracting the pre-Oedipal unity of the mother–child dyad. McGrath insists that Žižek, nevertheless, underplays Lacan's collaboration with Koyré (whose seminar on Boehme was attended by Lacan in 1934), which then carries over to an underestimation of Boehme's influence over Lacan.

McGrath (2011) also endeavours to explain why Žižek's Lacanian interpretation of Schelling appears to work so well. He suggests that this is because Schelling articulates a *transcendental materialist* theory of subjectivity: transcendental because Schelling begins with subjectivity and asks after the condition of its possibility; materialist because Schelling discovers that the condition of the possibility of subjectivity is actually a denial of materiality! However, in true Lacanian form, this ideal condition is grounded in a lie for the repressed always returns as irreducible remainder. In other words, McGrath (2011) warns that for Schelling, the eternal cycle of potencies becomes the infinite reflection of a primordial psychotic subject who must repress its "Oedipal psychosis" if it is to exist at all.

Moreover, McGrath observes that Žižek also accepts Hegel's critique of Schelling's dialectic as one that fails to resolve "the ideal–real dyad into a point of indifference between them (the dialectical as such)", instead, hypostasizing the "point of indifference into Godhead" (i.e. Lacan's Big Other), which as such, is situated entirely outside the dialectic. Supposedly, the Schellingian fantasy of transcendence is corrected by Hegel, for whom the dialectic of the ideal and the real is purely immanent. Hegel's dialectical "third" then becomes a spirit that is "eternally out of joint" because it has absorbed the real into the ideal, rendering it a constitutive moment of itself.

For Schelling, the *telos* governing the dual forces of nature is the principle of self-manifestation. He reasons that nature is driven to reveal itself, but this is an objective that can only be realized through self-consciousness. Accordingly, what was initially a primordial and unconditioned unity must divide itself into opposing forces so that it can become manifest. As McGrath (2011: 14) explains:

> One force is expansive and directed outward to infinity, the other is contractive and directed inward to a single point. The opposed forces collaborate in striving to bring about a return to the original unity and, at the same time, in blocking that return by producing finite beings. The end result is endless manifestation and concealment, ceaseless activity, which consists in tension (blockage of flow) and release (freeing of flow): the expansive power of *natura naturans* is infinitely countered by the contractive power of *natura naturata*.

Seen in this light, the metaphysics of Boehm and Schelling has a therapeutic significance that can be attributed to the notion of dissociation: in a negative sense, to dissociate from x is to render x unconscious and so a threat to the ego; in a positive sense, to dissociate from x is to render x an object of consciousness or to make x itself conscious, so that growth in consciousness is made possible by the contraction of some aspect of the individual's identity. What has been dissociated is not sublated, but rather, what subsists in the self as a grounding potency; i.e. it is personified by Boehme's Lucifer who is conceived as the telos of wilful unconscious (McGrath, 2011: 6).

Instead, Freud "effectively brackets teleology and abolishes organicism, refusing to see the dual drives as anything other than reactions of matter to the accident of life" (McGrath, 2011: 18). The Freudian eros is "a natural impulse to differentiate, a will to exteriority, a world-building drive, opposed by an antithetical drive that aims at the restoration of a primitive stage of inorganic equilibrium". Accordingly, the human being "no longer belongs to a greater whole, but is ultimately an absurd eruption of self-reflective and self-interested life in a mindless universe".

In contrast, for Schelling the negative force "is not a resistance to life but a will to individuation, a will to concrete, determinate existence, which, by blocking the ecstatic flow of *natura naturans*, congeals eros into a finite being and prevents it from totally emptying itself into *natura naturata*".

For Schelling, then, "it is the erotic principle, distributed throughout a living cosmos (as opposed to being concentrated in an atomistic ego, as in Freud), which if unchecked by the negative force, . . . would bring about the total death of nature" (McGrath, 2011: 17).

Nevertheless, some insight into Lacan's concerns about *Naturphilosphie* can be acquired by considering the criticism that he directed at the last work of his friend Merleau-Ponty. Lacan discusses the *Visible and Invisible* in his seminar on the 'Four Fundamental Concepts of Psychoanalysis'. This seminar is situated at the point where Lacan is moving beyond his earlier analysis of the dialectic between the imaginary and the symbolic dialectic to a new emphasis on the "traumatic" status of the real. Associated with this move is the introduction of the *objet petit a* which is situated at the *limit* where the Symbolic order is "incomplete". Correlated with this conception of the object is a notion of the subject whose structure is conceived as a discontinuity in the real accompanying the cut in the symbolic chain. In this context of psychoanalytic practice rather than philosophy, as such, Lacan discusses the 'gaze' and the 'voice' as respective objects of the scopic and vocative drives.

Lacan acknowledges the novelty of Merleau-Ponty's analysis of the flesh, which is manifest as both the flesh of the body and the flesh of the world, restructuring the subject–object relation. He also acknowledges that the *invisible* institutes the field of visibility at the very limit of classical phenomenology, subverting the reflexive nature of intentionality. At this site we find a gaze which comes from things themselves, and come upon ourselves as seen from without, such that our very vision is imposed upon us. Positioned between the seer (who constitutes corporeality) and the field of empirical positivity (which constitutes visibility) flesh undermines the anthropological!

However, Lacan's gaze comes not from the direction of the Other, but from the direction of the object, continuing itself in the very act of my perception. Nevertheless, in this role it manifests as a primordial passivity preceding the division between subject and object—a captivation by the gaze of the world. The subject not only makes himself the passive object of another will, but also an object of lack, thus veiling the lack in the Other. In other words, the apparatus of the subject is something lacunary insofar as it revolves around the primordially lost "Thing" making the Symbolic order incomplete and constituting castration anxiety.

In his analysis of the Abraham and Isaac myth, Lacan contends that the symbolic relation allows for substitution of ram for son, in the process defining a new relation between the Jewish people and the Other; but one characterized by the necessity for making an offering to obscure gods, in the pursuit of a divine *juissance*. And in his response to the rhetorical question—Is there no satisfaction in being under the gaze? —Lacan turns to the annihilation of the subject, to *aphanisis* as the fundamental mark of the death drive, which would seem to depart sharply from Merleau-Ponty's emphasis on the pleasure in which the subject finds its life!

A path to subjectivity

In this section I want to address some formal-*cum*-structural models of consciousness and anticipation. I will begin with the model first proposed by Robert Rosen in the context of his work on living systems. I then link Rosen's research to Whitehead's mathematico-philosophical analysis of the process of anticipation in higher organisms. This largely discursive overview leads into a formal discussion of strictly mathematical models of cognition that draws on topos and sheaf theory. Conclusions then follow.

Rosen's anticipatory systems

Like Herbert A. Simon, Marvin Minsky, Anatol Rapoport, and Alvin Weinberg, and Warren McCulloch and Walter Pitts, Robert Rosen studied under, and was greatly influenced by, the theoretical physicist, Nicholas Rashevsky, who pioneered research in the field of theoretical biology. Rosen's conception of a living system is predicated on the notion of complexity in a natural system. Natural systems can either be simple or complex depending on whether there is, or is not, a closed path of efficient causation. A natural system has a closed path of efficient causation (i.e. a system is closed to efficient causation) if its every efficient cause is entailed within the system itself. Rosen establishes that an organism must be complex.

Rosen describes a metabolism-repair and replication system by interpreting the diagram in Figure I.2 of interlinked morphisms, where hollow head arrows represent the flow from input (material cause) to output (final cause) and the smaller solid head arrows represent a constraint over the flow from the processor (efficient cause).

There are three mappings in an (M,R)-system on three hierarchical levels:

Metabolism: f

Repair: $\Phi \in H(B,H\,(A,B))$

Replication: $\beta \in H(H(A,B),H(B,H(A,B)))$

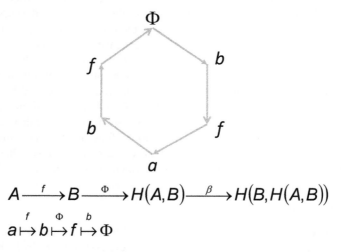

$$A \xrightarrow{\;f\;} B \xrightarrow{\;\Phi\;} H(A,B) \xrightarrow{\;\beta\;} H(B,H(A,B))$$
$$a \overset{f}{\mapsto} b \overset{\Phi}{\mapsto} f \overset{b}{\mapsto} \Phi$$

Figure I.2 Entailment within (M, R)-Systems
Source: Louie (2012: diagram/equation (6): 8)

According to Alphonse Louie (2008), the genius in Rosen's construction is that he establishes a correspondence between the hom-sets $H(H(A,B),H(B,H(A,B)))$ and B, so that the replication map β may be replaced by the isomorphic mapping b depicted in Figure I.2. Accordingly, the three (M,R)-system maps functionally entail one another in a cyclical permutation that spirals around in an iterative and hierarchical fashion, thus violating the computability conditions of the Church-Rosser-Turing theorem. However, I don't want to dwell on these controversial aspects of Rosen's arguments, turning, instead, to an application of this construction to anticipatory systems.

Rosen's work on anticipatory systems mirrors that of Alfred North Whitehead, whose work was, nonetheless, framed by a certain conception of anticipation grounded in projective geometry. Rosen had an advantage that was not available to Whitehead, namely: he had the machinery of category theory at his disposal. For Rosen, then, an anticipatory system "is a natural system that contains an internal predictive model of itself and of its environment, which allows it to change state at an instant in accord with the model's predictions pertaining to a later instant" (Louie, 2008: 296). In his reinterpretation of Rosen's research, Louie (2008) follows Rosen (1985) in considering anticipatory systems within theoretical biology as a special case of the more general (M,R)-systems. This relationship of specialization is captured in Figure I.3.

This anticipatory system is an (M,R)-Network, which has been decomposed into two pairs of components accounting for the anticipatory equivalents to metabolism and repair, $\{(S, E_s), (M, E_m)\}$, as shown in Figure I.4. Here, (M, E_m) is a predictive model of anticipatory system with internal time-scale running faster than the clock of (S, E_s). The map, $\varepsilon:S \rightarrow M$, completing the cycle, is the encoding of the object system S into its model M. Finally, the model-updating map (3): $E M$, is an inverse efficient cause.[5]

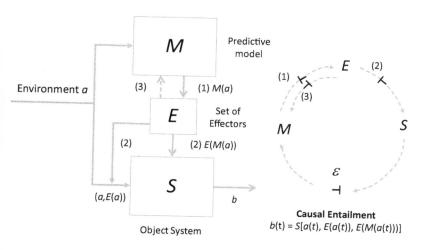

Figure I.3 (M,R)-Systems as Anticipatory
Source: Louie (2008)

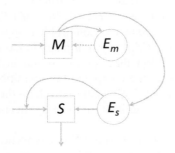

Figure I.4 Decomposition of the Effector Set
Source: Louie (2012: diagram (33): 18)

Therefore, the predictive model is analogous to metabolism while the response to prediction is analogous to repair. The whole system is hierarchical due to the presence of a recursive or iterative process, as depicted in Figure I.5.

By way of comparison, in *Second Nature*, Nobel laureate Gerald Edelman (2006: 25) expounds his notions of developmental and experiential selection and re-entry to "account for both the diversity and the regularity of brain responses in the absence of the control by logic and a precise clock that are the hallmarks of a computer". He argues that the development of neuronal circuits in the brain leads to enormous microscopic anatomical variation that is a result of a process of continual selection: "neurons that fire together wire together" (Edelman, 2006: 28). However, experiential selection occurs through changes in the strength of the synapses that already exist in the brain anatomy. The net result of developmental and experiential selection is that some neural circuits are favoured over others. Nevertheless, coherence obtains through the process of re-entry, which he describes as the continual signalling from one brain region (or map) to another and back again across massively parallel fibres (axons) that are known to be omnipresent in higher brains. In his explanation of consciousness, Edelman (206: 36) claims:

> The evidence suggests that consciousness is entailed by reentrant activity among cortical areas and the thalamus and by the cortex interacting with itself and with subcortical structures, thus linking perceptual categorization to value-category memory and allowing for the making of enormous numbers of discriminations and distinctions.

He contends that memory plays a crucial role in this process, "that consists of an enormous variety of so-called qualia: the discriminations entailed by the widely distributed and highly dynamic activity of the thalamocortical core" (Edelman, 2006: 37). Moreover, "the pattern of integrative activity in this thalamocortical reentrant neuronal network, called the dynamic core, would create a scene in the remembered present of primary consciousness, a scene with which the animal could lay plans" (Edelman, 2006: 36–37). This memory system "is likely to be mediated

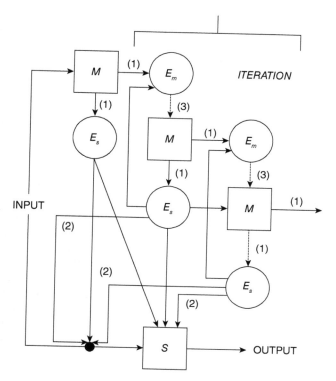

Figure I.5 Anticipatory Systems as Hierarchically Recursive
Source: Louie (2012: diagram (36): 20)

by more anterior cortical regions such as frontal and parietal cortex whereas ongo-ing perception is likely to be enabled by more posterior cortical regions".

At a critical point in his elucidation of consciousness as process, Edelman (2006: 72) complains about the adverse consequences of the Cartesian dualism between mind and body, suggesting that "[t]he strains and dilemmas that have emerged from the split [i.e. Cartesian mind–body dualism] have driven thinkers to extreme posi-tions as well as to penetrating observations". He further notes that "[t]he philosopher Alfred North Whitehead was deeply concerned with the issue and indeed constructed a whole metaphysics—the philosophy of the organism—to get around it".

Whitehead on anticipation

In the light of these comments by Edelman, I would like to briefly examine Whitehead's 'Pan-experiential' conception of anticipatory cognition to identify resonances with the Polanyian notion of tacit inference. These Whiteheadian deliberations are grounded in a philosophical critique of the Kantian emphasis on the subjective conditions of knowledge, even while remaining firmly grounded in experience. Whitehead (1978: 156) inverts Kant's "Copernican Revolution" for which "the process whereby there is experience is a process from subjectivity to apparent objectivity". Instead, he insists on turning this conception around. For him, the process proceeds "from objectivity to subjectivity, namely, from the objectivity whereby the external world is a datum, to the subjectivity, whereby there is one individual experience".

Of necessity, the following exposition of Whitehead's approach to anticipation must be brief. A more detailed treatment can be found in the texts of Epperson (2004) and Code (1985). In his description of the process of concrescence as a fundamental generative process, Whitehead distinguishes between a primary (or physical) phase, concerned with the determination of the definitiveness of the objective datum (i.e. with the initial datum as cause), and a secondary (or conceptual) phase, concerned with determination of the definitiveness of the subjective form (i.e. with the concrescent subject as effect).[6] For him, feelings are both conformal in their concern with forms of definiteness (i.e. with regard to real transmission, where the latter is understood as the process through which many actual occasions become one actual occasion), and conceptual in their concern for possibilities of subjective valuation (i.e. with regard to valuative operations and processes of adaptation and self-determination). Nevertheless, as he conceives it, the *mental pole* can be further sub-divided into two phases, namely: conceptual valuation (the actual process of ingress of ideas or "eternal objects" that give rise to a patterned contrast), and conceptual reversion (the conceptual prehension of alternatives in their potentiality). During the phase of conceptual reversion, propositions have the capacity to act as a *lure for* the creative emergence of novelty, specifically, through the feeling of absence achieved through negative rather than positive prehensions. According to Whitehead's *materialist principle*, while the prehended datum solely pertain to the *actuality* of physical inheritance, novelty obtains in the case where a *combination* of both the potential *and* the actual is entertained.

Significantly, Whitehead insists on the fact that that *consciousness* only emerges in the phase of conceptual reversion, when provoked by an abstract element within synthetic feeling, such that it becomes integrated with various potentialities for definiteness. For consciousness, propositions are manifest as a *hybrid* construct mediating between *potential* and the *actual*. Moreover, where true propositions are conformal, false propositions are non-conformal.

Whitehead's (1978: 224) fundamental notion of concrescence entails a 'decision' on the part of the concrescing actual occasion as to how it should relate both to its past and to its future; a decision guided by its "subjective aim", and when this decision is made, the occasion reaches satisfaction and perishes. The "subjective aim" embodies purpose, or final causation, and "one task of a sound metaphysics is to exhibit final and efficient causes in their proper relation to each other" (Whitehead, 1978: 84). Here, one species of cause is provided by 'concrescence', which (as physical prehension or conformal feeling) is internal to the act of becoming (Whitehead, 1978: 23, 210). The other aspect of the causal process is 'transition'—that whereby a past actual occasion is an element of the conformal phase of a new concrescence. Whitehead complains that an exclusive focus on sense data fails to account for "the mass of our moral, emotional, and purposive experience [that] is rendered trivial and accidental" (Whitehead, 1968a: 148). The essence of this purposiveness consists of "the rise of an affective tone originating from things whose relevance is given" (Whitehead, 1967a: 176).

When an actual occasion or nexus is perceived in the mode of presentational immediacy, the sense-data derived from antecedent states of our own bodies through an indirect process of "representing" or "inferring" (which is *precise* but *trivial*), is then *projected* into the contemporary space. Similarly, relevant eternal objects are derived from prehensions in earlier stages. The mode of causal efficacy involves a direct "seizing" or "grasping" (which is *vague but important*) and, through an 'anticipatory feeling' of actual occasions in the future these same eternal objects are projected into "future extensive regions". For Whitehead (1978: 168) human experience is a mixture of the two modes, which he terms "symbolic reference". Nevertheless, because the data of presentational immediacy, notwithstanding their "prominence in consciousness", are part of the "superficialities of experience", they conceal "the reality from which the occasion springs, the reality from which it derives its source of emotion, from which it inherits its purposes, to which it directs its passions" (Whitehead, 1967a: 280).

While developments in the neurosciences, linguistics, and computational analysis have cleared the way for new insights into the relationship between cognitive and linguistic aspects of human behaviour, advances in linear logic and combinatory algebra have also contributed to a flourishing of new forms of computational linguistics with category theory serving as an integrative mathematical framework for many of these advances.

Formal models of cognition

Jean Petitot's (1993) attributes to logical positivism the error of failing to recognize the sensible nature, and enduring importance, of the notion of the *"synthetic a priori"* both for post-Kantian critical thought in general, and for contemporary developments in logic and geometry in particular. His phenomenology of perception draws on qualitative physics, and sheaf mereology to illuminate Husserl's crucial distinction between totality (*verschmelzung*) and continuity, or part (*sonderung*), along with the notion of spreading or filling-in (*ausbreitung*) within a pre-specified boundary. Petitot concludes his discussion of the Husserlian phenomenology of perception by noting:

> The fact that truth-values are indexed on open sets and the forcing status of the Kripke-Joyal semantics shows that "space" is irreducible to logical analyticity and constitutes a *sui generis* geometrical dimension of the *a priori* stance. This geometrical dimension of truth corresponds exactly to what Husserl calls, after Kant, *synthetic a priori*. In this sense the concept of the "synthetic a priori" is a perfectly sane one. That it has been dramatically misunderstood by logical positivism must not hide the fact that it is basic for ontology.

Petitot's phenomenological approach to perception is more defensible than Husserl's broader concerns about consciousness and anticipation. An alternative formal representation of cognition is provided by Ehresmann and Vanbremeersch (1987) who also draw on the category-theoretic notion of limit as the basis for a good model for organization. In their work on "hierarchical and evolutive systems", they have clarified the emergence of properties, the 'complexification' of system, conditions governing the stability of hierarchical organization when component objects are replaced, as well as the stepwise formation of the system through creation and destruction of both objects and organization. An evolutive system is analysed by considering the categorical modelling of changes in system states over time, where changes of state are represented by a transition functor. In a series of papers, this category-theoretic approach has been extended to the cognitive domain, in terms of memory evolutive systems.

Kato and Nishimura (2013) have published a recent article applying topos theory to cognition. These topos-theoretic techniques that were originally developed for the analysis of quantum gravity as a core element of unified field theory— effectively, by achieving a structural and dynamic integration between quantum mechanics and general relativity theory—have been applied to a specific model of brain activity or thinking. To achieve a formal representation of quantum gravity, relativistic notions of phenomena such as the light cone, gravitational effect by mass, black holes, and the big bang have also been formulated. The main epistemological advantage of this specific application of the t-topos is that it provides a unifying theory of both microcosm and macrocosm based on mathematical notions of a (micro) decomposition of the associated presheaf and a (micro) factorization of the relevant morphism that can be associated with the t-site. It is this aspect of t-topos theory that comes to the fore in the authors' work on cognition. As Peter Johnstone (1977: 17) has explained:

> What, then is the topos-theoretic outlook? Briefly, it consists in the rejection of the idea that there is a fixed universe of "constant" sets within which mathematics can and should be developed, and the recognition that the notion of "variable structure" may be more conveniently handled within the universe of continuously variable sets than by the method, traditional since the rise of abstract set theory, of considering separately a domain of variation (i.e. a topological space) and a succession of constant structures attached to a point of this domain. In the words of F. W. Lawvere [1973], "Every notion of constancy is relative, being derived perceptually or conceptually as a limiting case of variation, and the undisputed value of such notions in classifying variation is always limited by that origin. This applies in particular to the notion of constant set, and explains why so much of naïve set theory carries over in some form into the theory of variable sets". It is this generalization of ideas from constant to variable sets which lies at the heart of topos theory; and the reader who keeps it in mind, as an ultimate objective, whilst reading this book, will gain a great deal of understanding thereby.

After concisely defining sheaves and pre-sheaves, the authors introduce two restrictions: the first based on restricting the state of the whole brain via a decomposition to the state of a sub-division of the brain into parts (e.g. the frontal, parietal, temporal, and occipital lobes); and, the second, based on a topological covering of what they describe as "generalized time periods", which ensures linear temporal ordering of relations. This is where variable or indexed sets come into play. Coherence conditions for both the decomposition and the covering are then examined. A key theorem is then proven, establishing *uniqueness* when the decomposition of whole-and-part relations is succeeded by the gluing of coverings to achieve a linear temporal ordering. It is this specific articulation of the "local–global" mechanism of topos, in the form of a temporal ordering that represents the main contribution of Kato and Nishimura's (2013) construction. They go on to explain how their *t*-topos formalism can represent information flows (and types of information—verbal and visual) in communication between two people or even interactions between different parts of the brain.

Nevertheless, Whitehead's distinction between two modes of perception—the visceral *mode of causal efficacy* conceived as direct operation of "seizing" or "grasping" (that is characterized as *vague but important*), and the more visual *mode of presentational immediacy* conceived as an indirect operation of "representing" or "inferring" (that is characterized as *precise but trivial*)—raises some doubts about the foundational character of Kato and Nishimura's distinction between verbal and visual modes of thinking. Whitehead's distinction was originally drawn in his efforts to combat Humean scepticism (i.e. in a manner that entirely avoided the Kantian subjective procedure of projecting intuitions of time and space onto things in the world). Nevertheless, this reasoning about visceral modes of perception would also appear to be entirely congruent with the contemporary and now extensive literature on situated and embodied cognition (see Wilson and Foglia, 2011 for a review, and Lakoff, 1987).

Moreover, from a computational and cognitive perspective, Kato and Nishimura's focus on time-ordering reflects tense logic (which is concerned with temporal notions such as: henceforth, eventually, hitherto, previously, now, tomorrow, yesterday, since, until, inevitably, finally, ultimately, endlessly, it will have been, it is being . . .) while the main thrust of their paper exemplifies geometric logic (which is concerned with transitions from local to global). Nevertheless, as the topos theorist, Robert Goldblatt (2006: 3), has explained, other forms of logic, of relevance to both computation and cognition, include: *deontic logic* (it is obligatory/forbidden/permitted/unlawful that . . .); *epistemic logic* (it is known to X that, it is common knowledge that . . .); *doxastic logic* (it is believed that . . .); *dynamic logic* (after the program/computation/action finishes, the program enables, throughout the task . . .); and *metalogic* (it is valid/satisfiable/provable/consistent that . . .).

This seemingly commonsensical dichotomy between verbal and visual types of information can also be questioned on a more formal basis. As argued above, string diagrams, which support visual intuitions about computational and business processes, can be manipulated to prove algebraic and logical theorems with *no loss of rigour!*

Following the lead of Samson Abramsky (2015), computer scientists at Oxford University (Coecke, Kissinger, Sadrzadeh, and Clark) have employed string diagrams derived from quantum mechanics to gain insights into the nature of natural language. These new techniques, based on Post-Mongovian linguistics, which have been incorporated into Coecke and Pulman's successful EPSRC grant (2011), may yet offer new ways of incorporating linguistic elements into our understanding of cognition, especially when coupled with other string-diagrammatic approaches to the representation of graphical logic, universal algebra, reaction-diffusion networks, signal flow graphs, Petri nets, and rewriting logic.

A summing up

In their review article on neuroeconomics, Camerer et al. (2005) make much of the distinction between controlled and automatic behaviour. Two other valuable but subtly divergent distinctions have also emerged within the pages of this paper, namely that between (i) visceral and visual modes of perception, and (ii) tacit and codifiable forms of knowledge or inference.

By firmly embedding itself within the Post-Cognitivist tradition, this Introduction has investigated the deployment of diagrammatic reasoning as a major component of semantic technology. By interpreting the process of tacit inference on the basis of Whitehead's distinction between the visceral mode of causal efficacy and visual mode of perceptual immediacy and linking this to recent arguments about embodied cognition, this Introduction has hopefully thrown new light on the strategic significance of semantic technologies in the digital economy. The limitations of contemporary approaches to so-called 'deep' machine learning and robotics have also been examined by drawing on the philosophically informed research of Herbert Dreyfus and Merleau-Ponty.

The efforts of one particular group of researchers in the field of Artificial General Intelligence to construct a psychoanalytical model of behaviour were then exposed to criticism on the basis of a Lacanian reading of Freud. Robert Rosen's category theoretic treatment of (M,R)-systems was then reviewed to shine a light on certain anticipatory aspects of cognition. Taking my cue from Gerald Edelman's Neural Darwinism, I also discussed Whitehead's pan-experientialist notion of anticipatory behaviour, which was then compared with its more subjectivist counterparts derived from the Husserlian notion of intentionality. This latter conception of anticipation was found to have influenced neo-Austrian conceptions of entrepreneurship. In summary, I suggest that the Whiteheadian approach provides an alternative, potentially fertile avenue for future research into the diagrammatic nature of both pre-conscious and unconscious structures of cognition.

The notion of strategic decision-making and competitive advantage has provided the context for these inquiries. Tacit inference plays a pivotal role in the Dynamic Capabilities approach to strategy because, by definition, it must be untraded. Although new forms of formal or codifiable knowledge are a rapidly developing feature of the digital economy, tacitness and visceral modes of perception will continue to operate as drivers of competitive advantage. For advances in robotics, cognitive computing, and AI to achieve their full potential in reasoning and communication they will have to exploit this aspect of human cognition. This paper suggests that researchers in these fields will have to combine Freudian procedures of reality testing with the kinds of anticipatory structure described by Rosen, Edelman, and Whitehead to achieve success in this endeavour.

An overview of the text

Chapter 1: Transcendental empiricism: From Schelling to Benjamin and Bloch

F. W. Schelling's influence extends far beyond the inner circle of Early Romanticism to include existentialist thinkers such as Søren Kierkegaard, the Pragmatist Charles Sanders Peirce, Karl Marx—directly or indirectly—and early researchers in the Frankfurt School: Walter Benjamin and Ernst Bloch. After an introduction to Schelling's philosophy, interpreted as a species of "transcendental realism", in accordance with the recent work of Gabriel Markus, the paper focuses on the work of Bloch and Benjamin, who have each, in their own way, contributed so much to our understanding of the role of art and creativity in an age of "mechanical reproduction". It seeks to partially answer or at least broach the following series of questions about the politico-cultural consequences of the new digital technologies of production and consumption that abound: What form should immanent critique (a notion understood by Benjamin to imply that the very criteria of critical judgement should be discovered or invented in the course of criticism) assume in the current epoch of technological development? Has the phenomenon of ubiquitous computing changed the mode of being of the historical collective? Does the "shock effect" of art, which Benjamin attributed to film and architecture, carry over to the technological developments associated with digital computation and its correlative "virtualities"? How, in an age of mechanical reproduction, can great works of art continue to embody the unclosed, and continue to realize the utopian function of living hope?

Chapter 2: Bourdieu and structuralism

Those conducting research into cultural aspects of the new digital economy and the role of the creative industries often draw on Pierre Bourdieu's conceptions of symbolic capital, which allows them to distinguish between dominant and subservient forms of communicative and cultural capability. There are two important elements that I want highlight in explaining why I have chosen to dedicate a whole chapter to Pierre Bourdieu. Firstly, I want to demonstrate his proximity to a certain Structuralist body of thought that is no longer "fashionable" and accordingly, in recent times, has been exposed to a barrage of criticism. However, I also want to insist that much of this criticism is superficial and misplaced.

Second, to demonstrate the reasons for this misperception, I want to highlight the fact that Bourdieu's Structuralist anthropology is far less rigid and deterministic than is usually supposed. To this end, I want to examine two of the most significant influences over Bourdieu's philosophical development by going back to the sociological work of Jean Piaget as well as to Merleau-Ponty's phenomenology of the flesh.

Chapter 3: 'Co-creation' in the creative industries: A new neoliberal technology of self?

This chapter interrogates the phenomenon of 'co-creation' by viewing it as a "technology of self". To this end, it focuses on the link that Foucault establishes in *The Birth of Biopolitics* between neoliberalism, on one hand, and the conception of market logic that is explicated within Austrian value theory. However, rather than conceiving of individuals who make "investments" in education and training as "entrepreneurs of themselves", in what follows, it is argued that "prosumers" or consumers as co-creators can also be viewed (and constituted) as self-regulating subjects, who share in the process of production and collaborate democratically in value-creating activity, but without remuneration. This 'theft of value' is seen to contribute to the profitability of private sector activity within the digital economy. The chapter briefly examines the role of computational ontologies in this process and reviews debates on the nature and importance of the creative industries to the digital economy.

Chapter 4: Neoliberalism, 'digitization', and creativity

This chapter extends Foucault's analysis of neoliberalism in *The Birth of Biopolitics*. More specifically, the chapter constructs and defends an anti-Husserlian approach to the labour process with the objective of investigating how collectively generated forms of intellectual labour have been appropriated under capitalist relations of production. It also interrogates the way that different notions of (computational) applied ontology influence both the nature of and our very conception of social creativity.

Chapter 5: Ubiquitous computing systems and the digital economy

This chapter examines the implications for economic analysis of the "ubiquitous computing system" (UBS) revolution, in its generality, with a more specific focus on concomitant calls for an "integrated" approach to design. This objective is approached in two main ways. First, the chapter examines knowledge representation and category-theoretic approaches to computation (which build bridges between logic, topology, algebra, and computation) before interrogating the literature on the economics of innovation as a means for understanding procedures of integrated design and new product development. In the popular media, the UBS is associated with the "internet of things", "Big Data", "Apps", and new forms of communication between business and business, businesses and customers, customers and customers, customers and machines, machines and machines, and businesses and machines. To this list, we should add concurrency and decentralized control. Process algebras provide a theoretical framework for understanding the communicative and interactive components of these developments. Other aspects of the UBS—including semantic technologies, cognitive computing, and artificial general intelligence—support procedures for massive data analysis. The chapter provides a critical overview of all these elements of the digital economy. It then examines how associated changes in computation feedback into economic analysis and modelling itself. This last section of the chapter promises to be the most provocative.

Chapter 6: The use of diagrammatic reasoning in teaching economics for the digital economy

This chapter demonstrates the precise relationship holding between Diagrammatic Reasoning (DR) and the diverse range of computational processes that characterize the operation of Ubiquitous Computing Systems (UCSs) in the digital economy. It goes on to justify their use as a pedagogical tool, with a view to identifying and foreshadowing the new kinds of insights and understandings that might flow from such an approach to teaching and learning. The chapter reviews Charles Sanders Peirce's conception of DR within the wider context of his pragmatic conception of semiotics. For Peirce, semiotics weaves together pathemata (i.e. thoughts as determinations of the mind, with matter conceived in a Schellingian manner as mind 'hide-bound' with habits), grammata (i.e. graphs as determinations on what he called the sheet of assertion, which records inscriptions of graphs and operations between graphs), and pragmata (i.e. things conceived as facts of the universe and the relations holding between things). This chapter argues that one of the major benefits of a diagrammatic approach to UCS would derive from the application of pedagogical technologies based on the very computational techniques, artefacts, and applications that would be studied and analysed in a course focusing on the drivers of the digital economy. For educational purposes, these formal techniques could then be supplemented by relevant case study material and a range of relevant simulation and modelling systems deployed within a blended learning environment.

Chapter 7: Category-theoretic approaches to semantic technologies

This chapter extends Meseguer's 1997 review article on "Research Directions in Rewriting Logic" up to this year focusing, in particular, on aspects of computation that are of relevance for the development of Semantic Technology. Research in this field is evaluated in terms of whether it: (i) is relatively straightforward to implement (i.e. it works categorically with sets and relations); (ii) represents current best-practice; (iii) has relevance to industry needs (specifically, to the process industries); (iv) can interact with a diverse range of data-base instances (including with the World Wide Web conceived as a giant global graph or hyper-graph, and with transition systems such as Petri nets, the π-calculus, reaction-diffusion systems, and dynamic systems); (v) supports diagrammatic reasoning (formal concept analysis, string diagrams, or existential graphs); and (vi) conforms to Willems' behavioural approach to open and interconnected systems, which is based on the notion that complex systems are constructed from a multitude of smaller components (e.g. PROPs, operads) that can be analysed by procedures of tearing, zooming, and linking. An accompanying appendix provides some of the technical and mathematical background to this review of the field.

Notes

1 Similarly, in one of his footnotes Brooks (1999: fn. 19: 155) cautions that an endorsement "of some of Dreyfus' views should not be taken as whole hearted embrace of all his arguments".
2 The CUBIST Project is discussed in more detail in the semantic technology section of Chapter 5.
3 As Esposito (1977) argues, Peirce was much influenced in his views on science by Schelling's nature philosophy and his later critiques of the Hegel dialectic. For an informed and detailed discussion of debates between Schelling and his contemporaries on the relationship holding between philosophical and strictly mathematical forms of reasoning, see Beiser (2010).
4 An alternative interpretation of this "clearing" to that provided by Dreyfus is that it is a transcendental opening that constitutes the conditions of possibility of structures; establishes the manner of their perturbations; and operates as the matrix within which the classical metaphysical oppositions and contradictions are engendered. On this conception, Heidegger's "clearing" is closer to Derrida's notion of the *Architrace* deployed so effectively in his critique of Husserlian phenomenology. For Derrida, the *architrace*—as the trace of an absence—is what constitutes the alterity or non-presence providing the "phenomenologically primordial" with the mark of minimal difference within which it can repeat itself infinitely as the same. This is accomplished insofar as the *Architrace* refers to an Other, in two related senses: first, to another of itself within itself (thus producing a spacing); and second, to a retention through which the self is, only insofar as the interval that constitutes it simultaneously divides it (thus accounting for temporalization). Dreyfus seems immune to this additional layer of metaphysical profundity.
5 Peter Wegner (1998) points to the case of interactive machines, which combine Turing machines with interaction between inputs and outputs, thus transforming dumb algorithms into smart agents. He contends that Interaction is not expressible on the basis of a finite initial input string (as finite sequences can always be extended); hence, the machine is transformed into an open system, as with real time and the real world that have to be modelled using real numbers, so that the system that ensues can't be described by sound and complete first-order logics (i.e. incompleteness is necessary to realize greater expressiveness or, in computational terms, we are obliged to move from the lambda to the pi calculus).
6 For a lucid discussion of the framework set out in this and the following paragraph of this Introduction, see Pomeroy (2001).

Bibliography

Abramsky, Samson (2015). Contextual Semantics: From Quantum Mechanics to Logic, Databases, Constraints, and Complexity. arXiv:1406.7386v1 [quant-ph]. 28 June 2014.
Abramsky, S. and M. Sadrzadeh (2014). Semantic Unification: A Sheaf Theoretic Approach to Natural Language. In C. Casadio, B. Coecke, M. Moortgat and P. J. Scott

(eds), *Categories and Types in Logic, Language, and Physics: A Festshrift for Jim Lambek*. Lecture Notes in Computer Science 8222. Berlin: Springer, 1–13.

Badiou, Alain (2004). *Badiou: Theoretical Writings*, ed. Ray Brassier and Alberto Toscano. London: Continuum Press.

Beiser, Frederick C. (2010). Mathematical Method in Kant, Schelling, and Hegel. In Mary Domski and Michael Dickson (eds), *Discourse on a New Method: Reinvigorating the Marriage of History and Philosophy of Science*. Chicago and La Salle, IL: Open Court, 243–258.

Brady, Geraldine and Todd Trimble (2000a). A Categorical Interpretation of C. S. Peirce's Propositional Logic Alpha. *Journal of Pure and Applied Algebra*, 149: 213–239.

Brady, Geraldine and Todd Trimble (2000b). A String Diagram Calculus for Predicate Logic and C. S. Peirce's System Beta, preprint.

Brooks, Rodney A. (1999). *Cambrian Intelligence: The Early History of the New AI*. Cambridge, MA: MIT Press.

Buchler, Justus (1939). *Charles Peirce's Empiricism*. New York, NY: Harcourt, Brace, and Company.

Camerer, C., G. Loewenstein and D. Prelec (2005). Neuroeconomics: How Neuroscience Can Inform Economics. *Journal of Economic Literature*, 63(March): 9–64.

Code, M. (1985). *Order and Organism: Steps to a Whiteheadian Philosophy of Mathematics and the Natural Sciences*. Albany, NY: State University of New York Press.

Code, M. (2005). Kindergarten Quantum Mechanics. In A. Khrennikov (ed.), *Quantum Theory: Reconsiderations of the Foundations III*. AIP Press, 81–98. arXiv:quant-ph/0510032v1.

Coecke, B. and R. Duncan (2011). Interacting Quantum Observables: Categorical Algebra and Diagrammatics. *New Journal of Physics*, 13(4): 043016.

Coecke, Bob and S. G. Pulman (2011). A Unified Model of Compositional and Distributional Semantics: Theory and Applications. Research Grant, EPSRC Project Ref EP/ I03808X/1: http://gow.epsrc.ac.uk/NGBOViewGrant.aspx?GrantRef=EP/I03808X/1.

Curien, Pierre-Louis (2008). *Category Theory: A Programming Language-Oriented Introduction*, mimeo. Accessed 16 September, 2016. www.irif.fr/~mellies/mpri/mpri-ens/articles/curien-category-theory.pdf.

Dau, Frithjof (2006). *Mathematical Logic with Diagrams, Based on the Existential Graphs of Peirce*. Habilitation thesis, to be published. Available at: www.dr-dau.net.

Deleuze, G. (2004). *Desert Island: And Other Texts 1953–74*. Los Angeles, CA: Semiotext(e) Foreign Agent Series.

Dietrich, Dietmar, Dietmar Bruckner, Gerhard Zucker, Brit Muller and Anna Tmej (2009). Psychoanalytical Model for Automation and Robotics. Paper presented at AFRICON, 2009 Conference, 23–25 September.

Dipert, Randall (2004). Peirce's Deductive Logic. In Cheryl Misak (ed.), *The Cambridge Companion to Peirce*. Cambridge: Cambridge University Press, 315.

Dreyfus, H. L. (1992). *What Computers Still Can't Do: A Critique of Artificial Reason*. Cambridge, MA: MIT Press.

Dreyfus, H. L. (1993). Heidegger's Critique of Husserl's (and Searle's) Account of Intentionality. *Social Research*, 60(1): 17–38.

Dreyfus, H. L. (2005). Overcoming the Myth of the Mental: How Philosophers Can Profit from the Phenomenology of Everyday Expertise. APA Pacific Division Presidential Address.

Dreyfus, H. L. (n.d.) *Being and Power: Heidegger and Foucault*, mimeo.

Edelman, Gerald (2006). *Second Nature: Brain Science and Human Knowledge*. New Haven, CT: Yale University Press.

Ehresmann, A. C. and J.-P. Vanbremeersch (1987). Hierarchical Evolutive Systems: A Mathematical Model for Complex Systems. *Bulletin of Mathematical Biology*, 49(1): 13–50.

Epperson, M. (2004). *Quantum Mechanics, and the Philosophy of Alfred North Whitehead*. New York, NY: Fordham University Press.

Esposito, J. L. (1977). *Schelling's Idealism and Philosophy of Nature*. Lewisburg, PA: Bucknell University Press.

Fenichel, Teresa (2016). *Uncanny Belonging: Schelling, Freud and the Vertigo of Freedom*. Boston College Electronic Thesis or Dissertation, Boston College Libraries, http://hdl. handle.net/2345/bc-ir:104819.

Fraenkel, A. A., Y. Bar-Hillel and A. Levey, with the collaboration of Dirk van Dalen (1973). *Foundations of Set Theory*. Amsterdam: Noord-Hollandsche U.M.

Franchi, Stefano (2006). Herbert Simon, the Anti-Philosopher. In L. Magnani (ed.), *Computing and Philosophy*. Pavia: Associated International Academic Publishers, 27–40.

Franchi, Stefano (2011). The Past, Present, and Future Encounters between Computation and the Humanities. Philosophy and Theory of Artificial Intelligence Conference (Pt-Ai). Thessaloniki, *Greece*. http://stefano.cleinias.org/sites/default/files/S_Franchi_ Digital_Encounters_Springer_FINAL.pdf.

Freud, Sigmund (1958). *The Standard Edition of the Complete Psychological Works of Sigmund Freud*, ed. and trans. James Strachey et al. 24 vols. London: Hogarth Press.

Ganter, B. and R. Wille (1999). *Formal Concept Analysis: Mathematical Foundations*. Berlin and Heidelberg: Springer (Trans. Formale Begriffsanalyse: Mathematische Grundlagen. Springer, Berlin-Heidelberg, 1996).

Geurts, Bart, David I. Beaver and Emar Maier (2016). Discourse Representation Theory. *The Stanford Encyclopedia of Philosophy* (Spring Edition), ed. Edward N. Zalta. http:// plato.stanford.edu/archives/spr2016/entries/discourse-representation-theory/.

Goldblatt, R. (2006). Mathematical Modal Logic: A View of Its Evolution. Revised version. In Dov M. Gabbay and John Woods (eds), *Logic and the Modalities in the Twentieth Century*. Handbook of the History of Logic 7. Amsterdam: Elsevier, 1–98.

Heidegger, Martin (2001). *Being and Time*. Trans. John Macquarrie and Edward Robinson. Oxford: Blackwell.

Hereth, Joachim, Gerd Stumme, Rudolf Wille and Uta Wille (2000). Conceptual Knowledge Discovery and Data Analysis. *Conceptual Structures: Logical, Linguistic, and Computational Issues*. Lecture Notes in Computer Science 1867. Berlin: Springer, 421–437.

Johnstone, Peter (1977). *Topos Theory*. New York, NY: Academic Press.

Joyal, A. and R. Street (1988). Planar Diagrams and Tensor Algebra. Unpublished manuscript, available from Ross Street's website, September.

Joyal, A. and R. Street (1991). The Geometry of Tensor Calculus I. *Advances in Mathematics*, 88(1): 55–112.

Kartsaklis, Dimitri, Mehrnoosh Sadrzadeh, Stephen Pulman and Bob Coecke (2013). Reasoning about Meaning in Natural Language with Compact Closed Categories and Frobenius Algebras. In A. Chubb, J. Eskandarian and V. Harizanov (eds), *Logic and Algebraic Structures in Quantum Computing and Information*. Cambridge: Cambridge University Press.

Kato, G. (2004). Elemental Principles of t-Topos. *Europhysics Letters*, 68(4): 467–472. DOI: 10.1209/epl/i2004-10234-2.

Kato, Goro C. and Kazuo Nishimura (2013). Grasping a Concept as an Image or as a Word: A Categorical Formulation of Visual and Verbal Thinking Processes. *Journal of Scientific Research and Reports*, 2(2): 682–691.

Keeler, Mary (1995). The Philosophical Context of Peirce's Existential Graphs. Available at: www.welchco.com/02/14/01/60/00/05/1501.HTM.

Lakoff, G. (1987). *Women, Fire, and Dangerous Things: What Categories Reveal about the Mind*. Chicago, IL: University of Chicago Press.

Lakoff, G. and R. E. Núñez (2000). *Where Mathematics Comes From: How the Embodied Mind Brings Mathematics into Being*, New York, NY: Basic Books.

Lambek, Joachim and Philip J. Scott (2011). *Reflections on the Categorical Foundations of Mathematics*. In G. Sommaruga (ed.) *Foundational Theories of Classical and Constructive Mathematics*. The Western Ontario Series in Philosophy of Science 76. New York, NY: Springer, 171–186.

Louie, A. H. (2008). Functional Entailment and Immanent Causation in Relational Biology. *Axiomathes*, 18: 289–302.

Louie, A. H. (2012). Anticipation in (M,R)-Systems. *International Journal of General Systems*, 41(1): 5–22.

Louie, A. H. (2013). *The Reflection of Life: Functional Entailment and Imminence in Relational Biology*. International Federation for Systems Research International Series on Systems Science and Engineering. New York, NY: Springer.

McGrath, S. J. (2011). Is Schelling's Nature-Philosophy Freudian? *Analecta Hermeneutica*, 3: 1–20.

Marsden, Daniel (2014). Category Theory Using String Diagrams. Accessed October 2016. https://arxiv.org/pdf/1401.7220.pdf.

Merleau-Ponty, Maurice (1968). *The Visible and the Invisible*. Trans. Alphonso Lingis. Evanston, IL: Northwestern University Press.

Müller, Vincent C. (ed.) (2016). *Fundamental Issues of Artificial Intelligence*. Synthese Library 377: Berlin: Springer.

Peirce, Charles Sanders (1906). Prolegomena to an Apology for Pragmaticism.

Peirce, Charles Sanders (1931–1935). *Collected Papers of Charles Sanders Peirce*, ed. Paul Weiss, Charles Hartshorne and Arthur W. Burks. Cambridge, MA: Harvard University Press.

Peirce, Charles Sanders (1931–1958). *Collected Papers of Charles Sanders Peirce*. 8 volumes, ed. Arthur W. Burks, Charles Hartshorne, and Paul Weiss. Cambridge, MA: Harvard University Press.

Peirce, Charles Sanders (1935). MS 478: Existential Graphs. Partly published in Charles Sanders Peirce (1931–1935), *Collected Papers of Charles Sanders Peirce*, ed. Paul Weiss, Charles Hartshorne and Arthur W. Burks. Cambridge, MA: Harvard University Press, 4.394–417.

Peirce, Charles Sanders (1992). *Reasoning and the Logic of Things*. In K. L. Kremer and H. Putnam (eds), *The Cambridge Conferences Lectures of 1898*. Cambridge, MA: Harvard University Press.

Petitot, Jean (1993). Phenomenology of Perception, Qualitative Physics, and Sheaf Mereology. 16th International Wittgenstein Symposium, Kirchberg, 15–22 August 1993. Accessed 31 October 2011. http://jean.petitot.pagesperso-orange.fr/.

Polanyi, M. (1965). The Structure of Consciousness. *Brain*, 88: 79–810. Accessed October 2016. http://polanyisociety.org/essays.htm.

Polanyi, M. (1966). *The Tacit Dimension*. Chicago, IL: University of Chicago Press.

34   *Introduction*

Pomeroy, Anne Fairchild (2001). Process Philosophy and the Possibility of Critique. *Journal of Speculative Philosophy*, 15(1): 33–49.

Price Waterhouse Coopers (2010). Final Demand-driven Mapping Report. Public report D3.2 from the research project value-it. , February 2010. Accessed September 2010. Available at www.value-it.eu.

Rosen, R. (1985). *Anticipatory Systems*. Oxford: Pergamon Press.

Rosen, R. (1991). *Life Itself: A Comprehensive Inquiry into the Nature, Origin, and Fabrication of Life*. New York, NY: Columbia University Press.

Rudrauf, David et al . (2003). From Autopoiesis to Neurophenomenology: Francisco Varela's Exploration of the Biophysics of Being. *Biological Research*, 36: 21–59.

Schelling, F. W. J. (1936). *Philosophical Inquiries into the Nature of Human Freedom*. Trans. J. Gutmann. Chicago, IL: Open Court Publishing.

Segall, Matthew David (2015). Philosophy of Mythology and Revelation (h/t Schelling). Blog entry, 11 December. https://footnotes2plato.com/2015/12/11/philosophy-of-mythology-and-revelation-ht-schelling/.

Stjernfelt, Frederick (2007). *Diagrammatology: An Investigation on the Borderlines of Phenomenology, Ontology, and Semiotics*. Synthese Library 336. Dordrecht: Springer.

Teece, D. J (2000). *Managing Intellectual Capital: Organizational, Strategic, and Policy Dimensions*. Oxford: Oxford University Press.

Teece, D., G. Pisano and A. Shuen (1997). Dynamic Capabilities and Strategic Management. *Strategic Management Journal*, 18(7): 509–533.

Varela, Francisco J., Eban T. Thompson and Eleanor Rosch (1991). *The Embodied Mind: Cognitive Science and Human Experience*. Cambridge, MA: MIT Press.

Wegner, Peter (1998). Interactive Foundations of Computing. *Theoretical Computer Science*, 192: 315–351.

Wells, A. J. (2002). Gibson's Affordances and Turing's Theory of Computation. *Ecological Psychology*, 14(3): 141–180.

Whitehead, Alfred North (1967a). [1933] *Adventures of Ideas*. New York, NY: The Free Press.

Whitehead, Alfred North (1967b). [1925] *Science and the Modern World*. New York, NY: The Free Press.

Whitehead, Alfred North (1968a). [1938] *Modes of Thought*. New York, NY: The Free Press.

Whitehead, Alfred North (1968b). *Essays in Science and Philosophy*. New York, NY: Greenwood Press.

Whitehead, Alfred North (1978). [1929] *Process and Reality* (Corrected Edition), ed. David Ray Griffin and Donald W. Sherburne. New York, NY: The Free Press.

Wilson, Robert A. and Lucia Foglia (2011). Embodied Cognition. In *The Stanford Encyclopedia of Philosophy* (Fall Edition), ed. Edward N. Zalta.

1 Transcendental empiricism
From Schelling to Benjamin and Bloch

Hope is nothing else but *an inconstant pleasure, arising from the image of something future or past, whereof we do not yet know the issue. Fear*, on the other hand, is *an inconstant pain also arising from the image of something concerning which we are in doubt.* If the element of doubt be removed from these emotions, hope becomes *Confidence* and fear becomes *Despair.* In other words, *Pleasure or Pain arising from the image of something concerning which we have hoped or feared.*

(Spinoza, 1955: II, Prop. XVIII, Note II, p. 144)

I have no right to continue my development as long as I have not accepted Kant or haven't proven him wrong inside me.

(Scholem, 2007: diary entry dated
27 September 1917: 183)

In this chapter I pursue a specific theoretical lineage, which begins with the active subversion of Kantian Transcendental philosophy both by certain contemporaries (such as Salomon Maimon) and by later contributors to the tradition of German Idealism (Hegel, Feuerbach and Marx), while choosing to focus, for reasons of brevity, on the overriding influence of F. W. Schelling on the German philosophers, Ernst Bloch and Walter Benjamin. Figure 1.1 maps out this trajectory, while seeking specifically to distinguish it from both the phenomenological and hermeneutic traditions of philosophy.

One of the objectives in tracing this lineage is to bring together two thinkers, Bloch and Benjamin, who have each contributed so much to our understanding of the role of art and creativity in an age of "mechanical reproduction". I shall be returning to this theme again and again at certain points.[1] To meet this objective, I have been obliged to spend less time than might otherwise be desirable in demonstrating the affinities, congruences, and isomorphisms that, in my view, clearly hold between the reasoning of Schelling and the that of my chosen pair of more contemporary philosophers.

Predecessors

The predecessors for Benjamin and Bloch's revolutionary aesthetics are the German Idealists, especially Novalis and Schelling. Novalis precipitated a breaking away

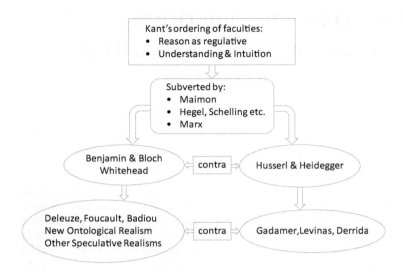

Figure 1.1 Two Post-Kantian Philosophical Trajectories

from efforts to ground knowledge in identical being, because he recognized that the very process of bringing consciousness into being veils consciousness from itself, thus imposing the necessity for self-critique. Moreover, the self's familiarity with itself is something that is both indeterminate and non-discursive.[2] For Novalis, then, finitude is subverted and exposed by the inescapable phenomenon of infinite regress, which the knowing subject is exposed to in virtue of the fact that higher forms of thinking are required to integrate both the thinking self and thought in itself. Much like modern theorists of computation, such as Peter Aczel, he argued that this infinite regression, must be actively embraced!

As Beiser (2002: 465) explains, it was Schelling "who fathered the basic principles and who forged the central themes of the absolute idealism that Hegel loyally defended and systematized from 1801 to 1804". And even "if we admit that Hegel eventually saw farther than Schelling—a very generous concession—it is also necessary to add that he did so only because he stood on Schelling's shoulders".

Beiser (2002: 466) also articulates the reasons for the contemporary neglect of Schelling's thought, saying that it "has much to do with the ill repute of metaphysics", for "no one nowadays wants to be near metaphysics, the bogeyman of positivists, pragmatists, neo-Kantians, and postmodernists alike". Beiser comments that Schelling's notoriety for being a full-blown metaphysician "is somewhat ironic, given that, after 1809, Schelling himself turned against the metaphysical tradition, developing an interesting critique of conceptual thought in his later *Positivephilosophie*". Nevertheless, Beiser (2002: 466) also explains the reasoning behind Schelling's "ontological turn" away from the Kantian question of legitimate knowledge, for:

The basic question of epistemology—"How do we know that our concepts correspond to the world?"—is resolvable, Schelling argued, only if we can also explain the interaction between the mental and physical, the subjective and objective, the ideal and real. If these terms refer to complete opposites—if they denote entities in separate worlds—then the correspondence between representation and object in knowledge becomes impossible, at best a complete mystery.

For the elder Schelling, the ontological question is captured by the existentialist conception that our existence necessarily precedes access to existence. In his terms, 'unprethinkable' being is both the presupposition of, and the beyond of thought. As I will demonstrate below, the distinction between logical being and historical being is exploited by Schelling in moving away from the flat ontology of logical space to the ordered ontology of historical time, with its movement from the logical past, to the present and future of being; especially, to the notion of personality as a "yet-to-be-completed" project. This ensures that human agency, itself, is exposed to the paradox that what comes later in logical time modifies what has come earlier, giving rise to an inexhaustible and indeterminable multiplication of the very means by which we refer to being and intervene in history: human freedom is vested in a profound contingency, in the historical possibility of things always being otherwise.

Gabriel makes this conception of Schelling's the very core of his own transcendental ontology, insisting that his temporal ordering contrasts markedly with Hegel's essentially timeless, circular logic. Nevertheless, he maintains that it should still not be conceived solely in subjective terms, because the self-relation of reality to itself is, in effect, achieved through our reference to it. He goes on to proclaim that both our thoughts about facts and the facts themselves are facts. Gabriel's objective is to promote a New Ontological Realism (NOR) that can overthrow both the stodgy old version of metaphysical realism, which implies a "world without spectators", and the contemporary version of Constructivism, which implies a "world with spectators". To achieve success, his NOR must not only be able to explain the existence of spectators, but also the fact that spectators do not exist at all times and in all places. Furthermore, given that phenomena such as thoughts, institutions, and dreams are just as much a part of the object domain as objects such as projectiles, bacteria, or quarks that are more familiar to the natural sciences, advocates of NOR refuse to reduce all ontological questions to those posited by natural sciences.

Walter Benjamin, too, rejects the Kantian position that absolute reason is something entirely removed from the determinate features of intuition, choosing, instead, to embrace the notion of the absolute as embedded within a potentially infinite network of interconnected reflections, with both a structure and a genealogy conditioned by a dialectical interweaving of surfaces and their configurations. Moreover he also holds to the idea that the self-relation of reality to itself is achieved through our reference to it; a view most notably manifest in his onomatopoetic conception of non-sensuous sensuality and his genealogical analysis of the mimetic faculty as it passes, disruptively, from the unmediated cognition of natural marks to the mediated re-cognition of written inscriptions.

For his part, Ernst Bloch also argues for a dialectical conception of matter, which is grounded in a displacement of transcendental inquiry away from epistemological questions to those of ontology. For him, matter is the substrate of the objectively real possible, and transcendental inquiry interrogates the conditions required for something to be possible.

Transcendental ontology

As Gabriel (2011: ix) pronounces, "*Transcendental ontology investigates the ontological conditions of our conditions of access to what there is*".[3] The analysis of the concept of existence is therefore methodologically prior to the analysis of the subject's access to existence. From the beginning, German Idealism was concerned with the question of the *phenomenalization* of being: What conditions have to be fulfilled by being (the world) in order for it to appear to finite thinkers who in turn change the structure of what there is by referring to it? However, the way that this question was approached from an Idealist perspective is cogently summarized by Slavoj Žižek (1996: 14):[4]

> [A]s with Hegel, the problem is not how to attain the noumenal In-itself beyond phenomena; the true problem is how and why does this In-itself split itself from itself at all, how does it acquire a distance towards itself and thus clear the space in which it can appear (to itself)?

Gabriel explains that,

> Kant was eager to prove that everything that exists has to be constituted by thought, given that thought can only grasp what is compatible with the logical form of referring to something, which differs from the fact of being referred to. Instead of laying out the structure of being as such, he assigned philosophy the task of reflecting on the constitution of objects qua objects of thought.
>
> (Gabriel, 2011: x)

In accordance with Kant's largely epistemological approach to the transcendental question, "there can be no absolute ontological gap between the order of things and the order of thought (of judging)", because "the given must itself have a form that is at least minimally compatible with being grasped by thought". As such, "the unifying activity that makes judgments about anything possible, yet which is not itself a judgment, had to be located within the subject" (Gabriel, 2011: xi)

For Kant, synthesis establishes relations within a given material, which is given through sensibility. In part, Hegel will attempt to replace the semantic atomism of this naïve "myth of the given" with a form of radical conceptual holism. For him, this very thought, that "what is given in sensory experience is conceptually structured", transcends sensory experience by investigating "the relation holding between how something is given and the position to which it is given", for the structure of experience "cannot itself be experienced among other objects". Moreover, Hegel believes that Kant is "right in understanding subjectivity as constituting logical forms of reference (categories) outside of which nothing determinate can be apprehended", however, he errs in not applying this thought to itself, for synthesis is a property of intentionality as such and, therefore, also applies to higher-order intentionality, that is, to theorizing about intentionality (Gabriel, 2011: xvi)!

> [I]ntentionality as such has an *as if* character: in order for us to have anything *in view*, which is even potentially distinct from our *having* it in view, we need to refer to it at least *as if* it was independent of this act of reference.

In summary, for Gabriel (2011: xvii), "*the Kantian metaphysics of intentionality is dialectically contradictory under self-application precisely because it does not reflect on its own position, on its own constitution*". In summary, "[a]ll of the so-called German idealists are looking for a transcendental method which is thoroughly dialectically stable under self-application. They all practice various forms of higher-order reflection thereby distinguishing between the levels of reflection".

In Fichte, for example, Gabriel (2011: xviii) notes that "Being" is "the name for the facticity of absolute knowing, for the fact that we make the concept of knowledge explicit after having already claimed some knowledge or other about something or other". Thus, Fichte's related notion of "objectifying performance, which takes absolute knowing and thereby being as its object, is being's self-reference". Similarly, in *The Grounding of Positive Philosophy*, Schelling points out that, in his first *Critique*, Kant draws a twofold distinction between two forms of reason: (i) reason in its application to the sensible realm; and (ii) reason in its self-application. According to Schelling, however, "Kant mainly considers reason in this first sense, that is, in its capacity to structure sensible experience with the help of regulative ideas. In this way, Kant neglects 'absolute reason', that is, reason insofar as it explicates itself". He also complains that for Kant, "Givenness is evidently not itself given, it is already a position within higher-order thought" (Gabriel, 2011: xix).

And Gabriel comments in approving terms, on Jacobi's protest that Kant's "transcendental idealism amounts to nihilism" for it "destroys the subject by reducing it to an empty logical form", for "the only way to preserve the possibility of freedom" for Kant, was for the subject to dissolve "into its judgments" so that it could not possibly judge itself.

For Hegel, too, this Kantian autonomy of the subject "is defined with recourse to spontaneity, and spontaneity is only defined in opposition to receptivity. Hence, autonomy is contingent on heteronomy, the possibility of freedom presupposes the actuality of necessity, and so forth". Nevertheless, Hegel also acknowledges that "the question to be answered remains Kantian: how is it possible to refer to anything that is not a judgment by a judgment?" (Gabriel, 2011: xii).

For Gabriel, himself, the thought that transcendental ontology adds to this Hegelian question is given by the maxim: "*our thoughts about the way the world is are themselves a way the world is*". On the basis of this maxim It is therefore necessary to refer "to the ontological conditions of the conditions of possibility of truth-apt reference". More profoundly, he asks, "how is it possible that the world refers to itself through our reference to it?" In answering these specifically ontological questions, Gabriel turns to the work of McDowell for whom the world turns out to be a totalizable domain of facts immediately available to truth-apt thought. Accordingly, Gabriel (2011: xiii) makes this "premodern notion of a thoroughly determined, totalizable world" into the focus of a sustained attack: for "there is no such thing as an all-encompassing entity, an 'all', even though the idea of an all regulates our epistemological enterprise": the all is nothing but a (necessary) illusion (Gabriel, 2011: xxi)!

In his efforts to examine the conditions of possibility of truth-apt reference, Gabriel commences with Frege's "description of the metaphysical situation—that is, some 'thing' or state of affairs on the one hand, and a plurality of ways of truthfully accessing *It* on the other—is partial" (Gabriel, 2011: xiii).[5] That is, "It still tries to identify It, thereby accessing the apparently unproblematically singular It under one description among others". In Frege's own words:

> The sense of a proper name is grasped by everybody who is sufficiently familiar with the language or totality of designations to which it belongs; but this serves to illuminate only a single aspect of the reference, supposing it to have one.
>
> (Frege, 1997: 154)

Gabriel expands on this fundamental insight, noting:

> [e]ven though sense should indeed not be conceived as a barrier or misleading veil between an objective state of affairs and our attempts to grasp it, there is an inherent plurality in the notion of sense. *Sense is a medium of difference, whereas reference is meant to limit the sheer proliferation of senses without a referent.*
>
> (Gabriel, 2011: xiv)

However, if it is

> a thoroughly individuated domain of referents on the one hand, and a plurality of senses on the other hand, which serves to make the determinacy of things available to truth-apt discourse, then the very ontology we use in this case to make finitude available to higher-order thought about thought itself turns out to be finite.
>
> (Gabriel, 2011: xiv)

In other words, "the very thought that tries to grasp this finitude and contingency becomes finite and contingent" (Gabriel, 2011: xiv). For Gabriel (2011: xv), therefore, "Being itself is the source of contingency" it is "nothing other than a side effect of the transfinite, nontotalizable plurality of fields of sense". Yet, inevitably, this very "plurality of fields of sense remains hidden to those who endorse either a metaphysics of common sense or that of scientism".

Opposing the views of the Speculative Realist, Quentin Meillassoux, Gabriel contends that, "Post-Kantian idealism is not a first-order theory according to which there would be no objects if there were not any subjects in the universe".

Gabriel also makes use of Brandom's distinction between: (i) *sense-dependence*: an idealism which claims that being given in a particular kind of way constitutes a particular kind of domain of objectivity; and (ii) *reference-dependence*: which claims that there is only a particular kind of object (say a spatiotemporal object) if there is a corresponding act of judging. That is, the ways in which objects are given "determine the possibility of getting something right *or* wrong about them": sense is therefore "the medium of different modes of presentation". While sense belongs to the "world", Gabriel insists that, "It is not the case that there is a stable, completely determined 'world' on the one side of a dividing line and a precarious, potentially contradictory domain of sense and reference on the other" (Gabriel, 2011: xx).

In a way that will be of great benefit to my subsequent analysis of Benjamin and Bloch, Gabriel goes on to demonstrate that the concept of "unprethinkable being", as set out in the mature phase of Schelling's writing, partakes of this sense of incompleteness and precariousness. The political context for Schelling's subsequent ascendancy to Hegel's vacated Chair in Berlin is clearly described by Terry Pinkard (2002: 317):

> Alarmed by what he saw as anti-Christian, republican, and revolutionary movements growing in Berlin, and being himself a great partisan of Romantic philosophy (which since the Congress of Vienna had departed from its origins and assumed an increasingly apologetic role for the conservative reaction in Germany), the king wished to summon to Berlin someone with both the intellectual profile and the political sensibility to be able to mount a successful counter-offensive against the Hegelian school. Famously, the minister encharged with recruiting Schelling quoted the king as hoping that Schelling's appointment would stamp out the "dragon-seed of Hegelian pantheism" in Berlin.

It is somewhat remarkable that the philosophical thought of someone willing to assume this burdensome role should have been taken to heart by such a wide variety of readers ranging from existentialists like Kierkegaard, Post Structuralist thinkers like Slavoj Žižek, scientific realists, and Marxists like Benjamin and Bloch.[6] Pinkard (2002: 319) provides us with valuable insight into the motivation for the radical re-thinking of his philosophical project that Schelling initiated:

After 1809, he worked intently on an alternative system of philosophy that would unite philosophy and a kind of narrative mythology into an account that would make good on the kinds of metaphorical claims Schelling had made in the 1809 essay. By 1833, however, he had ceased to see that approach as fruitful, and he began working out a new approach that repudiated entirely the "mythological" and "narrative" elements of his interim "system".

Subsequently, Schelling came to believe that "a thorough rethinking of Kantianism was demanded, which would both circumvent the post-Kantian movement altogether and return again to the original issue that had motivated the post-Kantian movement in the first place" (Pinkard, 2002: 319).

Pinkard observes that there were three main issues driving this rethinking: (i) the third Kantian Antinomy (i.e. the apparent contradiction between radical freedom we and the determinism in nature); (ii) the "Kantian paradox" of self-legislation (i.e. in so far as we deprive ourselves of our autonomy in subjecting ourselves to the principle of reason); and, (iii) the post-Kantian conflation between logic and existence (that we are obliged to think of the world in a certain way does not imply that the world has to be that way) (Pinkard, 2002: 319–320).

Ultimately, the subjective point of view was itself indebted to something that was not itself and on which it simply had to acknowledge its dependency (i.e. God and the Christian revelation)!

(Pinkard, 2002: 321)

As Pinkard (2002: 322–323) explains, this re-thinking led Schelling to move away from his earlier reliance on "intellectual intuitions" as "ways of re-describing our mode of being-in-the-world such that problems dissolved rather than were disproved".[7] After a brief flirtation with "a more literary way of "intuiting" what was at stake", articulated in the *Historische-kritische Einleitung in die Philosophie der Mythologie*, which argued for the creation of a new "philosophical mythology", Schelling moved on to a stage of re-thinking the absolute as "that which in itself neither has being nor does not have being" but is rather the "eternal freedom to be". The absolute, conceived by Schelling as "primordial essence", is split between a willing that wills nothing but could be everything (eternal God), and a willing that strives for existence, thus, initiating the "beginning of existence", which initially gives rise to the temporal world and ultimately "ends with the reconciliation (restoration of unity) of God and the world" (a conception that is re-interpreted by Whitehead in panexperientialist terms as the Principle of Creativity).

Pinkard (2002: 326–327) observes that for Hegel, "the key insight of the Schellingian system—that the difference between the subjective and the objective was itself neither subjective nor objective"—could only be implemented in a logical manner, which Schelling failed to accomplish. For Schelling, however, Hegel simply confused the way we must "logically" think of things with the system of the existing world, and that confusion lay at the basis of what was wrong with all post-Kantian idealism. Opposing such a "negative philosophy" would be a "positive philosophy" which started from some kind of metaphysical "fact" that it freely admitted could not be demonstrated by reason itself and which then elucidated developments out of that "fact", using reason to make its case but conceding that the development out of that "positive" beginning is always guided by something beyond human reasoning that is to guide reason itself.

Pinkard (2002: 327)

Moreover, "there is no 'dialectical transition' from negative to positive philosophy; the latter begins with the failure of the former, but it takes none of its principles from it" (2002: 328). As Jason Wirth (2007: 10) explains:

Schelling never dismissed Hegel or his own earlier negative philosophy but argued that negative philosophy cannot proceed from existence itself. Rather it transcends existence to reveal the free ground of existence. It begins with necessity and culminates with freedom. Positive philosophy, however, reverses the direction, beginning with freedom as its starting point.

For his part, Gabriel (2011: 61) begins his explication of "unprethinkable being" by noting the importance of Schelling's distinction between two conceptions of being: logical and historical. The first of these, Logical being, is based on the argument that "determinacy can only take place in a whole, in which everything determinate is so only by virtue of its being predicatively comprehensible and distinguishable from everything else". The second conception, Historical being, is correlative to a profound and vertiginous awareness that "all grounds, have an 'abyss [*Abgrund*]' (Heidegger) or a 'non-ground [*Ungrund*]' (Schelling) as their limit". Historical being is associated with an ordered rather than a flat ontology: one predicated on distinguishing between a being's logical past, its present and its future.

Under this logical conception, "being has to be determined as something determinate, as determinacy" so that the difference between being and nothingness is necessarily nullified (although this does not imply straightaway that everything determinate is actually known) (Gabriel, 2011: 63). Schelling goes on to identify the idea of ('blueprint' or 'figure' of) being with the Kantian "transcendental ideal of pure reason". Under its sway, "[t]he individual is hereby understood as *eo ipso* nothing more than a moment of the whole" in the search for "the highest and most general modes (the *summa genera*) of being" (Gabriel, 2011: 64; citing SWS, XI, 336) Nevertheless, the weakness of this Kantian conception of thought and subjecthood is that it "fails to account for the thinker's own *existential position*". Gabriel (2011: 65) champions Schelling's alternative discovery: in contrast to the *negativity* of such determinations, *positive* philosophy must

take into account the ontological significance of our thinking *personality*, if we are to succeed in giving a philosophical account of ourselves that can be distinguished from the thought according to which we are the impersonal instantiation of pure thought.

This new notion of personality, as a "yet-to-be-completed" project, opens out onto the Schellingian notion of contingency: while logical space (as the space of reasons within which judgements and their determinate objects are situated), *has* an outside, it cannot find its *reason* in what is outside it. Once this ontological incompleteness is acknowledged it can be wedded to a re-invigorated notion of freedom that escapes the antinomial trap of Kant: the 'historical' concept of being is brought under that of *personality* so that determinate being has the character of a project underway, a yet-to-be-completed doing, and must be thought to advance by acts of *will*, hence exhibiting freedom rather than rational necessity. Moreover, because *necessario existens* can only be manifest as necessary, "once the ontological modalities have been distinguished, this means that the 'possibility of another being', and therefore, the possibility of being's own contingency, cannot be excluded from unprethinkable being" (Gabriel, 2011: 66; citing SW, XI, 317; XIV, 346).

Hence, unprethinkable being, designates "that whose determinate being (*Dasein*) is necessary for thought" or "that which, no matter how early we come on the scene, is already there", i.e. it signifies the always-already as such (SWS, XIV, 341). Accordingly, Schelling's conception of the infinite does not arise from a Hegelian self-sublation of the finite but rather from the inexhaustible determinability of unprethinkable being, i.e. as Gabriel construes it, through "the possibility of multiplying indefinitely (though not arbitrarily) the senses by means of which we refer to a unitary reality". In fact, contingency is "shown as a logical-ontological condition of necessary being", because "without this other and therefore contingent being, the *necessario existens* would not itself be necessary" (i.e. the very structure of coming-to-be-determinate necessitates the contingency of determinacy!) (Gabriel, 2011: 66).

Schelling's doctrine of the three potencies, embodied in the judgement, provides us with a deeper insight into one of his key notions.[8] The first potency is the determinable as such. However, determinacy and therefore something, anything whatsoever, presupposes that something be determined: this is the "originary subject" as "pure being without any 'could', without any capability" (Gabriel, 2011: 68; citing SW, XI, 352, fn. 3; 292). The second potency features the figure of the predicate, which opens a logical space of possible instances, without there being *eo ipso* a determinate instance to sort out: this is the role of the "originary predicate" as "pure 'could' or capability without any being" (Gabriel, 2011: 69; citing SWS, XI, 292; 352, n. 3.) Finally, the third potency is conceived as the "originary synthesis of subject and predicate". Accordingly, subject and predicate must be coordinated: this is the role of the copula, or "spirit".

> The three potencies are what establish a logical space for raising the question of how there can be something rather than nothing. Moreover, Unprethinkable being is the first potency in its initial independence from judgment.
> (Gabriel, 2011: 69; citing SWS, XIV, 341)

Unprethinkable being is that "that which thinking cannot get behind or before, that which cannot be anticipated or anteceded by any thought whatsoever" (Gabriel, 2011: 70). Gabriel (2011: 71) goes on to articulate the Schellingian dialectical interplay between the logical and historical and necessity and contingency by noting

> *that* there is a logical space that is opened by and through the fundamental structure of judgments and the potencies cannot be explained or understood with recourse to judgment. The existence of logical space is therefore contingent, because no ground can be given to account for the fact that it exists.

As such, it obtains as "the actuality of all possibility, that is, all determinability prior to its becoming anything determinate as such". In this role, it serves as the "ground of ground" or the "abyss".

In what follows, I will attempt to describe the manner in which these philosophical conceptions of Schelling have been taken up, albeit in modified form, first by Marx, and subsequently, by both Benjamin and Bloch.

Marx and living labour

For Schelling,

> the construction of objects follows identical series in ideation as in matter: the introduction of a limit into the unlimited (first act), the object-becomings of the construct as repeatedly divided by this limit (second act), and the object-becoming-to-itself of the construct now recapitulating this division in itself (third act), i.e., between forces. [Moreover,] At each stage, the decomposition of intelligence parallels that of matter, while at no stage is the asymmetry of the process eliminated.
>
> (Grant, 2006: 187–188)

Schelling's hypothesis is "that *realism concerning the Idea* follows from the physical grounds of idea-generating organizations, or intelligence". Even his late definition of myth conceives of it as "still 'a kind of philosophy', only 'unconscious, naturalistic, *autophusis philosophia*' (XI, 258), or '*nature itself philosophizing*'" (Grant, 2006: 201).

> Dussel (1997) argues that Marx's emphasis on living labor as the "creative source" of surplus-value is based on Schelling's critique of Hegel. According to Hegel, Being passes into Essence as a result of its own self-development; no external element is necessary for this development. According to Schelling, on the other hand, the "creative source" of Being exists outside of and prior to Being. Being is explained as an effect of this "creative source". Similarly, Dussel argues that for Marx living labor is the economic "creative source", which also exists outside of and prior to capital. . . . This is Marx's "inversion" of Hegel's logic, according to Dussel. All the different individual forms of capital are explained as effects of living labor, as the forms of appearance of living labor, from the "exteriority" of capital.
>
> (Moseley, 2001: 4–5)

In particular, Dussel criticizes Lukács and Kosík for thinking that the key concept in Marx's theory is totality, suggesting that capital is self-sufficient in itself. However, according to Dussel, Marx's theory of surplus-value demonstrates that capital is not a self-sufficient totality. Capital can exist (i.e. produce surplus-value) only by incorporating living labour from outside of itself, in the "exteriority".

Dussel argues that Marx began work on *Theories of Surplus Value* as a means for deploying his own conception in a critique of rival theories. This includes "Smith's dogma", where Smith argues that the total price of the annual product could be entirely resolved into different forms of revenue (wages + profit + rent), without an additional component for constant capital. As this critique required a concept of circular flow, Dussel suggests that Marx modified the Physiocrats' tableau to suit this purpose. On this basis, Marx established that the total price of the annual product could not be entirely resolved into revenues.

> Instead, the total price includes another component, which is equal to the value transferred from the means of production, and the capital recovered from this component must be used to repurchase the means of production consumed in the last period.
>
> (Moseley, 2001: 8)

Dussel (2006: 63) points out that in his inaugural lecture in Berlin, Schelling made a crucial intervention, noting that "What is the beginning (*Anfang*) of all Thought is not yet Thought (*PO*, XII, 162)". He then continued:

> "The beginning of *positive* philosophy is that all Thought presupposes Being" (*PO*, IX, 156). But, to end, Schelling wanted to prove that even *before Being* there is *Reality*, as *prius* of Thought and of Being. Thus he asserts, from a creationist doctrine: "The Absolute consists in being the Lord of Being (*Herrsein über das Sein*), and it is the greatest function of philosophy to pass over from pure Being (*to on*) to the Lord of Being (*Herrn des Seins*)" (*PO*, XII, 172).
>
> (Dussel, 2006: 63)

In accordance with Dussel's (2006: 64) Schellingian reading of Marx,

> Value is the Foundation of capital, and this Foundation is in process. It is the valorization of value. Labour is the substance (in the Hegelian sense) of all value. When a worker works, he "reproduces" the value of salary in the necessary time. The reproduction of salary is production from the Foundation of capital (the value of salary is from capital). But, because he has no value-capital Foundation (works without a salary), in the surplus-time of the surplus labour the worker *creates* from nothingness surplus-value in capital. This kind of "making" the surplus-value of a product (commodity) without being founded in capital is what Marx technically calls: "creation of value" (*Wertshoepfung*).

Crucially, on this view, living labour is the source from which the creation of value derives. Moreover, not only does it involve mere reproduction but also the creation of new value because it is the objectification of new labour time in a use value. It is the negation of capital conceived as objectified labour; it is purely subjective and denuded; it is absolute poverty, not as a shortage but as a total exclusion of objective wealth. It has nothing outside its living personal corpo-reality or empirical materiality; it is the future creator of wealth out of nothing; the only positive and creative source of surplus-value. As Arthur (2003) points out, "Dussel distinguishes sharply between the value-totality of capital and what comes from outside, and—this is important—is necessarily *redetermined* catego-rially once subsumed by capital". Thus Dussel (2001: 8) writes:

> Can it be said that the "living labor", the reality and category, is the same as "wage labor" or labor already subsumed within the totality of capital? As subsumed, it is an *internal* determination of capital, and thus founded on the totality of capital. But while it has not yet been totalized, living labor is real-ity (the most absolute reality for Marx, and the measure of all de-realization in the totality of capital), it is exterior.

For example, Dussel insists "that in this manuscript 'labour capacity' refers to the exteriority that becomes 'labour power' when subsumed by capital and taken the shape of one of its determinations". Arthur (2003: 254) flags Dussel's focus on Marx's crucial insight that the negation of labour by capital "can be reversed through a second negation only if it is possible conceptually to sepa-rate living labour from its historically determinate form as wage-labour in the first place":

> I personally believe that Marx thought his greatest discovery was the cat-egory of surplus-value or the distinction between abstract and concrete labor, but both discoveries depend on the following (which I affirm was the most important of all, and of which Marx himself perhaps was not fully aware): the difference between living labor, substance "of" value "without" value, and objectified, labor "with" value.
>
> (Dussel, 2001: 172)

However, Arthur (2003: 255) distances himself from Dussel's presumption that Marx had come under the direct or indirect sway of Schelling in mounting his famous inversion of Hegelian logic, for

> in 1842, Marx wrote to Ludwig Feuerbach (3 October 1843) imploring him to take up the cudgels against Schelling: "The entire German police is at his disposal as I myself once experienced when I was editor of the *Rheinische Zeitung*. . . . You are just the man [to be the] opponent of Schelling".

Arthur also notes that Marx "went back to his doctoral dissertation to insert a passage reminding the Schelling of 1841 of some of his radical early views, and for Feuerbach, the positive is defined in terms of 'sensuousness' rather than 'existence'". Moreover, Arthur (2003: 255) discerns a more direct influence emanating from Feuerbach, himself, observing:

> Feuerbach had been working his way out of Hegelianism through the 1830s and published his definitive text Towards the Critique of Hegel's Philosophy in 1839. His *Essence of Christianity* followed in 1841. By the time Schelling gave his Berlin lectures of 1841, Feuerbach had already ensconced himself in rural isolation at Bruckburg, there to compose a flood of philosophical manifestos, no "thanks to Schelling".

Arthur commends Dussel for introducing the following important distinctions: "according to Marx, 'to be' value, 'to posit' value and 'to create' value, are three completely different concepts" (Dussel, 2001: 7). However, he goes on to suggest adding the concept 'source' as a fourth distinguishable concept. In summary, to posit value is to subject products to the exchange relation, to create value is to produce capital by means of capital, but to be the source of value is to be that out of which capital creates value (i.e. living labour, which nevertheless must be distinguished from the creation of value (Arthur notes that although a waterfall may be the actual source of the power generated by a hydroelectric power station, as the analogue of living labour, it does not 'create' the electricity itself, for that is done by the dynamos, which are the analogue of capital's dynamic, all the while drawing on alienated labour as the use-value of capital). In the very act of constituting labour as wage-labour, "capital constitutes itself and embarks on its inherent dynamic of accumulation" (Arthur, 2003: 258). When the concept of capital is developed it leads back to labour, "but, as labour's Other at the same time, it requires recognition of its own effectivity" (Arthur, 2003: 258).

The nub of Arthur's argument is that "[o]nce a system has achieved sufficient complexity, powers emerge that cannot be reduced to those of its constituent elements". For him, "[t]he capital system exhibits precisely such emergent powers, regardless of whether or not it emerges from some such original 'ontological act' as Dussel maintains" (Arthur, 2003: 258). That is, Dussel (2001: 96) erroneously insists that Marx's system of categories "is nothing but the development of the concept of 'living labor' . . . within which the development of the concept of 'capital' is a secondary and founded moment . . . Everything is labor: capital is nothing but labor". Here, capital is recognized as a "moment", moreover, it is recognized as a moment that is founded *within* (i.e. in a dependence upon) the development of living labour.

I would suggest that the seemingly sophisticated conceptual elaborations introduced by Arthur are effectively 'red herrings' insofar as they are already captured by Dussel's distinction between living labour and labour objectified as use-value and his arguments about alienation. With the deployment of his metaphor of the hydroelectric turbine, Arthur would have us believe that capitalism is the turbine actively converting kinetic energy into electrical energy! However, this transformation of energies is clearly a productive activity requiring various forms of labour directly and indirectly, rather than one that is merely reducible to a parasitic activity of recording for the sake of appropriation.

Arthur's philosophical arguments are substantially weakened once it is acknowledged that Schelling had already formulated his notions of positive philosophy by 1808 in his *Freedom* essay and went on to refine this conception in *The Ages of Man* (although he reworked the latter text, many times deferring publication). And Feuerbach, himself, would certainly have been influenced by these philosophical irruptions. Nevertheless, let us turn to Arthur's (2003: 257) summary of the conclusions to his conceptual analysis:

> Thus, living labour in the "exteriority" is Other than capital, but, subsumed under capital, it is at the same time Other than itself, alienated labour. The same thing happens to capital when it descends from the self-referring ideality of value to the materiality of production. But, of course, this process of mutual othering is not balanced; the struggle for dominance is won by capital, which successfully returns from the sphere of production with surplus-value, while living labour returns from the factory exhausted and deprived of its own product.

For my part I can't see Dussel disagreeing with any of the sentiments appearing in the above quote. In any event, the penultimate purpose behind Dussel's investigation of these philosophical constructs is the quest to identify and better understand the site and the particular motivation for Marx's departures from Hegel's dialectical logic. In my view Arthur's concerns do not detract from the force of Dussel's findings.

Benjamin on art and technology

Theorists in media and cultural studies have drawn on the insights of Walter Benjamin in their interpretation of the relationship between art and technology. The following review of Benjamin's thinking on this particular theme attempts to locate his position within a broader philosophical frame: specifically, his speculative critique of Kantian philosophy. In mounting this critique, Benjamin chose to focus on perception, which he conceived as a process entailing the reading of configurations on a surface, as depicted in Figure 1.2. Where the *speculative* dimension of his critique was concerned with the infinite set of possible surfaces that could be encountered, the *transcendental* dimension of his critique addressed the conditions of possibility for the legibility of a given inscription while recognizing that any surface could become the medium for an infinitude of possible inscriptions.

For Benjamin, the totality expressed by reason (conceived as both an 'active' and an 'absolute' faculty) already resides in intuitions (that were previously conceived by Kant as 'quasi-visual', 'passive', and 'receptive'). Moreover, this

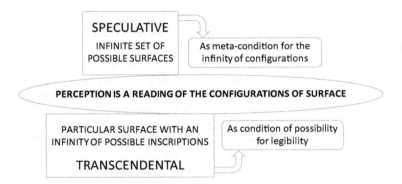

Figure 1.2 Benjamin's Speculative Critique of Kant

grounding totality can interact with the concepts of understanding (in stark contrast to Kant's view of concepts as entirely 'discursive' thinking). For Benjamin, it is the very plasticity of our intuitions, which allows them to encompass experiences of metre, accent, and rhythm while their absolute character enables them to become *constitutive* rather than merely *regulative* as Kant had supposed of the faculty of Reason, itself. Moreover, these *a priori* attributes of intuition, now re-framed, were conceived by Benjamin to be susceptible to historical influence and modification. In 1939, he asserted:

> Within broad historical epochs the mode of sense perception (*die Art und Weise ihrer Sinneswahrnehmung*) changes with the overall mode of being in the world (*Daseinsweise*) of the historical collective.

For example, in speaking of the power of film, Benjamin makes the following observation,

> *The function of film is to train human beings in the apperception and reactions needed to deal with a vast apparatus whose role in their lives is expanding almost daily.* Dealing with this apparatus also teaches them that technology will release them from their enslavement to the powers of the apparatus only when humanity's whole constitution has adapted itself to the new productive forces which the second technology has set free.
>
> (SW, III, 107–108)

Howard Caygill emphasizes the continuity of Benjamin's thinking about the mimetic nature of knowledge and experience stretching all the way back to his early work on children's perceptions of colour. For Benjamin, perception is an active reading of configured surfaces where any given surface is only one of a possibly infinite number of surfaces. At the dawn of history, tribal people, soothsayers, and shamans were engaged in a "reading of what was never written", whose conditions of legibility were supplied by nature.

The subsequent reduction of reading to the interpretation of written inscription marginalized this process of reading of what was never written, which had previously been grounded in a recognition of the 'non-sensuous similarity' between object and words. Benjamin explains the meaning of *nonsensuous similarity*, in the following quote, where he relates it to the concept of onomatopoeia (Bracken, 2002: 329):

> Every word—indeed, the whole language—is onomatopoetic. The key which makes all this fully transparent lies concealed in the concept of a nonsensuous similarity. For if words meaning the same thing in different languages are arranged about that signified as their centre, we have to inquire how they are all—while often possessing not the slightest similarity to one another—all similar to the signified at their center.
>
> (Benjamin, 1996: 696)

Non-sensuous similarity derives from the nature of knowledge itself which brings the self-reflection of the knowing subject together with the self-knowledge of other natural things,

> It is not only persons who can expand their knowledge through intensified self-knowledge in reflection; so-called natural things can do so as well. In their case, the process has an essential relation to what is commonly called their "being-known". That is, the thing, to the extent that it intensifies reflection within itself and includes other beings in its self-knowledge, radiates its original self-knowledge onto these other beings. In this way, too, the human being can participate in this self-knowledge of other beings.
>
> (Benjamin, 1996: 146)

If the term 'reflection' in the above quote were to be replaced by Whitehead's term 'prehension' then the resonance between Benjamin's notions of knowledge and Whitehead's *panpsychism* would become all too clear! Indeed, Benjamin engages in a reversal of Saussure's definition of linguistic sign, which is not a link between a thing and a name, but between a concept and a sound pattern.

In much the same manner, Salomon Maimon's objective ordering of experience departs from Kant's subjective ordering—which goes from the receiving of sensations to the ordering of them into intuitions of space and time, to the thinking of these intuitions under concepts, to the thinking of their totality under ideas of reason—in so far as it goes from the differentials of sensation, to the point of grasping these differentials through the concepts of understanding, before finally thinking the totality of concepts under the ideas of reason. For Kant, pure intuition is the form of empirical intuition so that *reality* is secondary to *objectivity*. For Maimon, differences and relations between them are prior to their objects. Difference is univocal, with spatio-temporal forms of difference grounded in real differences. *A priori* concepts are thus applied to differentials of sensation so that *objectivity* is secondary to *reality*. (Maimon, 2010: 19–20) states:

Considered in itself as a quality, every sensible representation [i.e. sensation abstracted from space and time] must be abstracted from all quantity whether extensive or intensive. For example, the representation of the colour red must be thought without any finite extension, although not as a mathematical, rather as a physical point, or as a differential of extension. It must further be thought without any finite degree of quality, but still as a differential of a finite degree. This finite extension or finite degree is necessary for consciousness of the representation, and is different for different representations according to the difference of their differentials; consequently, sensible representations in themselves, considered as mere differentials, do not yet result in consciousness.

For Maimon, differentials are determinate and relative rather than absolute unities. Moreover, through the addition (i.e. integration) of these unities both finite extensive and finite intensive sensations (i.e. *noumena*) are produced. As ideas of understanding, however, differentials have a constitutive, and not a regulative, role. Thus, understanding resides not in intuition; instead, what is required is that we get behind intuition to grasp its production. In other words, we must abandon both pure *and* empirical intuition to understand the real. Objects, for example, can only be thought as process, as a flowing or an arising by specifying both the way that they arise and the very rules by which they arise. Similarly, for Benjamin, neither intuition, as such, nor consciousness (needing extension in time) play a role in cognition:

Through the word, man is bound to the language of things. The human word is the name of things. Hence, it is no longer conceivable, as the bourgeois view of language maintains, that the word has an accidental relation to its object, that is a sign for things (or knowledge of them) agreed by some convention. Language never gives *mere* signs.

(Benjamin, 1996: 69)

Moreover, "The link between name and object is an immediate mediation. Since the word participates in the object through the name, the relation between word and object is one of mediate immediacy" (Benjamin, 1996: 87).

On this view, while criticism is a mediation that allows one thing to represent another, critique is a participation of the name in the thing named. At the same time, Benjamin distances himself from the residue of transcendental subjectivity that survives in the Phenomenological conception of intentionality:

While Husserl says that it is the thinking being that intends the object, Benjamin insists that the intentional process occurs exclusively in language: every statement is a statement *of* something. That *there is* meaning, however, does not entail that there is a *subject* of language. It is the act of meaning that produces the object, but it is not the cogito that performs the act of meaning.

(325–326)

In brief, "All knowledge is self-knowledge of a thinking being, which does not need to be an 'I'" (Benjamin, 1996: 144–145). This philosophical assault on the transcendental subject was coupled with a new, immanent conception of criticism:

> It is axiomatic for immanent critique that the criteria of critical judgement be discovered or invented in the course of criticism. This followed necessarily from the extension of the bounds of experience: if the absolute is immanent to experience, then the critical judgement of experience must also be undertaken immanently. There can be no externally given and secured criteria of critical judgement such as those Kant deduced from the nature of the apperceptive subject.
>
> (33)

Associated with this new form of immanent critique was an implied openness and pluralism of thinking. Benjamin's speculative concept of experience was predicated on a "theory of orders", for which, each order was conceived to correspond to its own, unique modality of configuration that naturally included its own categorical forms. In the case of a religious fundamentalism, literalism, or even a one-sided scientific understanding of world, one particular surface was taken up and spuriously privileged as absolute (Quadrio, 2009). Moreover, within any specific historical epoch—art forms would differ in their capacity to respond to the emancipatory potentialities afforded by technological developments.

Caygill (1998: 113) notes that, for Benjamin,

> The model for the future art of the technological epoch is architecture, the art which responds most readily to changes in the structure of experience. The architectural setting of the experience of technology had already been established in a footnote to reflection XIV, where Benjamin presented film as the "art form that is in keeping with the increased threat to life which modern humanity has to face"; it is through film that humanity can "expose itself to shock effects" and to learn to "adjust to the dangers threatening it" (1939: 252). Yet this aspect of film had already been anticipated by architecture, whose form cannot easily be separated from technique and which is for this reason close to the structure of technological experience.

A fundamental notion for Benjamin is the dialectical image.

> It is not that what is past casts its light on what is present, or what is present its light on what is past; rather, an image is that wherein what has been comes together in a flash with the now to form a constellation. In other words: image is dialectics at a standstill. For while the relation of the present to the past is purely temporal, the relation of what-has-been to the now is dialectical: not temporal in nature but figural [*bildlich*]. Only dialectical images are genuinely historical.
>
> (AP, 463)

For Benjamin, the dialectical image is one conceived in terms of a process of ecstatic suspension,

> This suspension or "the damming of the stream of real life, the moment when its flow comes to a standstill" momentarily frees action from necessity, "making life spurt up high from the bed of time and, for an instant, hover iridescent in empty space". This Experience is "felt as reflux, this reflux is astonishment".
>
> (Caygill, 1998: 74, quoting Benjamin, 1931: 13)

Both poetic creation and the task of criticism must attend to the inner form (Plotinus's *endon eidos* from the *Enneads*), which is conceptualized not as a subjective aesthetic principle (i.e. the poet's *Geschick*) to be actualized through technē, but as a process of *poetization* (*Gedichte*) now conceived as the essence of *objective* reflection—the "lawful calculus of the ancients"; not as the expression (*Ausdruck*) of beauty nor as a profound emotional diremption, as embodied in the *Genie* of *Sturm und Drang*, rather as a sober mechanics of form constituted within the infinite (as the limit value of limited forms) (Hanssen, 1997: 796).

Hanssen (1997: 797–798) observes that "inner form" plays an important role in the organicist interpretation of the arts functioning as an antidote to Aristotle's competing notion of empirical forms. Much like the Philosopher's stone, with its capacity to weld vessel, matter, fire, and cooling bath, inner form weaves together the intellectual/spiritual and the perceptual/intuitive faculties, to establish an order (much like the Greek *kosmos*), or a synthetic unity, in which the semantic, phonetic, aesthetic, and ethical realms are attuned to one another. In other words, a particular configuration (*gestalt*) is attained through which the poetized (as something given form or shape) is opened up to the realm of truth.

To better characterize this notion of poetization, Benjamin draws on the poetic doctrines of the early Romantics. Hölderlin's 'Principle of sobriety' is conceived as "the necessary limit to a perilous state of ecstatic self-loss". As Hanssen (1997: 795) explains, "[O]ne can fall upward just as well as downward. The latter is prevented by the flexible spirit, the former by the gravity that lies in the temperate presence of mind".

In his 1914 essay on Hölderlin's poetry, Benjamin provides us with two examples of this dialectical principle in action, instancing Homer's Apollonian "fire from heaven" that is counterpoised both to "occidental sobriety" as well as to the oriental and "holy pathos" of Greek art that must, in turn, be tempered by a "Junonian sobriety", when manifest in as its Hesperian mode of representation or constriction.

For Benjamin then, the poetic law (*das Leben im Gessange*) displaces the logos in so far as it serves as the creative ground for acts of object formation, while preventing the poem from sliding between the two extremes of dead mechanical form and artless, pure nature (Hanssen, 1997: 799).

Hanssen (1997: 801) insists that the poetized should never be interpreted along neo-Kantian lines as an infinite task, but as what escapes the grasp of finite cognition, and this, because no one element of the poetized "could be considered separately or in isolation without at once bringing into play an infinite series of other functional unities".

Benjamin considered his *The Arcades Project* to be an exemplar of what he termed a Copernican revolution in historical perception:

> Formerly, it was thought that a fixed point had been found in "what has been". And one saw the present engaged in tentatively concentrating the forces of knowledge on the ground. Now this relation is to be overturned, and what has been is to become the dialectical reversal—the flash of awakened conscious-ness. Politics attains primacy over history. The facts become something that just now first happened to us, struck us; to establish them is the affair of memory. Indeed, awakening is the great exemplar of memory: the occasion on which it is given us to remember what is closest, tritest, most obvious.
>
> (AP: 338–339)

In helping us to understand what Benjamin means by this notion of politics attaining priority over history, Bracken (2002: 344–345) compares his views on commodification with those of Marx. For example, where Marx saw the spir-itual powers of the commodity (value) emerging as an occulted form of the social (abstract labour), Benjamin saw the social as the form assumed by the occult pow-ers of creativity while leaving a residue in the (silent) language of things. For him, political transformation requires that we re-establish the worker's participation in the object, conceived in terms of a restoration of the material communication between worker and thing. Benjamin reasoned that "Capitalism was a natural phe-nomenon with which a new dream-filled sleep came over Europe, and, through it, the reactivation of mythic forces" (AP: 391). In turn, it is these cumulative forces that possess the potential to awaken us from the dream that is capitalism. On this view, revolution is effectively "an act of 'discharge' that releases the energies in things by folding together, in primitive fashion, the real with the ideal, matter with language, body with image". And "the name of this fold is technology, and it supplies a spasm that jolts the collective body towards its awakening" (Bracken, 2002: 348).

> Only when in technology body and image so interpenetrate that all revo-lutionary tension becomes bodily collective innervation, and all the bodily innervations of the collective become revolutionary discharge, has reality transcended itself to the extent demanded by the *Communist Manifesto*. For the moment, only the surrealists have understood its present commands. They exchange, to a man, the play of human features for the face of an alarm clock that in each minute rings for sixty seconds.
>
> (SW, II, 217–218)

Benjamin's work raises the question of how current developments in ubiquitous computing and new digital fabrication technologies such as 3-D printing will change the contemporary mode of being of the historical collective? It also raises the question of the form that immanent critique should assume in the current epoch? Finally, we could also ask whether Benjamin's views about the media of architecture and film, also hold true of these very same developments associated in digital technology.

Ernst Bloch

In what follows, I intend to emphasize the coherence of Bloch's philosophical itinerary with the purpose of overturning the false impression that his work is in any way anti-systematic. To this end, I will draw on Catherine Moir's analysis of Bloch's dialectical materialism. For his part, Habermas views Bloch as a "Marxist Romantic". Some insight into what he means by that particular label can be gleaned from the following quote:

> In Schelling's "System of Transcendental Idealism" the unconscious assumes the double meaning of an impulsive subconscious out of the "dark foundation of nature" and a winged superconsciousness out of the "voluntary favor of a higher nature"; likewise, Bloch separates the nightly dream's unconsciousness from the day dream's, the no-longer-conscious of memory from the not-yet-conscious of the future. In this view, the romantic pathos of an antiquarian approach misses an entire sphere of ciphers, symbols, mythical elements which appear not only in legends but in viewing nature and art, in dreams and visions, in poetry and philosophy.
>
> (Habermas, 1969–1970: 318)

Hudson (2013: 22–23) questions the Habermasian view of Bloch as merely a "Marxist Schelling", a "philosopher of German Expressionism who failed to develop", or "a religious leftist who never freed himself from metapolitical satisfactions . . .?" for

> [t]hese views fail to account for the shrewdness of Bloch's analysis of the Nazis, his evaluations of the political potential of a green politics, or *Naturpolitik*, and his commitment to an alliance of socialist and progressive Christian forces, as well as to the cause of women's liberation and to work for peace!

Central to his thinking is not just Schelling's paean to the blind spot of the moment, but also Kant's work on practical reason, and conceptions of the pre-Freudian unconscious in the work of critics such as von Hartmann.

The focus of Catherine Moir's paper accompanying Hudson's in the same 2013 volume, provides a crucial analysis of how Bloch transformed Schelling's late Idealism along dialectical materialist lines, while preserving its poetic force. She also helpfully compares Bloch's philosophical framework to two fashionable versions of Speculative Realism—propounded, respectively, by Alain Badiou and Quentin Meillassoux. She observes that, for Meillassoux, access to the absolute is what constitutes the very foundation for speculative thought, which he conceives as a break both with "correlationism" (the inability of the knowing subject to escape from the prison of its always, already constituted horizon of objectivity in the dance between knowing subject and known object) and "transcendentalism" (the incapacity of knowledge to escape the projected horizons of the transcendental subject). However, Moir (2013: 123), points out that "his question—'How is science able to tell us anything meaningful about reality anterior to the emergence of the transcendental subject?'—is essentially the same as Kant's question, 'What are the conditions of possibility of scientific knowledge of objective reality?'" By the same token, she warns that the danger associated with Badiou's "ontoligization of mathematical logic" is that it may "spill over into idealism" (Moir, 2013: 124).

Seen in this light, Bloch's alternative approach is the other side of the coin, in so far as it considers materialism as immanently speculative and views the absolute, from a human perspective, as immanently "not-yet-realized", while making use of the dialectic to overcome any residual "correlationist" dualism. For her, the injunction is, "to think being in a non-correlative, non-identical way, without denying any relation between thought and being" (Moir, 2013: 126). The maxim she posits as an initial response to the injunction is that "there can be *Sein* without *Bewusstsein*, but there can be no *Bewusstsein* without *Sein* (Moir, 2013: 127). Moreover, in this capacity of thought to reflect on being—and hence, on itself— she follows Bloch in her insistence that thought also retains a measure of freedom: that is, she suggests that Bloch holds to the principle that "to think is to transgress" (Moir, 2013: 128)! Moreover, she concludes that this "internalization of the undetermined in the (partially) determined" is none other than dialectic itself.

However, this raises another question of pertinence to a Marxist such as Bloch; namely: How is "being's reflection on itself . . . conceivable in materialist terms?" Her answer, which clearly resonates with the earlier overview of Schelling's thinking, is that "matter must be self-generative" and saturated with what Bloch calls the *Agens-Immanenz*, i.e. "the subject–object relation is immanent in being *qua* material reality" but in a manner that is entirely "incompatible with the equation of being with object and thought with subject" (Moir, 2013: 128)

In his efforts to articulate the relationship between the undetermined and the determined, Bloch insists that the resulting speculative method must be a "processual one, since no single concept in a speculative scheme can exhaust or be exhausted by any or all of the others". For him, matter "is inherently incomplete and inessential in itself, but the process of materialization consists in the expression of matter's essentiality in the relations between the forms it becomes" (Moir, 2013: 132)

Moir demonstrates that Bloch's process of materialization is characterized by dynamic agency, incomplete entelechy, and the material attributes of potential and *logikon*. Dynamic agency requires the possibility that things can be otherwise— i.e. matter is "open 'forwards' and as such necessarily incomplete. Accordingly, dynamic agency pertains to the mode of being-in-possibility (*dynámei on*), where possibility presupposes partial conditionality; complete unconditionality equates to necessity; and complete conditionality to impossibility" (Moir, 2013: 133).

For its part, potentiality entails the indissolubility of force and substance, attaining realization through the imposition of an immanent telos, for:

> Matter is dissolved energetically by the indivisibility of force and stuff just as little as it disappears when reason emerges from its idealist reservation and comes forth as that which is guiding and practicable in matter; thus potential and *logikon* are the attributes of matter.
>
> (Moir, 2013: 133)

Finally, "if we conceive of the fundamental unit of reality as radical potentiality, as Bloch does, the philosophical distinction between the material and the ideal all but dissolves" (Moir, 2013: 134). Moir includes a dense quote from Bloch's text on dialectical materialism to convey the idea that although "*thought is a form of material being*", it "is not identical with matter":

> Consciousness [*Bewußtsein*] emerges from being [*Sein*] as conscious being [*bewußtes Sein*] in that being, indeed first as organic, reflects itself. This self-reflexion is possible because matter is precisely not the external, indeed in the vulgar view the preeminently external, but rather the Agens has all later externality in itself and is as a whole the bearing womb on which the self of matter itself can finally meet its self-reflexion consciousness. However, being reflects itself here with such a strong transition from brain to so-called soul that there appears to be a rupture in what is usually in material terms called being.
>
> (Moir, 2013: 133; citing Bloch, 1972: 461)

In accord with this dialectic of material Being, Bloch's great work, *The Principle of Hope*, is structured in five major parts. The first of these, "Report" begins with the "small things" that always govern history, describing the dreams of the man in the street. For Bloch (1995: 3),

> The emotion of hope goes out of itself, makes people broad instead of confining them, cannot know nearly enough of what it is that makes them inwardly aimed, of what may be allied to them outwardly. The work of this emotion requires people who throw themselves actively into what is becoming, to which they themselves belong. It will not tolerate a dog's life which feels itself only passively thrown into What Is, which is not seen through, even wretchedly recognized.

The second part, "Foundation" provides analysis of anticipatory consciousness and the 'Not-Yet-Conscious' as a subterranean and brooding possibility. The utopian function is introduced along with the key notions of archetypes and ideal, along with the definitive Blochian categories of Front, Novum, Nothing, and Homeland. In this section, the key notion of forward dreaming is also introduced within the frame of a threefold form of creative production,

[T]his premonition is the feeling for what is on its way. When it becomes creative, it combines with imagination, particularly with that of the objectively Possible. This premonition with its potential for work is intellectual productivity, understood here as *work-forming*. More specifically, productivity extends threefold into the unarrived, growing in three directions: as incubation, as so-called inspiration, as explication.

(Bloch, 1995: 122)

To this end, Bloch (1995: 191) sets out the Aristotelean concept of entelechy. According to this principle, "realization is solely self-realization of the form-idea or entelechy which is inherent in things; the entelechy is thus itself the energy (or the actus) towards its Realization". Moreover, Bloch (1995: 168) detects a close correlation between entelechy and Kant's aesthetic version of the ideal:

[T]he "perfect embodiment of an idea in an individual phenomenon", passes, moreover, from a formal idealism straight into an objective one. Thus this concept of the ideal ultimately comes close to the Idea, which was taken by Aristotle from Plato's generic form above the phenomenon into goal-form or entelechy within the phenomenon. This entelechy, which does not perfectly reveal itself because of impeding secondary causes in individual things, is made visible for Aristotle by sculpture, and also by literature.

Ideas, for Bloch (1995: 144), thus

extend, in an anticipating way, existing material into the future possibilities of being different and better so that the thus determined imagination of the utopian function is distinguished from mere fantasizing precisely by the fact that only the former has in its favour a Not-Yet-Being of an expectable kind, i.e. does not play around and get lost in an Empty-Possible, but psychologically anticipates a Real-Possible.

Crucially, in accordance with the utopian function when viewed from Bloch's (1995: 146) materialist perspective, ideas become an active force of process and transformation,

[T]he *positive utopian function*; the *historical content* of hope, first represented in ideas, encyclopaedically explored in real judgements, is *human culture referred to its concrete-utopian horizon*. The docta spes [educated hope] combine operates on this knowledge as expectant emotion in the Ratio, as Ratio in the expectant emotion. And predominant in this combine is no longer contemplation, which for centuries has only been related to What Has Become, but the participating, co-operative process-attitude, to which consequently, since Marx, the open becoming is no longer sealed methodically and the Novum no longer alien in material terms.

In this part of the text we also find a detailed articulation of Bloch's (1995: 307) schema of moving world-substance, which possesses three principle moments—the Not, the Nothing, and the All:

> In such a way, however, that the *Not*, unable to bear the presence of itself, characterizes the intensive, ultimately interest-based *origin* (the That-based Realizing element) of everything. The *Not-Yet* characterizes the *tendency* in material process, of the origin which is processing itself out, tending towards the manifestation of its content. The *Nothing* or conversely the *All* characterizes the *latency* in this tendency, negative or positive towards us, chiefly on the foremost Front-field of material process. Even this latency, however, refers again only to the content of the intensive origin, i.e. to the filling of what is intended in its hunger, to the satisfaction of this interest which is breaking in.

Another important concept, with obvious Schellingian resonances, that is introduced by Bloch (1995: 307) is the "Darkness of the Now":

> The start of the beginning of all Being-Here lies here always in the darkness which is still unmediated with itself, namely in the darkness of the Now or of the just lived moment; the fiat of all world-movements occurs most immediately in this darkness. And the darkness is in fact not a far removed, not an immemorial darkness at the beginning of time, a long since passed beginning masked by continuation or cosmos. But on the contrary: the darkness of the origin remains, as immediate darkness, unchanged in nearest nearness or in the continuing That of all existing itself.

For his part, Hudson (2013: 32) argues that "Bloch's ontology of not-yet-being could be developed in new directions as an ontologically-oriented philosophy of the proterior". Here, the term 'proterior' "captures Bloch's insight that reality is not finished behind us and signals the possibility of an ontology that is not organized around the anterior".

Some inkling of this complexity of this 'ontology of the proterior' can be gained by considering Bloch's (1995: Chp. 18) decomposition of the respective layers of the category of possibility into: (1) The Formally Possible: as "that which can in any way be conceived as standing in relation, even those relations whose parts are related not only absurdly, but totally *disparately* to one another"; (2) The Factually-Objectively Possible: as the "condition or real ground existing according to cognition for an affirmative, factually valid statement itself does not exist in a complete form"; (3) The Fact-Based Object-Suited Possible: "in so far as it does not concern our knowledge of something, but this something itself, as something that could become this or that: i.e. what is more or less sufficiently conditioning in *Objects themselves and in their factual relations*"; (4) The Objectively-Real Possible: pertaining to matter as "the real possibility for all the forms which are latent in its womb and are delivered of it through process"; (5) Memory: as the

Logical-Static Struggle against the Possible: which distinguishes between partial conditions and partial knowledge of these conditions in accounting for the "*external worldly character of a large part of modality*"; and (6) Realizing Possibility: pertaining to "[f]ree people on free ground, grasped thus in a total way, this is the final symbol of the realization of what is realizing and hence of the most radical frontier-content in the objectively real Possible as a whole". This explication sets the scene for the next chapter in Bloch's work, which deals with Marx's "Theses on Feuerbach", that were set out in the first chapter of *The German Ideology*.

"Transition" sets up a contrast between the mirror presented to the people by the ruling class and the mirror that comes directly from the people. For its part, "Construction" considers utopias that have either been planned or set out as blueprints. From this constellation of hope-images emerges the promise of a society without deprivation. Finally, "Identity" describes the process of human venturing beyond the limits, ranging from fairy-tales, myths, and film montage, through to the experience of travel, childhood dressing-up, and the mysterious promises of shopping arcades.

Hudson (2013: 23) complains that for Habermas, Bloch is a "Marxist Schelling" (Habermas) and a "philosopher of German Expressionism" who failed to grow up, as well as a "a religious leftist who never freed himself from metapolitical satisfactions"! Nevertheless, he insists that views such as this fail to account for the shrewdness of Bloch's analysis of the Nazis, his evaluations of the political potential of a green politics, or *Naturpolitik*, and his commitment to an alliance of socialist and progressive Christian forces, as well as to the cause of women's liberation and to work for peace.

Of great moment for our purposes is Bloch's conception of the relationship between technology and nature. Habermas (1969–1970: 319) describes this from the perspective of ideology, suggesting that,

Only when the "ideological" view comprehends the phenomena as extrapolations of themselves as it were, the subjective purposes of human endeavor will no longer be suspended in empty air but will find the connection with a purposefulness suggested by nature itself.

He goes on (Habermas, 1969–1970: 320) to note:

Scientific theories and their technological application are indeed "alien to nature." Both dispose of nature according to stated laws defining its behavior "for use". The functional relationships determined by these laws are in-different to nature "per se" and productively ignorant of its "essence". Technology, which has to proceed according to such laws, lacks the relatedness to any favors of nature, to the "old, natural world". Bloch criticizes this lack of relatedness to the earth, which is the source of the exaggerated artificiality of "the bourgeoisie's mechanical universe", its specific misery and its specific ugliness.

In stark contrast, a great work of art, in exposing itself to the unclosed and expressing the unclosed,

> shows the pleasant and homogeneous aspects of its work-based coherence broken, broken up, leafed open by its own iconoclasm, wherever immanence is not driven to closedness of form and content, wherever it still poses as *fragment-like*. Here—completely incomparable with the mere contingency of the fragmentary in the avoidable sense—another hollow space of a factual, highly factual kind opens up, with *unrounded immanence*.

Moreover, "it is precisely in this space that the *aesthetic utopian meanings* of the beautiful, even the sublime make their presence felt" (Bloch, 1995: 219).

It remains to be seen how, in an age of mechanical reproduction, great works of art can continue to embody the *unclosed*, and can continue to realize the *utopian function* of living hope.

Notes

1 The French philosopher, Bernard Stiegler, whose work will be discussed in Chapter 4, effectively straddles both of these philosophical trajectories. In Chapter 8, I discuss how Stiegler's philosophical stance can be defended against that of his critics.
2 Benjamin acknowledges the direct influence of Novalis over his thinking. However, for a detailed though somewhat unforgiving critique of Benjamin's interpretation of Novalis, see Menninghaus (2002).
3 Gabriel's reliance on the works of the mature Schelling comes through more clearly in his *Transcendental Ontology: Essays in German Idealism* than it does in his more recent and more popular texts, which spend more time and intellectual effort in engaging with the contemporary philosophical scene.
4 See McGrath (2011), for a hard-hitting critique of Žižek's Lacanian reading of Schelling, which, to my mind, exhibits too much sympathy for Jung's libido theory over that of Freud.
5 See Rodin (2012: 181–182) for a more extensive discussion of Frege's notion of sense.
6 Pinkard (2002: 318) notes that Schelling delivered his inaugural address in Berlin to a full and anxious audience, "Among the people coming to hear him were the young Friedrich Engels, Søren Kierkegaard, and Mikhail Bakunin; other attendees at the full set of lectures included Friedrich von Savigny, Jakob Burckhardt, Henrik Steffens, Friedrich Trendelenburg, Leopold von Ranke, and scores of highly placed governmental, court, and military personages".
7 See Frank (2004: Lect. 5), for a rich and detailed discussion of the similarities and differences between Hölderlin's and Schelling's understanding of intellectual intuition during the early period of German Romanticism.
8 Much could be made here, of the affinities between Schelling's notion of the three potencies and Charles Sanders Peirce's conception of firstness, secondness, and thirdness. On this, see Esposito (1977: 203–206).

Bibliography

AP: Benjamin, W. (1999). *The Arcades Project*. Trans. Howard Eiland and Kevin McLaughlin. Cambridge, MA and London: Belknap Press.
GS: Benjamin, W. (1972–). *Gesammelte Schriften*, vols I–VIII, ed. Rolf Tiedemann and Hermann Schweppenhäuser. Frankfurt am Main: Suhrkamp Verlag.

SW: Benjamin, W. (1991–1999). *Selected Writings*, ed. Howard Eiland and Michael W. Jennings. Cambridge, MA and London: Harvard University Press.

SWS: Schelling, F. W. J. (1856–61). *Sämmtliche Werke*, ed. K. F. A. Schelling. I. Abteilung vols 1–10, II. Abteilung vols 1–4. Stuttgart: Cotta.

Arthur, Chris (2003). Review of "Towards an Unknown Marx: A Commentary on the Manuscripts of 1861–3", by Enrique Dussel, translated by Yolanda Angulo, edited by Fred Moseley. *Historical Materialism*, 11(2): 247–263.

Beiser, Frederick C. (2002). *German Idealism: The Struggle against Subjectivism, 1781– 1801*. Cambridge, MA: Harvard University Press.

Benjamin, Walter (1931). *Was ist das epische Theater?* (What Is Epic Theatre?). GS II.2; UB, 1–22.

Benjamin, Walter (1939). *Das Kunstwerk im Zeitalter seiner technischen Reproduzierbarkeit* (The Work of Art in the Epoch of Its Technical Reproducibility) [Final Version]. GS 1.2; I, 219–253.

Benjamin, Walter (1996). *Selected Writings. Volume I: 1913–1926*, ed. Marcus Bullock and Michael W. Jennings. Cambridge, MA: Harvard University Press.

Bloch, Ernst (1972). *Das Materialismusproblem: Seine Geschichte und Substanz*. Frankfurt: Suhrkamp.

Bloch, Ernst (1995). *The Principle of Hope: Volume 1*. Trans. Neville Plaice, Stephen Plaice and Paul Knight. Cambridge, MA: MIT Press.

Boer, Roland (2013). The Privatization of Eschatology and Myth: Ernst Bloch vs. Rudolph Bultmann. In Peter Thompson and Slavoj Žižek (eds), *The Privatization of Hope: Ernst Bloch and the Future of Utopia*. London: Duke University Press.

Bracken, C. (2002). The Language of Things: Walter Benjamin's Primitive Thought. *Semiotica*, 138(1/4): 321–349.

Caygill, Howard (1998). *Walter Benjamin: The Colour of Experience*. New York, NY: Routledge.

Dussel, Enrique (2001). *Towards an Unknown Marx: A Commentary on the Manuscripts of 1861–3*. Trans. Yolanda Angulo, with an Introduction by Fred Moseley. London: Routledge.

Dussel, Enrique D. (2006). Marx, Schelling, and Surplus Value. *International Studies in Philosophy*, 38(4): 59–69.

Esposito, J. L. (1977). *Schelling's Idealism and Philosophy of Nature*. Lewisburg, PA: Bucknell University Press.

Frank, Manfred (1992). *Der unendliche Mangel an Sein*. Munich: Wilhelm Fink Verlag.

Frank, Manfred (2004). *The Philosophical Foundations of Early German Romanticism*. Trans. Elizabeth Millán-Zaibert. New York, NY: State University of New York Press.

Frege, Gottlob (1997). On *Sinn* and *Bedeutung*. In M. Beaney (ed.), *The Frege Reader*. Oxford: Blackwell Publishing.

Gabriel, Markus (2011). *Transcendental Ontology: Essays in German Idealism*. Continuum Studies in Philosophy. London: Continuum Press.

Gabriel, Markus (2015). *Fields of Sense: A New Realist Ontology*. Edinburgh: Edinburgh University Press.

Grant, Iain Hamilton (2006). *Philosophies of Nature after Schelling*. London: Continuum International Publishing Group.

Habermas, Jurgen (1969–1970). Ernst Bloch: A Marxist Romantic. *Salmagundi*, 10/11 (Fall/Winter): 311–325.

Hanssen, Beatrice (1997). "*Dichtermut*" and "*Blodigkeit*": Two Poems by Hölderlin Interpreted by Walter Benjamin. *Modern Language Notes*, 112(5) (December) (Comparative Literature Issue): 786–816.

Hudson, Wayne (2013). Bloch and a Philosophy of the Proterior. In Peter Thompson and Slavoj Žižek (eds), *The Privatization of Hope: Ernst Bloch and the Future of Utopia.* London: Duke University Press.

Jones, Kristin Alise (2013). *Revitalizing Romanticism: Novalis' Fichte Studien and the Philosophy of Organic Nonclosure.* Doctoral dissertation, Harvard University. http://nrs.harvard.edu/urn-3:HUL.InstRepos:11124853.

McGrath, S. J. (2011). Is Schelling's Nature-Philosophy Freudian? *Analecta Hermeneutica,* 3: 1–20.

Maimon, Salomon (2010). *Essay on Transcendental Philosophy.* Trans. N. Midgley, H. Somers-Hall, A. Welchman and M. Reglitz. London: Continuum Press.

Menninghaus, Winfried (2002). Walter Benjamin's Exposition of the Romantic Theory of Reflection. In Beatrice Hanssen and Andrew Benjamin (eds), *Walter Benjamin and Romanticism.* New York, NY: Continuum.

Moir, Catherine (2013). The Education of Hope: On the Dialectical Potential of Speculative Materialism. In Peter Thompson and Slavoj Žižek (eds), *The Privatization of Hope: Ernst Bloch and the Future of Utopia.* London: Duke University Press.

Moseley, Fred (2001). Introduction to Dussel: The Four Drafts of *Capital. Rethinking Marxism,* 13(1): 1–9.

Osborne, Peter and Matthew Charles (2013). Walter Benjamin. *The Stanford Encyclopedia of Philosophy* (Winter 2013 Edition), ed. Edward N. Zalta. http://plato.stanford.edu/archives/win2013/entries/benjamin/.

Pinkard, Terry (2002). *German Philosophy: 1760–1860—The Legacy of Idealism.* Cambridge: Cambridge University Press.

Porter, Timothy (1994). Categorical Shape Theory as a Formal Language for Pattern Recognition? *Annals of Mathematics and Artificial Intelligence,* 10(1) (March): 25–54.

Quadrio, Philip (2009). Benjamin Contra Kant on Experience: Philosophising beyond Philosophy. Working Paper.

Rodin, Andrei (2012). Axiomatic Method and Category Theory. 5 October. arXiv: 1210.1478v1 [math.HO] 25 September 2012.

Scholem, Gershom (2007). *Lamentations of Youth: The Diaries of Gershom Scholem, 1913–1919.* Trans. Anthony David Skinner. Cambridge, MA: Harvard University Press.

Spinoza, Benedict (1955). *Ethics.* Trans. R. H. M. Elwes. New York, NY: Dover Publications.

Wirth, Jason M. (2007). Foreword in Schelling, F. W. J. *Historical-critical Introduction to the Philosophy of Mythology.* Trans. Mason Richey and Markus Zisselsberger. New York, NY: State University of New York Press.

Žižek, Slavoj (1996). *The Indivisible Remainder: An Essay on Schelling and Related Matters.* London: Verso.

2 Bourdieu and Structuralism

Introduction

There are two important elements that I want highlight in explaining why I have chosen to dedicate a whole chapter to Pierre Bourdieu. First, I want to demonstrate his proximity to a certain Structuralist way of thinking about systems—social, natural, and mathematical—that is no longer "fashionable" and, accordingly, has been exposed to a barrage of criticism. However, much of this criticism is both superficial and misplaced. Second, and for this very reason, I want to show that Bourdieu's Structuralist anthropology is far less rigid and deterministic than is usually supposed. To this end, I want to trace two of the most significant influences over Bourdieu's philosophical development by going back to the sociological work of Jean Piaget as well as Merleau-Ponty's phenomenology of the flesh. Despite this structural flexibility, I still intend to distance myself from Bourdieu's conceptual framework. On one hand, I want to raise doubts about Bourdieu's conceptions of symbolic or cultural capital. Moreover, it is this very social notion of capital that has been taken up by many commentators on the digital economy, as evidenced by the work of Lissitsa (2015), and Hesmondhalgh (2006), whereas other authors writing about the digital economy, such as Costa (2013) or Bolin (2012), have drawn, respectively, on Bourdieu's conception of habitus and field. On the other hand, I want to suggest that Bourdieu's interpretations of mathematics, in particular, *can* be accused of being somewhat rigid and outdated. In this domain, Bourdieu's structuralist orientation takes on a form that is especially conservative and restrictive in its effects. To this end, I have drawn on Merleau-Ponty's philosophy of the flesh as a counter-foil to Bourdieu's own reflexive sociology. Nevertheless, even Merleau-Ponty's philosophy is found to be wanting although, in this case, an efficacious remedy can readily be prescribed.

Wacquant on Bourdieu's method

For Evens (1999), "Bourdieu is a materialist who has failed to take into account the fundamental hermeneutic insight that even the most material aspects of social life are inherently meaningful, rendered possible only by wider cultural understandings".

In contrast, Wacquant argues that Bourdieu's work is a unified undertaking firmly grounded in a non-Cartesian social ontology: one whose methods and conceptual tools are opposed to any reduction of sociology to either an objectivist physics of material structures or a constructivist phenomenology of cognitive forms (Bourdieu and Wacquant, 1992: 5).

Thus, Bourdieu sees the task of sociology as an attempt to uncover the structures of social world and the underlying mechanisms that ensure their reproduction and/or transformation (Bourdieu and Wacquant, 1992: 7). In his work structures pertaining both to relations of power and to meaning lead a 'double life'. On one level—the first order—they are concerned with the distribution of material resources and the various means of appropriation of scarce values (i.e. these are the structures producing social existence as such). On another level—the second order—they concern the mental and bodily schemata and symbolic templates governing the practical activity of social agents.

Accordingly, a reflexive sociology must reject both a one-sided *mechanical structuralism* and a *teleological individualism*. Instead, Wacquant insists, both aspects are conceived as woven together within a social praxiology which replaces mundane representations by objective structures, and jointly reintroduces immediate lived experience and dispositions of agents.

Wacquant asks whether there might be a unified source of schemata or a singular mode of operation that would explain the correspondence between social and mental structures, and which would obtain in both primitive and modern societies (Bourdieu and Wacquant, 1992: 11–12). Answering in the affirmative, he argues that such modes or schemata are homologous because they are genetically linked through durable and transposable dispositions that are, in turn, instilled by a cumulative exposure to given social conditions (Bourdieu and Wacquant, 1992: 13).

The internalization of these transindividual and unconscious principals, which function politically by inscribing division and imposing domination, achieve a strictly ideological purpose when they represent structures as natural or necessary rather than as historical or contingent (Bourdieu and Wacquant, 1992: 14). However, certain schemata can also help both to constitute and to transform social relations and their representations. As such, existing schemata are always at stake in struggles between individuals and groups.

Through a rigorous *Methodological Relationalism*, Bourdieu acknowledges the ontological primacy of relations over either the system and actor or the individual and the collective (Bourdieu and Wacquant, 1992: 15). Thus, Bourdieu's key concepts of *habitus* and *field* should be viewed as designating 'bundles of relations': the *field* represents objective, historical relations between positions that are anchored in specific forms of power and capital; while *habitus* stands for the set of mental and corporeal schemata deposited in individual bodies (Bourdieu and Wacquant, 1992: 16). More precisely, it is defined as a constellation of:

> systems of durable, transposable dispositions, structured structures predisposed to function as structuring structures, that is, as principles which generate and organize practices and representations that can be objectively adapted to their outcomes without presupposing a conscious aiming at ends or an express mastery of the operations necessary in order to attain them.
>
> (Bourdieu, 1990: 53)

These regularities, governed by a subjective but non-individual system of cognitive and motivating structures, provides the basis for schemes of perception and thought and modes of collective action.

Crucially, the practices reflected through the notion of *habitus* possess a logic that differs from that espoused by the logician. Bourdieu emphasizes that symbolic systems owe their practical coherence to the fact that they are the products of practices, which are successful in achieving their targeted outcomes through their looseness, their convenience or susceptibility to manipulation and potential slippage of meaning and to their economy (Bourdieu, 1990: 86–87).

Under this relational logic *Society* is then conceived as an (effectively Weberian) ensemble of relatively autonomous *fields*—economic, political, aesthetic, intellectual—each possessing their own regulative principles, values, and norms. Moreover, the effects of the field on its objects and agents are like refractions of prism governed less by quantum effects than by the internal structure of a game (Bourdieu and Wacquant, 1992: 18). Simultaneously, the field serves as a space of conflict and competition over respective species of capital and their associated rewards, gains, profits, or sanctions.

Bourdieu rejects the duality between body and mind emphasizing Merleau-Ponty's notion of the intrinsic corporeality of pre-objective contact between subject and world (practical sense as precognizant) (Bourdieu and Wacquant, 1992: 20–21). There is an ontological complicity or mutual possession between habitus and the world, which determines it: the practical sense associated with *habitus* spontaneously constitutes the world as meaningful by anticipating likely manoeuvres without calculative reason. In this way, past, present and future interpenetrate one another.

While Phenomenological intentionality implies interest implying material gain, in turn, Bourdieu expands the notion of a sphere of interest by recognizing non-material forms of profit. However, both utility and consciousness are reduced to, while strategy is related to unconscious, objectively oriented regularities and (often non-economic) investments, which are seen to be mobilized by habitus (Bourdieu and Wacquant, 1992: 26).

Another key principle in Bourdieu's work is that of *epistemic reflexivity*, which he defines as the unthought delimiting the thinkable and observable (e.g. the unthought social origins and coordinates of researcher, and the always dominated field of power that cultural producers work within, and the related intellectualist bias of the researcher who is divorced from action, viewing world as a kind of spectacle) (Bourdieu and Wacquant, 1992: 39–40).

Yet another principle is *historicist rationalism* defined as the attempt to historicize reason without dissolving it: While acknowledging the possibility of scientific truth, and recognizing that knowledge has (symbolic) power, Bourdieu firmly rejects the notion of any transhistoric structures of consciousness (Bourdieu and Wacquant, 1992: 47). Nevertheless, according to Wacquant, Bourdieu evidently rejects Foucault's orthogonal bracketing of causality and totality (Bourdieu and Wacquant, 1992: 48, fn. 86).

Finally, Wacquant highlights Bourdieu's commitment to an ethos predicated on a distinction between necessity and freedom to define the scope for moral action.

Associated with this ethos is an undertaking to 'denaturalize' and 'defatalize' the social world by destroying the various myths cloaking power and questioning the apparent arbitrariness of conduct (Bourdieu and Wacquant, 1992: 49–50).

Bourdieu's approach to resolving the dichotomy between the subject and the object

In *The Logic of Practice*, Bourdieu warns that the phenomenological description of what characterizes 'lived' experience as self-evident and taken-for-granted cannot question the conditions of possibility of either "the coincidence of the objective structures and the internalized structures which provides the illusion of immediate understanding" or the social epoch which supports such a reflexive turning back onto doxic experience. On the other hand, he suggests that a semiotic analysis of the social world of words or practices is an essential complement to the phenomenological scientific project, which amounts to an articulation of pre-scientific experience by assembling constructs of the very constructs deployed by actors within the social field. Semiosis accomplishes this task by demonstrating the structural basis for the sedimentation of meanings that are independent of individual consciousness, and yet contribute to the immediacy of our experiences of the social world (Bourdieu, 1990: 26). In reflecting on the peculiarities of his own social background he posits the following:

> Perhaps because I had a less abstract idea than some people of what it is to be a mountain peasant, I was also, and precisely to that extent, more aware that the distance is insurmountable, irremovable, except through self-deception.
>
> (Bourdieu, 1990: 14)

Bourdieu rejects the fetishism of social laws, the reduction of social processes to a history without a subject, and the notion that social events are merely the transient, surface expression of a deeper and lawful unfolding of transcendental objective structures, immune to human creativity or intervention (1990: 41). Yet he is also opposed to those subjectivist anthropologies that emphasize the freedom and autonomy of human agents who are seen to create meaning out of nothingness and to impose their rational and consciously posited intentions over what would otherwise be an entirely chaotic and arbitrary realm (1990: 50). To this end, he also continues Max Weber's attempts to extend the "materialist mode of thought into areas which Marxist materialism effectively abandons to spiritualism" (1990: 17).

In this manner, Bourdieu is forced by the immanent logic of his research trajectory to engage in a Hegelian kind of sublation: the actual oppositions between subjectivism and objectivism are brought together as the alternate moments of a mediating continuum, whilst still preserving their separate identities within a unity of identity-in-difference. As such, all his critical instruments, the newly forged concepts of the *habitus*, doxa, and symbolic capital, are wielded with the intention of realizing this sublime goal.

For example, Bourdieu draws on the notion of *habitus* to question the validity of rational actor theory. He argues that economistic explanations for the 'rationality' of practices that relate them either mechanistically to narrowly defined economic interests, or teleologically to consciously posited ends (e.g. profit-maximization) are "unaware that practices can have other principles than mechanical causes or conscious ends and can obey an economic logic without obeying narrowly economic interests". For on one hand, intelligibility and coherence can obtain without intentionality or deliberation whereas, on the other hand, actions can be reasonable without necessarily being the products of reasoned design or rational calculation (1990: 50–51). On this view, Bourdieu suggests that scarcities, stakes, and choices over investment can occur across a range of 'economies', each involving different forms of capital—both symbolic and purely economic.

As far as the *doxic* is concerned, Bourdieu defines this concept as the pre-verbal, unmediated taking-for-granted of the world that is established in the relationship between the *habitus* and "the field to which it is attuned". Taking up the example of a sports game, Bourdieu discusses the way that players can develop a "feel for the game", which allows them to anticipate their opponents' moves and prepare for them in a totally non-reflexive way. In this doxic dimension of action the body operates as a "living memory pad" drawing the mind along behind it through automatic modes of behaviour and deep-rooted linguistic patterns, governed overall by a sensibility that operates behind the backs of those who exercise it (1990: 66–70).

Bourdieu's concept of *symbolic capital*, was first introduced in the context of a critique of objectivism and economism as ethnocentric processes that colonize gift-exchange with their vision of the counter-gift. Bourdieu contends that the practices of gift-exchange, which apply to kinship alliance, work, and neighbourhood, each require the performance of what he chooses to call *symbolic labour*. Through this labour the self-interest that might otherwise intrude into these sacred domains is both concealed and transmuted into an expression of reciprocity. The imperialistic conquest of gift-exchange by objectivism reduces the polythetic to the monothetic and replaces something that is improvised and strategic, in the face of high uncertainty and an undeclared calculus of interest, with something purely mechanical, something that falls into error itself. This is because it refuses to recognize the effects of misrecognition, that is, it ignores the practical consequences of a pretended abeyance of self-interest (1990: 112–113).

In Bourdieu's anthropological research, however, this misrecognition, or pretended abeyance of self-interest, is seen to have real effects. The workings of symbolic labour are illustrated through a comparison between the market and the "good-faith" economy, where the latter is seen to operate both by limiting and disguising the narrow self-interest that would otherwise be exercised in transactions between friends or in rites of marriage between those who are close neighbours. While friendly exchanges are characterized by the absence of money, guarantees, security, and witnesses, market exchanges feature a generalized mistrust of strangers and the mutual practice of fraud, deception, and trickery. In Kabyle peasant life, activity is valued as an end in itself, rather than valued for its economic contribution to productivity or profit, and the relationship to the land is also modelled on the basis of reciprocal obligation (1990: 114–116). In this context, symbolic capital is expressed in a group's ability to preserve its land, honour market transactions, or protect the integrity of its womenfolk.

The structuralist origin of Bourdieu's methodology

Attending to practical logics, Bourdieu attacks economistic and objectivist readings for obscuring the discrepancy between social representation and the objective reality of production and exchange. At one stage, he even defines symbolic capital as economic capital appearing in its denied and misrecognized form (Bourdieu, 1990: 118). As such, it is hardly surprising that the defence of 'useless' forms of symbolic capital can lead to conduct that can only be described as economically ruinous (1990: 121). Bourdieu describes various forms of behaviour—ethical and emotional, whose preservation requires a constant effort on the part of the master—that camouflage what might seem to be largely economic forms of obligation (lending of animals and land) with rites and practices that project an outward appearance of reciprocity and the sharing of mutual benefits (1990: 123–124).

It must be pointed out that Bourdieu's work has become unfashionable in sociological circles, but it will be argued herein that much of the criticism directed at Bourdieu has been misplaced. For example, a large number of sociologists (Schatzki, 1987, 1997; Bouveresse, 1995; Brubaker, 1985; Jenkins, 1982, 1993; DiMaggio, 1979; Garnham and Williams, 1980; Lamont and Lareau, 1988) have recently taken aim at Bourdieu's use of *habitus* by reasoning that "this concept slips back into exactly the kind of objectivism Bourdieu refutes" (King, 2000: 418)! Andrew King, himself, responds to this criticism by insisting that Bourdieu's emphasis on intersubjective virtuosity provides a vehicle for escaping the worst aspects of what would otherwise be an objectivist method. King (2000: 419) follows Bourdieu (1977: 79) in arguing that social agents are 'virtuosos' "who are not dominated by some abstract social principles but who know the script so well that they can elaborate and improvise upon the themes which it provides and in the light of their relations". In fact, as Bourdieu (1990: 12) opines:

> [I]f practices had as their principle the generative principle which has to be constructed in order to account for them, that is, a set of independent and coherent axioms, then the practices produced according to perfectly conscious generative rules would be stripped of everything that defines them as distinctively as practices, that is, the uncertainty and "fuzziness" resulting from the fact that they have as their principle not a set of conscious, constant rules, but practical schemes.

Bourdieu goes on to warn that even researchers, themselves, need to practise a certain kind of virtuosity to avoid falling into a trap of their creation, for the anthropologist "compensates for lack of practical mastery by creating a cultural map" (Bourdieu, 1977: 2), but takes this (static and timeless) map as spurious evidence for the existence of an objective system of rules over social interactions! When he remains unaware of the limits inherent in his point of view on the object,

> the anthropologist is condemned to adopt unwittingly for his own use the representation of action which is forced on agents or groups when they lack practical mastery of a highly valued competence and have to provide themselves with an explicit and at least semi-formalized substitute for it in the form of a repertoire of rules, or of what sociologists consider, at best, as a "role", i.e. a predetermined set of discourses and actions appropriate to a particular "stage-part".
>
> (Bourdieu, 1977: 2)

King (2000: 419, 421) observes that this same emphasis on intersubjective virtuosity is highlighted in Bourdieu's critique of structuralist accounts of gift exchange and his discussion of honour as an inculcated disposition among the Kabyle. For King (2000: 431), this notion of "practical theory" in Bourdieu's work helps to overcome "the impasse of objectivism and subjectivism because it recognizes that appeals to the existence of objective social structure or culture are reifications of particular moments in the social process which consists, in fact, of individuals interacting meaningfully with other individuals".

King concludes (2000: 431) by observing:

> The intersubjective social context in which we are always already thrown constrains practices and ensures that any practice we perform is social—it is always derived from shared understandings—but that context does not determine exactly what we will do or exactly what it is appropriate to do under any circumstance.

However, this naïve juxtaposition of *habitus* as an objectivist concept and "practical theory" as its subversive antidote can be overturned by a deeper interrogation of the intellectual influences behind Bourdieu's foundational concepts. In an informed paper, Lizardo (2004: 379) distinguishes between two major uses of *habitus*: first, as a *perceptual and classifying* structure, which he suggests can be traced back to Durkheim and Mauss, the Structuralist anthropology of Claude Levi-Strauss, and the structural psychology of Jean Piaget; and, second, as a generative structure of *practical action*, which he traces back to Merleau-Ponty's phenomenological reflections on embodied consciousness.

He observes that, in *The Logic of Practice*, Bourdieu (1990: 25) explicitly chides the phenomenological account of experience for failing to go beyond a "description of what specifically characterizes 'lived' experience of the social world, that is apprehension of the world as self evident, as 'taken for granted'". With a nod to the neo-Kantians, phenomenology is faulted for ignoring the "conditions of possibility" of knowledge (i.e. "the coincidence of the *objective structures and internalized structures* which *produce* the illusion of immediate understanding").

For Lizardo (2004: 379–380), any claim that *habitus* stands opposed theoretically to "practical theory" can only be sustained when "the *habitus* is seen simply as a passive perceptual and classificatory faculty or when the embodied *habitus* is simply seen as the docile clay where society leaves its stamp, and not as an *active* generative matrix of action". Instead, Lizardo traces Bourdieu's fundamental concepts of habitus and the doxic back to their sources in Piaget's version of genetic structuralism.

Of course,

> [i]n his mesolevel theory of structural change, Bourdieu of course made use of the field-theoretic metaphors derived from the social psychologist Kurt Lewin and the relational epistemology of Ernst Cassirer. . . . but at the level of individual action and cognition it was another psychologist (Piaget) who provided him with the tools of how to think of a conception of structure at a cognitive-practical level.
>
> (Lizardo, 2004: 380)

Accordingly, "[w]e must recuperate the Piagetian notion of a *psychological (cognitive) structure*" to appreciate how the *habitus* is a "structured structure" situated at "the intersection of field and internalized dispositions": "*two ontologically distinct but mutually constitutive structural orders* (objective and internalized)", rather than at the intersection between structure and agency (Lizardo, 2004: 381). When the character of structured wholes depends on their laws of composition, "these laws must of their very nature be *structuring*: it is the constant duality, or bipolarity, of always being simultaneously *structuring* and *structured* that accounts for the success of the notion of law or rule employed by structuralists" (Lizardo, 2004: 385, quoting Piaget, 1970: 10).

Nevertheless, Lizardo (2004: 382) also stresses the fact that Piaget "was one of the few scholars that rejected the static understanding of structuralism inherited from Saussure and adopted almost wholesale by Levi-Strauss". In fact, he notes that Piaget's infamous dismissal of Chomskyan nativism "centered precisely on Chomsky's inattention to the genesis of linguistic structure and his abandonment of the question of genesis to biology and neurophysiology (Piaget, 1970)". For Piaget then,

> Knowing reality means constructing systems of transformations that correspond, more or less adequately, with reality. They are more or less isomorphic to transformations of reality. The transformational structures of which knowledge consists are not copies of the transformations in reality; they are simply possible isomorphic models among which experience can enable us to choose.
>
> (Piaget, 1970: 15)

Kitchener (1991) observes that Piaget's sociological work is relatively unknown in the English-speaking world due to a lack of available translations. He goes out of his way to emphasize the *a priori* theoretical framework, which grounds Piaget's theories, rendering them immune to mere experimental confirmation or disconfirmation. He points out that Piaget was equally opposed to both Durkheim's (anti-reductionist) sociological holism and to Gabriel Tarde's individualism. Instead, Piaget defended a sociological relativism, which construed all social facts as being reducible to social relations. However, where psychology studies their inter-relations in the single mind, sociology studies their relations between minds. Furthermore, these relations can assume three forms: rules (which are cognitive), values (which are affective), and signs (which are symbolic). For their effective operation, the latter two also require normative rules and cognitive grounding.

Kitchener insists that, for Piaget, the process of actual social exchange is both visible and immediate, but virtual exchange is non-present, thus requiring norms of transitivity, so that values can be conserved over time, including through processes of normative reciprocity. Values originate in desires but become systematized through interaction into a regulatory equilibrium. Along Kantian lines, Piaget suggested that on taking up a disinterested, moral viewpoint we begin to treat the other person as an end-in-themselves. For Piaget desires and beliefs are effectively transmitted through imitation. However, the social exchange of values also involves action, satisfaction, debt and payment, with these aspects mediating between processes of organic maturation, on one hand, and mechanisms of social transmission, on the other hand. Similarly, with processes of intellectual exchange there must be the communication of judgement, leading to agreement with and attribution of validity to such judgements, leading in turn to a commitment to that conservation of accord between those who are engaged in communication. Our ability to confer value on these exchanges implies the existence of a common scale of values guaranteed by common language, meaning, and standards of reference; agreement over these values and their associated conserving obligations; and an actualization ensured by a reciprocity of views.

For Piaget then, morality and logic are often closer than thought itself to morality, and he feels bound to reject simplistic notions of self-interested action in favour of a rival conception of equality and reciprocity. This view is ultimately grounded in a *correspondence thesis*, which holds that inter-individual and individual equilibria are one and the same. Nevertheless, cooperation is still required for both to evolve, much as social life is necessary for logic to evolve. So too, rationality and objectivity presuppose social interaction, along with an *a priori* awareness of the distinction between self and non-self, and between thought and reality.

In accordance with this correspondence thesis, Piaget considers the stages of cognitive development to be isomorphic to those of social development. Each stage in the development of the individual, then, has a correlated social dimension: (i) the *sensori-motor* stage is correlated with autistic; (ii) the *pre-operational* with the egocentric stage; (iii) the *concrete-operational* with the stage of cooperation; and (iv) the *formal-operational* with the stage of full socio-cultural assimilation.

Piaget also ascribes an orthogenetic tendency towards increasing equilibrium in both logical and social development via a kind of "grouping" predicated in turn on an isomorphism that is seen to hold between operations on objects and operation on others. For example, cooperative actions are conceived as being similar, reciprocal, and complementary. Along these lines, Kitchener detects resonances between Piaget's genetic epistemology and Jurgen Habermas' theory of communicative action. For Habermas, genetic structuralism forms a bridge with historical materialism, thus providing a rational reconstruction of the history of social systems with respect to the moral, epistemic, and social problem-solving powers of a, now decentred, subject inscribed by ever more rational and ever more reciprocal relational structures. In the case of Habermasian theory, the grounding principle for communicative action is provided by his quasi-transcendental presupposition that, through sincere dialogue we can achieve a transparent, unforced consensus, which in turn implies the existence of universal validity claims and legitimate criteria of evaluation.

Lizardo (2004: 384) notes that Piaget sees the primary purpose of knowledge accumulation and development as one of

> change and transformation as well as the *conservation* of previously acquired cognitive structures, with cognitive and bodily structures alternating between states of equilibrium and shorter lived episodes of disequilibrium and subsequent re-equilibration, as the child attempts to cope with an ever changing experiential flux.

Crucially, he goes on to observe (Lizardo, 2004: 388) that Piaget entirely sidesteps "the problematic of order from shared representations or from domination through ideological manipulation inherited from Marx and Durkheim, both of which are dependent on the symbolic fallacy of interpreting cognitive structures in a purely representational manner". Instead, Piaget's sense of operation is "borrowed from the formal algebra of group theory and mathematical studies of general classes of structures (group, order, and topological) as advanced by the 'Bourbaki' group of early and mid 20th century French mathematicians". Both mathematical operations (i.e. addition, subtraction), and Boolean and logical operations (i.e. negation, union, intersection) are conceived as having as their early substrate the sensorimotor manipulations enacted upon real-world objects (e.g. moving an object away from the body is the "negation" of the operation composed by moving it towards the body, along the lines of Freud's famous "fort" and "da" analysis of the infant throwing away and then reeling in the spool on a string).

A critique directed specifically at the notion of symbolic capital

The notion of symbolic capital is problematic for two reasons. First, any framing of any conception of capital, as a social attribute, is in danger of falling into the trap first highlighted by Marx when, in Chapter 29 of *Capital* (Vol. III Part V)—"Division of Profit into Interest and Profit of Enterprise: Interest-Bearing Capital, Component Parts of Bank Capital"—he observed that the capitalization of wage services serves to obscure the nature of labour power as the very source of all value:

> We shall now consider labour-power in contrast to the capital of the national debt, where a negative quantity appears as capital—just as interest bearing capital, in general, is the fountain-head of all manner of insane forms, so that debts, for instance, can appear to the banker as commodities. Wages are conceived here as interest, and therefore labour-power as the capital yielding this interest. For example, if the wage for one year amounts to 50 and the rate of interest is 5%, the annual labour-power is equal to a capital of 1,000. The insanity of the capitalist mode of conception reaches its climax here, for instead of explaining the expansion of capital on the basis of the exploitation of labour-power, the matter is reversed and the productivity of labour-power is explained by attributing this mystical quality of interest-bearing capital to labour-power itself.

Second, there is a proximity between notions of human and social capital and neoliberal 'individualizing' conceptions of entrepreneurship. In his discussion of Chicago-style neoliberalism Foucault (2008: 219) analyses two exemplary cases: the theory of human capital, and the analysis of criminality and delinquency. In regard to each of these elements Foucault highlights the importance of neoliberalism's efforts to extend economic analysis into previously uncharted domains in providing an economic explanation for what was previously thought to be non-economic in nature. Nevertheless, in what follows, I will only discuss the first of these cases. Classical political economists such as David Ricardo have been blamed for reducing the analysis of labour solely to a comparison of durations. And even for Marx, the crucial issue was one of how concrete labour was transformed into its abstract and universal form under capitalist social relations. However, once this conception was displaced by its Robbinsonian counterpart—the relation between ends and scarce means that have mutually exclusive uses—then Chicago-based economists such as Becker and Schultz could place all emphasis on the internal, rational character of human behaviour.

Here rational choice is applied to an activity possessing a dual aspect: on one side there is a remuneration stream, and on the other side, there is a capitalized capability or skill. The character of *homo oeconomicus* is duly transformed from that associated with being a partner of exchange and a bearer of needs to that of an entrepreneur, but now in the new sense of being an *entrepreneur of oneself*, with responsibility for capability-enhancing investments. Likewise, from the perspective of exercising rational choices over patterns of consumption, economic man becomes the producer of his own satisfaction (Foucault, 2008: 225–226). Included in the mix are concerns about personal mobility, which can be expressed in terms of choices made about patterns of commuting or migration, the concerns of a mother over time she spends with her children, and even those over the genetic makeup of one's spouse, and concerns over health care and public hygiene (Foucault, 2008: 227–229). Foucault (2008: 225–226) notes that Schulz even traces an economy's capacity for innovation back to an increase in the level of investment in such forms of human capital. Seen in this light, however, Bourdieu's seemingly radical anthropologically oriented notions of capitalization appear to be far less benign.

Situating Bourdieu: from German Idealism to topos theory

Kant was eager to prove that everything that exists has to be constituted by thought, given that thought can only grasp what is compatible with the logical form of 'referring to something', which differs from 'the fact of being referred to'. Instead of laying out the structure of being, as such, he assigned philosophy the task of reflecting on the constitution of objects qua objects of thought.

Under Kant's logical rather than historical conception of being, "being has to be determined as something determinate, as determinacy" so that the difference between being and nothingness is necessarily nullified (although this does not imply straightaway that everything determinate is actually known) (Gabriel, 2011: 63).

Hegel believed that Kant was "right in understanding subjectivity as constituting logical forms of reference (categories) outside of which nothing determinate can be apprehended", however, Kant erred in not applying this thought to itself, for synthesis is a property of intentionality as such and, therefore, also applies to higher-order intentionality, that is, to theorizing about intentionality (Gabriel, 2011: xvi)!

For the early contributors to German Romanticism, the Kantian conception of thought and thinking "fails to account for the thinker's own *existential position*". Therefore, Schelling reasoned that, in contrast to the *negativity* of such determinations, what he defined as *positive* philosophy must "take into account the ontological significance of our thinking *personality*, if we are to succeed in giving a philosophical account of ourselves that can be distinguished from the thought according to which we are the impersonal instantiation of pure thought" (Gabriel, 2011: 65). This is because "the unifying activity that makes judgments about anything possible, yet which is not itself a judgment, had to be located within the subject" (Gabriel, 2011: xi). Nevertheless, for Gabriel (2011: xii), the contemporary German philosopher of the *New Realism*, "the question to be answered remains Kantian: how is it possible to refer to anything that is not a judgment by a judgment?"

As Gabriel (2011: xvii) points out, "[a]ll of the so-called German idealists are looking for a transcendental method which is thoroughly dialectically stable under self-application. They all practice various forms of higher-order reflection thereby distinguishing between the levels of reflection".

Moreover, for Kant, philosophy was discursive, while mathematics was constructive. For a constructivist, to construct a concept means to exhibit the *a priori* intuition corresponding to it. Nevertheless, for him mathematics has a double-determination based on a distinction between general logic (which he saw as dealing with concepts alone), and transcendental logic (which he saw as being concerned with the relation between concepts and the objects as exhibited in pure intuition).

For Schelling, however, philosophy relied on construction just as much as mathematics did. He questioned Kant's argument that mathematics accounts for the general in the particular (e.g. geometry), while philosophy accounts for the particular in the general, by pointing out that both arithmetic and algebra were also relational, discursive and conceptual. Instead, he contended that what was constructed in intellectual intuition was neither a concept nor an object but an "idea" conceived as a unity between the general and the particular.[1]

Similar considerations come to the fore in efforts to develop a philosophical foundation for Post-Bourbakian mathematics. The logician and one-time set-theorist, John T. Bell (1988: 236), makes the following observation about the Bourbakian project:

[While the Bourbakians were] manifestly structuralist in intention, their uncritical employment of (axiomatic) set theory in their formulation of the concept of mathematical structure prevented them from achieving the structuralist objective of treating structures as autonomous forms with no specified substance.

A similar concern is expressed by the mathematician and philosopher, Stephen Awodey (1996: 211), who notes:

The Bourbaki description of mathematical objects as sets-with-structure leads to a useful, structuralist perspective, which the language and methods of model theory do not serve to describe particularly well.

It is notable that late in his life, Piaget published a book on category theory that was co-authored with mathematical specialists in this field (Piaget et al., 1992). It seems that he came to realize the limitations of the Bourbakian tradition, in which he began to work, and was seeking out more flexible formal notions of structure. As Papert puts it in the Preface to this work (Piaget et al., 1992: xiii):

In the same way in which treating numbers as elements of an additive group gets away or goes beyond the specific content of numbers, treating mathematical systems as elements of a category gets away from their specific content; in the psychogenetic use of a category this way of thinking provides a new prism for looking at the passage from the concrete to the formal.

Nevertheless, the applications of category theory in this text are themselves highly restrictive in that most of the formal analysis is conducted in reference to the category of Sets and groups rather than more general categories (such as the symmetric monoidal categories that feature in coalgebraic models of process).

The category theorist, William Lawvere, one of the most interesting if enigmatic contributors to debates over mathematical foundations, takes off from Hegel's problem of wanting to reject Kant's subjective (transcendental) logic and his abandonment of the *a priori* / *a posteriori* distinction (which privileges pure thought over empirically grounded science), while preventing the return of a "figurative" metaphysics of God, Soul, and World. To this end, Lawvere advances an objective logic that privileges the geometric (i.e. presheaves in a topos, conceived as 'shapes' or test spaces, positioned within a larger space of co-presheaves, conceived as containers)—but one working with measurable quantities and ratios defined using strong monoidal categories—even while continuing to work with a coherent subjective logic of connectives, quantifiers, natural number objects, and subobject classifiers (with characteristic functions asserting 'truth'). In combination, this gives him access to the mathematical foundations of empirically-grounded scientific reasoning (Rodin, 2012).

However, with topos theory, there are now two logics at hand: the internal (intuitionist) logic of the topos itself (i.e. a multi-valued logic based on indexed sets and Heyting algebras) and an external (metamathematical) logic that could well be Boolean. Nevertheless, each of these logics is situated within mathematics itself. In rejecting Hegel's version of objective logic, Lawvere has provided the empirical scientist with no coherent ontology to support his topos-theoretic constructs, or to justify their instrumental effectiveness. However, it would seem that Bourdieu himself does possess such an ontology, which he has derived from the late Phenomenology of Merleau-Ponty.

For Merleau-Ponty (see Hamrick and Van der Haven, 2011: 3), the traditional "ontology of the object" that he opposes is represented by three fundamental, inter-locking, and mistaken beliefs: (i) that the externally real—matter, substance—is conceived in exclusively quantitative terms and therefore known only through mathematics and its practical applications; (ii) that all purposes and values, all "secondary" qualities, are exiled from nature; (iii) that nature is thus conceived as an object standing over against us as subjects, or spectators and, for Descartes, Leibniz, and Berkeley, the class of spectators includes God as well.

Concluding observations

Lizardo has commented on the influence of Merleau-Ponty over Bourdieu's development of the practical action-oriented aspects of *habitus*. Of course, in his efforts to distance himself from the subjectivist and Idealist character of Husserl's transcendental and formal logics, Merleau-Ponty drew on thinkers other than Piaget, including Schelling, Bergson, and Whitehead. In their analysis of Merleau-Ponty's late ontology, articulated during the 1956–1957 year at the Collège de France, Hamrick and Van der Veken (2011) trace each of these influences, in some detail, before arguing that Whitehead's metaphysics affords the best opportunity to defend Merleau-Ponty's version of Phenomenology against attacks on the part of some of his more sympathetic critics—most notably Barbaras (1998, 2008).

To inform his embodied philosophy of the 'flesh', Merleau-Ponty (1970: 74/105–106) drew upon two interwoven concepts of logic that he took from Stoic philosophy (Hamrick and Van der Veken: 104–110). On one hand, there was *logos endiathetos*, which he interpreted as that which is inherently intelligible in nature, but anterior to the contributions of consciousness (Merleau-Ponty, 2003: 3/19). Here, that is, we have a conception of "meaning before logic"; or the logos of "brute or wild Being (= perceived world)" (Merleau-Ponty, 2003: 170/223), which for Merleau-Ponty was "more than all painting, all speech, all 'attitude'"; that pronounced itself silently in each sensible thing" (Merleau-Ponty, 2003: 208/261)—it is "the sensible itself coming to itself'. On the other hand, there was *logos proforikos*, which he interpreted as the description of the perceptual logos (Merleau-Ponty, 2003: 179/233). Here, we have an explicitation of "meaning first held captive in the thing and in the world itself"; a universality that can be reached only in and through particularity "in virtue of that mysterious affinity which makes situations mutually understandable" (Merleau-Ponty, 1964b: 92/162); that which brings about "the junction of the individual and the universal" (Merleau-Ponty, 1964a: 73/91); thus, entailing all possible cultural forms of expression.

Barbaras (2008) has identified a fundamental impasse in Merleau-Ponty's ontology of the flesh, revolving around Husserl's notion of a reversibility between touching (i.e. flesh conceived as lived body or *sentant*) and touched (i.e. flesh of the world conceived as *sensible*). He nevertheless complains that the sensibility (in the ontic sense of 'flesh') required for this reversibility is not added to the body when it is conceived as a physical object (Hamrick and Van der Veken, 2011: 181–182). Accordingly, given that there is no direct passage to ontological 'flesh', it merely amounts to a "brute Being", anterior to the subject–object distinction, for which the sensed alone purports to account for the sensing. Hence, there is a contradiction between a sensibility that only makes the world appear because it is already on the side of the world and a sensibility that already belongs to that which it nonetheless constitutes.

Hamrick and Van der Veken (2011) turn to Whitehead's process philosophy as a means for overcoming the contradictions that arise from this unresolved impasse in Merleau-Ponty's thought. In a nutshell, for Whitehead there are "no brute, self-contained matters of fact" because the initial phase of an actual occasion incorporates its past actual world into its own becoming in a chiasmatic relation of *sentant* and *sensible*.

While I do not have time to demonstrate this rigour and coherence in Whitehead's ontology, instead, referring the reader to Chapters 7 and 8 in Hamrick and Van der Veken's (2011) text, I would like to point out the implications of their arguments for Piaget and Bourdieu's version of structuralism. A similar impasse between the *objective field* and the *internalized disposition* can be discerned in their work; one that cannot be resolved, except through the articulation of a rigorous and consistent ontology. If we add to these concerns an acknowledgement of contemporary efforts to distance mathematical reasoning from Bourbakian conceptions of structure, and the view argued for above, that notions of capitalization are both dangerous, from the very labourist perspective that Bourdieu himself wishes to espouse, and all too proximate to Austrian forms of economic analysis that justify contemporary forms of neoliberal policy, it would bode social scientists well to think twice about drawing on the social theory of Pierre Bourdieu, despite the obvious progressive sentiment and political motivation for his work.

Note

1 A similar conception of the "idea" can be found in the mathematical philosophy of Albert Lautman.

Bibliography

Awodey, Stephen (1996). Structure in Mathematics and Logic: A Categorical Perspective. *Philosophia Mathematica* 4(3): 209–237.

Barbaras, Renaud (1998). *Le Tournant de l'expérience, recherches sur la philosophie de Merleau-Ponty*. Paris: Librairie J. Vrin.

Barbaras, Renaud (2008). Les trois sens de la chair. Sur une impasse de l'ontologie de Merleau-Ponty. *Chiasmi International*, 10: 19–32.

Bell, J. T. (1988). *Toposes and Local Set Theories*. Oxford Logic Guides. Oxford: Clarendon Press.

Bolin, Göran (2012). The Forms of Value: Problems of Convertibility in Field Theory. *triple C*, 10(1): 33–41.

Bourdieu, P. (1977). *Outline of a Theory of Practice*. Cambridge: Cambridge University Press.

Bourdieu, P. (1984). *Distinction: A Social Critique of the Judgement of Taste*. London: Routledge and Kegan Paul.

Bourdieu, P. (1990). *The Logic of Practice*. Trans. Richard Nice. Cambridge: Polity Press.

Bourdieu, P. (1991). *Language and Symbolic Power*. Cambridge: Polity Press.

Bourdieu, P. and Wacquant, L. J. D. (1992). *An Invitation to Reflexive Sociology*. Cambridge: Polity Press.

Bouveresse, J. (1995). Rules, Dispositions and Habitus. *Critique* (5): 573–594.

Brubaker, R. (1985). Rethinking Classical Sociology: The Sociological Vision of Pierre Bourdieu. *Theory and Society*, 14(6):745–775.

Costa, Cristina (2013). The Habitus of Digital Scholars. *Research in Learning Technology*, 21: 21274.

DiMaggio, P. (1979). Review Essay: On Pierre Bourdieu. *American Journal of Sociology*, 84(6): 1469–1474.

Evens, T. (1999). Bourdieu and the Logic of Practice: Is All Giving Indian-Giving or Is "Generalized Materialism" Not Enough? *Sociological Theory*, 17(1): 3–31.

Foucault, M. (2008). *The Birth of Biopolitics: Lectures at the Collège de France, 1978–1979*. Trans. G. Burchell. Houndmills: Palgrave Macmillan.

Gabriel, Markus (2011). *Transcendental Ontology: Essays in German Idealism*. Continuum Studies in Philosophy. London: Continuum Press.

Garnham, N. and R. Williams (1980). Pierre Bourdieu and the Sociology of Culture: An Introduction. *Media, Culture and Society*, 2(3): 209–223.

Hamrick, William S. and Jan Van der Veken (2011). *Nature and Logos: A Whiteheadian Key to Merleau-Ponty's Fundamental Thought*. Albany, NY: SUNY Press.

Hesmondhalgh, David (2006). Bourdieu, the Media and Cultural Production. *Media, Culture and Society*, 28(2): 211–231.

King, Anthony (2000). Thinking with Bourdieu against Bourdieu: A "Practical" Critique of the Habitus. *Sociological Theory*, 18(3): 417–433.

Lamont, M. and A. Lareau (1988). Cultural Capital: Allusion, Gaps and Glissandos in Recent Theoretical Developments. *Sociological Theory*, 6(2) (Fall): 153–168.

Lissitsa, Sabina (2015). Digital Use as a Mechanism to Accrue Economic Capital: A Bourdieusian Perspective. *Innovation: The European Journal of Social Science Research*, 28(4): 464–482.

Lizardo, Omar (2004). The Cognitive Origins of Bourdieu's *Habitus. Journal for the Theory of Social Behaviour*, 34(4): 375–401.

Merleau-Ponty, Maurice (1964a). *Signs*. Trans. Richard C. McCleary. Evanston, IL: Northwestern University Press. Originally published in 1960 as *Signes*. Paris: Gallimard.

Merleau-Ponty, Maurice (1964b). *Sense and Non-Sense*. Trans. Hubert L. Dreyfus and Patricia Allen Dreyfus. Evanston, IL: Northwestern University Press. Originally published in 1948 as *Sens et non-sens*. Paris: Nagel. Reprinted in 1996. Paris: Gallimard.

Merleau-Ponty, Maurice (1970). *Themes from the Lectures at the Collège de France, 1952–1960*. Trans. John O'Neill. Evanston, IL: Northwestern University Press. Originally published in 1968 as *Résumés de cours, Collège de France 1952–1960*. Paris: Gallimard.

Merleau-Ponty, Maurice (2003). *Nature: Course Notes from the Collège de France*. Trans. Robert Vallier. Evanston, IL: Northwestern University Press. Originally published in 1994 as *La Nature, Notes, Cours du Collège de France*, ed. Dominique Séglard. Paris: Éditions de Seuil.

Piaget, Jean (1970). *Structuralism*. New York, NY: Basic Books.

Piaget, Jean, Gil Henriques and Edgar Ascher (1992). *Morphisms and Categories: Comparing and Transforming*, ed. Terrance Brown. Hillsdale, NJ: Lawrence Erlbaum.

Rodin, Andrei (2012). *Axiomatic Method and Category Theory*. 5 October. arXiv:1210.147 8v1 [math.HO] 25 September 2012.

Schatzki, T. (1987). Overdue Analysis of Bourdieu's Theory of Practice. *Inquiry*, 30(1–2): 113–135.

Schatzki, T. (1997). Practices and Actions: A Wittgensteinian Critique of Bourdieu and Giddens. *Philosophy of the Social Sciences*, 23(3): 283–308.

Wacquant, L. J. D. (1996). Foreword to the English-language Translation of Pierre Bourdieu, *The State Nobility*. Trans. Lauretta C. Clough. Cambridge: Polity Press, viii–xxii.

3 'Co-creation' in the creative industries

A new neoliberal technology of self?

We are capable of shutting off the sun and the stars because they do not pay a dividend. London is one of the richest cities in the history of civilization, but it cannot "afford" the highest standards of achievement of which its own living citizens are capable, because they do not "pay". If I had the power today I should surely set out to endow our capital cities with all the appurtenances of art and civilization on the highest standards of which the citizens of each were individually capable, convinced that what I could create, I could afford—and believing that the money thus spent would not only be better than any dole, but would make unnecessary any dole.

(John Maynard Keynes, 1933)

Introduction

In his lucid analysis of 'financialization' Langley (2007) interprets the constitution of "everyday investors" as the expression of a neoliberal technology of self. Drawing on two strands of Foucaultian theory—governmentality and the problem of *aphrodisia* in Rome—he focuses on the "contradictions, tensions, and ambiguities" inflecting self-regulating subjects that, in the words of Louise Amoore (2004), are both the "vehicles of discourse and the means by which those discourses are rendered fragile and vulnerable". This theoretical framework allows him to bring the phenomenon of "financial education" within the purview of a Foucault-inspired analysis of power-knowledge relations to reveal "the ways in which the practices of investment come to be represented as integral to a secure and autonomous life" (Langley, 2007: 10). The underlying and subversive intent of Langley's paper is to reveal how the rational, calculative neoliberal subjects are fractured and divided by contradictions between their disparate roles and objectives as investors managing the risk of portfolio management, workers controlling the risks of career change, redundancy, and job loss, consumers controlling income, savings, and property investment, and shareholders ensuring sound and profitable governance practices.

In this chapter I turn to another aspect of neoliberal governmentality—the phenomenon of 'co-creation', as popularized by Prahalad and Ramaswamy (2000), and subsequently discussed by Andersson and Rosenqvist (2007), Vargo and Lusch (2008), Chaney (2012), and Payne, Storbacka, and Frow (2008). I interrogate this particular phenomenon in a similar fashion to Langley, by drawing on Foucault's discussion of the Chicago and Ordo schools of neoliberalism. More specifically, I focus on the link that Foucault establishes in *The Birth of Biopolitics* between neoliberalism, on one hand, and the conception of market logic that is explicated within Austrian value theory. Moreover, in much the same way that Foucault interprets Gary Becker's treatment of human capital theory, as a framework that conceives of the individuals who make "investments" in education and training as "entrepreneurs of themselves", in what follows, I argue that "prosumers" or consumers as co-creators can also be viewed (and constituted) as self-regulating subjects, but subjects that are now conceived to share in the process of production and to collaborate democratically in value-creating activity. In a deep philosophical sense I argue that co-creation is rooted in the Austrian conception of the entrepreneur.

The notion of co-creation has been fostered by two major social transformations. On one hand, there is the advent of "ubiquitous computing", 'digitization', and the "internet of things". On the other hand, there has been a dramatic shift in policy orientation away from the cultural sphere onto what are described as the "creative industries", most notably in the UK under Tony Blair's New Labour government. Accordingly, I will frame the theme of "co-creation" in these terms by considering its relationship with both the Information Technology and Communication (IC&T) sectors and the Creative Industries.

In this light, I will hone in on the applied computational ontologies that are under on-going development within the information, communication, and research sectors. These initiatives bring computer scientists, philosophers, scientists, professionals, and technicians together with the intention of constructing domain-specific or reference ontologies to assist in the gathering, storage, retrieval, and analysis of data for a narrowly construed range of practices such as medical research and health services.

At the same time, however, there are groups working on foundational or 'upper level' ontologies, which are designed to foster consistency in the ways scientific results are described for the ulterior purpose of a more effective integration of scientific data, break down data silos, and overcome problems associated with the non-interoperable coding of data. For example, those working in medical research might deploy a foundational ontology to link together data with medical interventions, and other related processes across the domains of genetics, environmental research, biochemistry, and epidemiological studies. For Smith and Ceusters (2010) these problems boil down to one of finding a way to *minimize the number of ontologies* that are being constructed, while at the same time *maximizing their mutual consistency*. The down-side is that this activity may unduly constrain research activity through the construction of a "Procrustean bed"!

Co-creation

Prahalad and Ramaswamy's (2000) paean to "co-creation" had its precedents in research by Firat, Dholakia and Venkatesh (1995), who coined the ungainly neologism of "customerization" to represent what they saw as a buyer-centric evolution of the Fordist process of mass-customization, and Wikström (1996), who observed that customers were now "coming on stage". Even before this, the work of prominent systems thinkers such as Edgar A. Singer, C. West Churchman, and Russell L. Ackoff foreshadowed dramatic changes in both business activity and practices of scientific research that would be occasioned by developments in information and communications technology.

The role of customers was initially undervalued in the firm-centric approach that dominated in the 1970s and 1980s. At best, the management literature was driven by a self-service conception, which viewed customers as 'partial employees'. Nevertheless, over the following decade, new themes emerged, which placed more emphasis on the entire value-chain conceived as a system for creating value through feedback effects that emanated from final consumers to subsequently influence design, proto-type testing and production as well as distribution, building on the notion that 'value-in-use' was a superior source of competitive advantage to that of 'value-in-exchange'.

Inevitably, the notion of co-creation became a source of hubris and over-statement with suggestions that new technologies and production practices had the potential to usher in a new democracy of networked co-creation. A few selective quotes should serve to highlight this starting with Tapscott and Williams (2006: 10): "Welcome to the world of Wikinomics where collaboration on a mass scale is set to change every institution in society". Then Leadbeater (2006): "Welcome to the world of We-Think. We are developing new ways to innovate and be creative en masse. We can be organised without an organisation. People can combine ideas and skills without a hierarchy".

Time magazine's Lev Grossman (2006), commenting on social networking platforms such as *YouTube, MySpace,* and *Wikipedia,* declared, "It's about the many wresting power from the few and helping one another for nothing and how that will not only change the world, but also change the way the world changes". And in *A Cluetrain Manifesto: The End of Business as Usual,* Locke et al. (2000) asked us to,

> Imagine a world where everyone was constantly learning, a world where what you wondered was more interesting than what you knew and curiosity counted for more than certain knowledge. Imagine a world where what you gave away was more valuable than what you held back, where joy was not a dirty word, where play was not forbidden after your eleventh birthday. Imagine a world in which the business of business was to imagine worlds people might actually want to live in someday. Imagine a world created by the people, for the people not perishing from the earth forever.

Less eloquently, perhaps, Vargo and Lush (2008) asked us to focus more on a service-dominant logic than a goods-dominant logic, with some of the detail in their argument captured in Table 3.1:

Table 3.1 Vargo and Lusch's Service Delivery Logic

FP1	Service is the fundamental basis of exchange.	The application of operant resources (knowledge and skills), "service", as defined in S-D logic, is the basis for all exchange. Service is exchanged for service.
FP2	Indirect exchange masks the fundamental basis of exchange.	Because service is provided through complex combinations of goods, money, and institutions, the service basis of exchange is not always apparent.
FP3	Goods are a distribution mechanism for service provision.	Goods (both durable and non-durable) derive their value through use—the service they provide.
FP4	Operant resources are the fundamental source of competitive advantage.	The comparative ability to cause desired change drives competition.
FP5	All economies are service economies.	Service (singular) is only now becoming more apparent with increased specialization and outsourcing.
FP6	The customer is always a co-creator of value.	Implies value creation is interactional.
FP7	The enterprise cannot deliver value, but only offer value propositions.	Enterprises can offer their applied resources for value creation and collaboratively (interactively) create value following acceptance of value propositions, but can not create and/or deliver value independently.
FP8	A service-centred view is inherently customer oriented and relational.	Because service is defined in terms of customer-determined benefit and co-created it is inherently customer oriented and relational.
FP9	All social and economic actors are resource integrators.	Implies the context of value creation is networks of networks (resource integrators).
FP10	Value is always uniquely and phenomenologically determined by the beneficiary	Value is idiosyncratic, experiential, contextual, and meaning laden.

The critics of "co-creation"

In light of overstatements reproduced above, it is unsurprising that some forceful critics have responded to these clarion calls to pseudo-revolution by returning to the revolutionary classics. Christian Fuchs, for example, recommends that we engage in a detailed reading of Marx's dialectic of production-consumption-circulation that is set out in the *Introduction to the Critique of Political Economy*.

Fuchs follows Marx by decomposing the dialectical relationship into a fourfold taxonomy. The first link between Consumption and Production draws attention to the fact that consumption is also the production of new needs, and provides the basis for the production of commodities (MEW 13, 623). It also allows for the (re)production of the human mind and body and involves the production of meanings and ideologies. The second link between Production and Consumption points to the fact that production "supplies the material, the object of consumption . . . therefore, production creates, produces consumption" (MEW 13, 623). At the same time, production is a consumption of means of production and labour power. The link between Production and Circulation highlights the fact that production is based on the circulation of two commodities: the labour force and means of production. Moreover, it creates commodities that circulate on markets. The linkage between Circulation and Production/Consumption underscores the requirement for commodities to circulate on markets in order to be consumed by end-consumers and function as resources while sustaining the labour force during the production of new commodities. Fuchs observes that the moment of circulation also involves the production of meanings and ideologies that are inscribed into commodities (i.e. through advertising and marketing) and that these meanings must always be decoded in certain ways by consumers.

Fuchs goes on to ridicule the notion of the Internet and World-Wide Web as a progressive, democratizing vehicle by highlighting the 'bread and circuses' features of Web-based entertainment and the trivializing political compass of the new social media.

Many critics of the potential afforded by the new information and communication technologies (I&CT) have turned to Deleuze's "Postscript on Control Societies" for a more dystopian reading. On comparing the new system of control and surveillance with what preceded it—namely, the anatamo-disciplinary politics of confinement and embodied regimentation—Deleuze (1990: 181) observes: "Control is short-term and rapidly shifting, but at the same time continuous and unbounded, whereas discipline was long-term, infinite, and discontinuous. A man is no longer a man confined but a man in debt".

In a side reference to Marx's *Communist Manifesto* Deleuze cautions us with the remark about the serpentine nature of control, noting that "[a] snake's coils are more intricate than a mole's burrow". With Felix Guattari, he expands on his cryptic comments about indebtedness as a means of control by suggesting: "The infinite creditor and infinite credit have replaced the blocks of mobile and finite debts. . . . [D]ebt becomes a debt of existence, a debt of the existence of the subjects themselves (Deleuze and Guattari, 1984: 197–198).

For his part, Bernard Stiegler (2011) targets two myths that, in combination, resonate strongly with the idea of consumers as "co-creators". The first is that we are living and working in a "Post-industrial" society. The second is the myth of "autonomous" and individual consumers, who exercise their sovereignty over economic affairs. I want to come back to the work of Steigler after taking a detour through both the territory of ubiquitous computing and the policy domain of the creative industries. This will be followed by an interrogation of the relationship between philosophical positions (namely, those associated with Husserl and Whitehead) and by an investigation into the more specialized field of applied research in computational ontologies.

Here, emphasis will be placed on philosophical motivation behind the development of 'foundational' or 'upper' ontologies.

The world of ubiquitous computing

Robin Milner, winner of the Turing award for his contributions to the world of computation, which have included the ML language, the Calculus of Communicative Systems, and the Pi calculus, has defined the notion of "ubiquitous computing" as a system with a population of interactive agents that manage some aspect of our environment. This population "consist[s] of software agents that move and interact not only in physical but also in virtual space; they include data structures, messages and a structured hierarchy of software modules" (Milner, 2009: Introduction). In this context, his vision entailed the construction of a "a tower of process languages able to explain ubiquitous computing at different levels of abstraction" where the low level model of such a system would consist of "a conflation of physical and virtual space, and therefore a combination of physical and virtual activity".

In a *Computer Journal* lecture, which he gave shortly before his untimely death, Milner raised a series of questions about this new world that some have called "the internet of things". His social questions focused on the kinds of ubiquitous computing systems (UCSs) that people want or need, and the way that ubiquitous computing will change their behaviour. His technological questions asked how the hardware entities—i.e. the sensors and effectors whose cooperation represents such a system—acquire power, and by what medium they might communicate. In turn, his engineering questions converged on the design principles that should be adopted for the populations and subpopulations—including software agents—that make up a system at each order of magnitude, to ensure dependable performance. Finally, his foundational questions were concentrated on the concepts that would be needed to specify and describe pervasive systems, their subsystems, and their interaction.

His 2009 text proposed bigraphs as one modest response to this set of foundational questions. Like an ordinary graph, a bigraph has nodes and edges, and the edges link the nodes, but unlike an ordinary graph, the nodes can be nested inside one another so that a bigraph has both a *link* structure and a *place* structure. Bigraphs can encompass specialized versions of both the Pi calculus and Petri nets. Other candidates include Abramsky's domain theory, Winksel's event structures, and Hyland's notion of the effective topos. However, in this chapter, my concerns will be more narrowly focused on the philosophical motivation behind the computational ontologies currently under development and the implications they might have for practices in the social sciences.

The creative industries

In their analysis of the Creative Industries conducted for NESTA, Bakhshi, Freeman and Higgs (2013) begin with the classification used by the UK Department of Culture, Media and Sport (DCMS):

... those industries which have their origin in individual creativity, skill and talent and which have a potential for wealth and job creation through the generation and exploitation of intellectual property.

Having worked on the Greater London Area's "Creative Industries" policies, Freeman alongside his co-authors (Bakshi et al., 2013) complains about the conflict between industry-based and occupation-based classifications in the DCMS classification. He prefers to define the creative occupations on the basis of a 'grid-score' approach which rates their creativity on the basis of five production and service delivery oriented criteria: (a) the relevant process must be novel one; (b) it must be resistant to mechanization; accordingly, (c) it must be non-repetitive and/or non-uniform; (d) it must make a creative contribution to the value-chain; and, (e) it must involve interpretation, not mere transformation. The resulting definition of the Creative Industries stipulates that the relevant occupations must have, "a role within the creative process that brings cognitive skills to bear to bring about differentiation to yield either novel, or significantly enhanced products whose final form is not fully specified in advance".

(Bakshi et al., 2013)

Creative industries are then characterized by the creative employment intensity of their workforce, which enables Freeman to identify a set of industries outside those defined as creative by the DCMS, which nevertheless feature a creative intensity that is close to that of the existing set (c). While being characterized by new technology, Freeman suggests that the pertinent occupations should be more focused on service delivery rather than material production and they should be responsible for products that are directly life-enhancing, achieving sustainability in resource use, with the potential to revolutionize personal relations. While this sounds very much like the co-creative industries, he also emphasizes the negative side of the picture, highlighting the inequities in power/influence associated with media magnates such as Berlusconi or Murdoch, the phenomenon of "celebritization" which has seen huge incomes flowing to supermodels and superstars, and the direct challenge to private investment posed by the creative occupations around such phenomena as the open source movement.

For Freeman, major obstacles to the capitalist expansion of the creative industries include the fact that creativity cannot be mechanized and separated from labourer, so that the myopia of the private sector could lead to low levels of investment due to the fear that there will be a high turnover of workers. By the same token, there will be a tendency for real accumulation to be entirely displaced by fictitious capital, and for intellectual property rights to operate as a "parasitic" substitute for innovation. Freeman calls for a reconceptualization of the public sphere, with the interests of humans/artists placed at the centre of policy, corporate bodies defined on the basis of their capacity to develop individuals, and with cultural infrastructure developed on an unprecedented scale, so that "cities function as factories" for the creative sectors.

The imbrication of computation, creativity and neoliberalism

What first struck me when I began to investigate the role of computational ontologies in the framing and integration of scientific and business-related practices was the fact that many of those active in this field were aficionados of Brentanian and Husserlian phenomenology. In contrast, many social theorists had abandoned phenomenology under the influence of Post-Structuralist critiques of strains of thought that they accuse of "phallologocentrism" and a "Philosophy of Full Presence" (of the speaking subject to itself).

By the same token, these same social theorists have been obliged to acknowledged a direct influence over current neoliberal policies emanating from this very same phenomenological tradition through the Austrian School of Economics and the Ordoliberal School of Walter Eucken (1891–1950) which included his jurist associates, Franz Böhm (1895–1977) and Hans Großmann-Doerth (1894–1944) (see Foucault, 2008). It might seem less than surprising, therefore, that leading players in the development of foundational ontologies—specifically, the Basic Foundational Ontology or BFO system, such as Barry Smith (1987) and Peter Simons (Simons and Fabian, 1986)—have sought to promote the ideas of the Austrian School of Economics on metaphysics and value theory.

Significantly, Austrian and Czech universities in the late nineteenth century were imbued with Aristotelean realist metaphysics in contrast to their German counterparts, which had come under the sway of High Romanticism and Hegelian Idealism. Firmly grounded in this tradition, Brentano exerted notable influence over Husserl, the first Austrian School of Economics (Wieser, Böhm-Bawerk), and, subsequently, the second Austrian School (Marty, Meinong, Ehrenfels, Kraus).

On mereological grounds, Brentano (1924: Ch. 8, §7) gainfully distinguishes between a (summative) type of unity where parts are independent and a fusion (*Verschmelzung*) of non-independent (yet distinct) elements, which together constitute a real unity (*Reale Einheit*).

This distinction carried over to the descriptive psychology of Ehrenfels and Stumpf with their conception of *Gestalt* as a whole that is greater than its parts—for which the removal or transformation of a single part would change the very nature of the whole. This school of psychology followed Brentano's arguments that value-theory should be based on 'feeling-dispositions' which linked mental phenomena with feelings of pleasure/displeasure.

Nevertheless, Brentano (2004: Bk. II, Ch. 7, 65; Ch. 4, §§1–22) also assumed that the very unity of consciousness, itself, cold be based on a sedimentary grounding (*Fundierung*) of complex acts on simple ones, yielding a merely *summative* conception of increasing structural complexity. For Husserl, however, Brentano's additive conception of founding precluded multiple levels of consciousness and was predicated on a naïve Empiricist notion of the *giveness* of intuited facts to consciousness, with abstraction, in its turn, conceived as a process of *simplification* (achieved through the elimination of spatial, temporal, qualitative) determinations. Finally, complexity itself was seen to be a product of a straightforward combinative process of *synthesis*. Husserl rejected Brentano's view that empirical concepts were determined by external perception, (logical and mathematical) axioms by inner perception, and harmful concepts by judgements about modalities, contending that it precluded him from genuine universal thought. To see why, we have to understand Husserl's conception of an eidetic discipline.

In departing from his mentor, Husserl distinguished between acts (*reall*), the content of acts (*reall*), meaning (that can be thought of as the consciousness of something *as* something), and objects, which in turn are predicated on a three-fold distinction between attitudes that can be taken towards intentional objects, namely: Realization-positional (real objects); Imagining-positioning (irreal objects); and Ideal non-positioning (eidetic objects characterized by both an ontic and epistemic neutrality). He also describes a correlative three-fold structure of intentionality distinguishing between the intentional act, the object as it is intended (how it is given), and the object which is intended (with intuition as fulfilment) (Husserl, 1928: XIX/2, LU VI)

For Husserl, processes drawing on the eidetic attitude give rise to adequate knowledge, conceived as a form of complete fulfilment, insofar as the intended object (meaning intention) achieves a synthesis of coincidence with its intuited meaning (Husserl, 1928: XIX/1, LU I, §9). Nevertheless, Husserl regarded this ideal meaning as being entirely *independent* of intuition and the process of fulfilment, itself. Instead, such meanings must be discovered through ideal abstraction, conceived as a process of intuiting intending ideals (thus achieving full coincidence), while preserving the irreducibility of act-characters (as the basis for any qualitative distinction between acts). On this view, truth and universality are entirely independent of any subjective process.[1]

Husserl also advances a twofold claim to the effect that: first, all synthetic *a priori* connections (all intelligible connections between objects in the world) are mediate or immediate relations of necessary dependence between dependent and independent objects; and second, all synthetic *a priori* propositions, in whatever sphere, are capable of being derived from propositions expressing "Syntactical Forms and Syntactical Matters: Core Forms and Core Matters". Husserl (1929) observes that an *a priori* scientific theory can be coherently constructed out of propositions which are uniformly analytic only if the theory is committed to at most *one* core matter: propositions expressing nontrivial interrelations between several core matters are, by definition, synthetic.

Smith (1987) remarks that the Austrian conception of the entrepreneur is structured around a synthetic relationship of this very kind. For the Austrians, entrepreneurship is not a *factor* of production that can be substituted for others, but, rather, a *presupposition* of production. Entrepreneurial activity is dependent, first of all, on the perception of a certain kind of structural *moment of material reality* as this has, at some given time, been conditioned by the existing grid of production, distribution, and exchange relationships. It is dependent further "on the *knowledge or belief* engendered by the given perception that this structural moment *is* an economic opportunity (will generate a stream of profits)". And "it is dependent also, like the given moments of perception and knowledge, upon a *specific individual*—the *entrepreneur*—who is endowed with an appropriate background knowledge of the economic articulation of the relevant area of material reality" (Smith, 1987: 20). Of course, it is in regard to the last two of these dependencies that methodological individualism comes to fruition. For, in a nutshell, the entrepreneur is someone who can work out what commodities we are going to be wanting to consume at some distant or considerable time into the future and, of no less importance, the likely ways in which we are going to be producing them.

In conclusion, the Austrian economic conception of the entrepreneur is drawn from Husserl's notion of anticipation as a *temporally* grounded faculty operating on the basis of protensions and retentions. In contrast, the Austrian conception of the market as something imbued with an essential, pure (ideal) logic is predicated on the notion of eidetic intuition, which Husserl saw as being unconcerned with either questions of existence, or any other peripheral qualities that the object expresses, but rather, being a *logically* grounded faculty, oriented towards fulfilment. What links these idealist conceptions together with the interpretation and development of computational ontologies is Husserl's underlying mereology and its subsequent axiomatizations. Ironically, in this era of I&CT and "digitization", we are now confronted with theoretical privileging of a *formal* and mathematical ground over its *temporal* and *logical* counterparts. And what can be said, in this context, about *efficient* cause as opposed to formal and final cause? Finally, it is important to realize that there are other philosophers such as Alfred North Whitehead who have made notable contributions to mereology and its axiomatization, but on the basis of a clearly divergent ontological way of thinking.

Scope for Whitehead–Marx synthesis

I don't really have the space here to adequately consider the question of Whitehead's contributions to mereology and its axiomatization so I have, instead, decided to point to specific ontological zones or territories that might lend themselves to the question of a synthesis between Marx's historical materialism and the critique of political economy, on one hand, and Whitehead's speculative metaphysical interpretation of ontological inquiry, as grounded in both the physical and natural sciences, but also in the aesthetic and ethical sciences, for which even the latter could attain to mathematical formalization through his proposed logic of pattern. Whitehead rejects the Aristotelian foundation of BFO, specifically the notion of the universal, warning:

An actual entity cannot be described, even inadequately, by universals; because other actual entities do enter into the description of any one actual entity. Thus every so-called "universal" is particular in the sense of being what it is, diverse from everything else; and every so-called "particular" is universal in the sense of entering into the constitution of other actual entities.

(PR: 48)

And where Kant is concerned with "the conditions that make possible the cognition of universals and particulars, concepts and objects, i.e., with the conditions that make such distinctions possible", Whitehead is concerned with making *esse* or the act of existence the subject of analysis, so that his categories are the conditions, which make possible things and their distinct features (Bradley, 1994: 161). Where medieval transcendentalism thinks being in terms of its representable features, and Kantian transcendentalism thinks being in terms of the conditions of its representation, Whitehead's transcendentalism thinks being in terms of its immanent, serial conditions of self-actualization (Bradley, 1994: 163).

Klose (2007) notes that Whitehead wants to unify different views of nature and to overcome the dualistic tradition of Cartesianism in modernity with respect to: (i) the *ontological* dualism, which denotes the absolute difference between an infinite and a limited substantiality; (ii) the *ontical* dualism, which denotes the absolute difference between the physical and the spiritual being; and (iii) the *gnoseological* dualism, which denotes the absolute difference between two kinds of knowledge: those that are based in rational grounds, on one hand, and those that are based on the grounds of experience, on the other.

Whitehead takes up the notion, which Marx doggedly pursued in his critique of Hegel's *Philosophy of Right*, of the Idea conceived as freedom and self-determination, reinterpreting it in ontological terms as his Categorical Principle of the Ultimate—creativity—under which "The many become one, and are increased by one" (PR: 1).

Anne Pomeroy (2001) also suggests that Whitehead's fallacy of misplaced concreteness can be viewed as being isomorphic to Marx's identification of the errors committed by political economy: namely, those as arising from a spurious interpretation of what is merely concrete and contingent in social formations as generic and/or universal and trans-historical, respectively. One instance of this false imputation occurs when the labour process—which is an expression of the *metabolic process* occurring between human activity and nature—is reduced solely to a means for the extraction of surplus value (i.e. under specifically capitalist relations of production). Whitehead, for his part, deploys his well-known distinction between the *mode of presentational immediacy*, which functions in perception as an indirect faculty for the "representing" or "inferring" (of relations that are *precise* but *trivial*) and the *mode of causal efficacy* which instead operates as a direct "seizing" or "grasping" (of relations that are *vague* but *important*), to bolster his philosophical assault on Humean scepticism.

Nevertheless, critical Whitehead scholars such as Anne Pomeroy (2001, 2004) also point out that *critical consciousness* can only arise as a transcendental viewpoint, which is strictly *internal* to the current situation (Pomeroy, 2014). In Whitehead's analysis of the categorical obligations he observes that the *mental pole* can be sub-divided into two phases: on one hand there is *conceptual valuation* (wherein the actual process of ingress results in patterned contrast); on the other hand there is *conceptual reversion* (which arises through the conceptual prehension of alternatives in their potentiality). For Whitehead, propositions link together the virtual and the actual, the conceptual and the physical, the objective datum and the subjective form; and both the logical and the metaphysical subjects. During the phase of conceptual reversion, however, propositions also have the capacity to act as a *lure for* the creative emergence of novelty, specifically, through the *feeling of absence* achieved through negative rather than positive prehensions. Pomeroy suggests that critique can be construed along these lines as an anticipatory capacity that emerges from the current situation through the capacity of conceptual reversion to envisage alternatives in their potentiality. Rather than grounding the anticipatory nature of the human mind on Husserlian protensions and retensions, alone, Whitehead sees anticipation as emerging from an almost Heideggerian "clearing" or openness within which the dialectical dance of transcendence (the many in the one) and immanence (the one in the many) can take place.

> The ultimate metaphysical principle is the advance from disjunction to conjunction, creating a novel entity other than the entities given in disjunction. The novel entity is at once the togetherness of the "many" which it finds, and also it is one among the disjunctive "many" which it leaves; it is a novel entity, disjunctively among the many entities which it synthesizes. The many become one, and are increased by one . . . These ultimate notions of "production of novelty" and of "concrete togetherness" are inexplicable either in terms of higher universals or in terms of the components participating in the concrescence. The analysis of the components abstracts from the concrescence. The sole appeal is to intuition.
>
> (PR: 21–22)

Pulling the various threads together

So what is the philosophical fabric that weaves together the three fibres—Neoliberal cultural policy informed by Austrian value-theory, a Benjaminite neo-Marxist aesthetics, and a "co-creative" process of 'digitization', which in turn can be gainfully explored through the lens of, say, Callon and Latour's New Economic Sociology—into a resilient and attractive cloth? Or instead, do we end up with a raggedy cloth that is more hole than fabric? Where Steigler's emphasis on mnemotechnics and Deleuze's *Postscript* sound out a warning, Freeman accentuates a set of positive interventions that can gainfully influence the eventual outcome.

In his critical writing on the turn away from the 'cultural' towards 'creative' industries, the arch-cynic, Justin O'Connor (2015), advocates that we conceive of this turn along New Economic Sociology (NES) lines, rather than in terms of the (less fashionable) reflexive sociology of a Pierre Bourdieu; that is, as the product of a highly specialized socio-technical assemblage. For NES, desiring production weaves 'statements' and 'visibilities' together, within a fragile fretwork (a structure that Foucault himself described as one comprised of power–knowledge relations), but nevertheless one that is continuously exposed to disruption (i.e. the spiralling dance of territorialization and deterritorialization).

Of course, socio-technical assemblages are merely isomorphic, albeit somewhat more concrete, expressions of the very same creative activity. For example, the assemblage could be the complex and shifting grid of petroleum flows originating in the extractive industries and ending up in service stations and on supermarket shelves around the globe.

As Mitchell (2008, 2009) explains, the oil grid is fluid enough to overcome the threat posed by a general strike, which would have been far more effective (and thus democratizing) during the era of coal, due to the very rigidity of the dendritic networks of production and distribution in this industry and its periphery—a network linking coal miners, to canals and their bargees and railway locomotives and their drivers, and, of course, to steam ships, their boiler stokers, and the stevedores in their dock yards—all footholds for a militant trade unionism.

While debate can certainly ensue over whether a Deleuzean rather than a Foucaultian interpretation of these concrete assemblages might be an improvement (i.e. to the extent that it replaces the notions of power–knowledge relations and resistance to them with their Deleuzean counterparts—namely, desiring production and processes of deterritorialization), from a political economy perspective, these constellations can still be evaluated in terms of their efficiency and fitness for purpose. And this, on the basis of the "performativity" of the relevant theoretical constructs—given that they do not just describe the world, but also actively condition, circumscribe, and constitute it (albeit, under certain conditions of felicitation)!

Nevertheless, as I have demonstrated above, these constructs should include not only those pertaining to the "creative industries", but also the phenomena of ubiquitous computing or 'digitization', along with the faddish and populist term, "co-creation". The purpose of this chapter has been to articulate the at times closely related philosophical and computational underpinnings of various disciplinary practices and discourses feeding into the sphere of policy in regard to 'co-creation', creativity and 'digitization' with a view to subverting the philosophical agenda that has conditioned the currently dominant neoliberal regime of governmentality.

On the policy front, Bakhshi, Freeman and Higgs have signposted a series of interventions that, for Freeman, can gather together whatever instruments are required to promote his Marxist conception of the revolutionary potential of the "creative industries". These are strongly Keynesian in their orientation, express caution about the purported effectiveness of intellectual property regimes, and are suitably wary of other corrosive influences over the operations of governmentality, though not solely from the perspective of the heroic entrepreneur (who is, perhaps, better thought of as an automaton insofar as he or she is simply the determinate reflection of an inherent and largely unconscious ability to process the Knightian uncertainty associated with investments—both public and private—that are applied with equal success in both the cultural sphere and its non-cultural complement).

O'Connor's take on the DCMS embrace of the "creative industries", a ritual for which Freeman and his Queensland University of Technology colleagues operated as matchmakers extraordinaire, is both cynical and amusing. Personally, he suggests, rather than just fleshing out a policy term, they were developing a brand (for their "creative campus") so they felt compelled to ignore conceptual confusion of the classification and camouflaged the political realities of what was masquerading as a cultural and economic strategy. As far as New Labour's identification of importance of the Cultural Industries goes, he notes here, that the motivation for this policy-turn, as well as the likely effects of the convergence of technologies that was due to 'digitization', were already thrashed out in Cultural Industries literature of the 1980s and 1990s.

Nevertheless, a great deal of water has flowed under the bridge since the early days of the "creative industries", confirming conjectured growth trends and ensuring that the associated policies, for better or worse, have become mainstream. For surely we can recognize the promise offered by new socio-technical constellations, even while anticipating and heading off the imminent betrayals. And all this under conditions where the policies to support the 'Creative Industries' are continually under evaluation in comparative economic *and* political terms. The policy directions advocated by Freeman and his associates have apparently been shaped by the UK's radical geography traditions, which can be attributed to researchers such as Geoff McLeod and Ron Martin, who have developed detailed post-Keynesian critique of the UK government's strategies of "devolution", Social Entrepreneurship, and the New Regionalism. Members of this radical tradition have repeatedly emphasized the importance of central government leadership and management of effective demand, highlighting the strong link between innovation, creativity, training, and business cycle conditions. It is to this tradition that this chapter makes a modest contribution.

Note

1 In *Erfahrung und Urteil*, Husserl discusses ideal abstraction in terms of pure categorical intuition, which builds on sensible intuition to construct nonsensible objectualities, which include mathematical objects such as sets or manifolds. Moreover, categorical acts operating at a lower level can serve as founding acts for the categorical acts of a higher level, establishing a relation between two states-of-affairs. Restrictions come into play when these relations between states-of-affairs are no longer considered in terms of the syntactic possibility of forms of intuition, but in terms of their logical possibility (Hill and Haddock, 2000: 228).

Bibliography

Amoore, Louise (2004). Risk, Reward, and Discipline at Work. *Economy and Society*, 33(2): 174–196.

Andersson, P. and C. Rosenqvist (2007). Mobile Innovations in Healthcare: Customer Involvement and the Co-Creation of Value. *International Journal of Mobile Communications*, 5(4): 371–388.

Auh, S., S. J. Bell, C. S. McLeod and E. Shih (2007). Co-Production and Customer Loyalty in Financial Services. *Journal of Retailing*, 83(3): 359–370.

Bakhshi, Hasan, Alan Freeman and Peter Higgs (2013). A Dynamic Mapping of the UK's Creative Industries. Report prepared for NESTA. Accessed, 8 November 2014. www. academia.edu/5538116/A_Dynamic_Mapping_of_the_UKs_Creative_Industries.

Banks, John and Sal Humphreys (2008). The Labour of User Co-Creators: Emergent Social Network Markets? *Convergence*, 14: 401–408.

Brentano, F. (1973). [1924]. *Psychology from an Empirical Standpoint*, ed. L. L. McAlister. London: Routledge. German original, *Psychologie vrom Empirischen Standpunkt* (2nd ed.), 2 vols, ed. O. Kraus. Leipzig: Meincr.

Caves, R. E. (2002). *Creative Industries: Contracts between Art and Commerce*. Cambridge, MA: Harvard University Press.

Chaney, D. (2012). The Music Industry in the Digital Age: Consumer Participation in Value Creation. *International Journal of Arts Management*, 15(1): 42–52.

Comor, Edward (2010). Contextualizing and Critiquing the Fantastic Prosumer: Power, Alienation and Hegemony. *Critical Sociology*, (September) 20: 329–307.

Deleuze, G. (1990). *Negotiations: 1972–1990*. New York, NY: Columbia University Press.

Deleuze G. and Félix Guattari (1984). *Anti-Oedipus: Capitalism and Schizophrenia*. Trans. R. Hurley, M. Seem, and H. R. Lane. London: Continuum.

Firat, A. Fuat, Nikhilesh Dholakia and Alladi Venkatesh (1995). Liberatory Postmodernism and the Reenchantment of Consumption. *Journal of Consumer Research*, 22(3): 239–267.

Foucault, M. (2008). *The Birth of Biopolitics: Lectures at the Collège de France, 1978–1979*. Trans. G. Burchell. Houndmills: Palgrave Macmillan.

Fuchs, Christian, Kees Boersma, Anders Albrechtslund, Marisol Sandoval (2013). *Internet and Surveillance: The Challenges of Web 2.0 and Social Media*. London: Routledge.

Grenon, Pierre and Barry Smith (2004). SNAP and SPAN: Towards Dynamic Spatial Ontology. *Spatial Cognition and Computation*, 4(1) (March): 69–103.

Grossman, Lev (2006). You – Yes, You – Are TIME's Person of the Year. *Time Magazine*, Monday, 25 December.

Hill, Claire Ortiz and Guillermo Rosada Haddock (2000). *Husserl or Frege: Meaning, Objectivity, and Mathematics*. Chicago, IL: Carus Publishing.

Hoekstra, Rinke (2009). *Ontology Representation: Design Patterns and Ontologies That Make Sense*. Amsterdam: IOS Press.

Husserl, E. (1928). [1964]. *Vorlesungen zur Phanomenologie des inneren Zeitbewusstseins*, ed. M. Heidegger, in *Jahrbuch fur Philosophie und phenomenologische Forschung*, 9: 367–498. Translated as *The Phenomenology of Internal Time-Consciousness*. Trans. J. S. Churchill. The Hague: Nijhoff.

Husserl. E. (1929). Syntaktische Formen und syntaktische Stoffe. Kernfornen und Kernstoffe. Appendix to "Formale und Transcendentale Logik", *Jahrbuch für Philosophie und phänomenologische Forschung*, 10, 269–274 (English translation in, *Formal and Transcendental Logic*. The Hague: Nijhoff, 1969, 294–311).

Husserl, E. (1984). [2001]. Husserliana XIX (2 vols) *Logische Untersuchungen*, ed. Ursula Panzer. The Hague: Martinus Nijhoff, translated as *Logical Investigations*. Trans. J. N. Findlay. New York, NY: Routledge.

Keynes, John Maynard (1933). National Self-Sufficiency. *The Yale Review*, Summer. Reprinted in Keynes, John Maynard (1998). *The Collected Writings of John Maynard Keynes* (30 vols) (Hardback ed.). Cambridge: Cambridge University Press. Volume 21.

Klose, Joachim (2007). Process Ontology from Whitehead to Quantum Physics. Preprint, Dresden, 1 May.

Langley, P. (2007). The Uncertain Subjects of Anglo-American Financialization. *Cultural Critique*, 65 (Winter): 66–91.

Leadbeater, C. (2006). Are You Thinking What I'm Thinking?, *The Times*, 13 October. Accessed June 2007. http://timesonline.co.uk/tol/life_and_style/article599526.ece.

Leydesdorff, Loet (forthcoming). Luhmann's Communication-Theoretical Specification of the "Genomena" of Husserl's Phenomenology. In Edmundo Balsemão Pires (ed.), *Public Space, Power and Communication.* Coimbra: University of Coimbra.

Locke, C., R. Levine, D. Searles and D. Weinberger (2000). *A Cluetrain Manifesto: The End of Business as Usual.* New York, NY: Perseus Books. Available online at: http://cluetrain.com/book/apocalypso.html.

Merrill, Gary H. (2010). Ontological Realism: Methodology or Misdirection? *Applied Ontology*, 5: 79–108.

Michel, Stefan, S. L. Vargo and R. F. Lusch (2008). Reconfiguration of the Conceptual Landscape: A Tribute to the Service Logic of Richard Normann. *Journal of the Academy of Marketing Science*, 36: 152–155.

Milner, R. (2006). The Internet of Things: Competing Formalisms, Ubiquitous Computing: Shall We Understand It? *Computer Journal Lecture, BCS, The Chartered Institute for IT*, March. Accessed 6 November 2014. www.bcs.org/content/ConWebDoc/4708/*/setPaginate/No.

Milner, R. (2009). *The Space and Motion of Communicating Agents.* Cambridge: Cambridge University Press.

Mitchell, Timothy (2008). Rethinking Economy. *Geoforum*, 39: 1116–1121.

Mitchell, Timothy (2009). Carbon Democracy. *Economy and Society*, 38(3): 399–432.

O'Connor, Justin (2015). Intermediaries and Imaginaries in the Cultural and Creative Industries. *Regional Studies*, 49(3): 374–387.

Panigyrakisa, George and Anna Zarkadaa (2014). A Philosophical Investigation of the Transition from Integrated Marketing Communications to Metamodern Meaning Co-creation. *Journal of Global Scholars of Marketing Science: Bridging Asia and the World, Special Issue: Contribution of Philosophy to the Advancement of Marketing Thought*, 24(3): 262–278.

Payne A. F., K. Storbacka and P. Frow (2008). Managing the Co-creation of Value. *Journal of the Academy of Marketing Science*, 36: 83–96.

Pomeroy, Anne Fairchild (2001). Process Philosophy and the Possibility of Critique. *Journal of Speculative Philosophy*, 15(1): 33–49.

Pomeroy, Anne Fairchild (2004). *Marx and Whitehead: Process, Dialectics, and the Critique of Capitalism.* SUNY series in the Philosophy of the Social Sciences. Albany, NY: State University of New York Press.

Pomeroy, Anne Fairchild (2004). *Marx and Whitehead: Process, Dialectics, and the Critique of Capitalism.* SUNY series in the Philosophy of the Social Sciences. Albany, NY: State University of New York Press.

Prahalad, C. K. and V. Ramaswamy (2000). Co-opting Customer Experience. *Harvard Business Review*, January–February.

Prahalad, C. K. and V. Ramaswamy (2004). *The Future of Competition.* Cambridge, MA: Harvard Business School Press.

Ritzer, George and Nathan Jurgenson (2010). The Nature of Capitalism in the Age of the Digital "Prosumer". *Journal of Consumer Culture*, 10(1) (March): 13–36.

Simons, Peter (2005). Against Set Theory. In Johannes Marek and Maria Reicher (eds), *Experience and Analysis: Proceedings of the 2004 Wittgenstein Symposium.* Vienna: ÖBV & HPT, 143–152.

98   *'Co-creation' in the creative industries*

Simons, Peter and Reinhard Fabian (1986). The Second Austrian School of Value Theory. B. Smith and W. Grassl (eds), *Austrian Economics: Historical and Philosophical Background*. Beckenham: Croom Helm, 37–101.

Smith, Barry (1987). Austrian Economics and Austrian Philosophy. In Wolfgang Grassl and Barry Smith (eds), *Austrian Economics: Historical and Philosophical Background*. London: Croom-Helm, 1–36.

Smith, Barry and Werner Ceusters (2010). Ontological Realism: A Methodology for Coordinated Evolution of Scientific Ontologies. *Applied Ontology*, 5(3–4): 139–188.

Smith, Barry and Pierre Grenon (2004). The Cornucopia of Formal-Ontological Relations. *Dialectica*, 58(3): 279–296. Available at: http://ifomis.uni-saarland.de/bfo/.

Stiegler, B. (2010). *For a New Critique of Political Economy*. Trans. Daniel Ross, Cambridge: Polity Press.

Stiegler, B. (2011). Suffocated Desire, or How the Cultural Industry Destroys the Individual: Contribution to a Theory of Mass Consumption. Trans. Johann Rossouw. *Parrhesia*, 13: 52–61.

Tapscott, Don and Anthony D. Williams (2006). *Wikinomics: How Mass Collaboration Changes Everything*. New York, NY: Portfolio.

Vargo, Stephen L. and Robert F. Lusch (2008). Service-dominant Logic: Continuing the Evolution. *Journal of the Academy of Marketing Science*, 36: 1–10.

Wikström, S. (1996). Value Creation by Company-Consumer Interaction. *Journal of Marketing Management*, 12: 359–374.

4 Neoliberalism, 'digitization', and creativity

The issue of applied ontology

What, quite wrongly, has been thought of in Spinoza as pantheism is simply the reduction of the field of God to the universality of the signifier, which produces a serene, exceptional detachment from human desire. In so far as Spinoza says— desire is the essence of man, and in the radical dependence of the universality of the divine attributes, which is possible only through the function of the signifier, in so far as he does this, he obtains that unique position by which the philosopher— and it is no accident that it is a Jew detached from his tradition who embodies it—may be confused with a transcendent love. . . . This position is not tenable for us. Experience shows us that Kant is more true, and I have proved that his theory of consciousness, when he writes of practical reason, is sustained only by giving a specification of the moral law which, looked at more closely, is simply desire in its pure state, that very desire that culminates in sacrifice, strictly speaking, of everything that is the object of love in one's human tenderness—I would say, not only in the rejection of the pathological object, but also in its sacrifice and murder. That is why I wrote *Kant avec Sade*.

(Lacan, 1979: 275–276)

But it is like the story of the Resistance fighters who, wanting to destroy a pylon, balanced the plastic charges so well that the pylon blew up and fell back into its hole. From the Symbolic to the Imaginary, from castration to Oedipus, and from the despotic age to capitalism, inversely, there is the progress leading to the withdrawal of the overseeing and overcoding object from on high, which gives way to a social field of immanence where the decoded flows produce images and level them down. Whence the two aspects of the signifier: a barred transcendent signifier taken in a maximum that distributes lack, and an immanent system of relations between minimal elements that come to fill the uncovered field (some-what similar in traditional terms to the way one goes from Parmenidean Being to the atoms of Democritus).

(Deleuze and Guattari, 1987: 290–291)

Marx was vexed by the bourgeois character of the American working class. But it turned out that the prosperous Americans were merely showing the way for the British and the French and the Japanese. The universal class into which we are merging is not the revolutionary proletariat but the innovative bourgeoisie.

(McCloskey, 2009)

Introduction

The kernel of the argument that I make this chapter, is that critics of mainstream economics, in their efforts to understand the full impact of "digitization" on the labour process, have to go beyond hackneyed nostrums about (i) the reductionist evils of positivism; and (ii) the consequent need to replace an ethics grounded in negative notions of freedom from external domination with one grounded in positive notions of freedom, so as to realize and perfect both the innate and acquired capacities of the workforce. In this undertaking I have chosen a recent paper by García-Quero and Ollero-Perrán (2015), an earlier Constructivist Feminist contribution by Susan Feiner (1995), and a much earlier though more famous interrogative piece by Heidegger (1953), "The Question Concerning Technology", as my targets. As the instruments for my own critique I have chosen Lacan's "Four Discourses", as adumbrated in the Seminar of 1969–1970, *The Other Side of Psychoanalysis*, along with Deleuze and Guattari's (1984) *Anti-Oedipus*. I go on to examine how certain aspects of these works have been developed by thinkers such as Bernard Stiegler.

García-Quero and Ollero-Perrán (2015) begin their critique of neoclassical economics with Aristotle, for whom ethics entailed the pursuit of individual good whereas politics, in seeking the collective good, was obviously more expansive and meritorious. Moreover, in accordance with this political reading of the nature of the ethical, economy, too, can never be useful for its own sake. They turn to Immanuel Kant (1724–1804) as a fulcrum for their interpretation of the marginal revolution in economics, noting that Kant famously attempted to reconcile the rationalism of Descartes, Spinoza, Leibniz with the idealism of Bishop Berkeley and the radical empiricism of Locke and Hume, for whom true knowledge drawn from the senses is elusive.

Kant's Copernican inquiry into the 'conditions of possibility' of true knowledge, García-Quero and Ollero-Perrán suggest, allowed truth to be predicated on both a shared and an immutable cognitive structure (grounded in transcendental reason), which serves to mediate between the world and inner understanding. Thus speculative reason obtains material knowledge from the empirical senses, which can be universal. If practical reason is to attain a similar kind of universality, however, Kant cautions that it will have to refuse any efforts to ground this universality in the contingent and fleeting domain of feelings or wishes. Instead, it must attain to a unity and coherence through a pure formalism: that is, it must abandon any reliance on empirical content or emotional concern. This split between speculative and practical reason, however, implies that "ethics can never become science and science can never deal with ethical issues" (García-Quero and Ollero-Perrán, 2015: 58).

For García-Quero and Ollero-Perrán (2015), this bifurcation between ethics and science also allows for another split between economics and ethics, which is deployed by the so-called Marginalist economists—Jevons, Menger, Clark, Edgeworth, Pareto, Fischer, and Pigou—most notably in their penchant for treating economics as a natural rather than as a social science. This is most clearly seen in General Equilibrium economics which views the attainment of equilibrium as an optimizing process maximizing utility based on individual preferences given endowments of scarce resources. Here, the market plays the role of balancing supply and demand. Nevertheless, not only do the underlying assumptions of methodological individualism and rational choice, in combining hedonistic psychology with an originally theological conception of the market as an "invisible hand", lead to a ludicrous simplification of human behaviour, they also bear the consequences of a commitment to Kantian liberal philosophy.

For Kant, (negative) freedom from external authority and aggressive domination can only be guaranteed and achieved "in the public domain through the democratic dialogue of economically independent men", thus serving to divorce "universally applicable agreements" from the private sphere of personal ethical considerations (García-Quero and Ollero-Perrán, 2015: 61).

In contrast, García-Quero and Ollero-Perrán (2015: 64) turn to communitarian notions of (positive) freedom associated with the realization of potential capacities, and to the Marxist and Veblenian tradition of institutionalist economics for which history matters, because "[i]t is not the consciousness of men that determines their existence, but their social existence that determines their consciousness", and because "institutions *build* motivations, making individuals internalize them and change themselves".

Susan Feiner has outlined a psychoanalytic interpretation of the yearning for general equilibrium which resonates with García-Quero and Ollero-Perrán's (2015) ethically based arguments for a return to institutionalist economics. Feiner (1995) turns to the Object-relations School of Psychoanalysis for a conception of the mother/child unit as the basis for the 'primordially repressed' fantasy of fusion and total fulfilment. This repressed kernel, she argues, then provides the locus in the unconscious of internalized feelings of powerlessness, dependency, and frustration which, in turn, gives rise to feelings of guilt at the aggressive impulses that are released as a result. The feelings of guilt and frustration, however, can be denied and thus overcome through mastery, autonomy, and masculinist self-assertion (she refers to the erotic fantasies of science as a 'penetration' of nature's veils). When projected onto notions of the free market as a site of fair exchange, they become associated with the notion that scarcity can be resolved through the attainment of a general equilibrium with the fictitious Walrasian auctioneer functioning as a guarantor of fairness. Nevertheless, she complains that the reproductive and caring role of household labour is entirely neglected by this fantasy.

However, another reading of the ethical and unconscious ground for the marginal revolution in economic analysis is possible; one set out by Jacques Lacan, the Freudian psychoanalyst, in the essay *Kant avec Sade*. In this essay Lacan (2006: 645) compares the ethical philosophies of Kant and the Divine Marquis, arguing that Sade's work is not so much an *anticipation* of Freud but rather a clarifying set of practices, which functions more like an ancient school of philosophy insofar as it paves the way for science by rectifying one's ethical position. Thus, Lacan sees Sade as the first step in a subversion for which Kant is the turning point. He notes (Lacan, 2006: 646) that *Philosophy in the Bedroom* came eight years after the *Critique of Practical Reason*. Moreover, he suggests that Kant's reasoning is subversive at its core because it suppresses progress, holiness, and even love for the "alibi of immortality", insofar as it is predicated on the sheer will to render its object intelligible. For Kant, no phenomenon can claim a constant relation to the pleasure principle, conceived as the law of feeling good. The purity of moral will can arise only if we accept the necessity of sacrificing the pathological interest of the subject. As such, the Kantian maxim derives its force from the voice in conscience. Nevertheless, while the universality of its logic implies the validity of its manifestations in every case, this in turn implies that the maxim must allow for analytic deduction. Thus, Lacan (2006: 647–648) points to the necessity for a more synthetic foundation: finding the requisite ground in the erotic trace of the lost object withdrawn from intuition.

From a Psychoanalytic perspective, the source of the split between pure and practical reason can be traced to the operation of negation conceived in turn as the *aufhebung* of repression: that is, negation is not an acceptance of what is repressed, rather the repressed persists in the form of non-acceptance (Hyppolite in Lacan, 2007: 746–754). Moreover, the intellectual function is separated from the affective process because negation serves (in the order of myth) as the very genesis of thought: behind every affirmation is negation, but behind negation is expulsion (*ausstossung*). Freud describes two types of Judgement: that of *attribution*, affirming or disaffirming the possession by a thing of a particular attribute; and that of *existence*: asserting or disputing that a presentation has an existence in reality. Behind the first type, however, is both 'introjection' and 'ejection' where the latter is conceived as primordial, for the alien must first be expelled before the respective presentation can be refound once again. Thus, it is not a process involving some kind of Jungian remembrance but rather one of repetition. Where affirmation, as a substitute for unification, belongs to Eros, negation, as the successor to expulsion, belongs to Thanatos, for how can there be pleasure in negating that results from the withholding of the libidinal components? The performance of the function of judgement is only made possible by the *creation of the symbol of negation*, thus permitting a degree of freedom from both the consequences of repression and the relentless compulsion of the pleasure principle.

In his commentary on Lacan's celebrated essay, Slavoj Žižek (1998) observes that the conventional interpretation of Lacan's point is that Kant was a 'closet Sadean' whose rigour reflected a sadism of the Law. Instead, Žižek favours the inverse conception that Sade was a closet Kantian insofar as he epitomized the ultimate consequences and disavowed premises of Kantian ethical revolution: far from every 'pure' ethical act being grounded in a pathological motivation; desire, itself ungrounded in pathological interest, meets the criteria of an ethical act. He observes that Sade's fundamental fantasy—a beauty that survives endless torture—is formally equivalent to the Kantian soul's endless striving for perfection. Moreover, Sade's injunction to reduce one's fellows to instruments of one's own pleasure should not be thought of as merely contingent and pathological for it reflects the fundamental tension constitutive of the Cartesian subject: namely, the Kantian imperative is 'empty' so that it must be filled by contingent, empirical content, so that it can be rendered necessary. As such, this imperative cannot be reduced solely to the superegoic injunction, for it is equivalent to desire itself, uncompromised.

Žižek goes on to examine the political consequences of this perverted realization of Kantian ethics. While acknowledging the obvious fact that that libidinal structure of totalitarian regimes is perverse, he notes that responsibility is the crucial Freudian notion of the ethical: in assuming full responsibility for one's duty the Sadean position of serving as an object-instrument of the Other's *jouissance* is prohibited. In his concluding comments Žižek also insists that we must also avoid the ontological guilt of existentialism, which entails putting the blame on the Other (once we have escaped the inauthenticity of capture by the Other's 'look') through the embrace of a psychoanalytic ethics of duty "beyond the Good". The formal indeterminacy of Kantian ethics, for Žižek, is paradoxically not its weakness (i.e. its unrecognized historical contingency), but rather, its greatest strength (in requiring the subject to assume responsibility). As with aesthetic judgements, the invention of universal obligation raises the contingent object to the very dignity of the Thing! And here too, we arrive at a pure faculty of desire, given that it has a non-pathological object cause: namely, Lacan's *objet petit a*.

The characteristics of this lost object as it functions within economic discourse are brought out by Jeanne Schroeder (1997), who notes the fact that Juno Moneta, the Roman Goddess of womanhood, was the Latin source of the English word money. From a psychoanalytic perspective, both women and property function as phallic objects and objects of exchange. Schroeder introduces Hegel's distinction between possession (i.e. having the phallus), enjoyment (being the phallus), and alienation (exchanging the phallus), observing that the Law operates within the Symbolic register from which the Imaginary order can be perceived as a closed world. The legal order, however, is condemned to perpetually oscillate between juridical rights and duties. Nevertheless, the Real functions here as a quadratic term: it is the indivisible remainder, embodying an impossible and always-already lost completeness. From this perspective then, as what is expelled by the Symbolic, the phallus is the representative of the Desire of the Other—in both its unknowability and unattainability it is manifest as the *objet a*—insofar as it functions as what doesn't work, it is possessed by those who never had it, and it has no content.

Schroeder identifies both the fixity of subject and the tangibility of property as attributes that are correlated with the lost object. For her part, the subject is fixed by her subjection *to* the law and her existence as a subject *of* the law. For its part, property is conceived as both physical and tangible, reflecting the urge to privilege possession and exchange, which she argues, should be conceived as the impetus behind an ill-feted search for a 'perfect mate' who will heal the hole of castration. In this light, Schroeder goes on to interpret the neoclassical pursuit of market efficiency as something partaking of this perfection in that it can supposedly be attained, in fantasy at any rate: beyond time (instantaneously), beyond space (without movement), and beyond subjectivity itself (without differentiation). Nevertheless, while *Eros* serves as the principle of exchange, she cautions that *Thanatos*—the death drive—operates as the *jouissance* ruling over the 'perfect market'.

I have chosen the theme of digitization of the labour process, which can readily be interpreted within a broader "varieties of capitalism". An approach of this kind comes to the fore in the work of Robert Wade and Alice Amsden with their similar conceptions of the "developmental state" and Mazzucato's (2013) innovation-centred research on *The Entrepreneurial State*.

The question of how best to conceive of the different varieties of capitalism has been pursued by Regulation Theorists, for whom Marx's dialectic of forces and relations has been displaced by one of 'regimes of accumulation' and 'modes of regulation', so that the resulting framework serves as a vehicle for "bringing the State back" into the economic field. Nevertheless, I have never been happy with this approach because, in my view, it undermines the rigour of Marx's analysis of social formations and modes of production (characterized by their associated forces and relations of production). Accordingly, in the next section, I provide an overview of Foucault's analysis of Austro-German neoliberalism in *The Birth of Biopolitics* (2008), focusing especially on philosophical influences over this tradition emanating from Brentano and Husserl. This is followed, by a brief discussion of the concept of "digitization", which I have chosen to approach via the phenomenon of "ubiquitous computing" or the "internet of things". In the following section I begin some observations on Whitehead's notion of Creativity, segueing into a consideration of how the notion of creativity has been deployed in the UK context to identify creative occupations and industries. I then turn to Heidegger's 1953 work, "The Question Concerning Technology", to identify crucial gaps and omissions in his analysis. These omissions, which are ostensively political, are detailed in the next section, which deals with the theme of the appropriation of knowledge as it appears in Lacan's analysis of the Four Discourses and in Deleuze and Guattari's *Anti-Oedipus*, before arriving, in the section after that, at the contemporary research of Pagano and Stiegler. The process of theft or appropriation linking these seemingly diverse texts together is one that is completely ignored both by Heidegger and by those associated with the Austrian tradition of economics. Concluding comments follow in the final section.

Philosophical influences over Austro-Germanic neoliberalism

In this section of the chapter I review Foucault's interpretation of neoliberalism in *The Birth of Biopolitics* (2008), especially where he highlights the difference between classical liberalism and the neoliberalism of the Austro-German and Chicago school traditions. In addition, I focus on the links that he establishes between Austrian economics and Husserlian Phenomenology.

In his lectures on Biopolitics, Foucault extends his analytical notions of the assemblage or apparatus as a structure of power–knowledge relations— relations which, in turn, weave together the archaeological strata of visibilities (with their conditions of emergence) and statements (with their conditions of enunciation).

It was a matter of showing by what conjunctions a whole set of practices—from the moment they become coordinated with a regime of truth—was able to make what does not exist (madness, disease, delinquency, sexuality, etcetera), nonetheless become something, something however that continues not to exist. That is to say, what I would like to show is not how an error—when I say that which does not exist becomes something, this does not mean showing how it is possible for an error to be constructed—or how an illusion could be born, but how a particular regime of truth, and therefore not an error, makes something that does not exist able to become something. It is not an illusion since it is precisely a set of practices, real practices, which established it and thus imperiously marks it out in reality.

(Foucault, 2008: 19)

This familiar apparatus, however, is now applied to a new theme, that of governmentality, which requires an analysis of governmental practice as it reflects upon itself and is rationalized, in such a way that the mechanisms of state and society, and of sovereignty and subjection are formed. Foucault develops an anti-essentialist analysis eschewing all universal notions of sovereignty, the people, the state, or civil society, choosing, instead, to trace the emergence of a particular type of rationality, which enables ways of governing to be modelled on the basis of a state that is both pre-existent and continually reconstituted as its objectives and rules are transformed.

From this governmentality perspective, the German tradition of Ordoliberals is seen to be inscribed by the necessity to constitute a state under the supervision of the market rather than a market supervised by the state. The "Ordos" ask themselves the question of how the market economy could function as the principle, form, and model for a state. Nevertheless, for them market competition can no longer be viewed as a mere expression of innate appetites and the instinct to "truck and barter", rather, Walter Eucken and his followers turn to Husserlian Phenomenology for its conception of a market as something historical and contingent, but something that is nonetheless constituted to be the expression of an underlying economic logic. The Ordos also took from Nazis the Sombartian critique of capitalism as a system destructive of natural community: one displaced by the administrative machinery of the state, processes of mass consumption, and state-sanctioned spectacle.

Foucault observes that the various schools of neoliberal thought depart from their classical forbears in raising the issue of how the market economy can thus function as the principle, form, and model for a state. For Eucken, this process of governing the market included the control of inflation and price controls. Sectoral subsidies and programmes of public investment and systematic policies of job creation, however, had to be abandoned to ensure a necessary reserve of unemployment to 'support' workers in transition from less to more profitable activities. The Ordos thus opposed welfare policies designed to provide equality of access to consumer goods and socialization of risk. For them the management of social risk had to be privatized through the creation of mutual benefit organizations. The role of sectoral policies was reduced to the facilitation of population movement, the enhancement of techniques of production, improving the allocation of property rights, and even modifying the climate.

For the Ordos then, a protected economy, a state unified on Bismarckian principles, an economy characterized by wartime planning, and one featuring Keynesian-style interventions was seen as one allied to an unlimited growth of state power along fascist lines. Foucault argues that, for their part, the Chicago School embraced a conception of freedom that had been nurtured during the War of Independence, for which interventionist policies of a Keynesian variety were viewed as the alien and external imposts of a military and imperial state that could ultimately assume the mantle of Stalinist totalitarianism. For Chicago-style cold-warriors such as Gary Becker, the neoliberal conception of the market would even serve as a principle for "deciphering" social relationships. This same economic grid would also be deployed to assess the validity and value of government activity—a grid assuming material form with the 1943 establishment of *The American Enterprises Institute*—so that it could become a "permanent economic tribunal turned against government".

Philosophy, ontology, and Austrian economics

In the previous chapter it was argued that the Austrian and Czechoslovakian universities gave birth to both Phenomenology and the Austrian School of Economics because, in contrast to their German counterparts, which were mired in High Romanticism, they were imbued with a more Aristotelean tradition of realist metaphysics. In Brentano's hands this gave rise to a philosophical and descriptive psychology which aimed to capture the structural interconnections amongst the objectively existing elements and complexes obtaining within the psychological sphere itself. In opposition to Kant, Brentano argued that the laws governing these interconnections were of a synthetic rather than analytic nature. In this milieu, Ehrenfels' conception of a Gestalt (i.e. a whole that is greater than its parts; whose very nature would be transformed by the removal of a part) carried over to value-theory, which was grounded in 'feeling-dispositions' linking mental phenomena with feelings of pleasure and displeasure. Along similar mere-ological lines, Stumpf argued that relations of necessary dependence obtained not only between the parts of a single whole, but also between objects that were not comprehended within any independently recognizable surrounding complex object. Grenon and Smith (2004: 14) observe that Brentano applied this mereo-logical logic of dependency to the commodity itself:

> A commodity or economic good is a dependent object in this generalised sense. A commodity cannot, of necessity, exist, unless there exist also appropriately directed valuing acts which depend in their turn upon specific subjective beliefs and intentions of individual subjects. A medium of exchange cannot, by its nature, exist, unless there exist also economic value, economic transactions, and a generally dispersed readiness to accept.

Of course, Husserl's version of Cartesian asceticism played a crucial role in the subsequent distillation of neoliberal theory, especially due to his distinction between objective and subjective ideals. Where logic and mathematics focuses on objective ideals and the science of consciousness on subjective ideals with respect to their lawfulness, eidetic science focuses on subjective ideals through a process of abstraction, because ideals are grasped on an *a priori* basis in eidetic intuition not through the elimination of particular determinations, nor on the basis of a belief in actuality and existence, but through an ideal non-positioning that was designed to achieve ontic and epistemic neutrality. Through this process of abstraction, fulfilment would be accomplished in establishing an equivalence between meaning intention and intuited meaning:

> The object is not actually given, it is not given wholly and entirely as that which it itself is. It is only given "from the front", only "perspectively fore-shortened and projected" etc. . . . . The elements of the invisible rear side, the interior etc., are no doubt subsidiarily intended in more or less definite fashion . . . On this hinges the possibility of indefinitely many percepts of the same object, all differing in content.

> (Husserl, 1984: 712–713)

As described in the previous chapter, another of the *persona* populating the neo-liberal stage is that of the entrepreneur. In this case, the Phenomenological ground for entrepreneurship is granted by anticipation, which in turn relies on a three-fold weaving together of Husserl's primal impressions with protensions and reten-sions. In the last chapter I also explained how, the entrepreneur was viewed as someone who could overcome Knightian uncertainty by working out what kinds of goods and services we shall be wanting in the more distant future, how they might be produced, and what the prospective streams of remuneration are likely to be. As Smith and Grenon (2004) explain:

> Entrepreneurial activity is dependent, first of all, on the perception of a cer-tain kind of structural moment of material reality as this is, at some given time, articulated by the existing economic relations. It is dependent further on the knowledge or belief engendered by the given perception that this struc-tural moment is an economic opportunity (will generate a stream of profits). And it is dependent also, like the given moments of perception and knowl-edge, upon a specific individual—the entrepreneur—who is endowed with an appropriate background knowledge of the economic articulation of the relevant area of material reality [and the latter must also obtain!].

Derrida's immanent critique of Phenomenology

In Husserl's philosophy, a transcendental grounding is achieved through an intui-tive fulfilment of meaning-bestowing acts. A merely contingent connection is thus established between the ideal unities productive of meaning and the signs to which they are tied. Everything is predicated on an almost Platonic distinction between meanings-in-themselves and the meanings-expressed. Husserl argues that as image is to perception, so the meaning-intending act is related to meaning fulfilment: intuition is seen to make good the promise issued by the expression. It is hardly surprising that knowledge of fact and logic are thereby accorded precedence over both grammar and understanding.

In contrast, Derrida questions the metaphysical identity of meaning-intention on the basis of a temporal difference and otherness that is seen to constitute the intuitive re-presentation of the same object by extracting it from the spatio-temporal flux of experience. In internal time consciousness, intuition is made possible through the conjoint activity of compounding and productive protentions and retentions (i.e. most notably in the form of expectations and remembrance). Therefore, the supposedly unmediated living presence of intuition is illusory because identity is actually guaranteed by the sensible form that underpins the ideal character (the formal identity) of either the phoneme or the grapheme. For Derrida, however, the externality of expression brings forth the difference between signification itself and that for which it stands, between the inner-worldly sphere and the articulated linguistic meaning, underpinning the separation between both the speaker and the hearer, and between speech and the objects of speech: within a general structure of 'making-present' and 'coming-to-light'. Derrida argues that the basis for these distinctions is overlooked by Husserl due to the dominance in the Western tradition of a notion of the phoneme as something that obtains within an auto-affective act that is responsible for uniting sound-patterns, sensual self-affection, and intended meaning within a 'realm of ownness'. In opposition to this phonocentrism, Derrida articulates the play of *différance* as an archewriting, an event without a subject, which permits him to deconstruct the Western conception of Being as both the production and the recollection of beings within an abiding presence and mastery. As we shall see in below, Heidegger draws on the notion of unconcealment to articulate a similar conception of the *difference* at play in both technē and poiēsis. Nevertheless, I shall argue that Heidegger's analysis falls short precisely in relation to our chosen theme of the 'theft of knowledge'.

Digitization and the "internet of things"

So much has been written about the phenomenon of "digitization", much of it of dubious value. In an effort to "cut-through-the-clutter", in Chapter 3 I drew on Robin Milner—one-time recipient of the Alan Turing Award and developer of the Calculus of Interactive Systems characterized by concurrency, the Pi Calculus, Meta-language, and the encompassing Bi-graph formalism. In the next section of this Chapter I examine the relationship between creativity and digitization in more philosophical terms.

Digitization and creativity

In this section I briefly examine Alfred North Whitehead's conceptions of creativity, which leads on to Alan Freeman's Marxist-influenced analysis of its role in the identification of the creative industries. From there, I move on to consider Heidegger's analysis of "The Question Concerning Technology", where I identify two glaring omissions or elisions in his analysis.

In an introductory piece on the philosophy of Alfred North Whitehead, Stephen Myer (2005) cites Kristeller's cautious inference that it is Whitehead who is singularly responsible for introducing the modern conception of creativity into the English language:

> [W]e are led to infer that the word became an accepted part of the standard English vocabulary only between 1934 and 1961. We may even go back a few more years. The great philosopher, Alfred North Whitehead used "creativity" in his *Religion in the Making* (1927 [sic!]) and in his major work, *Process and Reality* (1929), and in view of the great influence of this last work, we may very well conjecture that he either coined the term or at least gave it wide currency.

In *Process and Reality*, Whitehead (1978: 21–22) went so far as to make creativity into a fundamental principle of his metaphysical system, as evidenced by the following quote:

> The ultimate metaphysical principle is the advance from disjunction to conjunction, creating a novel entity other than the entities given in disjunction. The novel entity is at once the togetherness of the "many" which it finds, and also it is one among the disjunctive "many" which it leaves; it is a novel entity, disjunctively among the many entities which it synthesizes. The many become one, and are increased by one . . . These ultimate notions of "production of novelty" and of "concrete togetherness" are inexplicable either in terms of higher universals or in terms of the components participating in the concrescence. The analysis of the components abstracts from the concrescence. The sole appeal is to intuition.

For Whitehead (1978: 16), then, the terms 'creativity', 'many', 'one', 'thing', 'being', and 'entity' are equivalent in the sense that an actual entity *is* a prehension and a prehension *is* an actual entity, so the many *are* one, and the thing *is* a creative being. Moreover "[e]ach task of creation is a social effort, employing the whole universe" (Whitehead, 1978: 223).

Under Tony Blair's New Labour, the UK Department of Communication, Media, and Sport (DCMS) realized that it could attract more funding from a recalcitrant Treasury by talking about the "Creative Industries" rather than the "Sphere of Culture". This led to a proliferation of efforts directed at determining the nature of creative employment and, thus, the industries characterized by a high intensity of creative to non-creative labour. Bakhshi, Freeman and Higgs (2013) summarize the DCMS definition of the Creative Industries in the following way: "those industries which have their origin in individual creativity, skill and talent and which have a potential for wealth and job creation through the generation and exploitation of intellectual property".

Their report, commissioned by the UK innovation quango, NESTA, defines "Creative Occupations" as those having "a role within the creative process that brings cognitive skills to bear to bring about differentiation to yield either novel, or significantly enhanced products whose final form is not fully specified in advance". In arriving at a more workable characterization of these occupations Bakhshi et al. develop a 'grid-score' approach based on the following five criteria: (i) a novel process must be involved; (ii) it must be mechanization resistant; (iii) labour activity must be non-repetitive and non-uniform; (iv) and it must make a creative contribution to value-chain entailing 'Interpretation' rather than mere 'transformation'.

The economic model of the creative industries that Bakhshi et al. (2015) adopt is on characterized by:

1   a common type of input or resource (the creative workforce);
2   common features of the output (emphasis on content, product differentiation, shorter, often smaller, production runs, preponderance of cultural or culture-related outputs, sale to discretionary markets, exploitation of both traditional IP and firstmover advantage);
3   common processes of production (pre-market selection, uncertainty-management contracts, just-in-time short-run production methods, 'open innovation' with an emphasis on collaborative contracts, geographical clustering at the micro level, and so on).

Alan Freeman, one of the co-authors in the Bakshi et al. (2015) report, has identified a series of major obstacles to the capitalist-driven expansion of the creative industries, which include the fact that creativity cannot be mechanized and separated from the labourer, so that the myopia of private sector could lead to low levels of investment due to the fear that there will be a high turnover of workers. By the same token, he warns that there will be a tendency for real accumulation to be displaced by fictitious capital, and for intellectual property rights to operate as a "parasitic" substitute for innovation. Freeman therefore calls for a reconceptualization of the public sphere, with the interests of humans/artists placed at the centre of policy, corporate bodies defined on the basis of their capacity to develop individuals, and with cultural infrastructure developed on an unprecedented scale, so that "cities function as factories" for the creative sectors.

Many writers on the Creativity have been influenced by Martin Heidegger's (1953) essay "The Question Concerning Technology". In this section I intend to review Heidegger's arguments about technology to identify some important elisions and gaps in his interpretation of the dichotomy he sets up between technē and poiēsis. Heidegger begins his thought-piece by asserting that the *essence* of technology is nothing technological, rather, it is a way of revealing the totality of beings. This thought of Being occurs prior to distinction between theory (contemplation) and practice (deed). In addition, "[t]he thinking that inquires into the truth of Being, and so defines man's essential abode from Being and towards Being is neither ethics nor ontology (Heidegger, 1953: 259).

Moreover, despite its contemporary prevalence and its apparent source in the Scientific Revolution, it precedes the latter. Heidegger warns that it is both an expansionist and reductionist ordering of man and nature in terms of a certain manipulability, which may overwhelm other forms of revelation, such as Art, which is also concerned with the dialectic of concealment and unconcealment.

> On one hand, enframing challenges forth into the frenziedness of ordering that blocks every view to the propriative event of revealing and so radically endangers the relation to the essence of truth. On the other hand, enframing propriates for its part in the granting that lets man endure—as yet inexperienced, but perhaps more experienced in the future—that he may be the one who is needed and used for the safekeeping of the essence of truth. Thus the rising of the saving power appears.
>
> (Heidegger, 1953: 338)

This quote captures the full panoply of Heidegger's network of concepts. On one hand we have the idea of enframing (*Gestell* = frame, apparatus, skeleton), which, much like Plato's *eidos*, is that which in everything endures as present; it is a "gathering together of the setting upon that sets upon man" (Heidegger, 1953: 324–325). And modern science, itself, is such an enframing, which, "as pure theory, sets nature up to exhibit itself as a coherence of forces calculable in advance" (Heidegger, 1953: 326). Heidegger (1953: 328) even goes so far as to consider the 'orderable' as a system of information, insofar as it functions as neither an occasioning, nor a making, nor a planning, but a mere reporting!

We also have the idea that human activity becomes history as a destining (*Geschick*) "That first starts man upon a way of revealing" (Heidegger, 1953: 329) in such a way that man can exhibit the freedom not merely to listen and obey but also "to conceal in a way that opens to light" (Heidegger, 1953: 330) Yet man is also endangered by this destining,

> Since destining at any given time starts man on a way of revealing, man, thus underway, is continually approaching the brink of the possibility of pursuing and promulgating nothing but what is revealed in ordering, and of deriving all his standards on this basis.
>
> (Heidegger, 1953: 331)

Yet it must be obvious that there is much that has been elided in this comparison between poiēsis and technē: on one hand we have the question of the State, as David Krell (1999: 310) concedes, whereas, in Heidegger's speeches of 1935,

> ... the deed that founds the political state participates in the revelation of beings, in 1953 the political state is in total eclipse. Not the political but the poetical appears as the saving power; not *praxis* but poiēsis may enable us to confront the essential unfolding of technology.

The other glaring political omission in Heidegger's deliberations is one situated at a more localized level at the very site of production and exchange: for it is here at this level that we must confront the theft of knowledge.

Digitization and the "theft of knowledge" in Lacan, Deleuze, and Guattari

In this section I set the scene for a review of more recent writing on knowledge-based production through a detailed reading of Lacan's notion of the "theft of knowledge" in his description of the Discourse of the Master. I go on to consider the reappearance of this theme of appropriation in Deleuze and Guattari's *Anti-Oedipus* and *A Thousand Plateaus*.

Kiarina Kordela observes that Lacan first points to the analogy between surplus enjoyment and surplus value in Seminar XXII. As surplus enjoyment is *extimate* to the chain of circulation of signification, so too is surplus value *extimate* to the chain of circulation of capital: each is produced by the chain as its effect and also as ontologically distinguishable from the chain (Kordela, 1999: 810–811). While surplus value is the structural condition for the transformation of money into capital enabling the latter to circulate and expand, Kordela (1999: 810) notes that money and the commodity, from the view of capital as self-producing and self-reproducing, are mere forms supporting capital's autonomy and self-expansion: in theistic and patriarchal terms, through the surplus (the son), the original amount expensed (the Father) can be reunited as one, even when there is no (blood) relation between them. It is the prohibition of incest (because the mother is always the property of the patriarch or father), which transforms need (i.e. blood) into demand (in the form of the law). Simultaneously, the law is representation (of meaning and power), enjoyment (the *objet a*), and enjoyment of meaning (the underside of desire), in this way, turning exploitation into something more tolerable.

Hence, Lacan suggests that unbeknownst to Marx, the Marxian notion of surplus value is the ground of the constitution of the subject as an effect of the unconscious. This is supported by Kordela's reading of Lacan's analysis of metonymy and metaphor which relies on the psychoanalytic interpretation of a line taken from Victor Hugo's *Booz endormi*, "His sheaf was neither miserly nor spiteful" ("sa grebe n'était pas avare ni haineuse"). Deploying his schema-L, Lacan (2007: 53) argues that metonymy is one side of the field constituted by the signifier, which guarantees that meaning will emerge there, whereas the other side is metaphor (Lacan, 2007: 506). The creative spark of the metaphor is a function of the fact that one signifier has taken the place of the other in the signifying chain, however, the occulted signifier remains present through its metonymic connection with the rest of the chain: the place of Booz is 'usurped' by the sheaf, so that his "asserted generosity is reduced to *less than nothing* by the munificence of the sheaf", but the metaphor also conveys the promise that the old man will give birth to a son, thus reproducing the 'paternal mystery' (Lacan, 2007: 507). Elaborating on Lacan's analysis, Kordela suggests that use value and the vulgar law of property is negated by the attribute of munificence, which metaphorically

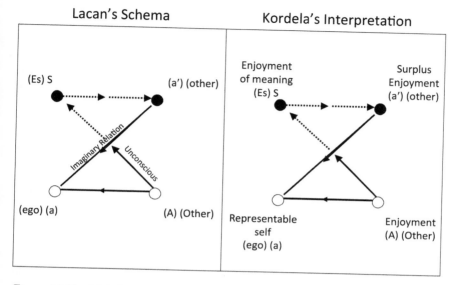

Figure 4.1 Kordela's Interpretation of Lacan's Schema-L
Source: Kordela (1999: 814)

transforms power and possession into an incomprehensible bounty—the surplus of poetic free-play (Kordela, 1999: 812–813). Kordela then maps this structural argument over Lacan's schema-L (Figure 4.1).

Kordela argues that, as surplus value was for Marx, surplus enjoyment is ambivalent in being precondition for both abundance and deprivation (Kordela, 1999: 814). In its capacity to designate lack, surplus enjoyment transforms the *jouissance* of the 'two' (the gap between master and slave) into the enjoyment-of-meaning derived from the harmony of the 'one' (where everything is substitutable for everything else, presumably through an equivalence of exchange). Here, she assigns the former to the node of the 'other' as the master signifier (S_1) and site of the dialectic between master and slave, while the latter is assigned to the position of the 'Subject' (*Es*). Finally, Enjoyment, as such, is assigned to the locus of the 'Other' embodying the real (antinomic) opposition between the presence and absence of miserliness and spite. Thus, under the sway of symbolic (capital) rather than real property (land), the mirage of the imaginary relation comes into play, rendering the 'spite and greed' of the masters, those who have real power (Spinoza's *potentia*), invisible, all the while instilling the illusion that the slaves, themselves, have power (Spinoza's *potentia*) (Kordela, 1999: 815). To summarize, in Marx's circuit of capital, the initial stock of money represents enjoyment-in-meaning, on its transformation into capital it represents enjoyment, while the surplus value added on at the completion of the circuit is surplus enjoyment (Kordela, 1999: 816).

In his seminar on "The Other Side of Psychoanalysis" Lacan (2007: 80) introduces a thermodynamic metaphor to explain his notion of surplus *jouissance*. In this metaphorical milieu, he interprets the master signifier (i.e. the unary trait) in machinic terms: S_1 is the dam holding the water, below it another S_1 is the pond that receives the falling water for powering the turbine, whereas *jouissance* is conceived as the energy released (i.e. insofar as the signifier serves as an apparatus of enjoyment). The power of the master is now interpreted as conservation of energy while the incidence of the signifier entails loss of energy or *jouissance*. That is, in obstructing *jouissance* the signifier is propelled by what it obstructs, but something disappears in the process: in mortifying the body, the signifier produces a residue, which is surplus *jouissance*. Only through the effect of entropy (wastage), however, does *jouissance* acquire a status by virtue of showing itself (Lacan, 2007: 50). In repeating the first signifier, however, the second becomes separated by the residue produced by entropy. Lacan suggests that S_1 frames the slave's knowledge, assigning it a place, so that it becomes knowledge in service of the master. This notion of assignment comes to the fore in Lacan's interpretation of the discourse of the master, the first of the four discourses depicted in Table 4.1.

The position of the symbol above the bar on the left represents the agent or sender of the message while the positon above the bar to the right represents the Other or the receiver of the message. Each symbol is moved a quarter turn in a clockwise direction as the analysis progresses in moving from the discourse of the university to that of the master, to the hysteric and finally, to that of the analyst. The position on the right below the bar represents what is produced by the communication whereas the position to the left and below the bar represents the unconscious truth of the message.

The discourse of the master portrays the unconscious truth of the drive in accordance with the matheme, $\$\Diamond a$ (i.e. the subject is constituted, as split, in relation to his desire for the *objet petit a*):

> What occupies the place there [of the Other, work, receiver of the message], which we will provisionally call dominant, is this S_2, which is specified as being, not knowledge of everything (*savoir de tout*)—we've not got to that point yet—but all knowing (*tout-savoir*).
>
> (Lacan, 2007: 31)

Table 4.1 Lacan's Four Discourses

Discourse of the Master	Discourse of the University
$\dfrac{S_1}{\$} \in \dfrac{S_2}{a}$	$\dfrac{S_2}{S_1} \in \dfrac{a}{\$}$
Discourse of the Hysteric	Discourse of the Analyst
$\dfrac{\$}{a} \in \dfrac{S_1}{S_2}$	$\dfrac{a}{S_2} \in \dfrac{\$}{S_1}$

For its part, the hysteric's discourse reveals the relation of the master's discourse to *jouissance*, in the sense that, in it, knowledge occupies the place of *jouissance*. (Lacan, 2007: 94) As Lacan (2007: 20) puts it,

> Of course, it wasn't Marx who invented surplus value. It's just that prior to him nobody knew what its place was. It has the same ambiguous place as the one I have just mentioned, that of excess work, of surplus work. "What does it pay in?" he says. "It pays in *jouissance*, precisely, and this has to go somewhere".

Lacan (2007: 22) situates the strictly philosophical origin of this conception of the theft of knowledge in Plato's *Meno*, noting:

> The entire function of the *episteme* insofar as it is specified as transmissible knowledge—see Plato's dialogues—is always borrowed from the techniques of craftsmen, that is to say of serfs. It is a matter of extracting the essence of this knowledge in order for it to become the master's knowledge. . . . Philosophy in its historical function is this extraction, I would almost say this betrayal, of the slave's knowledge in order to obtain its transmutation into the master's knowledge.

The dominant influence over Lacan's analysis, however, derives from Hegel's *Phenomenology of Spirit*, specifically the infamous dialectic of Lord and Bondsman. In a witty aside Lacan (2007: 32) observes:

> The slave knows many things, but what he knows even better still is what the master wants, even if the master does not know it himself, which is the usual case, for otherwise he would not be a master.

As Kordela (2007: 20) explains, Lacan named *jouissance* after the master's enjoyment not the slave's lust, for the sadist is no master, merely an instrument of the *jouissance* of the Other.

The theft of knowledge in Deleuze and Guattari's political economy

In this section I want to show how the notion of the 'theft of knowledge' is central to Deleuze and Guattari's notion of the axiomatic of capital.[1] Significantly, at a time when Husserlian conceptions of eidetic or essential logic are coming to play such an important role in grounding neoliberal policies, it is important to acknowledge that Phenomenology, when applied to the social sciences, seems immune to any considerations of this kind. Moreover, as I have reasoned above, Heidegger's post-Husserlian analysis of technology also ignores the issue of how technology could serve as a vehicle for the appropriation of surplus value and knowledge.

Deleuze and Guattari take from Artaud the key notion of the Body-without-Organs (BwO), a notion that is reframed in Marxist terms as the natural or divine presupposition of labour and this, insofar as it is conceived as a surface over which all the forces and agents of production are distributed and recorded. In relation to this surface of inscription the being of capital comes to operate as a quasi-cause from which all production seems to emanate. More specifically, as fixed capital it is seen to be productive of relative surplus value.

In more detailed terms, Deleuze and Guattari contend that there are three forms of the BwO with each one corresponding to one of the passive syntheses of the unconscious.[2] In regard to the flow-producing and flow-interrupting *connective synthesis of production*, the BwO is the non-identity of producing and the product operating via the non-organic though functioning singularities or elements of the machinic assemblage (i.e. the active inscription of the recording surface). In relation to the attracting, appropriating, and distributing of surplus value by the *disjunctive synthesis of recording*, the BwO is equivalent to capitalist being operating as a quasi-cause (i.e. the catatonic stasis of the non-productive recording surface). Finally, in regard to the subject constituted as an effect of the recording and determined by share of product assigned to it through the *conjunctive synthesis of consumption*, the BwO functions as an oscillating series of intensities set up between the other two syntheses.

Deleuze and Guattari embrace Foucault's diagrammatic approach to the analysis of social processes:

> [T]he diagram acts as a non-unifying immanent cause that is coextensive with the whole social field: the abstract machine is like the cause of the concrete assemblages that execute its relations; and these relations between forces take place "not above" but within the very tissue of the assemblages they produce.
>
> (Deleuze, 1999: 37)

Nevertheless, they call for a subtle 'transmogrification' of the Foucaultian assemblage along the following lines:

> Our only points of disagreement with Foucault are the following: (1) to us the assemblages seem fundamentally to be assemblages not of power but of desire (desire is always assembled), and power seems to be a stratified dimension of the assemblage; (2) the diagram and abstract machine have lines of flight that are primary, which are not phenomena of resistance or counterattack in an assemblage, but cutting edges of creation and deterritorialization.

Deleuze and Guattari (1987: 452) argue that, for capitalism to be realized, there had to be generalized conjunction or integration of the decoded flows. In the same way that specific production activities had to be constituted as production in general, and specific forms of wealth constituted as wealth in general, specific forms of labour had to be transformed into free labour in general and specific forms of circulating capital into capital in general in a manner that achieved an independence from state control. As capital becomes an active right, the law changes, abandoning its previous form as an overcoder of customs, it adopts the characteristics of an axiomatic. Capitalism is formed from a general axiomatic of decoded flows. Nevertheless, Deleuze and Guattari insist that this axiomatic can be realized in a variety of models across different industries or sectors and different state-forms, including through the integration of a variety of non-capitalist sectors or modes of production.

Three different state forms are thus distinguished: imperial archaic states constituting a machine of enslavement allow little diversity, while diverse feudal states—city states, systems and monarchies—proceeding through subjection—enable more decoding of flows. However, the greatest degree of decoding is permitted within the modern nation-state (Deleuze and Guattari, 1987: 459). This diversity of nation states, centred in the North and the West, is subtended by three great bipolarities (Deleuze and Guattari, 1987: 465, 468). On one hand, the isomorphy of states at the centre are confronted by the heteromorphous bureaucratic socialist states of the East. On the other hand, they are confronted by the polymorphous Third World states of the South (1987: 465). Moreover, there are Third Worlds inside as well as outside the centre (1987: 468). The third kind of bipolarity, Deleuze and Guattari identify as being one that operates within each state-form. To the extent that capitalism is axiomatic, Deleuze and Guattari (1987: 436) warn: "States tend to become isomorphic in their capacity as models of realization: there is but one centred world market, the capitalist one, in which even the so-called socialist countries participate".

Stiegler and Pagano on the appropriation of knowledge

In this section I trace the way that this Deleuzean notion of theft carries over to Bernard Stiegler's critique of "post-industrial" society and consumer sovereignty, and Ugi Pagano's analysis of intellectual monopoly capitalism.

Ugo Pagano (2014) applies a conventional Bravermanian approach to the analysis of contemporary changes in the labour process. While Braverman (1974) recognizes that modern techniques of scientific management involve an increase in the monopolization of knowledge by capital and management, Pagano suggests that he overlooks one possible development, namely: the inclusion of knowledge among privately owned assets of firms. He further contends that this process of inclusion was consolidated by the TRIPS negotiations that were concluded in the mid-1990s.

Where Adam Smith argued that division of labour would maximize "learning acquired by doing", Pagano (2014: 1411) observes that Babbage (1832) and Ure (1835) adopted a contrarian position in arguing that it would minimize both the "learning and strength required for doing". He follows Braverman in identifying an extension of this process of minimization of skill and effort from the handicrafts, to the mechanical crafts, and ultimately to all forms of work.

Braverman grounds his analysis in Marx's conception of workers under capitalism as a class confronted by the intellectual potencies of production manifest as the property of another. With the refinement of Taylorist management the process of dissociation of the labour process from the skills of workers continued unabated due to the separation of conception from execution and the deployment of the resulting monopoly over knowledge as a means to control each step of the labour process. Marx argued that workers with skills specific to certain production processes would be deprived of these craft-specific skills so that they became general purpose workers with general purpose abilities that could be controlled indirectly through the machine.

Pagano contends (2014: 1413) that the impetus for this long-run de-skilling, was due to the existence of well-defined property rights over machines alongside ill-defined rights over labour, although this could be partially offset by higher skill content in new production processes. In a further elaboration, Pagano emphasizes the difference in the *nature of human and non-human assets*. While the objects worked on by machines are circumscribed within a limited space, the objects of knowledge are not circumscribed in this way. While the enclosure of commons, for example, only affected the legal position of a few individuals, Pagano (2014: 1414) observes that the imposition of monopoly over knowledge affects the legal position of many individuals globally. He even goes so far as to suggest (Pagano, 2014: 1416–1417) that this imposition may have contributed to the Global Financial Crisis, for although tariffs can close off the market of a country imposing them, intellectual property agreements of the kind championed by the TRIPS agreement can effectively close off global markets for all other firms. Any countries prevented from specializing through TRIPS must import goods or licences resulting in forced trade. This may result in a global squeeze on investment opportunities. Moreover, the degree of patent inequality increases over time and amongst countries (augmented by cross-licensing and other alliances).

The policy requisites for overcoming the adverse consequences of such a monopoly include open science, open markets, and public intervention for public science, which should, Pagano argues (2014: 1425) be viewed in liberalizing pro-market terms. He further notes that the size of the multiplier is higher for such investments citing ARPANET, the IPC/TP protocol, and MILNET. He also endorses public buyouts of IPRs plus profit-sharing with the public sector (Pagano, 2014: 1426). In a global context he also acknowledges that policy makers must overcome the free-rider problem to promote higher global investment in public knowledge, suggesting that the WTO charter could impose a percentage of GNP threshold for public research activity. Finally, he supports the tax-based redistribution of assets (Pagano, 2014: 1427).[3]

In a 2011 paper entitled "Suffocated Desire" Stiegler launches into a critique of two increasingly prevalent myths about the contemporary world. The first of these is the myth that we are living in a 'post-industrial society'. Instead, Stiegler talks about a kind of 'hyper-capitalism' defined by an increasing control over both the means of production *and our* patterns of consumption that is accomplished through: (i) the power of media conglomerates; (ii) the prominence of the culture industry; and (iii) the resilience of the program industry. The second myth revolves around the notion of consumer sovereignty and autonomy. Here, Stiegler introduces Simondon's notion of the *co-constitution* of both group and individual which combines a *synchronous fund* of pre-individual knowledge, experience, and tradition with a *diachronous process* of inter-generational knowledge transmission and individual knowledge adoption, to suggest that we are now moving into a world of production which has been transformed into an on-going clash between industrial temporal objects (characterized by short termism and 'newness') and the pre-individual fund (emphasizing longevity and the values of the 'old').

In his 2010 text, *For a New Critique of Political Economy*, Stiegler (2010b) elaborates further on his theme of a cognitive proletarianization, which he defines as a loss of knowledge in the sense of *savoir-faire* (knowledge of making and doing) and *savoir-vivre* (knowledge of life). Like Pagano, he suggests that these procedures of knowledge theft have now been extended to the service sector (e.g. automated trading) to yield a pure cognitive (noetic) form of labour power devoid of knowledge. In explaining the mechanisms behind the loss of knowledge he draws on Derrida's distinction between *anamnesis* (i.e. the interior remembrance of the truth of being), and *hypomnesis* (i.e. the exterior mnemo-technics of memory). He also deploys another Derridean concept, namely, the logic of the *pharmakon* or drug partaking of the attributes both of poison and cure. So rather than functioning in terms of *opposition* or *sublation*, he suggests that technology partakes of this paradoxical logic; one consummated, in turn, through what he calls *grammatization*, which entails a procedure of discretization and abstraction from the continuum of memory. Since the industrial revolution this has occurred, not as an exceptional episode, but as a secular process of permanent innovation offsetting the Marxist tendency for the rate of profit to fall. Stiegler (2010b: 116) suggests that there is now a 'technization' of the social rather than an 'individuation' of the social which has occurred alongside both a disintegration of the interior milieu and an exhaustion of libidinal energies. At the same time, the technical system has become deterritorialized as its reach has been extended across the globe.

In his three-volume Heideggerian study, *Technics and Time*, Stiegler (1998, 2009, 2010a) argues that the genesis of technics corresponds not only to the genesis of what is truly called "human" but of temporality as such, and that a recognition of the dual character of this process provides us with insight into the future coevolution of humans and the technical. He extends the Lyotardian conception of a libidinal economy by suggesting:

> Now, the libido is constituted by technics: it's not an energy that develops spontaneously, but it is articulated on the basis of technics: of "fetishes" and, more generally, *prostheses*. It's *technè*, the artefactualization of the living, that constitutes the libido.
>
> (Stiegler, 2012: 10)

Nevertheless, he warns that, "This libidinal economy, in its current form, has reached the exhaustion of desire. As a result, it has become auto-destructive" (Stiegler, 2012: 10).

And this for the simple reason that, "*When desire is treated industrially, it leads to the destruction of desire,* which triggers the demotivation of the worker

and the consumer" (Stiegler, 2012: 10). In developing this theme of the destruction of desire, Stiegler introduces a distinction between two temporal circuits
of accumulation. On one hand, there are *individuating, long-circuits*, which
achieve an intensification of libidinal energy accomplished through the dona-
tion of (infinitely unachievable) objects of desire. On the other hand, there are
disindividuating, short-circuits, which ensure the destruction of libidinal energy
accomplished through finitizing processes of desublimation. It is his view that the
dominance of short-termism over the circuit has resulted in the systemic stupidity
of today's creative workers who only create "value" that is susceptible to evaluation by the market. As such, he suggests—citing the activities of press officers
and public relations staff—that they work towards an entropic adaptation of the
system rather than to create works. Moreover, in this myopic milieu the noetic
'intermittency' of arts workers (in relation to otium) is entirely ignored (including
by the seemingly radical proponents of 'basic income' policies).[4] Turning to the
Deleuzean theme of a control society, Stiegler (2012: 13) concludes:

> When Deleuze says we must try to invent an art of control, however, he
> means that we must depart from control, that is to say from calculation, to
> produce incalculable objects: incomparable and infinite singularities (one
> does not calculate only things that can be compared). We are in a dimension
> of immanence that cannot be calculated.

Concluding observations on the politics of computational ontologies

From process philosophy, from our reading of Deleuze and Guattari, and from
Marx's dialectic we derive the notion that capital is a process not a thing.
Moreover, it is a process in which money operates as the medium of production
as expressed in Marx's matheme for the monetary circuit $M \rightarrow C \rightarrow C' \rightarrow M'$.
Of course, the transition $C \rightarrow C'$ describes the labour process converting raw
materials and capital as congealed labour into products and services. This stage is
productive of the surplus value realized in exchange as profit, interest, and rent.
The transition $M \rightarrow C$ disguises the private appropriation of forces of production
that are otherwise collaborative and cumulative in nature.

In computational terms, the process of capital accumulation can be described as
the evolutionary algorithmic process of metabolism between inputs and outputs,
where the outputs support both repair and replication. For replication to occur,
however, systems interact and communicate with one another in such a way that
the progeny resulting from replication are more complex than their parents. In
other words, I am proposing to bring together John von Neumann's notion of self-
reproducing automatons (whose progeny are more complex than their parents)
with Robert Rosen's conception of metabolism-repair-and-replication systems
(which, through impredicativity, violate the conditions of the Church-Turing theorem: they cannot be mathematically simulated by a finite algorithmic program).[5]
What we end up with, then, is an evolving metabolism-repair-replication-and

super-replication system resulting in continuous improvements in the efficiency of the metabolic process itself! Thinking with Whitehead, we can certainly say that, in this setting, the many become the one plus one.

In this context, the genealogy I have traced above from the work of Lacan, mediated by Deleuze and Guattari, and further developed by Pagano and Stiegler, should not make the reader feel unduly pessimistic. Territorialization is always accompanied by deterritorialization. And at the very least, policy makers have to confront the grim realities of the system that they wish to effectively regulate. Moreover, a comprehensive analysis of both the national varieties of capitalism and the national varieties of socialism would do well to ground itself in the contemporary diagnoses on the part of Pagano and Stiegler of the dangers of digitization.[6] Nevertheless, I for one would hope that we could reach a little further than Stiegler has in his somewhat modest vision of a cooperative future:

> The question today for me is not the end of capitalism or the return of the communist horizon. Today we have to create a new industrial model. This new industrial model will possibly produce a new political organization, and an economical organization which may not be capitalist. . . . It is possible for example to produce a cooperative capitalism. I know of people exploiting capital in a cooperative way. It still is capitalism, because you have ownership of the means of production by a collective, but this collective is proprietary. It is not a collectivization in the communist sense. It is capitalist. But it is a new form of capitalism.
>
> (Stiegler in Lemmens, 2011: 39)

Notes

1 A more detailed exposition of Deleuze and Guattari's political economy is provided in Juniper (2006).
2 Desiring-production—conceived as the *natura naturans* of Spinoza or the will-to-power of Nietzsche—is composed of three syntheses, the connective, disjunctive, and conjunctive which perform, respectively, the three functions of production, recording, and enjoyment. The syntheses have no underlying subject; they are just immanent processes which constitute subjectivity through their conjoint activity. In *Difference and Repetition* these syntheses are formally interpreted, respectively, as the undetermined differentials (dx, dy), the reciprocally determined differential relation (dx/dy), and the singularities completely determined within the vector field (by the values of dx/dy). And in regard to the constitution of the subject they are, respectively, the foundation of time on the basis of living present (the binding action of *habitus* which endows pleasure with value as empirical principle), the foundation of time on the pure past (the disguising action of *Eros-Mnemonsyne* which conditions application of the pleasure principle to Ego), and the absence/groundlessness of the ground that has been prepared by the ground itself (the function of *Thanatos* which achieves a desexualization followed by resexualization of the drive by linking pleasure to pain).
3 Similar policy recommendations have been endorsed by Mazzucato (2013) in her influential book on *The Entrepreneurial State*. I discuss her approach in more depth in the section of Chapter 5 dealing with policy.
4 Stiegler (2010b: 51–52) sources the concept of *otium* to the work of Corsani and Lazarrato who highlight the importance of this form of studious leisure to arts workers.

More abstractly, he contends that Foucaultian 'technologies of self' establish an economy of otium and neg-otium (Stiegler, 2010b: 54). In policy terms, he warns that otium is ignored when the French Government calls for an increase in the time spent in employment by this category of workers (as happened in June, 2003).

5 I have examined these issues at further depth and more formally in Juniper (2007 and 2013).

6 In Juniper (2015) I examine the influence of Brentanian and Husserlian Phenomenology over the development of *foundational* computational ontologies (which are designed to achieve integration over and inter-operability amongst relevant clusters of domain-ontologies), arguing that this is another mechanism of transmission through which neoliberal discursive and strategic practices can adversely influence knowledge-related activities.

Bibliography

Aldea, Andreea Smaranda (2014). Husserl's Break from Brentano Reconsidered: Abstraction and the Structure of Consciousness. *Axiomathes*, 24: 395–426.

Bakhshi, Hasan, Alan Freeman and Peter Higgs (2013). A Dynamic Mapping of the UK's Creative Industries, Report prepared for NESTA. Accessed 8 November 2014. www. academia.edu/5538116/A_Dynamic_Mapping_of_the_UKs_Creative_Industries.

DCMS (2008). *Creative Britain: New Talents for the New Economy. DCMS.* Accessed April 29, 2008. www.culture.gov.uk/Reference_library/Publications/archive_2008/cepPub-new-talents.htm.

Deleuze, G. and Félix Guattari (1984). *Anti-Oedipus: Capitalism and Schizophrenia.* Trans. R. Hurley, M. Seem, and H. R. Lane. London: Continuum.

Deleuze, G. and Félix Guattari (1987). *A Thousand Plateaus: Capitalism and Schizophrenia.* Trans. Brian Massumi. Minneapolis, MN: University of Minnesota Press.

Deleuze, G. and Félix Guattari (1994). *What Is Philosophy.* Trans. Hugh Tomlinson and Graham Burchell. New York, NY: Columbia University Press.

Feiner, S. (1995). Reading Neoclassical Economics: Toward an Erotic Economy of Sharing. In Jolande Sap and Edith Kuiper (eds), *Out of the Margin: Feminist Perspectives on Economics.* Routledge, London.

Foucault, M. (2008). *The Birth of Biopolitics: Lectures at the Collège de France, 1978–1979.* Trans. G. Burchell. Houndmills: Palgrave Macmillan.

Freeman, Alan (2012). What Are the Creative Industries? Presentation to Chinese Academy of Social Sciences on Creative Industries, October. Accessed 15 February 2015. www. academia.edu/4394566/What_are_the_Creative_Industries_Presentation_to_Chinese_Academy_of_Social_Sciences_on_Creative_Industries_October_2012.

García-Quero, Fernando and Jorge Ollero-Perrán (2015). Is Neoclassical Economics Scientific Knowledge Detached from Ethics? A Kantian Answer, an Institutionalist Alternative. *Review of Radical Political Economics*, 47(1): 56–69.

Heidegger, M. (1993). [1953]. The Question Concerning Technology. In David F. Krell (ed.), *Basic Writings.* London: Routledge.

Hill, Claire Ortiz and Guillermo Rosada Haddock (2000). *Husserl or Frege: Meaning, Objectivity, and Mathematics.* Chicago, IL: Carus Publishing.

Husserl, E. (1928). (1964). *Vorlesungen zur Phanomenologie des inneren Zeitbewusstseins,* ed. M. Heidegger. In *Jahrbuch fur Philosophie und phenomenologische Forschung*, 9: 367–498. Trans. J. S. Churchill, *The Phenomenology of Internal Time-Consciousness.* The Hague: Nijhoff.

Husserl, E. (1984). [2001]. Logische Untersuchungen, E. Husserliana XIX (2 vols), ed. Ursula Panzer. The Hague: Martinus Nijhoff. Trans. J. N. Findlay. *Logical Investigations.* New York, NY: Routledge.

Hyppolite, Jean (2007). A Spoken Commentary on Freud's "Verneinung". Appendix I in J. Lacan, *The Seminar of Jacques Lacan.* Trans. Russell Grigg, ed. Jacques-Alain Miller. *Book XVII, The Other Side of Psychoanalysis.* New York, NY: W. W. Norton, 746–754.

Juniper, James (2006). Deleuze's Political Economy. Refereed paper presented at the 12th National Conference on Unemployment, Newcastle, NSW, December 8–10.

Juniper, James (2007). A Critique of Social Applications of Autopoiesis. *The International Journal of Interdisciplinary Social Sciences,* 1(3): 137–152.

Juniper, James (2013). A Classical Economic Perspective on Using Coalgebras to Model the Process of Accumulation. Paper presented at the Society of Heterodox Economists Conference. An earlier version of this paper was submitted to the Eighth International Conference on Interdisciplinary Social Sciences, Charles University, Prague, Czech Republic, 30 July–1 August 2013.

Juniper, James (2015). Ontological and Computational Aspects of Economic-Environmental Modelling. In Stephan K. Chalup, Alan D. Blair and Marcus Randall (eds), Artificial Life and Computational Intelligence Proceedings First Australasian Conference, ACALCI 2015, Newcastle, NSW, Australia, 5–7 February, 31–46.

Kordela, A. Kiarina (1999). Political Metaphysics: God in Global Capitalism (the Slave, the Masters, Lacan, and the Surplus). *Political Theory,* 27(6): 789–839.

Kordela, A. Kiarina (2007). $*urplus: Spinoza, Lacan.* Albany, NY: State University of New York Press.

Lacan, J. (1979). [1973]. *The Four Fundamental Concepts of Psychoanalysis,* ed. Jacques-Alain Miller, trans. Alan Sheridan. Originally published in French as *Le Séminaire, Livre XI, Les quatre concepts fondamentaux de la psychanalyse.* Paris: Les Editions du Seuil.

Lacan, J. (1988). [1978]. *The Seminar of Jacques Lacan,* ed. Jacques-Alain Miller. *Book II, The Ego in Freud's Theory and in the Technique of Psychoanalysis 1954–55.* Trans. Sylvana Tomaselli, with notes by John Forrester. Originally published in French as *Le Séminaire, Livre II, Le moi dans la théorie de Freud et dans la technique de la psycho-analyse, 1954–1955.* Paris: Les Editions du Seuil.

Lacan, J. (1992). [1986]. *The Seminar of Jacques Lacan,* ed. Jacques-Alain Miller. *Book VII, The Ethics of Psychoanalysis 1959–60.* Trans. with notes Dennis Porter. New York, NY: Routledge. Originally published in French as *Le Séminaire, Livre VII, L'ethique de la psychoanalyse, 1959–1960.* Paris: Les Editions du Seuil.

Lacan, J. (2006). [1963]. Kant with Sade. Trans. Bruce Fink. *Écrits: The First Complete Edition in English,* New York, NY: W. W. Norton. Section 29: 645–670.

Lacan, J. (2007). *The Seminar of Jacques Lacan.* Trans. Russell Grigg, ed. Jacques-Alain Miller. *Book XVII, The Other Side of Psychoanalysis.* New York, NY: W. W. Norton.

Lemmens, Pieter (2011). This System Does Not Produce Pleasure Anymore: An Interview with Bernard Stiegler. *Krisis: Journal of Contemporary Philosophy,* 1: 33–41.

McCloskey, Deirdre (2009). Bourgeois Dignity and Liberty: Why Economics Can't Explain the Modern World. MPRA Paper No. 16805. Accessed 27 February 2015. http://mpra.ub.uni-muenchen.de/16805/.

Marstellar, L. (2009). Towards a Whiteheadian Neurophenomenology. *Concrescence,* 57–66.

Mazzucato, M. (2013). *The Entrepreneurial State: Debunking Private vs. Public Sector Myths*. London: Anthem Press.

Meyer, Steven (2005). Whitehead: Introduction. *Configurations*, 13(1) (Winter): 1–33.

Milner, R. (2006). The Internet of Things: Competing Formalisms Ubiquitous Computing: Shall We Understand It? Computer Journal Lecture, BCS, The Chartered Institute for IT, March. Accessed 6 November 2014. www.bcs.org/content/ConWebDoc/4708/*/setPaginate/No.

Pagano, Ugo (2014). The Crisis of Intellectual Monopoly Capitalism. *Cambridge Journal of Economics*, 38: 1409–1429.

Pomeroy, Anne Fairchild (2001). Process Philosophy and the Possibility of Critique. *Journal of Speculative Philosophy*, 15(1): 33–49.

Pomeroy, Anne Fairchild (2004). Marx and Whitehead: Process, Dialectics, and the Critique of Capitalism. SUNY series in the Philosophy of the Social Sciences. Albany, NY: State University of New York Press.

Schroeder, Jeanne, L. (1997). Juno Moneta: On the Erotics of the Marketplace. Symposium on Lacan and the Subject of Law. *Washington and Lee Law Review*, 54: 995–1033.

Simons, Peter and Reinhard Fabian (1986). The Second Austrian School of Value Theory. In Wolfgang Grassl and Barry Smith (eds), *Austrian Economics: Historical and Philosophical Background*. London: Croom Helm, 37–101.

Smith, Barry (1987). Austrian Economics and Austrian Philosophy. In Wolfgang Grassl and Barry Smith (eds), *Austrian Economics: Historical and Philosophical Background*. London: Croom Helm, 1–36.

Smith, Barry and Pierre Grenon (2004). The Cornucopia of Formal-Ontological Relations. *Dialectica*, 58(3): 279–296. Available from BOP Website, http://ifomis.uni-saarland.de/bfo/.

Stiegler, B. (1998). *Technics and Time, 1: The Fault of Epimetheus*. Stanford, CA: Stanford University Press.

Stiegler, B. (2009). *Technics and Time, 2: Disorientation*. Stanford, CA: Stanford University Press.

Stiegler, B. (2010a). *Technics and Time, 3: Cinematic Time and the Question of Malaise*. Stanford: Stanford University Press.

Stiegler, Bernard (2010b). *For a New Critique of Political Economy*. Trans. Daniel Ross. Cambridge: Polity Press.

Stiegler, B. (2011). Suffocated Desire, or How the Cultural Industry Destroys the Individual: Contribution to a Theory of Mass Consumption. Trans. Johann Rossouw. *Parrhesia*, 13: 52–61.

Stiegler, B. (with Frédéric Neyrat) (2012). Interview: From the Libidinal Economy to the Ecology of the Spirit. Trans. Arne De Boever. *Parrhesia*, 14: 9–15.

Whitehead, Alfred North (1978). *Process and Reality: An Essay in Cosmology* (Corrected edition), ed. D. R. Griffin and D. W. Sherburne. New York, NY: Free Press.

Žižek, Slavoj (1998). Kant and Sade: The Ideal Couple. *Lacan Ink*, 13, 5 October. Accessed 4 January 2018. www.lacan.com/zizlacan4.htm.

5 Ubiquitous computing systems and the digital economy

Introduction

Let us consider the case of a well-known multinational mining corporation, with its headquarters in Australia. This company is moving towards the deployment of driverless trucks that are monitored, but not controlled, by on-site computers. Information is fed back to this on-site system from sensors located in each of the main bearings in each of the trucks, which allows the system to calculate when these bearings should be scheduled for maintenance. Sensors located on the trucks also feed information back to the central computer systems on the quality of ore and depth of overburden so that algorithms can determine how best to access the ore while saving on fuel used to remove the overburden. Other software modules on the central computer can calculate the number of railway carriages required per day to deliver the ore, that is still to be extracted, to port facilities based on extraction algorithms that draw upon a comprehensive three-dimensional map of all the relevant geological strata. It is important to emphasize that this particular case is not the creation of speculative fiction, but one that is already in operation.

In our efforts to understand the nature of these technological developments in communication, interaction, and decentralized control of concurrent systems, it may help to begin with an understanding of how computers and human beings make sense of the world—the domain of knowledge representation and computational ontologies—that will be considered in the next section of the chapter. Computational aspects of the digital economy bring together three closely related spheres of research: cognitive computing (or deep machine learning, sometimes associated with "Big Data" as in Varian, 2013) and artificial general intelligence; semantic technologies—to be considered in a later section of the chapter; as well as process algebras (another rapidly evolving field of research concerned with the formal representation of resource-using processes, also to be considered in a later section of the chapter. This formal sphere has also influenced organizational approaches to software engineering and new product development, which will also be examined in a later section. Policy and modelling aspects of these developments are briefly touched on with conclusions following in the last section of the chapter.

Knowledge representation

For researchers in the field of computational ontologies and knowledge representation, metaphysics continues to hold sway. Many practitioners have been influenced by Alfred North Whitehead's process philosophy (Sowa, 2000), Charles Sanders Peirce's analysis of diagrammatic reasoning (Dau, 2006), and his triadic conception of semiotics (Sowa, 2000), as well as Husserlian Phenomenology and Mereology (Barry Smith, Peter Simon and the Leipzig group). For example, John Sowa (2000) merges Peirce's triadic notions of independence (firstness), relation (secondness), and mediation (thirdness) with Whitehead's distinction between physical and abstract mediation to arrive at a foundational schema for classifying the world (see Table 5.1).

This endeavour to construct *foundational* ontologies is meant to promote interoperability and coherence between more concrete computational ontologies that are often driven by the minutiae of scientific research within a particular discipline or sub-discipline.

The stance adopted towards AI and Cognitive Computing in this chapter is one that acknowledges the strides taken by the "new AI" paradigm of perception-and-action-without-intelligence (Brooks, 1999). In loose terms, the previous paradigm positioned a central intelligence function, largely working in accordance with procedures of logical inference in a position of superiority over the subordinate procedures of perception/sensing and action/motility. The new paradigm involves two main departures: (i) intelligence obtains at the intersection between perception and action, largely reflecting the need to exploit mutually advantageous dependencies rather than privileging the logical requirements of achieving coordination and high levels of inter-operability. (ii) the very distinction between centre (i.e. centre of representation) and periphery (i.e. peripheral field of sensing or physical action) must be dissolved. In practice, as Rodney Brooks (1999: 89) concedes, certain non-conventional inferential procedures are adopted, but in a manner circumscribed by the need to remain entirely within the horizons of a previously defined zone of intersection:

> The purpose of the Creature (i.e. AI device or robot) is implicit in its higher-level purposes, goals or layers. There need be no explicit representation of goals that some central (or distributed) process selects from to decide what is most appropriate for the Creature to do next. . . . Just as there is no central representation there is not even a central system. Each activity producing layer connects perception to action directly. It is only the observer of the Creature who imputes a central representation or central control.
>
> (Brooks, 1999: 90)

Nevertheless, this chapter does pursue a "Post-Cognitive" (as described in the Introduction to the text) approach in recognizing Goertzel and Pennachin's (2007: 64) concerns about: (i) how far AI has departed from the goals and objectives that were pursued so optimistically in the early post-war period; and

Table 5.1 Matrix of Twelve Central Categories

Peircean Trinism	PHYSICAL		ABSTRACT	
	Contanuant	Occurrent	Contanuant	Occurrent
Independent	Object	Process	Schema	Script
Relative	Juncture	Participation	Description	History
Mediating	Structure	Situation	Reason	Purpose

	INDEPENDENT		RELATIVE		MEDIATING	
	PHYSICAL	*ABSTRACT*	*PHYSICAL*	*ABSTRACT*	*PHYSICAL*	*ABSTRACT*
	ACTUALITY Actual Occasions	*FORM* Eternal Objects	*PREHENSION*	*PROPOSITION*	*NEXUS*	*INTENTION* Subjective Form
c	Object	Schema	Juncture	Description	Situation	Reason
o	Process	Script	Participants	History	Execution	Purpose

Source: Sowa (2000)

(ii) the fact that "much is said about the information age, knowledge discovery, and the need for tools that are smart enough to allow human experts to cope with the unwieldy amounts of information in today's business and scientific world". However, they go on to argue that "the real answer for these analytical demands lies in AGI [Artificial General Intelligence], as the current narrow techniques are unable to properly integrate heterogeneous knowledge, derive intelligent inferences from that knowledge and, most important, spontaneously generate new knowledge about the world". Instead, it will be argued below that there are many paths that can be taken in achieving the cybernetic goal of knowledge integration, which entail working with a wide variety of different techniques across the domains of machine learning, cognitive computing, and robotics.

Theoretical aspects of computation

These philosophical arguments carry over into the domain of mathematical and computational reasoning. Category Theory—a branch of pure mathematics that weaves together formal representations of structures and dynamic transitions between structures that can be found in algebra, geometry, topology, computation, and the natural sciences—is often portrayed as an advance over earlier foundational approaches to mathematics that were grounded in Set Theory (Bell, 1988; Krömer, 2007; Marquis, 2009; Rodin, 2014). For example, Krömer (2007) complains that the Bourbakian approach to the formal representation of structure "begs the question" when it assigns a certain ontology to mathematical objects,

> But the Bourbaki ontology is subject to some criticism: what is claimed on the one hand is that structures are the real objects; on the other hand, this assertion asks for a definition of "structure", which Bourbaki in truth gives ultimately in relying on sets again. From the pragmatist point of view, such an ontological debate is empty since ontology is "wrapped up" in epistemology: and if one has no access to structures *but via sets* (as Bourbaki seems to believe), then the stressing of an ontological difference between structures and sets is useless, for lack of means of cognition enabling us to grasp the difference.

For his part, Jean-Yves Girard (2007) appeals to quantum-theoretic notions of an operator algebra:

> My personal bias, the one followed in this paper, is that the real hypostases are very different from our familiar (mis)conceptions: I shall thence propose a disturbing approach to foundations. This viewpoint is by no means "non standard", it is on the contrary most standard; but it relies on ideas developed in the last century and prompted by quantum physics, the claim being that operator algebra is more primitive than set theory . . . in the non commutative geometry of Connes, a paradigm violently anti-set-theoretic, based upon the familiar result: A commutative operator algebra is a function space.

Category theory provides those seeking to better understand 'Big Data' and the IoT with a variety of meaningful computational frameworks including the coalgebraic representation of automatons and transition systems, Domain theory, and the Geometry of Interaction, along with specific sites for formal modelling such as the elementary topos. Categorical logic serves to link inferential procedures and resource-using logics with functional programming, while string diagrams can represent everything from graphical linear algebra to signal flow graphs, Lawvere theories in universal algebra, and even functional relationships in topological quantum field theory (see Curien, 2008; Bonchi et al., 2015; Bonchi et al., 2016; Bartlett, 2005).

Semantic technologies

Semantic technologies provide users with integrated access to both structured and unstructured data by applying search and navigation techniques that are tuned to the computational ontologies of relevance to the organization. To this end, it draws on the WC3 standards for the World-Wide Web, in accordance with the Resource Description Framework, which can then be conceived in formal terms as a "giant global graph" (Lee and Kagal, 2016 and W3C website, 2016). Diagrammatic reasoning procedures and visual analytic processes are applied to the extracted information with a view to supporting business intelligence.

A recent example is the CUBIST Project. The CUBIST project largely drew on Peirce's existential graphs (Dau, 2014). It brings together a consortium of technological partners that includes: SAP—Germany (Coordinator and technological partner); Ontotext—Bulgaria (providing expertise in Semantic Technologies); Sheffield Hallam University—UK (providing expertise in Formal Concept Analysis); Centrale Recherche S.A.—France (providing expertise in FCA and Visual Analytics); and Case Partners that include Heriot-Watt University—UK (providing expertise in the analysis of gene expressions in mouse embryos); Space Applications Services—Belgium (providing expertise in the analysis of logfiles of technical equipment in space along with space system engineering, specification, operations engineering, training and software development) and Innovantage—UK (providing expertise in the analysis of the online recruitment activities of UK companies).

The core objective of the project is to investigate "how current semantic technologies can be applied in enterprise environments to semantically integrate information from heterogeneous data sources and provide unified information access to end users".

Under the architecture of the CUBIST Prototype there are different means of access to information, including through: semantic searching based on the domain ontologies specific to each of the three case studies; 'smart' query generation taking these computational ontologies into account, where the types and object properties form a 'query graph' that can actually contain more types than those selected, with their associated datatype properties being used for the filtering and characterization of formal attributes; more explorative search techniques; conceptual scaling as described above; and visual analytics.

To this end, it draws on the Resource Description Framework of the WWW, which can be pictured as a "giant global graph".[1] In this context, it pursues 'semantic integration', which essentially means transforming the information into a graph model of typed nodes (e.g. for products, companies) and typed edges (e.g. for the relationship "company-produces-product"), then performing Formal Concept Analysis (FCA) on the transformed information.[2] In this way, it aims to provide unified access by letting users search, explore, visualize and augment the information as if it was from one single integrated system.

Cognitive computing and 'deep' machine learning

A far from quiet revolution occurred in deep machine learning and robotics, in the 1980s, occasioned by the discovery that very large and hierarchical neural-networks could 'train themselves' to recognize a variety of patterns for purposes of image recognition, natural language communication and translation, and causal analysis. As Rodney Brooks (1999) explains, the revolutionary breakthrough arose from the recognition "that the so-called central systems of intelligence—or core AI as it has been referred to more recently—was perhaps an unnecessary illusion, and that all the power of intelligence arose from the coupling of perception and actuation systems".

One of the chapters in Brooks' history of AI is entitled "Intelligence without Representation". Brooks (1999: 79) concedes "that the title is a little inflammatory—a careful reading shows that I mean intelligence without conventional representation, rather than without any representation at all". He also complains that one of his seminal papers is "often criticized for advocating absolutely no representation of the world within a behavior-based robot". Instead, Brooks (1999: 177) insists that what he rejects is traditional Artificial Intelligence representation schemes as well as the explicit representations of goals within the machine:

> There can, however, be representations which are partial models of the world—in fact I mentioned that "individual layers extract only those aspects of the world which they find relevant—projections of a representation into a simple subspace" (Brooks 1991c). The form these representations take, within the context of the computational model we are using, will depend on the particular task those representations are to be used for. For more general navigation than that demonstrated by Connell it may sometimes need to build and maintain a map.
>
> (Brooks, 1999: 177)

Despite the seeming power of the latest generation of convolution, recurrent, echo-state and liquid-state neural networks, it is important to realize that human intervention in the form of feature engineering continues to be fundamental to the success of the deep machine learning program, not only in the choice of the data for feeding into the process of self-training, but also to curb 'hallucinatory' forms of overfitting (Goertzel, 2015; Nguyen et al., 2014; Szegedy et al., 2013).

Bengio et al. (2013) note that techniques for greedy, layerwise, unsupervised, pre-training were a significant technical breakthrough, enabling deep learning systems:

- to learn a hierarchy of features one level at a time, using unsupervised feature learning to learn a new transformation at each level;
- to be composed with the previously learned transformations (i.e. each iteration of unsupervised feature learning adds one layer of weights to a deep neural network);
- finally, by combining the set of layers, to initialize a deep supervised predictor, such as a neural network classifier, or a deep generative model, such as a Deep Boltzmann Machine.

Researchers within the field of Artificial General intelligence (AGI) are seeking the "holy grail" of robotics and computation, first characterized by John von Neumann in terms of interacting automatons whose progeny are continuously evolving to be smarter than their parents.

Goertzel and Pennachin (2007) cite as examples of AGI the General Problem Solver, CYC, Alan Newell's *SOAR* project, *ACT-R*, Bayesian networks, Pei Wang's *NARS* system, de Garis' evolutionary programming, Voss's *a2i2* architecture, classifier systems, program search-based AGI, and their own *Novemente*. Nevertheless, they concede that "none of these approaches has yet proved itself successful". Even the *Novamente* system, although "completely designed", has only been "partially implemented".

Representation of processes

Another computational approach grounded in the formal modelling of concurrent and communicative systems, conceived as transition systems, is process algebra. Baeten (2004: 9) observes that on,

> [c]omparing the three most well-known process algebras CCS (Calculus of Communicative Systems), CSP (Calculus of Sequential Processes) and ACP (Algebra of Communicative Processes), we can say there is a considerable amount of work and applications realized in all three of them. Historically, CCS was the first with a complete theory. Different from the other two, CSP has a least distinguishing equational theory. More than the other two, ACP emphasizes the algebraic aspect: there is an equational theory with a range of semantical models. Also, ACP has a more general communication scheme: in CCS, communication is combined with abstraction, in CSP, communication is combined with restriction.

Contemporary approaches to Business Process Modelling are typically based on stochastic versions of Milner's Pi Calculus or stochastic Petri nets. Towards the end of what was a remarkably productive life, acknowledged by his receipt of an Alan Turing Award, Robin Milner began to work on formal ways of merging both the Pi calculus and Petri nets using Bigraphs as a diagrammatic framework. Since then, computational research has blossomed into the best way to build bridges between process algebras and particular kinds of categories.

Category theory provides ubiquitous computing systems with a variety of formal approaches including the coalgebraic representation of automatons and transition systems, Domain theory, and the Geometry of Interaction, along with specific mathematical substrates such as the elementary topos. For its part, categorical logic links inferential procedures based on resource-using or linear logics with functional programming and algebraic topology, while string diagrams can represent everything from graphical linear algebra to signal flow graphs and topological quantum field theory (with the latter using string diagrams to account for the functional relationships holding between quantum phenomena and the cobordisms deriving from general relativity theory).

Integrated design and new product development

Under the impact of the "ubiquitous computing" revolution, researchers and practitioners within the professions of architecture, the visual arts, industrial design, and engineering have embraced the notion of "integrated design" as a means for meeting customer requirements in the development of new products, services, and socio-technological artefacts. This approach to design is typically regarded as one that brings together different design functions and specializations that would otherwise be applied separately and also adopts principles of life-cycle management and through-life support with greater consideration for the needs of end users. Often, the process of design will be applied concurrently to both the product (or family of products) and the assembly or production system that is intended to produce it (or in the case of model development engineering, to both hardware and software components). For these reasons, there is a notable congruency between integrated design principles and those of environmental sustainability in both products and processes.

By way of contrast, Stevens, Moultrie and Crilly (2009: 7) have identified three important themes emerging from the study of how efforts directed at design integration can fail:

1   Partial design: design is only used to a limited degree, such as in superficial cosmetic styling of a product, or in marketing communications.
2   Disparate design: design activity may be widespread throughout all operations, but is not co-ordinated holistically to realize its synergistic potential.
3   Silent design: design is driven by people who are not designers and who are not aware that they are participating in design activity.

The authors argue for the importance of reconciling "theoretical models of strategy with the practice of design professionals". Unfortunately, they rely solely on Michael Porter's (1985) interpretation of sustainable competitive advantage, in particular his value-chain model. Stevens et al. (2009) point out that "Porter's generic value chain describes an organisation's internal environment in terms of primary and support value activities", where the value and associated cost of each are "assessed with a view to maximising the former and minimising the latter".

Stevens et al. (2009) complain that "Porter only recognised design in its technological sense, as a primary activity in 'operations' and 'technology development'", with these functional areas treated as separate activities in a manner subservient to marketing and engineering (see Figure 5.1). Instead of viewing design as "a cosmetic, decorative treatment applied late in development", however, they draw on recent research that argues for an extension of design activities beyond a concern for "image" alone, into "value, process, production". In this light, they propose to treat the "holistic design function as a secondary (support) activity, which spans the breadth of the operation".

Of course, this notion of integrated design has been around for some time. One of Porter's contemporaries, Stephen Kline, from the Engineering Faculty of Stanford University, also propounded his conception of the "Chain-Linked" model of innovation back in 1985. This model depicts inputs of knowledge into research as well as the various design functions, with an emphasis on the need for both proximate feedback loops linking each of the stages of design, prototype development, production and distribution processes together, and with nested feedback loops extending from a common source: the final user or customer situated at the final distribution and marketing stage feeds back into earlier stages of design, testing, and production; as depicted in Figure 5.2 (Kline, 1985).

Where Kline highlights the importance of feedback between different design phases, critics within the software engineering community have gone even further.

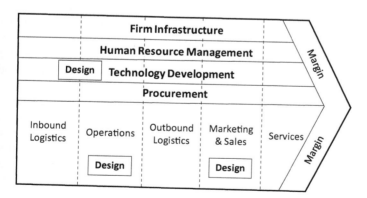

Figure 5.1 Porter's Value-Chain (Modified)
Source: Stevens, Moultrie and Crilly (2009, Fig. 3: 230/7)

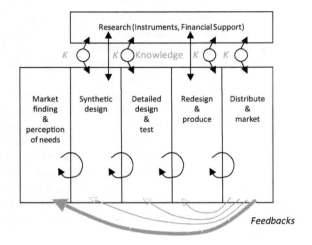

Figure 5.2 Kline's Chain-linked Model
Source: Kline (1985)

Larman and Basili (2003) set out a detailed history of developments in iterative and incremental development beginning with IBM Defence projects in the 1960s that eventually led the Department of Defence to revise their standards for large software engineering projects—partially in 1987, and completely in 1994. The old "waterfall" system had also been heavily criticized by leading computer science academics such as Joseph Goguen (1994). Goguen complains that, in most large-scale projects, there is no orderly progression from one stage to the next, for it is more of a zig-zagging backwards and forwards with phases constantly overlapping. In this context, managers of the process have great difficulty in assigning actions and events to each unique phase. This is especially true of the requirements engineering phase, which, Goguen suggests, is the most critical because, in turn, its failures are the most costly; it is the phase that is most exposed to error and uncertainty and, thus, to the necessity for iterative and zig-zagging development (insofar as high-level design often needed in defining requirements and code must often be delivered before requirements are fully specified).

It would seem that Porter's theoretical framework for analysing strategic questions of design is completely inadequate. However, this is so not only for the reasons discussed above, but also because Porter has chosen to work within the mainstream structure-conduct-performance framework, where market structure (i.e. size and number of firms, homogeneity or heterogeneity of product, and existence or non-existence of barrier to entry and exit) is seen to determine the conduct of firms and, thus, their performance.

In Porter's work, this underlying framework is extended by placing detailed emphasis on entry barriers, the threat of substitution from products produced by rival firms, the relative bargaining power of buyers and suppliers, and the degree of rivalry amongst incumbents. Accordingly, for Porter, economic rents are largely viewed as monopolistic in nature, while industry structures are deemed to be more or less attractive to prospective entrants due to various opportunities that might exist for erecting 'impediments' to competition (Teece et al., 1997).

Porter's more recent work on the competitive advantage of clusters and regions still falls into this category. Effectively, Porter argues that the intensity of interaction between firms within the 'competitive diamond' can be heightened if firms are geographically localized (see Martin and Sunley, 2003, for a lucid overview and insightful critique). Moreover, he suggests that most globally competitive industries are likely to be clustered. Hence the national economy, in Porter's eyes, has become manifestly 'spatial' with spatial clustering conceived as both a driving force and as an expression of sustainable competitive advantage.

In stark contrast, approaches to competitive advantage informed by Classical Political Economy place more emphasis on the capacity of firms to take labour—living and 'dead'—out of production faster than their rivals. In the "economics of strategy" literature, for example, emphasis is placed on whatever might serve as a *barrier to imitation* (i.e. 'replication of routines' or ways of doing things in the evolutionary economics of Nelson and Winter) so that unique sources of value, and thus, competitive advantage, can be sustained in the face of increasingly intense and increasingly global forms of competitive rivalry. For Resource Based Value theorists like Jay Barney, who focus on the selection and coordination of resources, the major barrier is *causal ambiguity* or uncertainty over what makes a particular constellation of resources successful. For this school of strategy, uncertainty is conceived in Knightian terms, which implies that the capacity to determine the relevant state space for a given species of commercial risk is unevenly distributed. Moreover, its presence or absence within organizations and firms can only be detected by those who already possess it, which explains why it does not attain a fair price in factor markets. In contrast, Keynesian forms of uncertainty are objective rather than subject in nature, and thus immune to any conquest on the part of human (or machine) understanding.

For their part, Dynamic Competency Theorists, focus on the development of competencies (rather than resources) through 'bottom-up' or collaborative processes of learning. Constellations of competencies are viewed as spanning a wide range of products and product families, reside at a deeper level than products, and evolve more slowly than do products, themselves, thus serving as the true locus of rivalry over competitive advantage. Here, the major barrier to replication on the part of rival firms is the non-codifiable and thus, non-traded, attribute of *tacit knowledge*, which not only complements and amplifies the advantages derived from codifiable knowledge, but can only be deployed or transmitted through face-to-face and collaborative forms of learning-by-doing. In the 'competency-approach', therefore, emphasis is placed on the development, accumulation, combination, and protection of unique skills and capabilities; alongside the coordination, renewal, and deployment of competencies that are congruent with modification to the commercial environment (Teece et al., 1997).

According to David Teece (2000), not only does the tacit knowledge embodied in individuals and organizations operate as a barrier to replication on the part of rival firms, but on a more extensive scale, it is untraded, thus becoming ever more critical to the firm as trade barriers are reduced and as copyright legislation is strengthened, by virtue of its unique, non-imitable qualities. While their impact can be amplified by network economies, customer 'lock-in', and the consolidation of dominant technology and product standards, the tacit knowledge that grounds them can only be transferred through face-to-face interaction, and learning-by-doing.

Increasingly, theorists of strategy and innovation (such as Neo-Schumpeterians, who emphasize the importance of national and regional systems of innovation) investigate the role of *co-evolutionary* processes through which firm organization, political institutions, and networks develop through mutual influence, in a mutually beneficial way (especially in the case where institutional bridges are built between the public science sector and both public and private industry or, in terms made familiar by Robert Reich—Bill Clinton's advisor on labour relations—where interactions between 'problem identifiers' and 'problem solvers'—i.e. users and producers of new technologies—are coordinated and augmented by 'strategic brokers' (of course, for sociologists following the dubious lead of Granovetter institutions, themselves, are merely 'congealed networks")).

While evolutionary theories do well in explaining how competencies can develop at the level of firm routines, they suffer, in a strictly empirical sense, from the absence of any convincing metrics for the measurement of their importance, strength, and resilience (which applies equally to the related concept of capabilities) in regard to sustainable competitive advantage at the level of the firm, region, or nation. This is especially the case for capabilities based on tacit knowledge and intangible forms of capital, with most metrics focusing, out of necessity, on knowledge that is more tangible and codifiable.

One way of getting around this problem of non-measurability has been revealed by César Hidalgo and Ricardo Hausmann (2009). Drawing on a global trade database, the authors construct a series of proximity measures based on derived probabilities that, in turn, in simple terms reflect the likelihood that a nation exporting one type of product is also likely to export another. They go on to construct a minimal spanning network based on these proximity measures. They end up with a model of a forest where each product is a tree and at any point in the network we can think of a monkey trying to jump from tree to tree.

The traditional assumption made when thinking of this kind of metaphor is that there is always a tree within reach so that the monkey can readily jump from tree to tree to reach a more productive part of forest (i.e. through continuous variations in factor intensity at the margin). Nevertheless, many factors may combine to explain relatedness between products. Hidalgo and Hausmann (2009) argue that countries with many capabilities are more diversified in their networks and can make products requiring many capabilities. Few rivals, however, will possess necessary capabilities to compete with them. Instead, less diversified countries will make less ubiquitous products. This kind of analysis helps to explain how nations can be locked in to slow development trajectories and throws some light onto the hurdles and constraints that apply to entrepreneurial activity.

The work of William Lazonick addresses the fundamental question of how productive resources are developed within an innovating enterprise. In viewing strategy solely as a form of predatory behaviour, mainstream approaches to the economics of strategy can only conceive of the enterprise as a site of 'market imperfections' that impede the free flow of resources. This misconception, however, flows from a deeper error which views markets as a cause rather than as a consequence of economic development. From this market-based perspective, firms are advised to create 'high-powered' incentives with no obligation for the sharing of returns: instead, salaries merely serve to segment and separate remuneration out from productive effort.

In the seemingly different work of Coasians such as Oliver Williamson, who emphasize the importance of transaction costs above all else, the role of firms is confined to that of 'working things out', that is, to optimizing outcomes subject to technological (asset specificity), behavioural (guileful opportunism), and cognitive (bounded rationality) constraints. In this context, Lazonick (1991: 195) protests, Transaction Cost Theory bases itself entirely on the analysis of adaptive firms. There is no concept of dynamics of capitalist development, nor of business as a value-creating organization. Instead, the focus is on "adaptive, sequential decision-making" in the face of "disturbances", which economizes on bounded rationality (Lazonick, 1991: 209). The core presumption is that "in the beginning there were markets", and "[o]nly as market-mediated contracts break down are the transactions in question removed from markets and organized internally" (Williamson, 1985: 143). For Lazonick, however, through processes of organizational innovation and collaborative learning, firms can transform bounded rationality into collectivized forms of rationality, while high-powered incentives have the ability to transform opportunism into collective purpose (Lazonick, 2002: 3065). For transaction cost theorists, then, there is little or no understanding of the role business enterprises play in the innovation process, and this because, when they consider the basis on which firms allocate resources for innovation, markets are accredited with most of the responsibility for these allocations when it is, instead, fundamentally an issue of organizational rather than market control.

Similarly, Lazonick's complaint about Dynamic Capabilities Theory is that it has nothing to say about such issues as the location of strategic control, the allocation of financial returns, the re-integration of learning and strategy, and how to develop a strategic response to new competitors and environments, when firms are confronted with the obsolescence of existing asset positions (Lazonick, 2002: 3069). No doubt, this overstates the case (especially in regard to the last point), but it does highlight what is cogent and unique about the theoretical framework that Lazonick (along with his erstwhile collaborator, Mary O'Sullivan) has constructed.

Lazonick (1991: 198–206) presents a cogent summary of his theory of the innovative organization. He argues that the crucial problem faced by business organizations is that of fixed costs. Because neither production nor sale are certain or instantaneous, firms must choose between two opposing strategies. On one hand, they can be innovative, developing productive capabilities and resources. On the other hand, they can be adaptive, staying with known technical specifications and existing capabilities. This choice is made in the context of two forms of uncertainty. Productive uncertainty is concerned with the internal organization of firms, while competitive uncertainty concerns rivalry on the part of other firms. Both forms of uncertainty obtain over the two sequential stages of development and utilization of capabilities.

Lazonick (1991: 203–204) emphasizes the fact that higher levels of innovation imply more uncertainty as the firm must invest in vertically integrated activities, R&D, planning and coordination. These costs are minimized for the adaptive firm, which maintains a lower level of fixed commitments. The innovative enterprise must invest in management capabilities, the development and coordination of specialized skills, coordination mechanisms that increase the speed of throughput, and higher levels of backward and forward integration. All these activities are associated with both the transformation of variable into fixed costs, and competitive uncertainty into productive uncertainty. Nevertheless, the firm can exercise more control over the process by trading off a higher risk of failure against enhanced opportunities for growth (Lazonick, 1991: 201). Moreover, Lazonick cautions that even late movers face some uncertainty over their ability to manage the requisite investments and, more often than not, they are exposed to an increased threat of 'creative destruction'. Accordingly, oligopolies always confront the dangerous temptation of relaxing into regimes of adaptation. At the same time, Lazonick (1991: 206) notes that effort-saving technological change creates opportunities for achieving high throughput. However, this imposes the need for extensive backward and forward integration, the conversion of variable into fixed costs, the conversion of competitive into productive uncertainty, and the successful exploitation of both scale and scope economies so that fixed costs can be spread over larger production volumes.

From this exposition is should be clear that macroeconomic policies that successfully achieve full utilization of capacity are highly conducive to innovation at the level of the individual enterprise. In her evolutionary analysis of innovation and corporate governance O'Sullivan (2000) identifies three characteristics of the innovation process that, she suggests, render it immune to neoclassical understanding: development, organization, and strategy. By development she means the irreversible commitment of resources over an unknown period of time for uncertain returns. Her reading emphasizes the exploratory nature of the innovation process, its dependence on the learning of skills that may quickly become obsolete, the productive uncertainties associated with the building of capabilities, and the competitive uncertainty associated with rivalry. As such, in terms that should now be increasingly familiar, she suggests that states of the world are not so much defined as discovered. O'Sullivan interprets organization as referring to a cumulative process of collective learning: integrative capabilities are developed around problem definition and shaping, the transmission and transformation of know-how, and the sharing of experience or complementary skills (O'Sullivan, 2000: 408). This collective process is therefore difficult to replicate although, infrequently, it can be rendered completely obsolete.

Moreover, it is difficult if not impossible to isolate the contribution made by individuals to the overall outcome. Finally, O'Sullivan (2000: 409) interprets strategy as referring to the development of new means-ends structures as a response to learning and the unfolding of new insight. Associated with this set of characteristics, O'Sullivan (2000: 410–411) distinguishes three conditions of corporate governance, namely: financial commitment, organizational integration, and insider control. Financial commitment refers to the need for on-going commitment of resources to irreversible forms of investment that yield uncertain returns. Organizational integration refers to the need to integrate human and physical resources and provide incentives for the development and effective utilization of technology. Finally, insider control refers to the need to vest strategic control in the hands of those with the ability and incentive to allocate resources for learning and innovation.

Policy and modelling implications

I do not wish to arbitrarily or carelessly separate more macro-level policies from those situated at a more micro-level, although I will subsequently return to interrogate these issues for modelling. The importance of financial commitment as an arm of innovation or science and technology policy comes to the fore in Mariana Mazzucato's (2013) book, *The Entrepreneurial State*, where she talks about the significance of "mission-oriented finance" for the US economy. Introduced by the Eisenhower administration in the context of the Cold War rivalry between the US and Soviet Union, continued by all future administrations, and managed by the military-industrial complex, not only did the mission to "land a man on the moon" support NASA, but it also drove a huge volume of *strategic* (though certainly not solely *applied*) research that guided the US innovation system along lines that were largely immune to the destructive myopia of the Anglo-Saxon (if not the global) system of corporate governance. This source of dedicated finance also assisted in diversifying the investment activity of the domestic private sector at a time when the forces of centralization and concentration were pushing things in exactly the opposite direction (Vitali et al., 2011). Mazzucato's research serves as a counter-weight to the current dominance of neo-Austrian, individualizing conceptions of market-oriented development and privatized entrepreneurship. She highlights the fact that not only does the state regulate markets, it effectively creates them. Her emphasis on mission-oriented finance highlights the crucial, if not guiding, role of government in the construction and social coordination of sociotechnical assemblages that are emphasized by advocates of the New Economic Sociology—grids, metrologies, devices, market mechanisms.

More recently, Mazzucato has collaborated with L. Randall Wray on a Levy Institute-funded project with the aim of achieving a new "Keynes-Schumpeter-Minsky" synthesis. This synthesis draws together the Keynesian understanding of effective demand, endogeneity of the money supply, and the uncertain and volatile nature of investment (and consumption streams that are increasingly driven by fluctuations in wealth rather than income), with Schumpeter's conception of how the process of "creative-destruction" has been institutionalized by large corporations through the establishment of large-scale industrial research laboratories, and Minsky's notions of how the fragility caused by the movement of banks, households, and firms into ever-increasing and precarious financial positions inevitably contributes to a cyclical 'boom-and-bust' dynamic that he referred to as financial instability. Mazzucato and Wray (2015) apply this new theoretical framework to the global process of 'financialization', which they interpret as a growth in the share of value added and an even larger share of total corporate accounted for by the financial sector. Nevertheless, they claim that this growing financialization has led to a retreat of finance from production into speculative investment, driven by a heightened myopia or short-termism on the part of large institutional investors.

In the US context, this problem of financial retreat is largely offset by massive, long-term public subsidies and grants from organizations such as DARPA, ARPA-E, and other organizations associated with the "military-industrial complex". Mazzucato and Penna (2015) draw on the same framework to argue for a growing role for state investment banks such as the IBRD, the German KfW, the Export Bank of Japan, Brazil's BNDES, Korea's KDB, Canada's BDBC, and the China Development Bank. Moreover, this role extends beyond Keynesian concerns for countercyclical expenditure and large-scale capital development (infrastructure projects etc.) into new venture support (i.e. venture capitalist services) and also has a challenge-role (which Mazzucato chooses to call "mission-oriented finance"). One of the best examples of this challenge role was Eisenhower's call

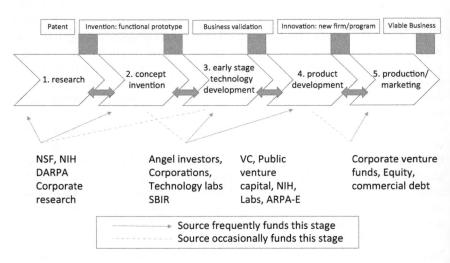

Figure 5.3 Public Financing of Innovation across Entire Innovation Chain

Source: Mazzucato and Wray (2015, Fig. 4: 29)

for the US to "put a man on the moon" before the Russians could. This mission-oriented finance continued throughout the Kennedy years and LBJ's Presidency into the current era, with Defense Advanced Research Projects Agency (DARPA) grants alone amounting to a total of $2.973 bn, under the Obama administration in 2016.[3] Mazzucato and Wray (2015) provide the diagram in Figure 5.3 of how various kinds of major funding bodies in the US contribute to different stages of the innovation chain.

Implications of ubiquitous computing systems for economic modelling

Supposed revolutions in the technology of production, communications, and distribution have presaged earlier calls for an analogous revolution in techniques of economic analysis. The work of Dixit and Nalebuff (1991) and Varian and Shapiro (1998) that erupted during the short-lived "dot-com" boom, comes to mind. More recently, Varian (2013) has taken on the responsibility for transforming econometrics (along the lines of statistical learning theory) in the epoch of "Big data". Nevertheless, I would like to begin with the unremarkable observation that for computationally feasible application, mainstream techniques of microeconomic analysis require very strong assumptions about representative agency, as well as homogeneity of preferences and techniques, and the rational formation of forward-looking expectations. Historians of economics thought have traced the origin of such techniques to nineteenth-century energetics, including mathematical techniques based on Lagrangians and Hamiltonians. Unfortunately, instantly recognizable and wide-spread developments within the digital economy are rendering these same techniques less and less relevant for economic analysis.

As acknowledged in the recent literature on changes to the technology and organization of industrial production and distribution systems, increasing levels of networked interaction, moves towards decentralized forms of control, and more broadly dispersed but concurrent processes (i.e. those that compete for and/or share resources within the boundaries of a given corporate establishment or entity) are omnipresent.

New engineering and operations research textbooks appear on the shelves every day, dealing with current developments in deep machine learning, statistical learning theory, and signal processing for systems that are increasingly characterized by hybridity, network-control and decentralization. And within the field of computer science, process algebras are continually being created, extended and improved to better model and control complex, interactive, and concurrent systems. Activity in areas of overlap between these computational developments and economic modelling is certainly increasing, but early initiatives have had mixed results (the Sante Fe Institute's efforts with multi-agent modelling using Swarm software come to mind along with the use of cellular automatons to represent heterogeneous and distributed processes of decision-making). While explanatory conceptions of emerging complexity along the lines of Conway's "game of life" or of multi-fractal processes are certainly seductive, the results of actual applications often disappoint, with pertinent software capabilities lagging behind developments in theory.

Although deep machine learning has transformed data-analysis and pattern-recognition, economists have a right to be suspicious when told that these same techniques will soon render professional modellers redundant. For their part, semantic technologies are an aid to analysis and have the potential to become an indispensable source of business and policy intelligence, yet I have argued above that they require substantial input of tacit knowledge and inference from those who deploy them. Production engineers are the main users of process algebras for purposes of business process modelling. In my view, one of the most promising sets of formal techniques for economic modelling is that of string diagrams, along with their varying families of generators and sets of axioms. This is because they have the capacity to represent a wide variety of transitions systems and dynamic structures.

One example should suffice to illustrate this. Permutation and product categories (PROPs) can represent signal flow graphs by drawing on a set of generators that can amplify, copy and delete signals, or emit a zero signal, while 'cups' and 'caps' allow signals to be changed in direction, thus allowing for processes of positive and negative feedback. They also meet the requirements of a graphical linear algebra. The fact that scalar amplifiers can be z- or s-transform operators as well as real numbers means that a PROP can represent a linear or hybrid system of differential or difference equations as well as generating polynomial equations and such mathematical sequences as the Fibonacci series and recursive fractal equations. A slightly different set of generators allows PROPs to represent the Petri nets that are used widely in Business Process Modelling. However, the most impressive advantages to be derived from working with PROPs is that they: (i) support diagrammatic reasoning in the design and construction of models; (ii) allow modellers to assemble larger and more complex models from smaller components—each PROP being a matrix building-block with n-column vectors of input and m-row vectors of outputs; (iii) potentially accommodate a hierarchy of feedback control loops with control processes at the bottom of the hierarchy being more dispersed or decentralized.

Notes

1　On this aspect of the WWW see Tim-Berners Lee, the inventor of WWW at http://dig. csail.mit.edu/breadcrumbs/node/215. The fact that the W3C syntax treats RDF graphs as basic data structures is articulated at www.w3.org/Consortum/technology.

2　In FCA, a concept is typically divided into two mutually dependent parts: its extensions are all objects that share all the attributes of the concept, whereas its intensions are the attributes which precisely describe the objects of the concept. The concepts also form a hierarchy, where: a concept C1 is a subconcept of C2, if the extension of C1 is a subset of the extension of C2 and the intension of C2 is a subset of the extension of C1. For a given universe, it can be shown that the concept hierarchy is a complete lattice. As FCA genuinely deals with Boolean data only, conceptual scaling is introduced as a means for "translating" non-boolean data attributes of entities into formal contexts. The conceptual scales can be manually or semi-automatically created (Dau, 2014; Gantner and Wille, 1999).

3 Department of Defense Fiscal Year (FY) 2016 President's Budget Submission, available at: www.darpa.mil/attachments/%282G1%29%20Global%20Nav%20-%20About%20 Us%20-%20Budget%20-%20Budget%20Entries%20-%20FY2016%20%28 Approved%29.pdf.

Bibliography

Baeten, J. C. M. (2004). A Brief History of Process Algebra. Report CSR 04-02, Vakgroep Informatica, Technische Universiteit Eindhoven.

Bartlett, B. (2005). Categorical Aspects of Topological Quantum Field Theories. Masters Thesis, Utrecht University.

Bell, J. L. (1988). *Toposes and Local Set Theories: An Introduction.* Oxford: Clarendon Press.

Bengio, Y., A. Courville and P. Vincent (2013). Representation Learning: A Review and New Perspectives. *IEEE Transactions on Pattern Analysis and Machine Intelligence,* 35(8): 1798–1828.

Bonchi, F., P. Sobociński and F. Zanasi (2015). Full Abstraction for Signal Flow Graphs. *Proceedings of the 42nd Annual ACM SIGPLAN-SIGACT Symposium on Principles of Programming Languages,* POPL'15, Mumbai, 15–17 January 2015, 515–526.

Bonchi, F., P. Sobociński and F. Zanasi (2016). Lawvere Theories as Composed PROPs. Accessed 10 April 2018. http://users.ecs.soton.ac.uk/ps/papers/lawvere.pdf.

Brooks, Rodney A. (1999). *Cambrian Intelligence: The Early History of the New AI.* Cambridge, MA: MIT Press.

Chedmail, Patrick, G. Cognet, C. Fortin, C. Mascle and J. Pegna (eds) (2013). *Integrated Design and Manufacturing in Mechanical Engineering: Proceedings of the Third IDMME Conference Held in Montreal, Canada, May 2000.* New York, NY: Springer Science & Business Media.

Curien, Pierre-Louis (2008). *Category Theory: A Programming Language-oriented Introduction,* mimeo. Accessed 16 September 2016. www.irif.fr/~mellies/mpri/mpri-ens/articles/curien-category-theory.pdf.

Dau, Frithjof (2006). Mathematical Logic with Diagrams, Based on the Existential Graphs of Peirce. Habilitation thesis, to be published. Available at: www.dr-dau.net.

De Lit, Pierre and Alain Delchambre (2011). *Integrated Design of a Product Family and Its Assembly System.* New York, NY: Springer Science & Business Media.

Dixit, Avinash K. and Barry J. Nalebuff (1991). *Thinking Strategically: The Competitive Edge in Business, Politics, and Everyday Life.* Chicago, IL: The University of Chicago Press.

Ganter, B. and R. Wille (1999). *Formal Concept Analysis: Mathematical Foundations.* Berlin and Heidelberg: Springer (Trans. *Formale Begriffsanalyse: Mathematische Grundlagen.* Berlin-Heidelberg: Springer, 1996).

Girard, Jean-Yves (2007). Truth, Modality and Intersubjectivity. *Mathematical Structures in Computer Science,* 17(6): 1153–1167.

Goertzel, Ben (2015). Are There Deep Reasons Underlying the Pathologies of Today's Deep Learning Algorithms? Accessed 10 April 2018. http://goertzel.org/DeepLearning_v1.pdf.

Goertzel, Ben and Cassio Pennachin (2007). The Novamente Artificial Intelligence Engine. In Ben Goertzel and Cassio Pennachin (eds), *Artificial General Intelligence.* Cognitive Technologies Series. Heidelberg: Springer, 63–130.

Goguen, Joseph A. (1994). Requirements Engineering as the Reconciliation of Technical and Social Issues. In Marina Jirotka (ed.), *Requirements Engineering: Social and Technical Issues.* New York, NY: Academic Press, 165–199.

Hidalgo, César, A. and Ricardo Hausmann (2009). The Building Blocks of Complexity. *PNAS*, 106(26): 10570–10575.

Kline, S. (1985). Research, Invention, Innovation and Production: Models and Reality, Report INN-1, March 1985, Mechanical Engineering Department, Stanford University.

Kline, Stephen (1985). The Chain-linked Model. Accessed 10 April 2018. https:// en.wikipedia.org/wiki/Chain-linked_model.

Krömer, Ralf (2007). *Tool and Object: A History and Philosophy of Category Theory*, ed. E. Knobloch and O. Darrigol. Vol. 32. Berlin: Birkhäuser.

Larman, Craig and Victor R. Basili (2003). Iterative and Incremental Development: A Brief History. *Computer*, 36(6) (June): 47–56.

Lawvere, William (1984). Functorial Remarks on the General Concept of Chaos. Accessed 10 April 2018. www.ima.umn.edu/Functional-Remarks-General-Concept-Chaos.

Lazonick, W. (1991). *Business Organization and the Myth of the Market Economy*. Cambridge: Cambridge University Press.

Lazonick, W. (2002). Theory of Innovative Enterprise. In *International Encyclopedia of Business and Management* (2nd ed.). London: Thomson Learning, 3055–3076.

Lazonick, W. (2003). The Theory of the Market Economy and the Social Foundations of Innovative Enterprise. *Economic and Industrial Democracy*, 24(1): 9–44.

Lazonick, William (2016). Innovative Enterprise or Sweatshop Economics? In Search of Foundations of Economic Analysis, mimeo. Accessed 10 April 2018. www.hbs.edu/ businesshistory/Documents/Lazonick%20final.pdf.

Lazonick, W. and M. O'Sullivan (2002). *Corporate Governance, Innovation, and Economic Performance in the EU: Project Policy Report*. Research Report funded by the Targeted Socio-Economic Research Programme of the European Commission (DGXII) under the Fourth Framework Programme.

Lee, Tim Berners and Lalana Kagal (2016). Map and Territory in RDF APIs. Decentralized Information Group. Accessed 10 April 2018. http://dig.csail.mit.edu/breadcrumbs/ node/215.

Mabsout, Ramzi (2015). Abduction and Economics: The Contributions of Charles Peirce and Herbert Simon. *Journal of Economic Methodology*, 22(4): 491–516.

Marquis, Jean-Pierre (2009). *From a Geometrical Point of View: A Study of the History and Philosophy of Category Theory*. New York: Springer.

Martin, R. and Sunley, P. (2003). Deconstructing Clusters. *Journal of Economic Geography*, 3: 5–35.

Mazzucato, Mariana (2013). *The Entrepreneurial State: Debunking Private vs. Public Sector Myths*. London: Anthem Press.

Mazzucato, Mariana and Caetano C. R. Penna (2015). Beyond Market Failures: The Market Creating and Shaping Roles of State Investment Banks. Levy Economics Institute of Bard College, Working Paper No. 831.

Mazzucato, Mariana and L. Randall Wray (2015). Financing the Capital Development of the Economy: A Keynes-Schumpeter-Minsky Synthesis. Levy Economics Institute of Bard College, Working Paper No. 837.

Minsky, H. P. (1985). The Financial Instability Hypothesis: A Restatement. In P. Arestis and T. Skouras (eds), *Post Keynesian Economic Theory: A Challenge to Neo-Classical Economics*. Sussex: Wheatsheaf Books.

Moe, Kiel (2008). *Integrated Design in Contemporary Architecture*. Princeton, NJ: Princeton Architectural Press.

Nguyen, Anh, Jason Yosinski and Jeff Clune (2014). Deep Neural Networks Are Easily Fooled: High Confidence Predictions for Unrecognizable Images. arXiv:1412.1897.

O'Sullivan, M. (2000). The Innovative Enterprise and Corporate Governance. *Cambridge Journal of Economics*, 24: 393–416.

Porter, Michael E. (1985). *Competitive Advantage: Creating and Sustaining Superior Performance*. New York, NY: Simon and Schuster.

Porter, Michael (1985). *The Value-chain*. Accessed 10 April 2018. https://upload. wikimedia.org/wikipedia/commons/thumb/7/70/Porter_Value_Chain.png/256px-Porter_ Value_Chain.png.

Rodin, Andrei (2012). Axiomatic Method and Category Theory. 5 October, arXiv:1210.1478v1 [math.HO] 25 September 2012.

Sowa, John F. (2000). *Knowledge Representation: Logical, Philosophical, and Computational Foundations*. Pacific Grove, CA: Brooks Cole Publishing.

Stevens, John, James Moultrie and Nathan Crilly (2009). Design Dis-integration Silent, Partial, and Disparate Design. Undisciplined! Design Research Society Conference 2008, Sheffield Hallam University. Available at: http://shura.shu.ac.uk/544.

Stjernfelt, Frederick (2007). *Diagrammatology: An Investigation on the Borderlines of Phenomenology, Ontology, and Semiotics*. Synthese Library, 336, Dordrecht: Springer.

Szegedy, Christian, Wojciech Zaremba, Ilya Sutskever, Joan Bruna, Dumitru Erhan, Ian Goodfellow and Rob Fergus (2013). Intriguing Properties of Neural Networks. arXiv:1312.6199.

Teece, D. J. (2000). *Managing Intellectual Capital: Organizational, Strategic, and Policy Dimensions*. Oxford: Oxford University Press.

Teece, D., G. Pisano and A. Shuen (1997). Dynamic Capabilities and Strategic Management. *Strategic Management Journal*, 18(7): 509–533.

Varian, Hal (2013). Big Data: New Tricks for Econometrics. *Journal of Economic Perspectives*, 28(2): 3–28.

Varian, Hal and Carl Shapiro (1998). *Information Rules: A Strategic Guide to the Network Economy*. Boston, MA: Harvard Business School Press.

Vitali, Stefania, James B. Glattfelder and Stefano Battiston (2011). The Network of Global Corporate Control, *PLoS ONE*, 6(10): e25995. doi:10.1371/journal.pone.0025995. www.plosone.org/article/info%3Adoi%2F10.1371%2Fjournal.pone.0025995.

Wikipedia (2016). Integrated Design. Accessed 1 April 2016. https://en.wikipedia.org/ wiki/Integrated_design.

Williamson, Oliver E. (1985). *The Economic Institutions of Capitalism: Firms, Markets, Relational Contracting*. New York, NY: Free Press.

Wojtowicz, Ralph L. (2004). Symbolic Dynamics and Unpredictability Defined by Right Adjointness. AIP Conference Proceedings 718, 268. Accessed 10 April 2018. www. adjoint-functors.net/aipcasys2.pdf.

6 The use of diagrammatic reasoning in teaching economics for the digital economy

Introduction

During the dot-com boom a coterie of influential economists argued that the new technologies and changes to systems of production, distribution, and exchange required entirely new ways of thinking about valuation, pricing and modelling (Dixit and Nalebuff, 1991; Varian and Shapiro, 1998). A lot of attention was placed on supposedly transformative developments such as the move to "close-to-zero" costs of reproduction, dynamic network economies of scale, the role of strategies in game theory, and heterogeneous agent-based modelling. Nowadays, with the on-going revolution in information and communication technology, commentators are talking in much the same manner about the "internet-of-things", which enables communication to occur amongst and between businesses, suppliers, consumers or end-users, and machines, in the context of a constellation of technological advances referred to as the new digital economy (Teece, 2012–2013), or the "fourth industrial revolution" (as it has been called in Germany since 2010).

Documentation prepared for the recent World Economic Forum, for example, waxed lyrical about "the seven technologies changing your world", which include: computing capabilities, storage, and access; Big data; digital health; the digitization of matter; the internet of things; Blockchain; and the wearable internet (see https://www.weforum.org/agenda/2016/01/a-brief-guide-to-the-technologies-changing-world). In this context, neo-Austrian commentators continue to delude themselves about the potential for Bitcoin and Blockchain to transform the nature of exchange, taking us beyond the dichotomy between "state" and "market" (Davidson et al., 2016). And those who have abandoned evolutionary economic thinking about strategy for its neo-Austrian (and thus, neoliberal) counterpart (Foss et al., 2007) talk incessantly about the entrepreneurial imperative to manage heterogeneous capital, while largely ignoring the theoretical implications of the capital debates from the 1960s (Burmeister, 2000; Garagnani, 2012).

However, if these changes in the digital economy are to be properly understood we need to turn to inter-disciplinary research drawn from some of the most influential computer scientists around the world. In contrast, computer science researchers such as Robin Milner (2006) simply refer to the attributes of what is being described as a Ubiquitous Computing System (UCS), conjecturing that: (a) it will continually make decisions hitherto made by us; (b) it will be vast, maybe 100 times today's systems; (c) it must continually adapt, on-line, to new requirements, and (d) a constellation of individual UCSs will interact with one another (http://www.cl.cam.ac.uk/archive/rm135/). For information science researchers, then, a UCS is characterized by a population of interactive agents that manage some aspect of our environment, and consisting of software agents that move and interact not only in physical but also in virtual space: as such, they include data structures, messages, and a structured hierarchy of software modules. Accordingly, the low level model of such a system must consist of a conflation of physical and virtual space, and therefore a combination of physical and virtual activity.

Milner identified four sets of questions that needed to be answered about the phenomenon of ubiquitous computing, namely:

Social questions: what ubiquitous computing systems (UCSs) do people want or need, and how will they change people's behaviour?

Technological questions: how will the hardware entities—the sensors and effectors whose cooperation represents such a system—acquire power, and by what medium do they communicate?

Engineering questions: for the populations and subpopulations—including software agents—that make up a system, what design principles should be adopted at each order of magnitude, to ensure dependable performance?

Foundational questions: what concepts are needed to specify and describe pervasive systems, their subsystems and their interaction?

Milner's vision was of a tower of process languages able to explain ubiquitous computing at different levels of abstraction.

Another leading professor of computer science, Joseph Goguen, has spoken about the need to integrate both the "Wet" and the "Dry", where the Wet represents the informal, socially situated aspects of information, and the Dry represents the formal syntactical and semantic rules of computation (see https://cseweb.ucsd.edu/~goguen/). In particular, he highlights the enormous cost of failure in large software engineering projects, tracing failure to the requirements phase of a project, which is the most error prone, most costly, most immune to technical analysis, and thus the phase affording the greatest economic leverage (Goguen, 1994). His solution to this problem of integration is framed in terms of the need to bridge the "great divide" between theory and practice. More specifically, he identifies the need to overcome the dichotomy between the four cultures of computing: hardware; software; the "shrinkwrap" or "Zine" culture; and theoretical computing, although he sees theory as a potentially unifying force for "social aspects of computing", once researchers become willing to engage with such theoretical frameworks as Bruno Latour's Actor-Network-Theory, ethnomethodology,

Heidegger's musing about Technology, Lyotard's critique of the grand narratives of modernity, Maturana and Varela's conception of autopoetic systems, and fuzzy logic. In his own work, Goguen (1999) also draws on Algebraic Semiotics, Unified Concept Theory, and the notion of Concept Blending in his own efforts at integration between the "Wet" and the "Dry".

Long before the notion of "Agile" New Product Development became fashionable, software engineers had abandoned rigid, linear approaches to Model Engineering Development, such as the well-known "waterfall" technique, for more iterative, spiralling approaches (Goguen, 1994; Larman and Basili, 2003). And of course, the notion of "Scrum", popularized by Takeuchi and Nonaka (1986), originally, and without acknowledgement, derived from AI research into "subsumption architectures" for behaviour-based robotics, that conducted by Rodney Brooks (1987) and his colleagues in the mid-to-late-1980s.

All this raises the obvious question of how and what students from an Economics or Social Sciences background should be taught about the workings of the contemporary digital economy. In my own research into computational aspects of UCS, I have drawn on knowledge of theoretical computing programmes that are taught in leading international universities such as Oxford, Cambridge, Edinburgh, Amsterdam, Nijmegen, and Stanford, as well as relevant research activities within leading public-cum-private research centres such as Microsoft Research, SAP, and the MIT Media Laboratories. I have also investigated approaches to the teaching of Business Information Systems and Business Process Management at leading European technical universities such as those located in Karlsruhe and Vienna. In most of these institutions, category theory or topos theory is the chosen mathematical framework for teaching formal computation. However, in recent years, more diagrammatic approaches to category theory have come to the fore, especially for representing transition systems (including automatons, Petri nets, Bayesian networks etc.). Along with these developments, large companies such as SAP have started to recruit researchers who have completed PhDs on semantic technologies, in general, and various approaches to Diagrammatic Reasoning (DR), such as Venn-Peirce diagrams, existential graphs, concept graphs and formal concept analysis, and from a cognitive computing perspective, large graph theory and recurrent neural networks.

This chapter draws specifically on Charles S. Peirce's insights into relational logic and the diagrammatic or graphical nature of the relationship between the knowing subject and known object (Zamalea, 2001–2003). Peirce's pragmatic conception of the iconic, indexical, and symbolic elements of 'semeiosis' weaves together *pathemata* (i.e. thoughts as determinations of the mind, with matter conceived in a Schellingian manner as mind 'hide-bound' with habits), *grammata* (i.e. graphs as determinations on what he called the sheet of assertion which records inscriptions of graphs and operations between graphs), and *pragmata* (i.e. things conceived as facts of the universe and the relations holding between things).

On this view (Fabbrichesi, 2011), diagrammatic reasoning, for Peirce, achieves an integration of Firstness (qualitative potentiality with evolution conceived as *tychastic*, mechanical necessity), Secondness (actual reactive existence characterized by *anachastic*, or fortuitous evolution), and Thirdness (or the generality and continuity of mediated existence, and *esse in futuro* with evolution conceived as *agapeistic* or influenced by the force of creative love). In more prosaic terms it will be argued that diagrammatics weaves together *ontology* (i.e. the processual generators of the digital economy), *epistemology* (the graphical logic through which we gain an understanding of the character and attributes of this economy), and *pedagogy* (with Semiotics viewed as a process of reasoning or 'learning through diagrams'). Peirce's "Pragmaticist Maxim" then is to: "Consider what effects which might conceivably have practical bearings we conceive the object of our conception to have. Then, our conception of these effects is then whole of our conception of the object" (Peirce, 1931–1958: CP5.402; 1878 Mimeo: 47). Fabbrichesi (2011: 117) modifies this quote to express the maxim in terms of an imperative about diagrammatic reasoning:

> Consider what graphical effects, which might conceivably have practical (experimental) bearings, we conceive the object of our conception to be expressed in. Then, our conception of these (sign, graphical, visual) effects is the whole of our conception of the object.

In this light, it behoves me, in the remainder of this chapter, to first demonstrate the precise relationship holding between these diagrams and the processes

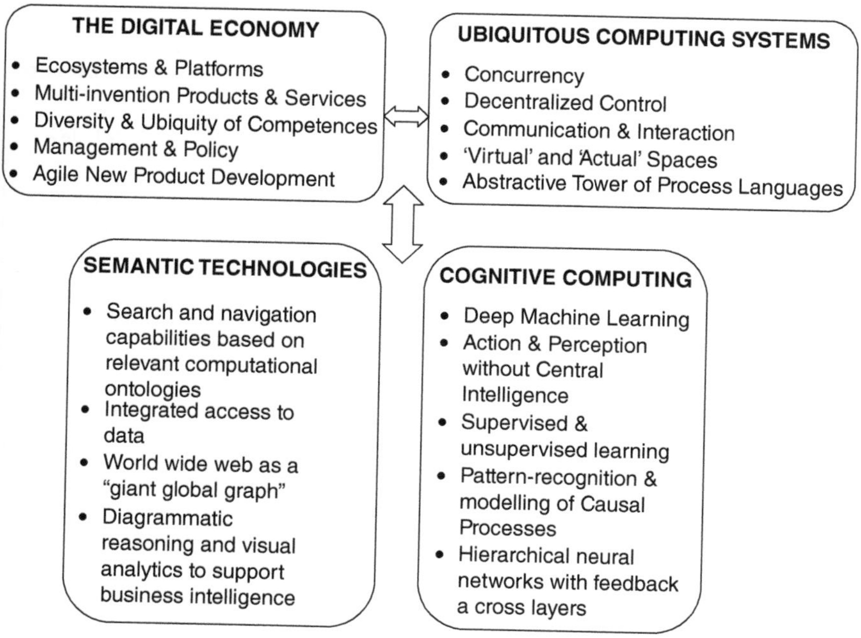

Figure 6.1 Computational Aspects of the Digital Economy

characterizing the operation of UCSs within the digital economy, second justify their use as a pedagogical tool, and third identify and foreshadow the kinds of new insights and understandings that might flow from such an approach to teaching and learning. Figure 6.1 highlights the linkages between each of the sections of the chapter.

Diagrams and the digital economy

Teaching along these Pragmatic lines would encourage students to think about information and communication technologies (ICTs) and Business Information Systems (BIS) from a strategic perspective informed by an understanding of contemporary and evolving computational technologies. Emphasis would be placed on the characteristics of ubiquitous computing systems (UBSs) that were associated with the search for, exchange of, and analysis of information, along with the capacity of these technologies to support communication between businesses, suppliers, customers, government agencies, and service providers, including those organizations offering ICT services. To this end, teachers would have to (i) ensure that students acquired a largely conceptual grasp of the way that ubiquitous computing systems communicate with, support, coordinate, and manage business processes; (ii) provide students with a largely diagrammatic insight into computational modelling, simulation and control of business processes, supply chains, process algebras, control systems, functional programming procedures, graph-based logics, and rewriting rules; and (iii) acknowledge the crucial importance of semantic technologies and cognitive computing by investigating how

Category Theory	Physics	Topology	Logic	Computation
Object X	Hilbert Space X	Manifold X	Proposition X	Data type X
Morphism $f:X \to Y$	Operator $f:X \to Y$	Cobordism $f:X \to Y$	Proof $f:X \to Y$	Program $f:X \to Y$
Tensor product of objects $X \otimes Y$	Hilbert space of joint system $X \otimes Y$	Disjoint union of manifolds $X \otimes Y$	Conjunction of propositions $X \otimes Y$	Parallel execution $X \otimes Y$
Tensor product of morphisms $f \otimes g$	Parallel processes $f \otimes g$	Disjoint union of cobordisms $f \otimes g$	Proofs in parallel $f \otimes g$	Programs in parallel $f \otimes g$
Internal hom $X -o\ Y$	Anti-X and Y $X^* \otimes Y$	Orientation reversed $X^* \otimes Y$	Conditional proposition $X -o\ Y$	Function type $X \to Y$

Figure 6.2 The "Rosetta Stone"

Source: Baez and Stay (2008; Table 4: 63)

they are, or could be, applied within commercial and public sector environments to integrate information from a variety of data sources while providing unified information access to end users, by exploiting Tim Berners-Lee's notion of the World-Wide Web as a "giant global graph" (see Lee and Kagal, 2016).

Category theory and topos theory have largely taken over the field of formal computation because categories can link the structures found in algebraic topology, together with the logical connectives and inferences to be found in formal logic, as well as with recursive processes and other operations in computation. Figure 6.2, taken from Baez and Stay (2008; Table 4), highlights this capability.

John Bell (1988: 236) succinctly explains why it is that category theory also possesses enormous powers of generalization:[1]

> A category may be said to bear the same relation to abstract algebra as does the latter to elementary algebra. Elementary algebra results from the replacement of *constant quantities* (i.e. numbers) by *variables*, keeping the operations on these quantities fixed. Abstract algebra, in its turn, carries this a stage further by allowing the *operations* to vary while ensuring that the resulting mathematical structures (groups, rings, etc.) remain of a prescribed kind. Finally, category theory allows even the *kind* of structure to vary: it is concerned with *structure in general*.

Category theory can also be interpreted as a universal approach to the analysis of process. As shown in Figure 6.3, this integrative capacity is supported by the existence

Economics and Finance?: Kirchoff's law $\Leftrightarrow$ non–arbitrage

	Displacement q	Flow q'	Momentum p	Effort p'
Electronics	Charge	Current	Flux linkage	Voltage
Translation	Position	Velocity	Momentum	Force
Rotation	Angle	Angular velocity	Angular momentum	Torque
Hydraulics	Volume	Flow	Pressure momentum	Pressure
Thermodynamics	Entropy	Entropy flow	Temperature momentum	Temperature
Chemistry	moles	Molar flow	Chemical momentum	Chemical potential

Figure 6.3 Physical Analogues across Different Dynamic Systems
Source: Baez and Fong (2014: 63)

of analogies to the phenomenon of effort, momentum, flow, and displacement across electronic, mechanical, hydraulic, chemical, and thermodynamic systems:

Peirce wrote almost 40,000 pages of unpublished manuscripts on what he called Existential Graphs (EG's). Where Alpha Graphs are closely related to propositional logic, Beta Graphs relate to predicate calculus, and the Gamma Graphs to modal and higher order logic (see Dau, 2016). Hoffman's interpretation of Peirce's approach to diagrammatics is summarized in Figure 6.4.

Figure 6.5 provides an example of a simple Alpha Graph, along with its representation as a sequence of morphisms, a proposition within a propositional logic, and in the form of a tree diagram. The closed curves, here, are called 'seps' and serve to negate whatever they enclose. Seps can also be nested. The empty sep represents the negation of 'true'.

The rules of Inference pertaining to Alpha Graphs are (Dau, 2016):

1   Erasure: Any evenly enclosed subgraph may be erased.
2   Insertion: Any graph may be scribed on any oddly enclosed area.
3   Iteration: If a subgraph G occurs on the sheet of assertion or in a cut, then a copy of the graph may be scribed on the same or any nested area which does not belong to G.

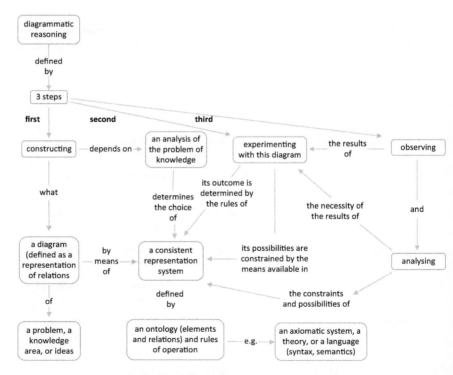

Figure 6.4 A Diagrammatic Definition of Diagrammatic Reasoning
Source: Hoffman (2011, Fig. 1: 195)

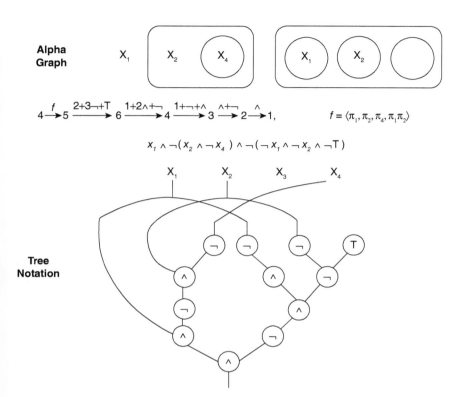

Figure 6.5 Representation of Propositions with Peirce's Alpha Graphs
Source: Brady and Trimble (2000a: 216, 220)

4   Deiteration: Any subgraph whose occurrence could be the result of iteration may be erased.
5   Double Cut: Any double cut may be inserted around or removed from any area.

To convey some feeling for Beta Graphs, Figure 6.6 depicts some simple examples with their accompanying interpretations (Dau, 2016: 12).

The rules of inference for Beta Graphs are extensions of the five rules for Alpha Graphs, designed to cover the properties of the lines of identity (Zamalea, 2001–2003: 125):

A1. Erasure: Any evenly enclosed subgraph and any evenly enclosed portion of a line of identity may be erased.
A2. Insertion: Any graph may be scribed on any oddly enclosed area, and two portions of two lines of identity which are oddly enclosed on the same area may be joined.

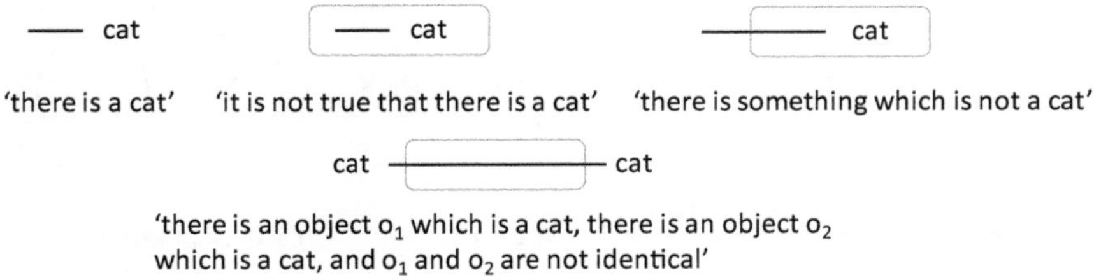

—— cat   —— cat   —•—— cat

'there is a cat'   'it is not true that there is a cat'   'there is something which is not a cat'

cat ——————•— cat

'there is an object o_1 which is a cat, there is an object o_2 which is a cat, and o_1 and o_2 are not identical'

Figure 6.6 Peirce's Beta Graphs and Lines of Identity
Source: Dau (2016: 12)

A3. Iteration: For a subgraph G on the sheet of assertion or in a cut, a copy of this subgraph may be scribed on the same or any nested area which does not belong to G. In this operation, it is allowed to connect any line of identity of G, which is not scribed on the area of any cut of G, with its iterated copy. Consequently, it is allowed to add new branches to a ligature, or to extend any line of identity inwards through cuts.

A4. Deiteration: Any subgraph whose occurrence could be the result of an iteration may be erased.

A5. Double Cut: Any double cut may be inserted around or removed from any area. This transformation is still allowed if we have ligatures which start outside the outer cut and pass through the area of the outer cut to the area of the inner cut.

   The correspondence between Alpha rules and those of Classical Propositional Calculus is illustrated by the natural translation rules set out in the following set of points (Zamalea, 2001–2003):

- Erasure and Insertion: rule of conjunction $p \wedge q \rightarrow p$ and contrapositive $\neg p \rightarrow \neg(p \wedge q)$
- Iteration and Deiteration: generic intuitionistic rule of negation $p \wedge \neg q \leftrightarrow p \wedge \neg(p \wedge q)$
- Double Cut: classical rule of negation $\neg\neg p \leftrightarrow p$

The resulting natural translation identifies a set of morphisms, Alpha-*wfg* $\rightarrow$ CPC-*wff*, between well-formed Alpha Graphs (Alpha *wfg*) and well-formed formulae for the Classical Propositional Calculus (CPC-*wff*): which are defined recursively by:

$(void)^* = T, p^* = p, (F,G)^* = F^* \wedge G^*,$ and

$(\boxed{F})^* = \neg(F^*)$

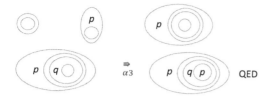

Figure 6.7 Inference of $[p \rightarrow (q \rightarrow p)]^{*-1}$
Source: Zamalea (2001–2003: 126)

For example, the following inference of $[p \rightarrow (q \rightarrow p)]^{*-1}$ can be demonstrated by the sequence of diagrams in Figure 6.7 (where È G implies G is an Alpha-theorem) (Zamalea, 2001–2003: 126):

Similarly, the modus ponens rule, the double cut rule, completeness, and the deduction theorem also have diagrammatic counterparts (Figure 6.8) (Zamalea, 2001–2003: 129–130).

Caterina and Gangle (2013) establish the diagrammatic proof of Heyting implication and further demonstrate how alpha graphs can be deployed to account for the logical connectives $\wedge$, $\vee$ and $\Rightarrow$ of the propositional calculus (Figure 6.9).

The axioms of Heyting algebra are set out below using Heyting implication and these logical connectives (Caterina and Gangle, 2013: 1040–1041). The algebra is defined over a set endowed with the logical connectives $\wedge$, $\vee$ and $\Rightarrow$ plus T and $\perp$, for which:

- $g \rightarrow$ T for any $g \in S$
- $g \wedge h \rightarrow h$
- $g \wedge h \rightarrow g$

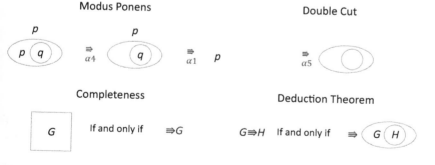

Figure 6.8 Modus ponens Rule, the Double Cut Rule, Completeness, and the Deduction Theorem

Source: Zamalea (2001–2003: 129–130)

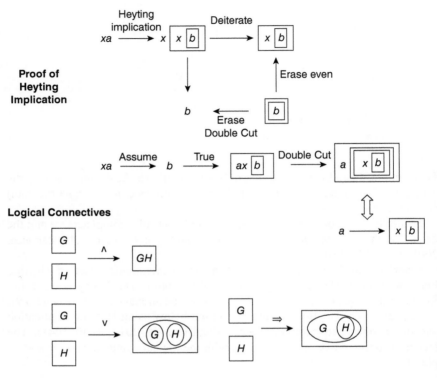

Figure 6.9 Heyting Implication and the Logical Connectives
Source: Caterina and Gangle (2013: above, 1039; below, 1040)

- $g \to h$ and $g \to k$ implies $g \to h \wedge k$
- $\bot \to g$ for any $g \in S$
- $g \to g \vee h$
- $h \to g \vee h$
- $h \to g$ and $k \to g$ implies $h \wedge k \to g$
- $g \to (h \Rightarrow k)$ iff $g \wedge h \to k \neg g$
- $\neg g = (g \Rightarrow \bot)$

The commutative diagrams in Figure 6.10 represent the categorical notion of adjunction defined over the category G, which is then deployed in characterizing the adjunctive nature of Heyting implication (Caterina and Gangle, 2013: 1037–1039).

Heyting algebras, which conform to intuitionist rather than classical propositional logic, play an important role in algebraic topology. Caterina and Gangle (2013) establish this relationship between logic and topology in a lemma reproduced

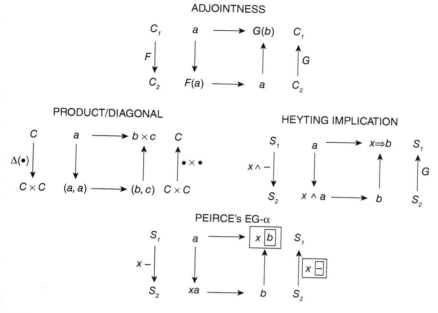

Figure 6.10 Adjunctions and their Applications

Source: Caterina and Gangle (2013: 1037–1039)

below, immediately after the definition of an "upper set" of G, a notion required by the lemma concerned:

> The upper set for any $g \in G$, is defined as $g \uparrow = \{h \in G: g \rightarrow h\}$ (i.e. $g \uparrow$ represents the collection of "the futures" of g). A subset U of G is an upper closed set if $g \uparrow \subseteq U$ for any $g \in U$.

Lemma:

> The set $UC(G)$ of all upper closed sets of G is a topological space (because the denumerable union of upper closed sets and the finite intersection of upper closed sets are both upper closed sets).

Gamma-EGs (Zamalea, 2001–2003: 136):

- γ-1: in any even area, any Alpha cut may be *half-erased* to become a Gamma cut.
- γ-2: in any odd area, any Gamma cut may be *half-completed* to become an Alpha cut.

- Coupled with the Alpha double cut rule (α-5), γ-1 provides immediately the *-1 translation of the modal T axiom ($P \rightarrow$ P), while γ-2 ensures $P \rightarrow \Diamond P$ (Zamlea, 2001–2003: 137).
- Other Gamma rules pertaining to restrictions on eventual *iterations* along broken cuts give rise to Gamma systems equivalent to Lewis S and S4 systems (Zeman, 1964: 162–168).

Gamma Graph axioms (Zamalea, 2001–2003: 136):

1   In a broken cut already on the Sheet of Assertion any graph may be inserted.
2   A broken cut in an area enclosed by an odd number of cuts (which may be either alpha or broken cuts) may be transformed to an alpha cut (by "filling in" the breaks in it).
3   An alpha cut in an area enclosed by an even number of or by no cuts may be transformed to a broken cut (by erasing parts of it).

Brady and Trimble (2000a, 2000b) have interpreted Peirce's Alpha and Beta Graphs using string diagrams, observing that, while Alpha Graphs are isomorphic to Boolean algebra, Beta Graphs are isomorphic to fibered categories, and Gamma Graphs to freely generated Boolean toposes.[2] They also explicate the nature of Beta Graphs using string diagrams, which are modified with surgery (i.e. specific conditions imposed on graph transformations) (Brady and Trimble, 2000b).

This kind of diagram, which first appeared in the work of physicists such as Roland Penrose and Richard Feyneman, represents an alternative approach to that of commutative diagrams for articulating concepts in category theory. Although string diagrams had their origins in Feyneman's work on quantum electrodynamics and Roland Penrose's teaching of tensor calculus, these deployments were primarily heuristic. The work of Joyal and Street, from the Australian School of Category Theory, has established that string diagrams are planar diagrams that possess all the formal properties and the rigour of symbolic algebra (see Theorem 1.5 from Joyal and Street, 1988, and Theorem 1.2 from Joyal and Street, 1991, which establish coherence for planar monoidal categories). For this reason, string diagrams are now being used to represent much of the underlying mathematical structure of category theory, but in a far more abbreviated form than can be achieved by resorting to the usual kind of "diagram-chasing" to establish commutative properties (Curien, 2008; Marsden, 2014).

String diagrams have been applied in a wide variety of domains with the objective of gaining a deeper understanding of the properties of signal flow graphs (Bonchi et al., 2015), Bayesian Networks (Fong, 2013), Petri nets, universal algebra (Bonchi, Sobociński and Zanasi, 2016), Rewriting Logics (Bonchi, Gadduci and Kissinger, 2016), first-order propositional logic (Kissinger and Quick, 2015), quantum mechanics (Coecke and Parquette, 2009), topological quantum field theory (Bartlett, 2005), and even formal aspects of computation theory itself (Pavlovic, 2012). They are also increasingly applied to the mathematics of process, resource usage, and transition (Coecke et al., 2014).

When deployed as building blocks for Signal Flow Graphs (Bonchi et al., 2015) and Bayesian Networks (Fong, 2013), these components consist of constants, as well as blocks composed in sequential and parallel arrangements. These blocks make up a circuit where wires carry elements of a field, k, enter and exit through boundary ports. Computation in the circuit proceeds synchronously according to a global "clock", where at each iteration fresh elements are processed from input streams on the left and are emitted as elements of output streams on the right. The generators for each circuit include (i) a copier, duplicating its input signal; where (ii) its counit accepts any signal and discards it, producing no output; (iii) an adder that takes two inputs and emits their sum, where (iv) its unit constantly outputs the signal 0; (a delay, x, which is a 1-place buffer that initially holds the 0 value); and finally, (v) an amplifier, k, which multiplies its input by the scalar k (Baez and Fong, 2014). Together with "cups" and "caps" (i.e. wires bent around to turn downward signals into upward signals and vice versa) these components suffice to construct a conventional feedback control circuit.[3] Bonchi, Sobociński and Zanasi (2015) establish that the semantics and syntax for such a PROP meet the conditions for soundness and completeness.

Potential for the application of DR in political economy

It has been argued above that category theory can be interpreted as a universal approach to the analysis of process. Monoidal categories and monads serve as a unifying mechanism for modelling digital aspects of the economy in a variety of different ways. First, they provide a formalism for describing the structure borne by an object of a category where the resulting structures are called algebras. In this context, two such monads can be "composed", with the resulting algebra for the composite monad consisting of an algebra for each of the original monads, subject to certain compatibility conditions between the two algebra structures. For example, the structure of a ring, involves an abelian group (the additive structure) and a monoid (the multiplicative structure) subject to the compatibility condition of distributivity (i.e. there is a distributive law between the monad for abelian groups and the monad for monoids, and the composite monad is precisely the monad for rings). Monads can also be deployed in the constitution of polynomial functors, which can in turn be used to represent dynamic systems such as weighted automatons and Markov processes. Benton and Wadler (1995) have shown that a categorical model of the Monadic Lambda Calculus could be derived from a strong monad with "tensorial strength". This formalism has now been built in to functional programming languages such as Haskell. Benton (2015) notes that a great range of effects can be modelled this way, including errors, non-determinism, partiality due to recursion, and continuous maps rather than sets. In a PROP each matrix representing inputs (column vectors) and outputs (row vectors) thus functions like a building block (with composition of blocks representing matrix multiplication), so that more complex systems can either be constructed from smaller ones or decomposed into their underlying components.

Category theory and its string diagrammatic counterparts possess the potential for a wide range of applications in modelling. For example, string diagrams are now being applied by researchers in game theory to provide an abbreviated language for the representation of games and strategies (Hedges et al., 2016). I would suggest that the modelling of joint production within a multisectoral production system (Wright, 2013, 2014) along with the modelling of the monetary circuit as a process (Foley, 1982; Graziani, 2003; dos Santos, 2011; Parguez and Seccareccia, 2000; Tymoigne, 2014) can also benefit from the application of string diagrams. The ability of string diagrams to represent automatons as well as more conventional dynamic systems would suggest that they could be deployed in diagrammatic representations of Stock-Flow-Consistent Macroeconomic models when these are coupled with Agent-Based Modelling using automatons (Caiani et al., 2016).

In the analysis of dynamic systems, so-called hybrid systems, which combine discrete and continuous sub-systems together, are assuming increasing importance. Economic applications, which go back to the writings of Kalecki, are also proliferating (Matsumoto and Szidarovszky, 2009). In continuous time, researchers work with time lags associated with transfer functions, whereas discrete time delays give rise to more complex integro-differential equation systems. In a string diagram context, the generators for scalar amplification can represent both z-transforms and Laplace transforms thus accommodating hybrid systems. Furthermore, the capacity of string diagrams to characterize signal flow graphs with a small set of generators means that not only can they be combined sequentially and in parallel but also in nested hierarchies to represent complex and decentralized control networks

Research on thermodynamic networks has been fundamental to the explanation of arbitrage within markets (Ellerman, 2000). The applicability of network diagrams to "far-from-equilibrium systems characterized by emerging complexity and self-organization", means that these techniques can also be applied to open economic networks (Baez et al., 2015).

Petri nets are a major formalism supporting Business Process Management (Russell et al., 2006). However, they have also been interpreted as models of economic processes (Bonnano, 1995). In more general stochastic versions, any Markov process can be represented by a Petri net, affording flexibility in choosing the correspondence between the states of the Markov process and the actual system it is to model. In this context, it is worth mentioning that Markov processes are the fundamental building blocks of modern quantitative finance.

More generally, semantic technologies, sometimes described under the rubric of cognitive computing, are a rapidly growing field within artificial intelligence.[4]

A recent example is the CUBIST Project that was described in the section of Chapter 5 dealing with Semantic Technologies. As described there, the CUBIST project largely drew on Peirce's Existential Graphs (Dau, 2016). The core objective of the Project was to investigate "how current semantic technologies can be applied in enterprise environments to semantically integrate information from heterogeneous data sources and provide unified information access to end users".

Under the architecture of the CUBIST Prototype there are different means of access to information, including through: semantic searching based on the domain ontologies specific to each of the three case studies; 'smart' query generation taking these computational ontologies into account, where the types and object properties form a 'query graph' that can actually contain more types than those selected, with their associated datatype properties being used for the filtering and characterization of formal attributes; more explorative search techniques; conceptual scaling as described above; and visual analytics.

It is certainly conceivable that, as their capabilities improve, semantic technologies and cognitive computing software suites will be used in a growing variety of economic modelling and analysis tasks. However, at this stage it is both tempting and dangerous to exaggerate the modelling capabilities of cognitive computing, despite the increasing availability of huge data sets.

Conclusions

It has been argued above that the major benefits of a diagrammatic approach to UCS in the digital economy would derive from the application of pedagogical technologies based on the very computational techniques, hardware and software artefacts, networks, and applications that would be studied and analysed in a course focusing on drivers of the digital economy.

For educational purposes, these formal techniques could readily be supplemented by relevant case-study material sourced from local and global players in the field. A range of relevant simulation and modelling systems could also be deployed within a blended learning environment, with user-friendly, object-oriented software modules providing an integrative environment for the simulation of elementary Petri nets, signal flow graphs, automatons, and other relevant transitions systems and networks. Pedagogically, computational concepts are easier to grasp when taught in a diagrammatic manner because visual and geometric rather than algebraic cues and demonstrations are closer to the embodied nature of categorical and logical thinking. Also, graphical proofs are often more abbreviated than commutative diagrams in category theory and certainly more abbreviated than their algebraic counterparts.

Grounding this alternative conception of teaching economics is the view that techniques derived from late nineteenth-century energetics (e.g. Lagrangians, Hamiltonians and optimal control theory) are no longer suitable for modelling behaviour in a digital economy increasingly characterized by concurrency, interaction, algorithmics, and decentralized control.

Notes

1 William Lawvere, one of the more interesting contributors to on-going debates over mathematical foundations, takes off from Hegel's problem of wanting to reject Kant's subjective (transcendental) logic and his abandonment of the *a priori* / *a posteriori* distinction (which privileges pure thought over empirically grounded science), while preventing the return of a "figurative" metaphysics of God, Soul, and World. To this end, Lawvere advances an objective logic that privileges the geometric (i.e. presheaves in a topos, conceived as 'shapes' or test spaces, positioned within a larger space of co-presheaves, conceived as containers)—but one working with measurable quantities and ratios defined using strong monoidal categories—even while continuing to operate with a coherent subjective logic of connectives, quantifiers, natural number objects, and subobject classifiers (the latter, giving rise to characteristic functions asserting 'truth'). In combination, this gives him access to the mathematical foundations of empirically-grounded scientific reasoning (Rodin, 2014).
2 Brady and Trimble (2000a, 2000b) draw on both linear logic and closed symmetric monoidal categories (CSMC) in providing conceptual explanation for Peirce's illative transformations (i.e. rules of inference). Linear logic and the technical notion of tensorial 'strength' also allow them to drop the global form for the contraction and weakening rules in this logic, through the application of exponential modal operators), which enables them to overcome the problem of exponential explosion in the size of proofs when cuts are 'pushed' past contractions (the very problem that motivated the development of linear logic in the first place), while also revealing that the indeterminacy property of a cut elimination algorithm (also known as the Church-Rosser property) is not satisfied.
3 More detail on category theoretic approaches to signal flow diagrams is provided in Chapter 7's Technical Appendix.
4 A notable example of cognitive computing is the Large-Scale Integrating Knowledge Collider (LarKC) Project (see www.larkc.org/). The aim of this project, funded by the European Union 7th Framework Program, is to develop a platform for massive distributed incomplete reasoning that will remove the scalability barriers of currently existing reasoning systems for the Semantic Web. Similarly, Microsoft's Cognitive Toolkit—previously known as CNTK—empowers researchers to harness the intelligence within massive datasets through deep learning (via deep—many-to-many—recurrent neural networks) by providing uncompromised scaling, speed, and accuracy with commercial-grade quality and compatibility with the programming languages and algorithms you already use (see www.microsoft.com/en-us/research/product/cognitive-toolkit/). Finally, IBM System G (http://systemg.research.ibm.com/), which was partially assisted by DARPA, is a comprehensive set of Graph Computing Tools, Cloud, and Solutions for Big Data. "G" stands for graphs—large or small, static or dynamic, topological or semantic, and property or Bayesian. It includes: (i) Graph Database; (ii) Graph Visualizations; (iii) a Graph Analytics Library; (iv) Graph Middleware for various hardware, for in-memory, and for distributed clusters; and (v) Network Science Analytics tools, including: Cognitive Networks, Cognitive Analytics, Spatiotemporal Analytics, and Behavioural Analytics.

Bibliography

Baez, John C. and Brendan Fong (2014). A Compositional Framework for Passive Linear Networks. arXiv:1504.05625 [math.CT] 28 April 2015.

Baez, John C., Brendan Fong and Blake S. Pollard (2015). A Compositional Framework for Markov Processes. arXiv:1508.06448v2 [math-ph] 3 September 2015.

Baez, J. and M. Stay (2008). Physics, Topology, Logic and Computation: A Rosetta Stone. Accessed 26 August 2010. http://math.ucr.edu/home/baez/.

Bartlett, B. (2005). Categorical Aspects of Topological Quantum Field Theories. Masters Thesis, Utrecht University. arXiv:math/0512103v1 [math.QA] 5 December 2005.

Bell, J. T. (1988). *Toposes and Local Set Theories: An Introduction.* Oxford Logic Guides 14. Oxford: Oxford University Press.

Benton, Nick (2015). Categorical Monads and Computer Programming. London Mathematical Society Impact 150. *Stories*, 1: 9–14.

Benton, Nick and Philip Wadler (1995). Linear Logic, Monads and the Lambda Calculus. Eleventh Annual IEEE Symposium on Logic in Computer Science, 1996. LICS '96. Proceedings.

Bonchi, Filippo, Fabio Gadducci, Aleks Kissinger (2016). Rewriting Modulo Symmetric Monoidal Structure. arXiv:1602.06771v2 [math.CT] 23 February 2016.

Bonchi, F., P. Sobociński and F. Zanasi (2015). Full Abstraction for Signal Flow Graphs. In *Proceedings of the 42nd Annual ACM SIGPLAN-SIGACT Symposium on Principles of Programming Languages*, POPL'15, Mumbai, 15–17 January 2015, 515–526.

Bonchi, F., P. Sobociński and F. Zanasi (2016). Lawvere Theories as Composed PROPs. Accessed 10 April 2018. http://users.ecs.soton.ac.uk/ps/papers/lawvere.pdf.

Bonnano, G. (1995). Modelling Production with Petri Nets. Accessed 18 February 2013. www.econ.ucdavis.edu/faculty/bonanno/PDF/petri.pdf.

Brady, Geraldine and Todd Trimble (2000a). A Categorical Interpretation of C. S. Peirce's Propositional Logic Alpha. *Journal of Pure and Applied Algebra*, 149: 213–239.

Brady, Geraldine and Todd Trimble (2000b). A String Diagram Calculus for Predicate Logic and C. S. Peirce's System Beta, preprint.

Brooks, R. A. (1987). Planning Is Just a Way of Avoiding Figuring Out What To Do Next. Technical report, MIT Artificial Intelligence Laboratory.

Burmeister, Edwin (2000). The Capital Theory Controversy. In Heinz D. Kurz (ed.), *Critical Essays on Piero Sraffa's Legacy in Economics*. Cambridge: Cambridge University Press.

Caiani, Alessandro, Antoine Godin, Eugenio Caverzasi, Mauro Gallegati, Stephen Kinsella, and Joseph E. Stiglitz (2016). Agent-based-Stock Flow-consistent Macroeconomics: Towards a Benchmark Model. *Journal of Economic Dynamics & Control*, 69: 375–408.

Caterina, G. and R. Gangle (2013). Iconicity and Abduction: A Categorical Approach to Creative Hypothesis Formation in Peirce's Existential Graphs. *Logic Journal of IGPL*, 21(6): 1028–1043.

Coecke, Bob, Tobias Fritz and Robert W. Spekkens (2014). A Mathematical Theory of Resources. arXiv:1409.5531v3 [quant-ph] 28 November 2014.

Coecke, Bob and Eric Oliver Paquette (2009). Categories for the Practising Physicist. arXiv:0905.3010v2 [quant-ph] 12 October 2009.

Curien, Pierre-Louis (2008). Category Theory: A Programming Language-oriented Introduction, mimeo. Accessed 16 September 2016. www.irif.fr/~mellies/mpri/mpri-ens/articles/curien-category-theory.pdf.

Dau, Fritjof (2014). CUBIST: Your Business Intelligence. Presented at Fourth European Business Intelligence Summer School (eBISS 2014). www.cubist-project.eu.

Dau, Frithjof (2016). Mathematical Logic with Diagrams, Based on the Existential Graphs of Peirce. Habilitation thesis, to be published. Available at: www.dr-dau.net.

Davidson, S., Primavera De Filippi and Jason Potts (2016). Economics of Blockchain, 8 March. http://ssrn.com/abstract=2744751.

Dixit, Avinash K. and Barry J. Nalebuff (1991). *Thinking Strategically: The Competitive Edge in Business, Politics, and Everyday Life.* Chicago, IL: The University of Chicago Press.

Ellerman, David (2000). Towards an Arbitrage Interpretation of Optimization Theory. World Bank, December. Available at: www.ellerman.org/.

Fabbrichesi, Rossella (2011). Iconic Thought and Diagrammatical Scripture: Peirce and the Leibnizian Tradition. *Semiotica*, 186(1/4): 111–127.

Foley, D. (1982). Realization and Accumulation in a Marxian Model of the Circuit of Capital. *Journal of Economic Theory*, 28(2): 300–319.

Foley, Duncan (1991). Maximum Entropy Exchange Equilibrium. https://sites.google. com/a/newschool.edu/duncan-foley-homepage/home/downloads.

Fong, Brendan (2013). Causal Theories: A Categorical Perspective on Bayesian Networks. arXiv:1301.6201v1 [math.PR] 26 January 2013.Foss, Kirsten, Nicolai J. Foss, Peter G. Klein and Sandra K. Klein (2007). The Entrepreneurial Organization of Heterogeneous Capital. *Journal of Management Studies*, 44(7): 1165–1186.

Ganter, B. and R. Wille (1999). *Formal Concept Analysis: Mathematical Foundations.* Berlin-Heidelberg: Springer (Trans. Formale Begriffsanalyse. *Mathematische Grundlagen.* Berlin-Heidelberg: Springer, 1996).

Garagnani, Pierangelo (2012). On the Present State of the Capital Controversy. *Cambridge Journal of Economics*, 36: 1417–1432.

Goguen, Joseph A. (1994). Requirements Engineering as the Reconciliation of Technical and Social Issues. In Marina Jirotka (ed.), *Requirements Engineering: Social and Technical Issues.* New York, NY: Academic Press, 165–199.

Goguen, Joseph A. (1999). An Introduction to Algebraic Semiotics, with Applications to User Interface Design. In Chrystopher Nehaniv (ed.), *Computation for Metaphor, Analogy and Agents*, Springer Lecture Notes in Artificial Intelligence, 1562. Berlin: Springer, 242–291.

Graziani, A. (2003). *The Monetary Theory of Production.* New York, NY: Cambridge University Press.

Hedges, Jules, Evguenia Shprits, Viktor Winschel and Philipp Zahn (2016). Compositionality and String Diagrams for Game Theory. arXiv:1604.06061v1 [cs.GT] 20 April 2016.

Hoekstra, Rinke (2009). *Ontology Representation: Design Patterns and Ontologies that Make Sense.* Amsterdam: IOS Press.

Hoffman, M. H. G. (2011). Cognitive Conditions of Diagrammatic Reasoning. *Semiotica*, 186(1/4): 189–212.

Joyal, A. and R. Street (1988). Planar Diagrams and Tensor Algebra. Unpublished manuscript, available from Ross Street's website, September.

Joyal, A. and R. Street (1991). The Geometry of Tensor Calculus I. *Advances in Mathematics*, 88(1): 55–112.

Kissinger, A. and D. Quick (2015). A First-order Logic for String Diagrams. arXiv:1505. 00343v1 [math.CT] 2 May 2015.

Larman, Craig and Victor R. Basili (2003). Iterative and Incremental Development: A Brief History. *Computer*, 36(6) (June): 47–56.

Lee, Tim Berners and Lalana Kagal (2016). Decentralized Information Group, "Map and Territory in RDF APIs". Accessed 10 April 2018. http://dig.csail.mit.edu/breadcrumbs/ node/215.

Marsden, Daniel (2014). Category Theory Using String Diagrams. Accessed October 2016. https://arxiv.org/pdf/1401.7220.pdf.

Matsumoto, Akio and Ferenc Szidarovszky (2009). Delay Differential Nonlinear Economic Models. In G. I. Bischi, C. Chiarella and L. Gardini (eds), *Nonlinear Dynamics in Economics, Finance and Social Sciences.* Berlin: Springer-Verlag, 195–214.

Milner, Robin (2006). Ubiquitous Computing: Shall We Understand It? BCS Chartered Institute for IT website. Accessed 10 April 2018. www.bcs.org/content/ConWebDoc/4708/*/setPaginate/No.

Parguez, A. and M. Seccareccia (2000). The Credit Theory of Money: The Monetary Circuit Approach. In J. Smithin (ed.), *What Is Money?* London: Routledge, 101–123.

Pavlovic, Dusko (2012). Monoidal Computer I: Basic Computability by String Diagrams. arXiv:1208.5205v2 [cs.LO] 29 December 2012.

Peirce, Charles Sanders (1931–1958). *Collected Papers of Charles Sanders Peirce* (8 vols), ed. Arthur W. Burks, Charles Hartshorne and Paul Weiss. Cambridge, MA: Harvard University Press.

Peirce, Charles S. (1992). Reasoning and the Logic of Things. In K. L. Kremer and H. Putnam (eds), *The Cambridge Conferences Lectures of 1898*. Cambridge, MA: Harvard University Press.

Rodin, Andrei (2014). *Axiomatic Method and Category Theory*. Syntheses Library 364. Cham: Springer.

Russell, N., A.H.M. ter Hofstede, W.M.P. van der Aalst and N. Mulyar (2006). Workflow Control-Flow Patterns: A Revised View. BPM Center Report BPM-06-22, BPMcenter.org.

Santos, Paulo dos (2011). Production and Consumption Credit in a Continuous-Time Model of the Circuit of Capital. *Metroeconomica*, 62(4): 729–758.

Shin, S.-J. (1994). *The Logical Status of Diagrams*. Cambridge: Cambridge University Press.

Stiegler, B. (2009). Desire and Knowledge: The Dead Seize the Living. Accessed 10 April 2018. http://arsindustrialis.org/desire-and-knowledge-dead-seize-living.

Stiegler, B. (2011). *The Decadence of Industrial Democracies: Disbelief and Discredit*. Cambridge: Polity Press.

Takeuchi, Hirotaka and Nonaka, Ikujiro (1986). The New Product Development Game. *Harvard Business Review*, 86116 (January–February): 137–146.

Teece, David (2012–2013). Understanding How Innovation Shapes Competition and Policy in the Digital Economy. *Journal of Law, Economics and Policy*, 9(1): 97–118.

Tymoigne, E. (2014). Modern Monetary Theory, and Interrelations between the Treasury and Central Bank: The Case of the United States. *Journal of Economic Issues*, 48(3): 641–662.

Varian, Hal and Carl Shapiro (1998). *Information Rules: A Strategic Guide to the Network Economy*. Boston, MA: Harvard Business School Press.

Wright, I. (2013). Pasinetti's Hyper-integrated Labor Coefficients and the "Pure Labor Theory of Value". Accessed 28 January 2015. http://ssrn.com/abstract=2255732.

Wright, I. (2014). A Category-Mistake in the Classical Labour Theory of Value. *Erasmus Journal for Philosophy and Economics*, 7(1): 27–55.

Zamalea, Fernando (2001–2003). Peirce's Logic of Continuity: Existential Graphs and Non-Cantorian Continuum. *Review of Modern Logic*, 9, 1–2(29): 115–162.

Zeman, Jay J. (1964). Peirce and Philosophy. Accessed 10 April 2018. http://users.clas.ufl.edu/jzeman/csphiloflogic.htm.

7   Category-theoretic approaches to semantic technologies

Introduction

This review chapter not only addresses the influence of the computational sciences over the social sciences, but also those influences extending in the opposite direction. And this is especially true of sociology, where it is helpful to recognize the impact of methodological debates occurring at the time when Max Weber was attempting to lay down the foundations of modern sociology. Emerging from an active engagement in the German *Methodenstreit* debates, Weber emphasized the importance of motivation and purpose in human society. However, he insisted that these motives and purposes were socially determined. That is, his version of "methodological individualism" was fiercely anti-psychological and opposed in ontological terms to any simplistic social atomism.[1]

In *The Order of Things*, Foucault characterizes the nineteenth-century episteme governing the human sciences as one inscribed by three faces: the mathematical and physical sciences; philosophy as an analytic of finitude; and the three positivities of labour, life, and language. Foucault argues that from the nineteenth century onwards—conditioned by a breakthrough in the structuring of scientific knowledge in the natural sciences, political economy, and general grammar—the latter positivities came to be conceived as somehow folded back upon themselves, and in this way possessed by their own densities, by their own historical laws and temporalities.

Contemporaneous with the birth of the new sciences of economics, linguistics and economics, Foucault suggests that Man began to be conceived as being governed by each of the respective positivities: i.e. as a living being, an instrument of production, and a vehicle for words which exist before him, thus marked by them in his finitude. In anthropological terms, Man is seen to be the being who renders all knowledge possible, but not in a Kantian manner through representation (reminiscence, imagination, self-consciousness), rather, in his finitude (i.e. as determined by his anatomo-physiology or the given historico-social conditions that mould him). And in this 'anthropological slumber', truth must now be perceived in a variety of forms: as something expressed through the body and perception, as an historical illusion overcome, and as true discourse. This is the meaning Foucault attributes to what he labels as Man conceived by philosophical anthropology as an "*empirico-transcendental doublet*". Clearly, this doublet still weighs heavily on those labouring on the sciences of cognition and artificial intelligence.

As detailed in earlier chapters, my own research into the Digital Economy, has adopted a sceptical *Post-Cognitive* stance towards AI, robotics, algorithmics, machine learning, and semantic technology. To this end, I have drawn on the philosophies of Schelling, Marx, Peirce, Whitehead, and Merleau-Ponty, along with insights from embedded cognitive science, the "New AI", and neural Darwinism. Central to this approach is the notion that the sciences of artificial intelligence have been obliged to enfeeble 'intelligence' for the purpose of achieving progress in self-directed or 'deep' machine-learning which, at present, amounts to little more than a sophisticated form of pattern recognition and approximation.[2] Arguably, this enfeebling applies both to image recognition and natural language processing, despite the obvious strides that have been made in these fields of machine learning.

On this view, digital technology should be deployed as an instrument for the application of creative labour and not a mere mechanism of control, surveillance, subordination, and displacement of human labour. Moreover, it also implies that, at least in the near future, humans are unlikely to be *replaced* by machines in a range of tasks that includes planning, forecasting, education, and decentralized control, due to: (i) the messy (i.e. incremental and interactive) nature of new product development and innovation; (ii) including, the crucial role of requirements engineering in driving the success of large engineering and construction projects; (iii) the incompleteness and undecideability of expressive logics; (iv) the impact of uncertainty on decision-making; (v) the inability of machines, at present, to demonstrate true creativity (notwithstanding impressive new developments in self-directed learning). In conclusion, there is a need to pursue genuinely collaborative forms of tacit knowledge and inference that can be brought to bear on cognitive and communicative problems within organizations.

The Australian Federal Government's publication, "The Advanced Manufacturing Growth Centre's Sector Competitiveness Plan 2017", argues that "[v]alue in manufacturing is shifting from production to pre- and post-production intangibles such as R&D and Services". Support for this view is garnered from a recent OECD (2013) report on "Interconnected economies benefiting from global value chains".

This emphasis on the contribution of 'design' and 'servitization' to profit merely restates arguments regularly aired within IT circles, from the late 1950s onwards, about the need to position "requirements engineering" at the forefront of software development endeavours, especially to reign in huge cost blow-outs in major projects. Joseph Goguen's insistence that this aspect of software engineering was also the most error prone and the least amenable to technical analysis underpinned his later efforts to adopt a variety of methodological approaches drawn from disciplines as diverse as Ethnomethodology, the Sociology of Technological Change (i.e. Actor-Network-Theory), and semiotic approaches informed by Pragmatism, and Concept-Blending in Linguistics.

Graph-based logic and computation

In traditional research on graph-based logic, informed by category theory, commutative diagrams are typically employed to establish the 'validity' of 'hypotheses' that are entered into on the grounds of certain 'claims', where each step of validification, hypothecation, and claiming are captured by diagrams through the use of limit and colimit diagrams (Bagchi and Wells, 2008; Rydeheard and Burstall, 1988). It would be hard to go past José Meseguer's (1997) survey for both comprehensiveness and depth. However, some indication of recent and significant developments in the field, as well as some guidance on promising future trajectories, would be highly desirable. This is the main intent of these notes.

Meseguer (1997: 2) explains how rewriting logic expresses the essential equivalence between logic and computation: system states are in bijective correspondence with formulas (modulo certain axioms that they satisfy such as associativity and commutativity) and concurrent computations are in bijective correspondence with proofs (modulo requisite definitions of equivalence). This means that the derivation of one formula from another mirrors the transition from one system state to another.

Meseguer (1997: 12) goes on to observe how William Lawvere made the seminal discovery that, when given a sigma-algebra satisfying an equational theory, the assignment of a functional interpretation to each equation (where the latter is defined in terms of its equivalence class) can be represented by a set of product-preserving functors in the category of what are now called Lawvere Theories. Meseguer (1997: 13) shows that this readily generalizes to the 2-category case where objects are natural numbers expressing the arity of algebraic operations, morphisms are equivalence classes of proof terms, and the assignment of a rule to each natural transformation between product-preserving functors extends naturally to the (2-product preserving) 2-functor extending from Lawvere theories to the 2-category.

Using linear combinatory algebra, Abramsky, Haghverdi and Scott (2002) apply traced monoidal categories to the representation of the logical connectives that feature in linear (i.e. resource-using) logic. Linear logic has found application to proof nets, functional computing, including various lambda calculi, and the modelling of resource-using processes (e.g. as seen in business process modelling). This is both a rich and promising focus of on-going research.

More recently, Bonchi, Gadducci and Kissinger (2016) have investigated (double pushout) rewriting rules by deploying PROPs in the form of a Span: $L \leftarrow K \rightarrow R$. Here, L forms the left-hand side of the rewrite rule and R forms the right-hand side, while K, common to both L and R, is the sub-structure that remains unchanged as rule is applied. To apply the rule to a structure C, one first needs to find a match $L \rightarrow C$ of L within C. The rule is then applied by constructing the missing parts (E, D, and arrows) of the following diagram in a way which ensures that the two squares are pushout diagrams.

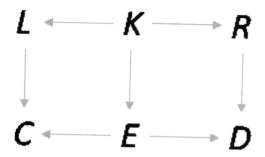

Once such a diagram is constructed we may deduce that C → D, that is, *C* rewrites to *D*. When formulated in categorical terms, the process of rewriting is then portable to structures *other than* directed graphs. For example, Stephen Lack and Pawel Sobociński (2005) point to the mathematical advantages of operating within the framework of quasi-adhesive categories and the effective topos.

This category-theoretic approach is closely related to the process-oriented research of Kissinger and Uijlen (2017) into the semantics of causal structures, and David Myers' (2017) on string diagrams for double categories, which he shows to be well-suited to analysis of sets, functions, and relations. Other relevant graph-theoretic research includes Koch et al.'s (2010) work on formalizing opetopes using a combination of nested rings and trees. Significantly, this same formalism was also utilized by the late Robin Milner (2009) in his efforts to integrate the (asynchronous) Pi calculus with Petri nets. The additional structure to account for natural transformations of representative functors is provided by 2-categories.

In his work on string diagrams, Myers (2017) draws on 'equipments' in enriched categories, pointing out:

> [W]here categories consist of objects and arrows between them, equipments consist of four kinds of things: objects, vertical arrows which are meant to behave like functions, horizontal arrows which are meant to behave like relations, and 2-cells which act like implications between relations.

For the equipment of sets, functions, and relations, objects are sets, vertical arrows are functions, horizontal arrows are relations, and 2-cells are implications. For the equipment of rings, homomorphisms, and bimodules, for example, 2-cells manifest as bimodule morphisms. For the equipment of categories, functors, and profunctors, 2-cells are profunctor morphisms. Finally, for the equipment of categories enriched in V, we have V-functors, and V-profunctors, whose 2-cells are morphisms of V-profunctors. In my view, the extended discussion of admissibility and composability of tilings in Myers' (2017) work affords a range of invaluable insights into invariance properties for these rich mathematical structures.

Courser's (2016) paper views dynamic networks as representatives of a "decorated cospan category", or labelled directed graph with inputs, outputs and weighted edges all specified by the pertinent cospans (which are dual to spans). Fong (2015) has provided a general recipe for the construction of these categories and characterized functors between them. Courser shows that when a category with pullbacks has finite limits, decorated cospans are morphisms in a symmetric monoidal bicategory, while maps of spans are 2-morphisms. Crucially, he extends Fong's approach to characterize an isomorphism between two networks rather than just equality. To this end, he draws on Michael Shulman's technique for constructing the requisite symmetrical monoidal bicategory by first constructing a symmetric monoidal pseudo-double category. Incidentally, Shulman is one of the main players in Vladimir Voevodsky's Homotopy Type Theory Project based at the Institute of Advanced Studies at Princeton University.

Baez and Courser's (2017) paper focuses on coarse-graining of open Markov processes that are accommodate non-equilibrium steady-states where there is a nonzero flow of probability through the process. Coarse-graining is a standard method of extracting a simple Markov process from a more complicated one by identifying states.

Eugene Lerman (2017) and David Spivak have chosen to work with operads in a 2-category setting, to characterize maps between dynamical systems that are, in turn, viewed as maps in the 2-category. They also utilize Shulman's 2-category framework, which allows them to build systems out of collections of smaller open subsystems, while keeping track of the maps between open systems. They cite the influential paper by Willems (2007) as a precursor of their own approach, which they show to be a generalization of groupoid-based work by Golubitsky, Stewart and Torok (2005).

In their efforts to specify an operational semantics for the π-calculus, Stay and Meredith (2015) also deploy a 2-category framework. They acknowledge Milner's seminal work on the π-calculus, which he presented as a freely generated algebra quotiented by a structural equivalence relation, then subject to further rewrite rules. They further note that Milner drew on category theory to interpret both these rewrite rules and the notion of bisimulation which, to this day, still provides the basic agenda for operational semantics. However, Stay and Meredith observe that this seminal research was the precursor for a variety of 2-categorical constructions, in which bisimulation could be characterized as a 2-morphism. Where Hirschowitz (2013) tried to encompass the whole domain of operational semantics using higher-order category theory, they note that Seeley (1987) and Hilken (1996), adopted a more direct account, which subsequently came to inform their own research on the π-calculus. Where Seeley (1987) modelled a denotational semantics for the lambda calculus in Scott domains, to represent the adjunction between β-reduction and η-conversion, Hilken (1996) applied categorical logic to proof theory. Using similar methods (atoms in Fraenkel-Mostowski set theory), Gabbay and Pitts (2002) examine nominal set theory, while Clouston (2014), like Meredith and Stay (2017), draws on Lawvere theories. However, by utilizing Schönfinkel's 1922 SKI combinator calculus, the latter pair of authors eliminate nominal features as "so much syntactic sugar", in effect, interpreting Lawvere theories enriched over graphs.

Spivak et al. (2016), draw on sheaf theory in their categorical approach to dynamic systems, which allows them to account for both continuous- and discrete-time through the use of functors in a 2-category framework. This approach also accounts for synchronized continuous time, in which each moment is assigned a phase $\theta \in [0, 1)$.

Baez et al. (2017) introduce 'network models' to encode different ways of combining networks both through overlaying one model on top of another and by setting each model side by side. In this way, complex networks can be constructed using simple networks as components. Vertices in the network represent fixed or moving agents, while edges represent communication channels

The components of more general networks defined over coloured operads include vertices representing entities of various types and edges representing the relationships between these entities. Each network model gives rise to a typed operad O_F, with a canonical algebra A_F, whose operations are ways of assembling a network of the given kind from smaller parts, each characterized in turn by a set of types and a set of operations. The different ways to compose operations characterize a more general notion of an operation, along with different permutations of an operation's arguments (determined by the pertinent permutation group of inputs and outputs).[3]

In Stell's (1994) work, sesqui-categories are applied to term rewriting conceived in terms of 2-morphisms. Since then, Stell has participated in the IEEE Upper Ontology Project (along with the Digital Built Britain Project, as well as activities relating to ISO standard 18876, and 15926). Under this umbrella, he has also engaged in theoretical research projects explicating a more generalized approach to Formal Concept Analysis, which involve the application of techniques derived from mathematical morphology to hypergraphs (Stell, 2013), and the deployment of Boolean connection algebras to construct a four-dimensional mereotopology designed to facilitate data exchange and data integration between firms in the process engineering sector (Stell, 2000).[4]

Parsimonious approaches to semantic technology

Industry-relevant aspects of the developments described immediately above can be gathered together under the general rubric of a semantic technology. It is a matter of constructing parsimonious formal approaches to knowledge representation, data exchange and integration, extraction of information from the World-Wide Web, while taking advantage of the graph-based semantics of the latter. Parsimony is derived from the application of enriched structures that are of minimal rather than maximal complexity required to characterize morphisms between pertinent hyper-graph, multi-graph, or weighted hyper-graph constructions.

Meseguer worked closely with Joseph Goguen, who developed the MAUDE programming language. The tree diagram in Figure 7.1 identifies the trajectories of ancestral descent between different specializations of concurrent rewriting.

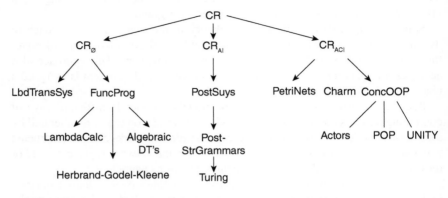

Figure 7.1 Specializations of Concurrent Rewriting
Source: Meseguer (1992)

Stell's (Stell and West, 2008) research develops a parsimonious approach to both Formal Concept Analysis and upper-level process ontology. The requisite machinery includes Boolean connection algebras and Galois connections. In Stell (2013) the pertinent devices include hypergraphs and a mathematical morphology supporting weaker versions of the usual Boolean complement, which, in turn, allow Stell to define notions such as boundary, expansion, and contraction for sub-graphs along with node-opening and node-closure. All this lets him define a 'strong concept', in graph-theoretic terms, which consists of all those properties holding throughout a given sub-graph. Stell reveals how the resulting framework not only allows him to identify properties that hold throughout a time interval, but also at end-points and, not only for a region as whole but for any points in the region and, not only for low resolution objects but for their high-resolution counterparts; and finally, those that not only hold at a specific level but also at higher levels of generality.

My motivation in dwelling on Stell's work has been to indicate how much can be accomplished while remaining within the familiar framework of sets, relations, and Galois connections. Recent developments within the 2-category formalism that I have described above relate more specifically to open dynamic networks and control systems. This literature is strongly connected to Meseguer's (1997) Chapter 3 review of "Semantic frameworks for concurrency models", which focuses on Petri nets, the π-calculus, algebraic nets, chemical machines, tile models, neural nets, and graph rewriting. The indications here point to a considerable amount of research, still to come, that will investigate concurrency, semantics, and rewriting along open network lines, in large part building on the foundations provided by Lawvere theories.

Patterson (2017) introduces a third knowledge representation formalism that interpolates between description logic (e.g. OWL, WC3) and ontology logs.

He observes that, where description logics are logical calculi designed specifically for knowledge representation, relational ontology logs or *relational ologs* are, by default, *typed*, which, he claims, can mitigate the maintainability challenges posed by the open world semantics of description logic.

Relational ologs are based on Rel, the category of sets and relations. As such, they mainly rely on relational algebra (intersections, unions, etc.). They lie somewhere between propositional logic and first-order predicate logic, striking a trade-off between computational tractability and expressivity. They can be distinguished from functional ologs to avoid confusion, because the latter are based on Set—the category of sets and functions.

Patterson observes that functional ologs achieve their expressivity through categorical limits and colimits (products, pullbacks, pushforwards, etc.) The advantages of the relational olog framework is that relevant functors allow *instance data* to be associated with an ontology in a mathematically precise way, by interpreting it as a relational or graph database, Boolean matrix, or category of linear relations. Moreover, relational ologs have a friendly and intuitive—yet fully precise—*graphical syntax*, derived from the string diagrams of monoidal categories.

While the internal language of relational ologs is the regular $(\exists,\wedge,T,=)$ fragment of first-order logic, Patterson has gone on to develop a more expressive form of relational olog, called a distributive relational olog, which satisfies the coherent $(\exists,\wedge, \vee, T,\perp,=)$ fragment of first-order logic. Nevertheless, unlike the case for description logics, Patterson observes that inference in a relational olog is undecidable. He goes on to argue that this undecideability could be resolved either through: (a) language restrictions; or (b) accepting approximate inference. He also complains that the development of a suitable graphical language must await a satisfactory extension of string diagrams to categories with multiple monoidal products. Moves in this direction require working with higher dimensional category theory, which I have deliberately avoided in this paper, because it imposes the obligation of having to work with more complex algebraic structures such as polyopetopes. However, those who are interested in pursuing these developments can consult David Yau's manuscript (2008) and Samuel Mimram's (2014) analysis of three-dimensional rewriting logic.[5]

Concluding comments

The fundamental premise of my research on the digital economy is that digital technology should serve as an instrument for the enhancement of creative labour, rather than as a mechanism of control, surveillance, displacement, and subordination. It is therefore crucial to develop a trans-disciplinary framework that helps us to describe the world of ubiquitous computing from a viewpoint that is broad enough to encompass the concerns of critical *social theory* as well as those of computational mathematics and *mathematical computing*. Only in this way will it serve both as a guide for policy and assist in the development of a range of political interventions that are justified from a *worker*-centric rather than the usual *manager*-centric perspective.

In particular, this premise reflects the view that, in the near future, humans cannot be entirely displaced by machines when it comes to planning, forecasting, learning, and decentralized control. This is a conclusion based on the following observations (i) the requirements engineering stage is crucial to the success of complex software engineering projects and other innovative activities; thus, (ii) new product development is both an incremental and interactive process characterized by overlapping and zig-zagging stages, with multiple feedback loops that span the entire innovation chain from design to final distribution and customer service; (iii) systems and logics of relevance to AI are characterized by uncertainty, incompleteness, and undecideability; (iv) a range of different logics come into play as formalisms for interpreting the WWW, managing business processes, and supporting human reasoning, which are often immune to translation; (v) from a formalist perspective, creativity is a more important feature than invariance of structure or semantics (i.e. abduction rather than a coupling of induction and deduction), but is much harder to model. Accordingly, there is a profound need for diverse forms of tacit knowledge and tacit inference to be brought to bear on commercial and scientific problems. Some brief indications of how this can be achieved, using the categorical machinery described above, will now be identified.

It is important to realize that computational systems can be integrated at different levels. Figure 7.2 (informed by the research of Paulheim and Probst, 2010) distinguishes between integration at the level of user interfaces, business or organizational logics, and data sources. Paulheim and Probst have worked at the level of user interface integration to develop an emergency services management system for the Dortmund region in Germany. The upper-level ontology DOLCE is deployed to link a core domain ontology together with a

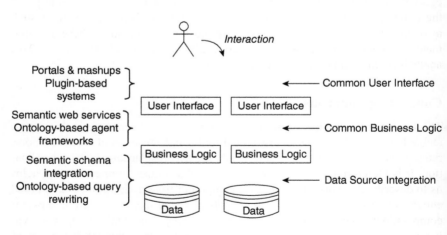

Figure 7.2 Levels of System Integration
Source: After Paulheim and Probst (2010)

user interface interaction ontology. In turn, each of these ontologies draws on inputs from an ontology on deployment regulations and various application ontologies, while improved search capabilities are achieved through the adoption of ONTOBROKER and F-Logic systems.

When navigating the terrain marked out by the work of Stell and Patterson, three main observations come to mind. First, Patterson's (2017) work links database schemas and relational and distributive logics (ologs) to dynamic systems (through instance data congruent with the field of linear relations). In this regard, Patterson cites research by members of the Categorical Informatics Group, who offer services to achieve "high-assurance data integration with mathematical rigor" (see the work of Schultz et al., 2016, on algebraic databases and that of Spivak et al., 2016, on dynamical systems and sheaves). The research of this active group of category theorists privileges Willems' (2007) notion of "interconnection", which interprets complexity as arising from the combination of simple components to produce a wide variety of interactive structures (in categorical terms, this is achieved via the compositionality of 'lax monoidal functors').

Second, Patterson's (2017) use of the string diagram formalism to represent generators and relations within (bi-) monoidal categories, which can also express a wide variety of logical connectives and algebraic axioms (e.g. axioms of Hopf and Frobenius algebras as well as interactions between them), has also been applied to networks (i.e. Petri nets, the π-calculus), calculi of concurrency, signal flow graphs and Existential Graphs, thus supporting various forms of diagrammatic reasoning that have been deployed by users and designers of semantic technologies (with the objective of transforming 'information' into 'intelligence').

Third, Stell and West's (2008) research into four-dimensional mereotopologies has influenced the drafting of ISO standards 18876, and 15926, for the Process Industry (i.e. coal and gas industry supply chain). They have also participated in the IEEE Upper Ontology Project, and the Digital Built Britain Project for the building and construction sector. Stell's (2013) more general approach to Formal Concept Analysis, involving application of techniques derived from mathematical morphology to hypergraphs, also helps to link semantic technology to these more narrowly-construed ontological initiatives.

Notes

1 I shall return to the *Methodenstreit* debates in the concluding chapter of the text.
2 MIT Media Lab and the Berkman Klein Center for Internet and Society at Harvard University have recently embarked on a new US$27m initiative aimed at addressing the global challenges of artificial intelligence (AI) from a multidisciplinary perspective. In particular, this project has the goal of developing intelligent communicative machines through the application of cognitive research into how infants acquire language.
3 One of the co-authors of the paper works for Metron, VA—a company involved in the development of systems and software to support search-and-rescue operations. Some examples in the paper deal with constraints that can be imposed with respect to proximity between vertices that represent thresholds on viable communication distance.

4 Seminal work on the axiomatic foundations for mereotopology were laid out independently by Husserl and Whitehead in the early twentieth century and perfected as a mathematical scaffold for contemporary developments in GIS systems.
5 Yau (2008) follows the approach advocated by Baez and Dolan in a number of publications (available on ArXiv), who apply what they call an 'upgrading process' to create higher-dimensional categories using the slice category construction. Yau works with (non-unital) coloured operads and PROPs, which he shows to be related by an adjunctive pair of morphisms. He demonstrates (Yau, 2008: 22) that the slice construction $O^\wedge+$ over the coloured operad O is a higher operad in the sense that "operations in O are now the colours in $O^\wedge+$, while operations in $O^\wedge+$ are reduction laws in O, which are equations stating that the composite of certain operations is equal to some operation". Moreover, "the reduction laws in $O^\wedge+$ are the ways of combining reduction laws in O to obtain other reduction laws". The upgrading process can then be repeated multiple or infinitely many times. Furthermore, there is "an analogous slice construction for coloured PROPs, giving rise to higher PROPs".

Bibliography

Abramsky, S., E. Haghverdi and P. J. Scott (2002). Geometry of Interaction and Linear Combinatory Algebras. *MSCS*, 12(5): 625–665.

Baez, J. C. and K. Courser (2017). Coarse-graining Open Markov Processes. arXiv:1710.11343v1 [math-ph] 31 October 2017.

Baez, J. C. and J. Erbele (2014). Categories in Control. arXiv:1405.6881v1 [math.CT] 27 May 2014.

Baez, J. C., J. Foley, J. Moeller and B. Pollard (2017). Network Models. arXiv:1711.00037v1 [math.CT] 31 October 2017.

Bagchi, Atish and Charles Wells (2008). Graph-based Logic and Sketches. arXiv: 0809.3023v1 [math.CT] 18 September 2008.

Barr, Michael and Charles Wells (2005). Toposes, Triples and Theories. *Reprints in Theory and Applications of Categories*, 12: 1–288. www.tac.mta.ca/tac/reprints/articles/12/tr12.pdf.

Barr, Michael and Charles Wells (2012). Category Theory for Computing Science. *Reprints in Theory and Applications of Categories*, 22.

Bonchi, Filippo, Fabio Gadducci and Aleks Kissinger (2016). Rewriting Modulo Symmetric Monoidal Structure. arXiv:1602.06771v2 [math.CT] 23 February 2016.

Bonchi, F., P. Sobociński and F. Zanasi (2017). Interacting Hopf Algebras. *Journal of Pure Applied Algebra*, 221(1): 144–184.

Clouston, Ranald (2014). Nominal Lawvere Theories: A Category Theoretic Account of Equational Theories with Names. *Journal of Computer and System Sciences*, 80(6): 1067–1086.

Coecke, Bob and Eric Oliver Paquette (2010). Categories for the Practising Physicist. In Bob Coecke (ed.), *New Structures for Physics*. Berlin and Heidelberg: Springer, 173–286.

Courser, Kenney (2016). A Bicategory of Decorated Cospans. arXiv:1605.08100v1 [math. CT] 25 May 2016.

Fong, Brendan (2015). Decorated Cospans. arXiv:1502.00872v3 [math.CT] 11 Aug 2015.

Gabbay, Murdoch and Andrew M. Pitts (2002). A New Approach to Abstract Syntax with Variable Binding. *Formal Aspects of Computing*, 13(3–5): 341–363.

Golubitsky, Martin, Ian Stewart and Andrei Torok (2005). Patterns of Synchrony in Coupled Cell Networks with Multiple Arrows. *SIAM Journal on Applied Dynamical Systems*, 4(1): 78.

Hilken, Barney P. (1996). Towards a Proof Theory of Rewriting: The Simply Typed 2lambda-Calculus. *Theoretical Computer Science*, 170(1–2): 407–444.

Hirschowitz, Tom (2013). Cartesian Closed 2-categories and Permutation Equivalence in Higher-order Rewriting. *Logical Methods in Computer Science*, 9(3): 1–22.

Kent, R. E. (2003). The IFF Foundation for Ontological Knowledge Organization. In N. J. Williamson and C. Beghtol (eds), *Knowledge Organization and Classification in International Information Retrieval*. Binghampton, NY: The Haworth Press, 187–203.

Kissinger, Aleks and Sander Uijlen (2017). A Categorical Semantics for Causal Structure. arXiv:1701.04732v3 [quant-ph] 21 April 2017.

Koch, J., A. Joyal, M. Batanin and J.-F. Mascari (2010). Polynomial Functors and Opetopes. arXiv:0706.1033v2 [math.QA] 21 February 2010.

Lack, Stephen and Pawel Sobociński (2005). Adhesive and Quasi-adhesive Categories. *RAIRO-Theoretical Informatics and Applications*, 39: 511–545.

Lerman, Eugene (2017). Networks of Open Systems. arXiv:1705.04814v1 [math.OC] 10 May 2017.

Meredith, L. G. and Michael Stay (2017). Representing Operational Semantics with Enriched Lawvere Theories. arXiv:1704.03080v1 [cs.LO] 10 April 2017.

Meseguer, José (1992). Conditional Rewriting Logic as a Unified Model of Concurrency. *Theoretical Computer Science*, 96: 73–155.

Meseguer, José (1997). Research Directions in Rewriting Logic. *Computational Logic*, Computer Science Laboratory, NATO ASI Series, 165: 347–398.

Milner, Robin (2009). *The Space and Motion of Communicating Agents*. Cambridge: Cambridge University Press.

Mimram, S. (2014). Towards 3-dimensional Rewriting Theory. *Logical Methods on Computer Science*, 10(2): 1–47.

Myers, David Jaz (2017). String Diagrams for Double Categories and Equipments. arXiv:1612.02762v3 [math.CT] 9 July 2017.

OECD (2013). *Interconnected Economies: Benefitting from Global Value Chains—Synthesis Report*. Accessed 10 April 2018. www.oecd.org/sti/ind/interconnected-economies-GVCs-synthesis.pdf.

Patterson, Evan (2017). Knowledge Representation in Bicategories of Relations. arXiv:1706.00526v1 [cs.AI] 2 June 2017.

Paulheim, H. and F. Probst (2010). Application Integration on the User Interface Level: An Ontology-based Approach. *Data and Knowledge Engineering*, 69: 1103–1116.

Rydeheard, D. E. and R. M. Burstall (1988). Computational Category Theory. Englewood Cliffs, NJ: Prentice-Hall.

Schultz, P., D. Spivak, C. Vasilakopoulou and R. Wisnesky (2016). Algebraic Databases. arXiv:1602.03501v2 [math.CT] 15 November 2016.

Seely, R. A. G. (1987). Modelling Computations: A 2-categorical Framework. *Proceedings of the Symposium on Logic in Computer Science (LICS '87), Ithaca, New York, USA, June 22–25*. IEEE Computer Society, 65–71.

Shulman, M. A. (2010). Constructing Symmetric Monoidal Bicategories. arXiv:1004.0993 [math.CT] 7 April 2010.

Spivak, D. I. (2014). *Category Theory for the Sciences*. Cambridge, MA: MIT Press. On-line (2013) version, *Category Theory for Scientists*. Accessed 10 April 2018. http://math.mit.edu/~dspivak/CT4S.pdf).

Spivak, David and Robert E. Kent (2012). Ologs: A Categorical Framework for Knowledge Representation. *PLOS One*, 7(1):e24274.

Spivak, David I., Christina Vasilakopoulou and Patrick Schultz (2013). Category Theory for Scientists. arXiv:1302.6946v1 [math.CT] 27 February 2013.

Spivak, David I., Christina Vasilakopoulou and Patrick Schultz (2016). Dynamical Systems and Sheaves. arXiv: arXiv:1609.08086v2 [math.CT] 28 September 2016.

Stay, Michael and L. G. Meredith (2015). Higher Category Models of the Pi-calculus. arXiv:1504.04311v4 [cs.LO] 22 September 2015.

Stell, John, G. (1994). Modelling Term Rewriting Systems by Sesqui-Categories. Technical Report TR94-02, Keele University, January.

Stell, J. G. (2000). Boolean Connection Algebras: A New Approach to the Region-Connection Calculus. *Artificial Intelligence*, 122: 111–136.

Stell, J. G. (2013). Formal Concept Analysis over Graphs and Hypergraphs. Conference Paper, August. www.researchgate.net/publication/258801178.

Stell, J. G. and M. West (2008). A 4-Dimensionalist Mereotopology. July. www.research gate.net/publication/249754393.

Vickers, Steven (1989). *Topology via Logic*. Cambridge Tracts in Theoretical Computer Science 5. Cambridge: Cambridge University Press.

Willems, J. C. (2007). The Behavioral Approach to Open and Interconnected Systems: Modeling by Tearing, Zooming, and Linking. *Control Systems Magazine*, 27(46): 99.

Wojtowicz, Ralph L. (2009). Non-Classical Markov Logic and Network Analysis. Paper presented at The 12th International Conference on Information Fusion, Seattle, Washington, July 2009. www.isif.org/fusion2009.htm.

Yau, D. (2008). Higher Dimensional Algebras via Coloured PROPs. arXiv:0809.2161v1 [math.CT] 12 September 2008.

Technical appendix: Category theory and sematic technology

Ologs and the information flow framework

Mathematicians such as John Foley and Ralph L. Wojtowicz who work for Metron Corporation in Virginia and San Diego, have collaborated with John Baez and his fellow travellers to exploit current research on network models. Wotjowicz (2009) applies non-classical Markov logic to detect network incursions under conditions of uncertainty.

Meanwhile, David Spivak's work on the development of ologs as a category-theoretic way of thinking about data management has been combined with Robert E. Kent's diagrammatic re-interpretation of the information flow framework originally proposed by Burstall and Goguen to inform research by *Categorical Informatics*, a company established at MIT. The efforts of researchers in this company to apply the resulting diagrammatic way of thinking about database schemas to real-world problems has led to a series of successful Office of Naval Research grants of particular relevance to the field of semantic technology (ST), including that of Evan Patterson.

Spivak and Kent (2012) interpret ologs as categories and their presentations. Where the more traditional view conceives of a category as consisting of objects and arrows with mathematical structures determined by algebraic laws of associativity law, unital laws, and categorical quotient operations, where functors are construed as morphisms between arrows and natural transformations as morphisms between structure-preserving functors, the olog view of category also begins with objects and arrows, but goes on to define congruence (equivalence relation) on paths (respecting end points and closed under composition from both the left and the right).

This olog category is resolved and presented as a specification, while morphisms between specifications are functors. The presentation separates the *graphical* part (types and aspects) of the olog from the *propositional* part (its facts), thus separating *information* flow from the *mechanism* of flow.

In his downloadable text on category theory, Spivak (Spivak et al., 2013: 20) demonstrates that the concept of an olog provides a linguistic interpretation of key categorical structures including products and coproducts (2013: 31, 35), pullbacks and pushforwards (2013: 39 and 49, respectively). Spivak uses ologs to interpret each of these "limits over a diagram" (2013: 34, 37, 40, 50, respectively).

A type is an abstract concept. Each type in an olog is represented by a box containing a singular indefinite noun phrase. The label on that box is what one should call *each example* of that class or type of thing. Many types have compound structures; i.e. they are composed of smaller units. The text in any given box should: (i) begin with the word "a" or "an"; (ii) refer to a distinction made and recognizable by the olog's author; (iii) refer to a distinction for which instances can be documented; and (iv) declare all variables in a compound structure. An aspect of a thing x is a way of viewing it, a particular way in which x can be regarded or measured. By aspect Spivak observes that we simply mean a function. The domain A of the function $f : A \rightarrow B$ is the thing we are measuring, and the codomain is the set of possible "answers" or results of the measurement. Spivak defines "facts" as simply the "path equivalences" within an olog. Path equivalences mean that the relevant diagram "commutes". An equivalence between paths in a commutative diagram means that if there is more than one path going from one node in the diagram to another, each of these paths are equivalent. Figure 7TA.1 depicts the olog of a product diagram.

Associated with any product is a series of projections. Figure 7TA.2 should suffice to explain the nature of a projection. Here, the product, depicted as a table of ordered pairs, represents a set of playing cards numbered from 1 to 6, which has been selected from each of the four suits. The projection operators are indexed to represent, in turn, the first and second member of each ordered pair.

Figure 7TA.3, taken from Spivak et al. (2013: 40), depicts the Olog of the pullback.

Let I and G be graphs. A diagram in G of shape I is a homomorphism $D: I \rightarrow G$ of graphs. I is called the shape graph of the diagram D (Barr and Wells, 2012: 94). Figure 7TA.4 depicts a variety of shape graphs together with their associated diagrams representing the diagonal, the pushforward (which is dual to the pullback), and the coproduct.

The particular example of a pushout, depicted in Figure 7TA.5, is a union where the cells in the shoulder are not double counted as would occur when using a coproduct (Spivak et al., 2013, olog 2.37: 50). This property is of special importance when dealing with unions of topological spaces to ensure that points of overlap or intersection are not counted twice over.

One feature of diagrams when they appear within a category-theoretic context is the property of universality. For example, consider the universal property

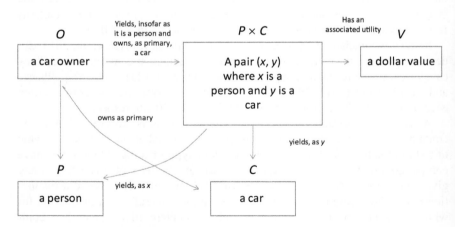

Figure 7TA.1 An Olog Product
Source: Spivak et al. (2013: 34)

$$X \times Y = \{(x, y) \mid x \in X, y \in Y\}$$
$$\pi_1 : X \times Y \rightarrow X$$
$$\pi_2 : X \times Y \rightarrow Y$$

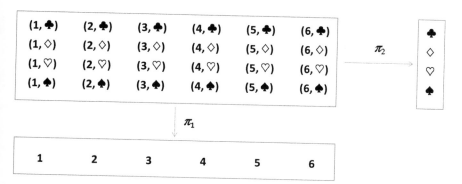

Figure 7TA.2 Products and Their Projections
Source: Spivak et al. (2013: 31)

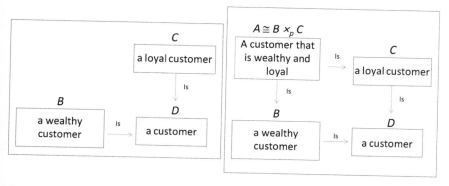

Figure 7TA.3 An Olog Pullback
Source: Spivak et al. (2013: 40)

of products. Let X and Y be sets. For any set A and functions $f : A \rightarrow X$ and $g : A \rightarrow Y$, there exists a unique function $A \rightarrow X \times Y$ such that Figure 7TA.6 commutes (see Spivak et al., 2013, equation 2.25: 32, for a proof).

Spivak (Spivak et al., 2013) explains how the universal property of coproducts formalizes the following intuitively obvious fact: If we know how economy class seats are priced and we know how first-class seats are priced, and if we know that every seat is either economy class or first class, then we automatically know how all seats are priced.

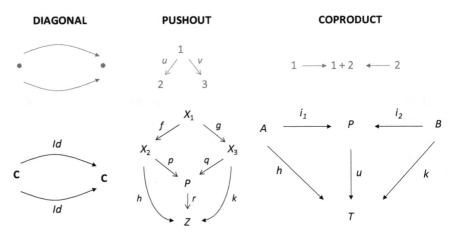

Figure 7TA.4 Shape Graphs and Their Diagrams

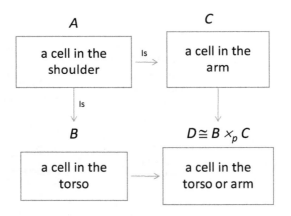

Figure 7TA.5 An Olog Pushout
Source: Spivak et al. (2013: 50)

In his text on category theory Spivak (Spivak et al., 2013: 85) highlights the importance of preorders, partial orders, and linear orders, before going on to interpret a preorder as a kind of graph. Next, Spivak (Spivak et al., 2013: 91–92, 95, 98, 120, 146–147, 188) introduces the notion of a *schema* as a category that can represent interlinked tables of information within a structured database, clarifying how homomorphisms, functors, and natural transformations apply both to schemas and their instances.

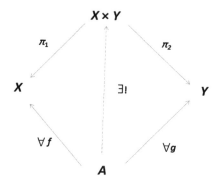

Figure 7TA.6 The Universal Property of Products
Source: Spivak et al. (2013, equation 2.25: 32)

To define preorders and partial orders, let S be a set and $R{\subseteq}S{\times}S$ a binary relation on S; if $(s, s') \in R$we will write s $\leq$s'. Then we say that R is a *preorder* if, for
all s, s', s"$\in S$ we have:

Reflexivity: s $\leq$s, and

Transitivity: if s $\leq$s' and s'$\leq$ s", then s $\leq$s".

We say that R is a *partial order* if it is a preorder and, in addition, for all s, s'$\in$
S we have

Antisymmetry: If s $\leq$s' and s'$\leq$s, then s = s'.

We say that R is a *linear order* if it is a partial order and, in addition, for all s,
s'$\in S$ we have

Comparability: Either s $\leq$1 or s'$\leq$s.

Finally, we denote such a preorder (or partial order or linear order) by $(S, \leq)$.
It will be helpful to expand somewhat on Spivak's coverage of these. Let P
be a preorder. We define a binary relation $\equiv$ on P by $a{\equiv}$ biff $a \leq b$ and $b \leq a$. If
the elements of a poset are thought of as propositions then $\leq$ can be thought of as
meaning "$\Rightarrow$" or logical entailment.
Let P be a poset such that $X \subseteq P$ and $y{\in}P$. Then y is a *meet* (or *greatest lower
bound*, glb or *infimum*) for X if and only if:

a y is a lower bound for X (i.e. if $x{\in}X$ then $y{\leq}x$)
b   If z is any other lower bound for X then $z{\leq}y$

In symbols we write $y = \wedge X$. Let P be a poset and X a subset. Then X can have at most one meet (proof by symmetry) (Vickers, 1989, Prop. 3.3.2: 15). Let P be a poset such that, $X \subseteq P$ and $y \in P$. Then y is a *join* (or *least upper bound*, lub or *supremum*) for X iff:

a y is an *upper bound* for X (i.e. if $x \in X$ then $y \geq x$)
b   If z is any other upper bound for X then $z \geq y$

A poset is a *lattice* if and only if every finite subset has both a meet $\wedge$ and a join $\vee$. A function between two lattices is a *lattice homomorphism* if and only if it preserves all finite meets and joins (Vickers, 1989, Def. 3.4.1: 18). A poset is a lattice if $\varnothing$ and all two-element subsets have meets and joins (Vickers, 1989, Def. 3.4.3: 19). A lattice P is *distributive* iff for every x, y, and z $\in$ P we have $x \leq y \Leftrightarrow x \wedge y = x \Leftrightarrow x \vee y = y$. In a distributive lattice P, $\vee$ also distributes over $\wedge$. The algebraic properties of meets and joins are listed below (Vickers, 1989, Props. 3.4.4, 3.3.5):

i   Commutativity: $x \wedge y = y \wedge x$ $x \vee y = y \vee x$
ii   Associativity: $(x \wedge y) \wedge z = x \wedge (y \wedge z)$ $(x \vee y) \vee z = x \vee (y \vee z)$
iii Unit laws: $x \wedge \textbf{true} = x$ $x \vee \textbf{false} = x$
iv   Idempotence: $x \wedge x = x$ $x \vee x = x$
v   Absorption : $x \wedge (x \vee y) = x$ $x \vee (x \wedge y) = x$
vi $x \leq y \Leftrightarrow x \wedge y = x \Leftrightarrow x \vee y = y$

A poset is a *frame* if and only if (Vickers, 1989, Def.3.5.1: 21):

a   Every subset has a join
b   Every finite subset has a meet
c   Binary meets distribute over joins

Frame *distributivity* is a property which holds when:

$$x \wedge \vee Y = \vee \{x \wedge y : y \in Y\}$$

In such a case, we write **true** for every empty meet (top) and **false** for every empty join (bottom).

A function between two frames is a *frame homeomorphism* iff it preserves all joins and finite meets. Let P be a poset in which every subset has a join. Then every subset has a meet. Such a poset is called a *complete lattice* (Vickers, 1989, Prop. 3.5.2).

Spivak engages in a detailed analysis of categorical interpretations of databases and schemas, which is germane to contemporary debates over the meaning of "digital devices". He notes (Spivak, 2014: 92) that a *database* is a collection of tables, each table T of which consists of a set of columns and a set of rows. The existence of table T suggests the existence of a fixed methodology for observing objects or events of a certain type. Each column c in T prescribes a single kind or method of observation, so that the datum inhabiting any cell in column c refers to an observation of that kind. Each row r in T has a fixed sourcing event or object, which can be observed using the methods prescribed by the columns. The cell (r, c) refers to the observation of kind c made on event r. All of the rows in T should refer to uniquely identifiable objects or events of a single type, and the name of the table T should refer to that type.

Each table has a primary ID column, found on the left, as well as some data columns and some foreign key columns. The primary key column is tasked with uniquely identifying different rows (Spivak, 2014: 92). Foreign key columns link one table to another, creating a connection pattern between tables (Spivak, 2014: 93).

A database *schema* (or simply schema) C consists of a pair $C := (G, \cong)$ where G is a graph and $\cong$ is a *categorical path equivalence relation* (CPER) on G. Let $G = (V, A, src, tgt)$ be a graph. A *path equivalence declaration* (or *PED*) is a phrase of the form $p \cong q$ where $p, q \in \text{Path}_G$ have the same source and target, $src(p) = src(q)$ and $tgt(p) = tgt(q)$. A *categorical path equivalence relation* (or *CPER*) on G is an equivalence relation $\cong$ on Path_G that has the following properties (Spivak, 2014: 96):

1 If $p \cong q$ then $src(p) = src(q)$.
2 If $p \cong q$ then $tgt(p) = tgt(q)$.
3 Suppose $p, q : b \to c$ are paths, and $m: a \to b$ is an arrow. If $p \cong q$ then $mp \cong mq$.
4 Suppose $p, q : a \to b$ are paths, and $n: b \to c$ is an arrow. If $p \cong q$ then $pn \cong qn$.

Any set of categorical path equivalence declarations generates a categorical path equivalence relation (CPER).

Spivak introduces monads on pages 203–204 of his text, then relates them to the categories of graphs (Spivak, 2014: 206). One page later, he introduces the unifying concept of a Kleisli category of monads, applying it to a wide variety of mathematical objects including probability distributions, discrete dynamical systems, graphs, Markov chains, finite state automatons, Turing machines, and multigraphs.

In a series of papers Robert E. Kent elaborates on the underlying metalogic of the Information Flow Framework (IFF) developed by Jon Barwise and Jerry Seligman (1997) (see Kent, 2003). The metalogic for IFF uses modularity to support semantic inter-operability (Spivak and Kent, 2012: 191). As depicted in Figure 7TA.7, an IFF hypergraph provides the formal prerequisites for the representation of an ontology, where hypergraph edges link two or more nodes together with functions or relations determining tuple and arity, with entity and relation types linking substances as universals to qualities as universals and with instance entities and relations linking individual substances to individual qualities (Spivak and Kent, 2012: 200). In turn, hypergraphs are related to one another by hypergraph morphisms, which map source nodes and edges to target nodes and edges.

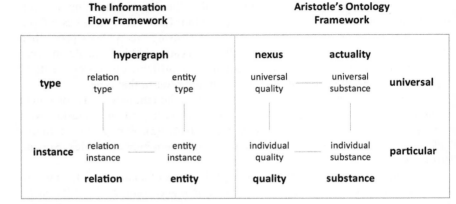

Figure 7TA.7 Information Flow Framework
Source: Kent (2003: 190)

An IFF model is then a hypergraph of classifications where its nodes are responsible for the classification of entities, its hyperedges for the classification of relations, the set of entity instances is responsible for representing the universe of discourse, the set of relation instances is responsible for representing the tuple space, while the instance aspect of model forms an instance hypergraph, and the type aspect of model forms a type language.

Entailment relations are required to conform to a lax notion of satisfaction: for an expression to hold of a tuple the arity of the expression must be a subset of the arity of the tuple and the restriction of the tuple to that subset must satisfy the expression in the usual sense. An expression then classifies a tuple when that expression holds for that tuple. A model satisfies an expression in its type language when that expression holds for all tuples (i.e. has maximal extent in the expression classification).

Spivak and Kent's (2012) interpretation of IT System Architecture is supported by a utopian vision of how the resulting semantic technology has the potential to constitute a working community of participants. As they see it, the technology achieves this by: (i) promoting communication due to the capacity to establish n-way (functorial) morphisms between ologs representing worldviews (a feature that allows for a translation of ideas between group members and assists in the creation of new ideas, with mathematical interactions supported by more specialized olog-Coq interface APIs); (ii) serving as a more accurate human–computer interface (drawing on the semantic web); (iii) overcoming the need for an unachievable single universal ontology, a capability in large part derived from the translation infrastructure associated with the functorial olog connections that were described in the last observation (in particular, the system could achieve semantic integration and inter-operability across each of the ontologies established by individual centres of research.

String diagrams

By way of an introduction to string diagrams, this section reviews the work of Baez and Erbele (2014) on the application of string diagrams to the signal flow graphs (SGF) deployed in signal processing and control theory. The ambient category is $FinRel_k$ of finite-dimensional vector spaces over a certain field k, but with linear relations rather than linear maps as morphisms, and direct sum rather than tensor product providing the symmetric monoidal structure. A linear relation from k_m to k_n is thus a system of linear constant-coefficient ordinary differential equations relating m 'input' signals and n 'output' signals. Baez and Erbele (2014: 2–4) begin their exposition by introducing the five generators in Figure 7TA.8.

The first generator amplifies a signal through scalar multiplication (presuming that the signals, as drawn, flow from left to right). The second adds two signals together while the third copies or duplicates a signal. The last two generators, respectively, delete a signal and emit a zero signal. The operations of addition and emission of zero make k a commutative monoid as shown by the diagrammatic equivalences, in Figure 7TA.9, which express associativity, the unital laws and commutativity, respectively (Baez and Erbele, 2014: 4).

The next set of diagrams, in Figure 7TA.10, reveal that duplication and deletion make k into a cocommutative comonoid (Baez and Erbele, 2014: 5).

The monoid and comonoid operations are compatible, as shown by the labelled bialgebraic interactions depicted in Figure 7TA.11 (Baez and Erbele, 2014: 5).

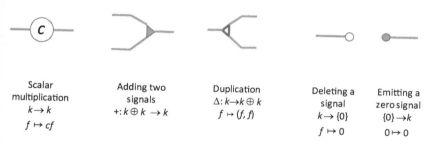

| Scalar multiplication $k \to k$ $f \mapsto cf$ | Adding two signals $+: k \oplus k \to k$ | Duplication $\Delta: k \to k \oplus k$ $f \mapsto (f, f)$ | Deleting a signal $k \to \{0\}$ $f \mapsto 0$ | Emitting a zero signal $\{0\} \to k$ $0 \mapsto 0$ |

Figure 7TA.8 Monoidal Categories for Linear Control
Source: Baez and Erbele (2014: 2–4)

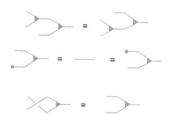

Figure 7TA.9 A Commutative Monoid (via Addition and Zero)
Source: Baez and Erbele (2014: 15)

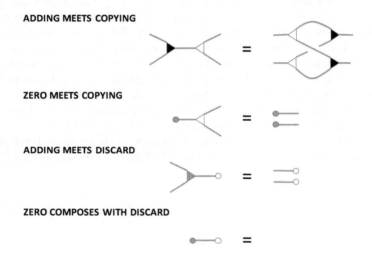

Figure 7TA.10 A Cocommutative Comonoid (via Duplication and Deletion)
Source: Baez and Erbele (2014: 15)

ADDING MEETS COPYING

ZERO MEETS COPYING

ADDING MEETS DISCARD

ZERO COMPOSES WITH DISCARD

Figure 7TA.11 The Bimonoid Compatible with Monoid and Comonoid Operations
Source: Baez and Erbele (2014: 5)

The set of equivalences in Figure 7TA.12 show how the ring structure of k can be recovered from the generators depicted.

Scalar multiplication is linear (i.e. compatible with addition and zero) as shown in the pair of string diagrams in Figure 7TA.13.

Once again, duality reveals that scalar multiplication is 'colinear' (i.e. compatible with both duplication and deletion) (Figure 7TA.14).

Next, Baez and Erbele (2014: 7–8) introduce two more generators—the 'cup' and 'cap'—depicted in Figure 7TA.15, which allow them to represent feedback control. Cup and cap obey the zig-zag relations shown in the figure.

The addition of the cup and cap generators to the other five generate $FinRel_k$, the category of finite-dimensional vector spaces over k and linear relations, as a symmetric monoidal category (Baez and Erbele, 2014: lemma 3, 22). Furthermore,

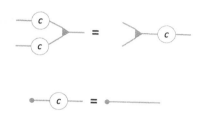

Figure 7TA.12 The Ring Structure of k
Source: Baez and Erbele (2014: 16)

Figure 7TA.13 Linearity of Scalar Multiplication (i.e. Compatibility with Addition and Zero)
Source: Baez and Erbele (2014: 16)

Figure 7TA.14 Colinearity of Scalar Multiplication (i.e. Compatibility with Duplication and Deletion)
Source: Baez and Erbele (2014: 16)

Figure 7TA.15 Zig-Zag Relations for Cup and Cap
Source: Baez and Erbele (2014: 23)

Figure 7TA.16 "Turning Around" of Morphisms
Source: Baez and Erbele (2014: 9)

they make FinRel$_k$ into a compact closed category where k, and thus every object, is its own dual (Baez and Erbele, 2014: 8). The cup and cap generators permit any morphism to be "turned around" including integration, which is thereby turned into differentiation, as shown in Figure 7TA.16.

We now have all the elements required to construct a basic feedback control system, which is depicted in Figure 7TA.17 (Baez and Erbele, 2014: 7).

Region-Connection Calculus

Def. A model of the Region-Connection Calculus consists of (Stell, 2000: 116):

- a set R,
- an element $u \in R$,
- a singleton set {n} disjoint from R,

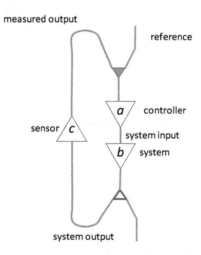

Figure 7TA.17 Basic Feedback Control System
Source: Baez and Erbele (2014: 7)

- a unary operation

    ○ compl : R - {u} → R - {u},
- binary operations

    ○ sum: R × R → R, and
    ○ prod : R × R → R ∪ {n}, and

- a binary relation C on R.

These data are required to satisfy the following axioms:

R1. $\forall x \in R.\ C(x, x)$

R2. $\forall x, y \in R\ C(x, y)$ implies $C(y, x)$

R3. $\forall x \in R\ C(x, u)$

R4a. $\forall x \in R\ \forall y \in R - \{u\}\ C(x, \text{compl } y)$ iff not NTPP(x, y)

R4b. $\forall x \in R\ \forall y \in R - \{u\}\ O(x, \text{compl } y)$ iff not P(x, y)

R5. $\forall x, y, z \in R\ C.x; \text{sum}(y, z)$ iff $C(x, y)$ or $C(x, z)$

R6. $\forall x, y, z \in R\ \text{prod}(y, z) \in R$ implies $C(x, \text{prod}(y, z))$ iff $\exists\ w \in R\ P(w, y)$ and $P(w, z)$ and $C(x, w)$

R7. $\forall x, y \in R\ \text{prod}(x, y) \in R$ iff O(x, y)

R8. $\forall x \in R\ \exists\ y \in R\ \text{NTPP}(y, x)$

N.B. Stell (2000) observes that axiom R7 is redundant. Also, binary relations on *R* *are defined in terms of C*, with part (P), proper part (PP), overlap (O), external connection (EC), and non-tangential proper part (NTPP) defined as follows: (i) P(x, y) iff For every region z; $C(z, x)$ implies $C(z, y)$; (ii) PP(x, y) iff P(x, y) and not P(y, x); (iii) O(x, y) iff There is some region z such that P(z, x) and P(z, y); (iv) EC(x, y) iff $C(x, y)$ and not O(x, y); and, (v) NTPP(x, y) iff PP(x, y) and no region z satisfies EC(z, x) and EC(z, y).

Boolean Connection Algebra

A Boolean Connection Algebra (BCA) clarifies the mereotopological content of the RCC axioms. Formally, it is a structure $\langle A, C \rangle$, where A is a Boolean algebra $A = \langle A, \top, \bot, ', \vee, \wedge \rangle$, C is a connection relation on A, satisfying the following (for completeness, the next two sections reproduce material from Stell, 2000). "In what follows the expression R_ denotes R – {⊤}.

- A1, A2: C is symmetric and its restriction to R is reflexive
- A3: $\forall x \in R\_.C(x, x')$
- A4: $\forall x, y \in R.C(x, y \vee z)$ iff ($C(x, y)$ or $C(x, z)$)
- A5: $\forall x \in R\_.\exists y \in R.\mathbb{C}(x, y)$ (where $\mathbb{C}(x, y)$ holds if $C(x, y)$ doesn't hold)

For a BCA $\langle A; C \rangle$, the relations derived from C can be characterized as follows:

- P(x, y) iff $x \leq y$
- PP(x, y) iff $x < y$
- O(x, y) iff $x \wedge y > \bot$
- EC(x, y) iff C(x, y) and $x \wedge y = \bot$
- NTPP(x, y) iff $x < \top$ when $y = \top$ or $\mathbb{C}(x, y)$ when $y \neq \top$

Theorem 5 (Stell, 2000: 119): Let $\langle A; C \rangle$ be a BCA and define:

- R= $A - \{\bot\}$
- n = $\top$
- Sum(x, y) = $x \vee y$, $\forall x, y \in$ R
- Prod(x, y) = $x \wedge y$, $\forall x, y \in$ R
- Compl x = x', $\forall x \in$ R $- \{\top\}$
- u = $\top$

Then the structure $\langle$ R; $\{n\}$, u, compl, prod, sum, C $\rangle$ is a model of the Region-Connection Calculus.

In a lattice A, a *pseudocomplement* of $a \in A$ is:

- an element $m \in A$ s.t. for all x in A, $a \wedge x = \bot$ iff $x \leq m$
- m is a pseudocomplement of a iff m is the greatest element of $\{x \in A|\ a \wedge x = \bot\}$.
- If a does have a pseudocomplement then it is unique

A pseudocomplemented distributive lattice is:

A distributive lattice A equipped with a unary operation $*$: $A \rightarrow A$, s.t. for all $a \in A$, a^* is a pseudocomplement of a, for which, the equations in Table 7TA.1 hold.

Table 7TA.1 Equations Holding for a Pseudocomplemented Distributive Lattice

$(x \vee y)'=x' \wedge y'$	$(x \vee y)'=x' \wedge y'$
$(x \vee y)''=x'' \wedge y''$	$(x \vee y)''=x'' \wedge y'')''$
$\bot'=\top$	$\top'=\bot$
$x'''=x'$	$x' \vee x''=x''$
$x \wedge x' = \bot$	

Source: Stell (2000, Theorem 19: 123)

Hypergraphs

An undirected graph $G = (G_N, G_A)$ has a set, G_N, of nodes and a set, G_A, of arcs.

- Every arc $a \in G_A$ has a set of two end nodes, or just one in the case of a loop.
- Dually, a set, N, of nodes determines a set arcs$N$, containing all arcs with both ends in N. A subgraph, H, of a graph, G, is a graph $H = (H_N, H_A)$, where $H_N \subseteq G_N$ and $H_A \subseteq G_A$, and where for every $a \in H_A$, ends $a \subseteq H_N$.

Given subgraphs, $H = (H_N, H_A)$ and $K = (K_N, K_A)$,

- their meet is $H \wedge K = (H_N \cap K_N, H_A \cap K_A)$, and
- their join is $H \vee K = (H_N \cup K_N, H_A \cup K_A)$.

The relative pseudocomplement is defined as follows:

- $(H*K)_N = H'_N \cup K_N$, and $(H*K)_A = H'_A \cup K_A$ arcs $(H'_N \cup K_N)$
- where H'_N is the set-theoretic complement of H_N in G_N.

From the relative pseudocomplement, we obtain the pseudocomplement,

- $(H_N, H_A)* = (H'_N, \text{arcs}(H'_N))$.

Figure 7TA.18 depicts the construction of Graph G.

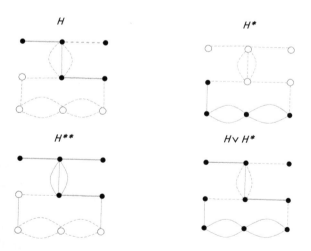

Figure 7TA.18 Construction of Graph G
Source: Stell (2000, Fig. 2: 128)

Formal Concept Analysis and dilation and erosion

What follows is set out in Stell (2013). Given a formal context (U,R,V), R^Δ: $PU \rightarrow PV$ is defined for any $X \subseteq U$ by

- $R^\Delta(X) = \{v \in V : \forall x \in X(xRv)\}$

  For any $Y \subseteq V$, the converse operator $\check{R}^\Delta : PV \rightarrow PU$ is described explicitly by

- $\check{R}\Delta(Y) = \{u \in U : \forall y \in Y(uRy)\}$

A formal concept belonging to the context (U,R,V) is a pair (X,Y) where $X \subseteq U$, $Y \subseteq V$, such that $R^\Delta(X) = Y$ and $\check{R}\Delta(Y) = X$, where the sets X and Y are respectively the *extent* and *intent* of the concept.

Given two sets, U and V, and a binary relation $R \subseteq U \times V$, and given any subsets, $X \subseteq U$ and $Y \subseteq V$, we can define:

$$X \oplus R = \{v \in V : \exists u \ (uRv \ and \ u \in X)\}$$

$$R \ominus Y = \{u \in U : \forall v \ (uRv \ implies \ v \in Y)\}$$

These operations are known respectively as dilation and erosion.

The pseudocomplement, $\neg X$, and the dual pseudocomplement, $-X$, satisfy both $X \cup -X = U$ and $X \cap \neg X = \varnothing$ but not necessarily $X \cup \neg X = U$ or $X \cap -X = \varnothing$.

$$\neg X = H \ominus (-X)$$

$$-X = (-X) \oplus H$$

Figure 7TA.19 illustrates these dual notions of complementarity along with derived notions of boundary, expansion and contraction.

A four-dimensional mereotopology

Stell and West's (2008) work on mereotopology departs from Stell (2000) in that axiom A4 quantifies over all elements including the null, $\perp$, so $R\_ = A - \{\top, \perp\}$. Hence, the null region (uniquely) is not connected to anything. Furthermore, Stell and West (2008) note that, in a Region-Connection Calculus, the parthood relation P is defined from C whereas, in a Boolean Connection Algebra, parthood is primitive. The partial order $\leq$, is definable by $x \leq y$ iff $x + y = y$. Moreover, the following property can be derived from the axioms A1–A5 above for the Boolean Connection Algebra: $x \leq y$ *iff* for all z, zCx implies zCy.

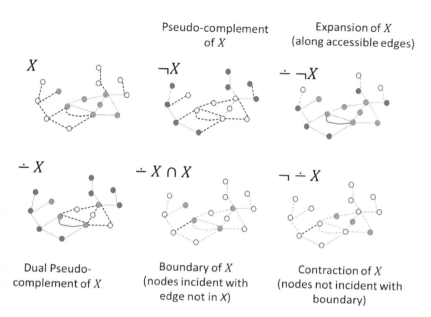

Figure 7TA.19 Complementarity, Boundary, Expansion and Contraction
Source: Stell (2013, section 2.3)

Next, Stell and West (2008) introduce three axioms for **historical closure**:

- **LCL-1** $xCy \Rightarrow xCy$
- **LCL-2** $xCy \Rightarrow xCy$
- **LCL-3** $y^* = y^*$

Historical closure enables them to subsequently define temporal part, historical part, and historical connection. Historical closure is itself a spatio-temporal region consisting of all the space-time that obtains during the existence of a given entity.

They **next** define a *topological* closure operator.

Definition. *A* **topological closure operator** *on a Boolean algebra, A, is a function* $\Theta : A \rightarrow A$ *such that, for all* $a, b \in A,$

- (Θ *is increasing*). $a \leq \Theta a,$
- (Θ is idempotent) $\Theta \Theta a = \Theta a,$
- (Θ is additive):

   i Θ null = null,

   ii $\Theta (a + b) = \Theta a + \Theta b$

Stell and West (2008) observe that the historical closure operator – is a topological closure operator on the Boolean algebra of spatio-temporal regions. Moreover, they note that two entities are *historically connected* if their historical closures are spatio-temporally connected. They use ◊ to denote historical connection.

Definition. (Historical Connection). x ◊ y *if and only if xCy.*

- **Theorem 2.** *Historical connection has the following properties*

  ○   *1 It is reflexive and symmetric*
  ○   *2 xCy implies x*◊ *y*
  ○   *3 (x + y)*◊ *z if and only if x*◊ *z or y*◊ *z*

- Historical Part:

  ○   Historical connection is used to define historical part
  ○   **Def.** $x \leq_{hist} y$ if and only if $x \leq y$

Lemma 3. $x \leq_{hist} y$ if and only if $\forall z(z$◊ $x \Rightarrow x$◊ $y)$ if and only if $\forall z(zCx \Rightarrow zCy)$

Lemma 4. $x \leq y$ implies $x \leq_{hist} y$

- **The Temporal Part:**

  ○   **Def.** for regions x and y, the temporal part of x induced by y is defined to be $x.y = y$

- **Stell's Theorem 5.**

  ○ $x \leq y$ if and only if $\begin{cases} x \leq y, \text{ and} \\ \forall z\, z \leq y \wedge z \leq_{hist} x \Rightarrow z \leq x \end{cases}$

- **Corollary.**

  ○   Let x,y be regions where $x \leq_{hist} y$. Then x,y is a temporal part of y and is historically equivalent to x; that is, $x \leq_{hist} x.y$ and $x.y. \leq_{hist} x$

The respective temporal orders are defined in Table 7TA.2.

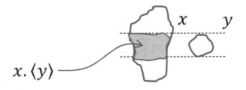

Figure 7TA.20 The Temporal Part of x Induced by y
Source: Stell and West (2008, Fig. 2)

Table 7TA.2 Definition of Temporal Orders

Temporal Order	Label	Definition
Pre-history	pre	Region of space-time extending from the beginning of time to the start of the entity
Post-history	post	Period of space-time from last existence of the entity onwards in time
Extended history	–	That part of space-time covering the period from first existence of the entity to the last
Extended pre-history	xpre	$xpre(x) = pre(post(x)) = $ pre-history plus extended history
Extended post-history	xpost	$xpost(x) = post(pre(x)) = $ post-history plus extended history

Source: Stell and West (2008, Fig. 1)

HST-1. For all x, **xpre**$(x) = $ **post**(x)'

HST-2. For all x, **pre**$(x) = $ **pre**(x)

HST-3. For all x, y $xCy \Rightarrow$ **pre**(x).**post**$(y) = $ null

Galois Connection Axiom (GAL): For all x,y $x \leq$ pre(y) iff $y \leq$ post(x)

Patterson's (2017) string-theoretic extension of description logic

Patterson draws on Coecke and Paquette (2010), where **Rel** is viewed as a "quantum-like" category, in contrast to the "classical-like" category **Set**

- Objects of **Rel** are sets
- morphisms $R: X \rightarrow Y$ are subsets $R \subseteq X \times Y$
- composition of $R: X \rightarrow Y$ and $S: Y \rightarrow Z$, written $R \cdot S: X \rightarrow Z$ or $RS: X \rightarrow Z$ is given by $xRSz$ iff $\exists y \in Y : xRy \wedge yRz$

Rel is a local posetal 2-category such that, between any two morphisms f, $g: A \rightarrow B$ with common domain and codomain each hom-set $C(A,B)$ is a poset (partially ordered set) under the relation $f \Rightarrow g$) (Patterson, 2017: 10).

Moreover, this natural transformation obeys the rules of vertical and horizontal composition i.e. $R \Rightarrow S$ if there is a set containment $R \subseteq S$ and: (i) Vertical composition says that set containment is transitive; while (ii) Horizontal composition says that containment is preserved by composition, while $R \subseteq R$ and also $R = S$ whenever $R \subseteq S$ and $S \subseteq R$ (NB. $\Rightarrow$ can be read either as a generic 2-morphism or as *logical implication*). The Cartesian product makes **Rel** into a monoidal category where $X \otimes Y := X \times Y = \{(x,y) : x \in X, y \in Y\}$. N.B. The tensor product is not strictly associative, only up to isomorphism (i.e. although the Cartesian product is not strictly associative, there is a natural isomorphism $X \times (Y \times Z) \cong (X \times Y) \times Z$, mapping $(x,(y,z))$ to $((x,y),z)$ that allows us to identify these two sets). Accordingly, strict associativity and units must be replaced with *associator* and *unitor* natural isomorphisms, subject to some coherence conditions. In addition, given morphisms $R: X \rightarrow Y$ and $S: Z \rightarrow W$, $R \otimes S : X \otimes Z \rightarrow Y \otimes W$ is defined by $(x,z)(R \otimes S)(y,w)$ *iff* $xRy \wedge zSw$. The monoidal unit is any singleton set, which we write as $I=\{*\}$.

The hom-set **Rel**(I, I) has only two members: (a) The identity relation $1_I=\{(*,*)\}$; and, (b) the empty relation $\varnothing$. Defining $\mathrm{T}:=1_I$ and $\bot:=\varnothing$, Patterson interprets relations $B: I \rightarrow I$ as Booleans. He goes on to establish a correspondence between the Distributive bicategory of relations (**DistBiRel**) and Coherent logic with product and sum types (conceived as a classifying category, $\mathrm{Cl}(\mathrm{T})$, for every coherent theory, T, whose objects are types of theory) i.e. for every small distributive bicategory of relations, B, there is an equivalence of categories $\mathrm{Cl}(\mathrm{Lang}(B)) \approx B$ in **DistBiRel** (Patterson, 2017: 48, 73). As shown in the Figure 7TA.21, Patterson deploys string diagrams to represent the concept constructors applying to Description Logic.

Figure 7TA.22 provides a summary of all the morphisms and some of the pertinent axioms applying to the bicategory of relations.

Concept Constructors in Description Logic	String Diagrams
"limited" existential quantification $\exists R.\mathrm{T}$	
Full quantifiction w.r.t. class $\mathcal{C}$, $\exists R.$ $\mathcal{C}$	
all pairs $(x,y) \in X \times Y$ satisfying $xRy \wedge xC *\wedge yD *$	
Local maximum $\mathrm{T}_{X,Y}$	
$f\Delta_B = \Delta_A(f \otimes f)$	
$f\boxtimes_B = \boxtimes_A$	
2-morphisms for relation $R: X \rightarrow Y$	
Unit & counit morphisms	

Figure 7TA.21 Concept Constructors Applying to Description Logic

Source: Patterson (2017, Table 3: 46, and string diagrams from section 9.1)

Structure	Name	Definition
Category	Composition	$R \cdot S := xRSz$ iff $\exists y \in Y : xRy \wedge yRz$
Monoidal category	Product	$R \otimes S := X \times Y = \{(x, y): x \in X, y \in Y\}$
	Braiding	$\sigma_{X,Y}: A \otimes B \to B \otimes A$
Diagonal	Copy	$\Delta_X: X \to X \otimes X$
	Delete	$\boxtimes_X = \{(x, *): x \in X\}$
Codiagonal	Merge	$\nabla_X = \Delta_X^\dagger X : X \otimes X \to X$
	Create	$\square_X = \boxtimes_X^\dagger : I \to X$
Compact closed	Unit	$\eta_X : I \to X \otimes X := \square_X \cdot \Delta_X$
	Counit	$\varepsilon_X : X \otimes X \to X := \nabla_X \cdot \boxtimes_X$
Dagger	Dagger	$R^\dagger := (\eta_X \otimes 1_Y)(1_X \otimes R \otimes 1_Y)(1_X \otimes \varepsilon_Y)$
Logical	Intersection	For $R, S: X \to Y$, $R \cap S = \Delta_X(R \; S)\nabla_X$
	True	$T = T_{I,I} = \boxtimes_I \cdot \square_I = 1_I$
	Local maximum	$T_{X,Y} := \boxtimes_X \cdot \square_Y$

Figure 7TA.22 Morphisms and Axioms for the Bicategory of Relations
Source: Patterson (2017, Table 3: 21, and string diagrams, sections 3.1 to 3.3)

8   Conclusion

A recapitulation of the narrative

The Introduction set the context by discussing the overarching Post-Cognitivist approach I have chosen to pursue in this text. It introduced the inter-related themes of embodied cognition, the criticism mounted by Herbert Dreyfus against AI, the New AI of Rodney Brooks, which some commentators—erroneously I my opinion—consider to be a resolution of the problems identified by Dreyfus, Edelman's Neural Darwinism, the psychoanalytic position of Freud and Lacan, and other more formal approaches to consciousness and cognition, drawing on topos theory.

Chapter 1 interrogated the Schellingian heritage of Peirce, Benjamin, and Bloch, which, at least in one respect, was taken up by other academics in the Frankfurt School. Theodore Adorno examined the ramifications of his insight into the phenomenon of universal commodification, which first arose when exchange value came to obliterate the last remnants of use value as an influence over the worth of works of art. Not only did this process threaten to undermine the autonomy of creative arts, when compared to their industrial counterparts, it also refracted the characteristics of value in all spheres of production because up to that point in time works of art were distinguishable by the unique use values that they embodied.

Chapter 2 was designed not only to counter erroneous interpretations of Structuralism as both rigid and mechanistic, but also to identify and neutralize any residual Platonic Idealism at play in the work of both Piaget and his admirer, Bourdieu—most obviously at play in his otherwise powerful analysis of symbolic and cultural capital.

Chapter 3 focused on co-consumption, which was initially analysed against the backdrop of Christian Fuchs' reading of Marx's dialectic of production and, in this light, then re-interpreted as a technology-of-self along Foucaultian lines. Here, the intention was to subvert any naïve vision of digital technology under contemporary conditions (i.e. neoliberalism), as a mechanism for democratic collaboration and co-creation.

In Chapter 4, Stiegler's conception of technics was admired for its ability to question the tool-maker conception of human nature. However, the Heideggerian aspects of this alternative must also be subject to criticism given Heidegger's proximity to fascism and the linkage between Phenomenology and Austrian economics. For me, the chosen instrument of critique was the Foucaultian assemblage—conceived as both abstract and concrete—rather than its Derridean counterpart: the notion of an exteriorized arche-trace or inscription. This analysis has now been complemented by the extended discussion, in this, the last chapter of the text.

Chapter 5 examined New Product Development and processes of Integrated Design because these are seen as central to the innovative capacity of the new digital economy. However, where many commentators have drawn on Michael Porter's concept of the value-chain, instead I chose to focus on Kline's "Chain-Link" model of innovation. This served two purposes: first, it allowed me to introduce notions of iterative and incremental design, which pertain especially to the requirements engineering stage of large software engineering and new product development projects. Second, it opened the door to broader considerations of policy associated with Mariana Mazzucato's conception of the 'Entrepreneurial State'. In this context, I reviewed her argument for active intervention by the State in the direct financing of investment and innovation-related activities.

Chapter 6 examined Peirce's work on Diagrammatic Reasoning within a broad philosophical context of "semeiosis" and agapeistic evolution. It extended the discussion of semantic technology, not only by considering issues of pedagogy around collaborative learning, but also by demonstrating the virtues of Peirce's three systems of existential graphs.

Chapter 7 was the most demanding in technical terms, insofar as it reviewed recent category-theoretic developments in rewriting logic and network modelling. Here, the intention was to demonstrate how complex systems could be constructed from a variety of simpler components: ologs, PROPs, operads, and opetopes. The resulting formalisms could then be applied to a variety of tasks including: Formal Concept Analysis; the construction of mereotopologies; the deployment of rich description logics for accessing the semantic web; as well as the estimation of Markov Logic networks, and the representation of a variety of network models including signal flow graphs and hybrid dynamic systems.

In what follows, I want to return to some of the issues raised in the text, but from a position grounded in a history of debates over methodology in the Economic and Social Sciences. To this end, I want to consider the role Max Weber played in the *Methodenstreit* debates. This will provide the backdrop for a return to some of the issues raised by Bernard Stiegler, whose Heideggerian approach to technology was discussed briefly in Chapter 4. I want to reassess Stiegler's contribution defending him against some of his critics before examining how his approach could be reinforced by drawing on the philosophical trajectory that I have defended in this text.

The *Methodenstreit* debates and anti-psychologism

For those ignorant of intellectual history within the Social Sciences, it may come as a surprise to realize that much of what passes for contemporary debate over issues of methodology mirrors similar debates that took place at the end of the nineteenth and beginning of the twentieth centuries. These *Methodenstreit* debates were in full swing at a time when scholars such as Max Weber, Edmund Husserl, and Heinrich Rickert sat on the same editorial board of the journal *Logos*. At stake were fundamental questions about the purported ontological differences between the social and natural sciences, in this context, how human behaviour should be characterized and, following from this, the ethico-political question of human freedom as a possible source of such differences. Other major players in these debates included Wilhelm Dilthey and Carl Menger and members of the German School of Historical Economics, who were anti-deterministic but empiricist, along with Logical Positivists from the Vienna Circle.

These issues were subsequently taken up by others including Whitehead and Merleau-Ponty. Moreover, towards the end of the twentieth century, the very same methodological conflicts would be resurrected in the post-empiricist thinking of Paul K. Feyerabend, Thomas Kuhn, Imré Lakatos, and Karl Popper.

For the purposes of this concluding chapter, I want to highlight one of the issues that arose during the first wave of methodological debates, which specifically concerned the role of psychology in social analysis. It is well known that Frege savagely attacked Husserl's PhD thesis, *The Philosophy of Arithmetic*, after it was first published in 1891, for being too "psychologistic". In this context, it is understandable that Husserl, in his *Logical Investigations*, would question the reliance of Franz Brentano, his one-time mentor, on the immediate and self-evidential nature of inner perception. Nevertheless, Husserl came to rely on the very same property when it came to describing the process of "essential intuition", which was responsible for grounding Phenomenology as a science of "essential Being" rather than a mere "science of facts". In Brentano's hands, this notion of inner experience also served to separate the human sciences from other sciences of the natural world. 'Reason', 'motive' and 'purpose' were bracketed off so that descriptive psychology would have unmediated access to human meaning, conceived in its most abstract form as a process of 'intentionality'. Of course, Brentano's 'essential intuition' and Husserl's 'exemplary intuition' afforded insight into the essential structures of cognition within the transcendental subject rather than the empirical ego, so in this sense we are dealing with a strictly philosophical psychology.

Through his own interventions during the period of the *Methodenstreit*, Max Weber (1903–1906) firmly rebuffed the notion of any difference between the natural and the social sciences (Huff, 1984). His approach was both anti-psychological and anti-nomological: anti-psychological because he rejected the notion of direct, undistorted access to sense impressions, and anti-nomological because he rejected the existence of general "laws of history". This aversion carried over to Diltheyan hermeneutics because Weber correctly viewed it as predicated on Brentano's conception of radical sensationalism. For Brentano and Dilthey, "Inner experience" was conceived as both the empathetic tool and the object of a new descriptive psychology. However, Brentano insisted that the grounding concept of "intentionality" had to be entirely removed from cultural contexts, so that any notions of purpose or motive were displaced by the idea of unmediated access to a 'relived' experience of mental connection. The very same notion also carried over to the naturalistic monism of Carl Menger and the German Historical School of Roscher and Knies. Instead, Weber argued that the very concept of "natural laws" had to be replaced by a causal explanatory model decoding, as causal factors, such social phenomena as 'motives', 'maxims' and 'rules of the game'.

His chosen methodology would be grounded in a hypothetico-deductive approach, but one that would also draw on observed empirical regularities. Crucially, these regularities were to be conceived neither in psychological terms nor as an irrational expression of the soul's "inner freedom". Instead, they were to be construed as socially determined, for the decisive point, for Weber (1975: 137), was that,

> history is simply not confined to the domain of 'mental life'. On the contrary, it 'conceives' the entire historical constellation of the 'external' world as both motive and as a product of the 'mental life' of the bearers of historical action. That is to say, things which, in their concrete multiplicity, have no place in a psychological laboratory.

We can find the same sentiment at work in Weber's (1975: 102) critique of Wundt's argument that "creative synthesis" was a unique product of mental life:

> From a logical point of view, the physical and chemical processes which pro-duced a seam of coal or a diamond constitute a "creative synthesis" in the same sense as the chain of motives which link the intuitions of a prophet to the formation of a new religion. The two sorts of "creative synthesis" can be sub-stantively differentiated only by reference to differences in the predominant value in terms of which we conceive them.

This stance is evocative of Whitehead's pan-experientialism, but it is also one emphasizing the claim that a value reflection that is securely focused on this very question of value relevance, should serve as the ultimate basis for any historical interest (Huff, 1984: 44). The aim of Weber's (1975: 257) intervention, then, was to "combat all those errors which have their source in every sort of psychologism, a confusion between the psychological processes responsible for the origins of objective knowledge and the concepts in which this knowledge is articulated"!

Stiegler: desire and knowledge

Stiegler's Heideggerian approach to technology is also positioned resolutely against both Cognitivism and its mathematical counterparts. On one hand, against Turing and many contemporary cognitive scientists, Stiegler insists that the organ of the brain is *not* a machine. Instead, he conceives of the brain as primarily a living and fallible memory, operating under the sway of finitude. On the other hand, he also observes that machines functioning as brains simply do not exist.

In escaping this dichotomy between life and machine, Stiegler views technics as a condition of (human) life itself. Rather than turning to a mathematical idealization that excludes genesis and is thus unable to think the defining characteristics of a machine, Stiegler calls for an organology (treating knowledge as desire), because the relation between the living and the dead constitutes libido. He posits a hierarchy of three levels: first, there is the human body (brain, nose, foot . . .) as substrate of the 'I'; second, the prosthetic technical system; and, finally, the social or the 'we'. Crucially, the biological subject is not the "pilot" of this co-determining process. Interactions within the body—including brain as body—are seen to produce *jouissance* and the circuit of desire, while internalizing hierarchy within both social organizations and the psyche in the form of the superego.

Turning to Stiegler's summary of his argument in "Desire and Knowledge" (n.d.) he contends: (i) the 'I' can only be thought in relation to a 'we'; that is, 'I' is a *process* (a tendency to become one) rather than a *state*. Within this process, I can recognize myself in particular non-ancestral pasts of my own choosing; however, (ii) *individuation* is never completely realized due to its confrontation with a counter-tendency (much like the Freudian drives) and the individuation of 'we's only occurs through the 'I's making them up; nevertheless, (iii) both are linked together by pre-individual *retentional apparatuses*. Enactment through particular technical objects is forcefully unified and inter-laced by the 'technical system', which in turn, is responsible for both grammatization and the constitution of retentional apparatuses; (iv) 'technical tendencies' (laws of physics and human physiology) are represented by (the first adjunctive relation) while 'technical facts' are, themselves, an expression of these very laws (the second adjunctive relation). For Stiegler, these adjunctive (i.e. functorial) morphisms are responsible for the fact that technical objects are situated at the interface between the organized and the inorganic; however, he does concede that (v) the pace of technical individuation is speeding out of control.

Stiegler goes on to expand on his observation about the Freudian nature of the dialectic between tendency and countertendency in the process of individuation. He notes that the emergence of desire was troublesome for Freud who, unlike him, had no access to the notion of epiphylogenesis (as distinct from epigenesis)! This notion is then interpreted along Husserlian lines, as a tertiary variety of retention responsible for overdetermining both the primary retention (i.e. flux) and the secondary retentions (i.e. the memory of primary retentions). Mnemo-technical examples of what serves the purpose of retention, for Stiegler, are diverse, including both aboriginal *churinga* and mythograms. He notes that through their action, the secondary retentions, themselves, are modified in two different ways: first, there is a process of synchronous repression/reinforcement involving a stereotyping of expectations (through screen- and proto- or arche-memories); and second, there is a diachronous process of integration of trauma types (concentrically set around the pathogenic kernel that was first revealed in Freud's *Studies in Hysteria*). For Freud, the pathogenic is derived from an *intense* exterior stimulus (that leaves no trace). However, Stiegler insists that, here, Freud is compelled to oppose the inside and the outside because he is unable to distinguish primary from secondary (in the very passage from one to another within consciousness). While it is certainly true that there can be no other site for the unconscious than consciousness itself, the id operates as a retentional apparatus for both the living (i.e. the brain) and the dead (here he cites the Lacanian notion of 'name-of-the-father')!

In his comprehensive critique of Stiegler's work Vaccari (2009) concedes that Technics is the metaphor of our times. However, this owes much to the fact that Stiegler views culture and language as 'engulfed' by technics because it is defined as what makes humans functional, speaking, and meaning-making beings. From a cognitive perspective, technics is a tertiary retention to supplement the primary and secondary retentions that ground Husserl's inner consciousness of time and his conception of intentionality. Nevertheless, it is also a process of exteriorization that co-conditions the interior of the mind. In this form it operates along Derridean lines as 'pharmakon' (in the ancient Greek sense that combines conceptions of both poison and cure) and an 'arche-writing'. However, whereas for Derrida, grammē is life itself; for Stiegler, technics is seen as a break from pure life. This, Vaccari points out, is because Stiegler wants to re-configure the opposition between nature and culture as one superimposed on the epigenetic/epiphylogenetic doublet.

Another way of thinking about what Stiegler is attempting to achieve here is to see his reliance on Derrida's arche-trace or generalized writing as the basis for a critique of Phenomenology (i.e. a return to the eidos as the pre-linguistic and ideal source of all meaning). In Derrida's hands, the arche-trace is responsible for constituting alterity or non-presence which provides the phenomenologically primordial with the mark of minimal difference within which it can repeat itself infinitely as the 'same' by referring to an 'Other' that is also another of itself within itself (in the sense of both a spatial and temporal as well as a diacritical differentiation). As such, it is anterior to the ontic-ontological difference between presencing and presence, presence and absence, or the truth of Being and the meaning of Being.

For Derrida, Husserlian Phenomenology is grounded in a distinction between indication (reference or empirical motivation) and expression (purity or the ideal self-presence of the 'speaking' subject to itself). Although expression is privileged over indication, as arche-trace the latter inhabits the former by way of a generalized indication, thus serving as the condition of meaning and self-presence, in turn, constituting auto-affection as non-presence, as the mark of minimal difference.

Vaccari (2009) is troubled by the two-fold approach that Stiegler advances in his philosophy of technics. First, his repetition of the history of metaphysics aims to uncover technics as the suppressed, foundational supplement—the originary prostheticity of thought. Second, Stiegler actively inhabits the work of certain figures (in particular Simondon, Husserl, and Leroi-Gourhan) from whom he adopts and adapts some key conceptual tools, such as tendency, individuation, tertiary retention, exteriorization and program. He observes that this strategy enables Stiegler to advance a notion of technics as the condition of possibility for all individuation, thus, overcoming the difficulty of furnishing a foundation for knowledge that is not circular (i.e. a consciousness that always, and in every case, resides in the *a posteriori* of its contents). He observes that, for its part, deconstruction can only approach technics as a case of writing, the interrogation of whose meaning and origins then merges with a certain type of question about the meaning and origin of technics. To this end, Stiegler sets out to *materialize* the trace partly in an effort to historicize the Derridean approach. However, the problem for Vaccari (2009) is that technics has some difficulty playing the role of metaphysical figure—namely, a transcendental vanishing point of the real—while attempting to provide a unifying framework that sets out to trace the essence and logic of technics across its concrete differentiation and diversity.

For Vaccari, one reflection of this tension arises when Stiegler tries to combine quite distinctive approaches (such as Leroi-Gourhan's, Simondon's, and Derrida's), which have distinctive philosophical origins and fields of application. However, Vaccari also has concerns about Stiegler's mobilization of informatic models that are subsequently applied to a diverse range of phenomena including processes of enculturation, the barrier between the living and the nonliving, and the depiction of processes of technical contamination of the living. To overcome this incongruency Stiegler must work with a formal, universal, and informatic notion of the program. However, in the interest of avoiding any determinism, he is then obliged to inject indeterminacy into both the work of transmission and of reproduction. To this end, Stiegler turns to Simondon's conception of "individuation". Nevertheless, this concept must be narrowly construed as a process of 'inscription' rather than bodily or organizational 'incorporation' (i.e. through social norms, schemas of enaction, and skills). In contrast, Vaccari insists that tools do not remember, instead, whole societies do! Furthermore, in strengthening his opposition to Stiegler's narrow interpretation, Vaccari also observes that Simondon, himself, refuses to conflate the technical (conceived as a multiplicity through his phenomenological notion of pre-individual, tertiary retentions) with human memory and social direction (conceived as a unifying force due to the formative role of productive labour).

Finally, Vaccari takes up Leroi-Gourhan's notion of *tendency*, which he observes was originally inspired by Bergson's *élan vitale*. For Leroi-Gourhan, tendency selects from the forms pertaining to the self-organizational relation of human living being to the matter it organizes and through which it organizes itself. In this light Vaccari insists that it must be logically posterior to epiphylogenesis, insofar as it is responsible for producing a rupture, a new techno-cultural milieu allowing the technical object to affirm its autonomy (if not incompatibility) in respect to the other layers of society. Vaccari suggests that this is all too close to whatever *determines* morphogenesis of organisms in their respective milieus. Human can only be an after-thought for something with this constitutive role.

While all this has major implications for the struggle against philosophical idealism, Vaccari highlights two major weaknesses. On one hand, technics becomes an overpowering ontological agency, which is nevertheless deprived of the theoretical resources required to mount an *internal* critique of philosophy. On the other hand, Stiegler's critique is obliged to fall back onto a liberal humanism offering schemas for correction and improvement of cultural production.

As a final riposte, Vaccari draws on Latour's (1999: 190–191) argument that while 'technical' is a good adjective, 'technics' is a lousy noun, which is not required for the purpose of separating humans from the multifarious assemblages with which they combine. To this particular end, Vaccari turns to the mytheme, setting Inanna (Ishtar) up against Stiegler's Prometheus: both seen as responsible for stealing, through deception, the cultural skills and artefacts from their original guardian (for Stiegler informatics is subsumed by writing, which in turn is articulated by an arche-writing). However, although Inanna steals this *me* from the drunk Enki, unlike Prometheus, she does not require a prophylactic receptacle (i.e. inscription conceived in Derridean terms both as memory and a safeguard of truth). Viewed in specifically ontological terms, however, there is no prior 'we' because the 'we' must first be constituted by the articulate matter of the *me*.

In his recent *Stanford Encyclopedia* entry David Introna (2017) also mounts a critique of Stiegler's approach. He too wants to distinguish between Heideggerian Phenomenology as a basis for critiquing the technological attitude as seen in the work of Dreyfus, which focuses on the technological attitude as it applies to particular technologies (i.e. AI), and Stiegler's notions of original technicity. However, he turns to Ihde's (1990) post-phenomenological analysis of the human/technological relationship to ground his Post-Phenomenological position. For Introna, Ihde (1990) convincingly argues for a turning away from the transcendental towards the empirical, especially the relational, interactive, and co-constitutive aspects of particular technologies (including mathematics) that are subsequently captured by a series of case studies. These aspects are interrogated in a four-fold manner as to: (i) the 'embodiment relations' operating as the media of subjective experience; (ii) the hermeneutic (i.e. referential) qualities of technology; (iii) alterity as the construction of alternative ('I'-technology) worlds; and (iv) processes of 'background withdrawal' associated with the 'taken-for-granted' characteristics of technology. In this way, Introna insists that we can first turn Phenomenology against the Constructivists, and then, overturn Heidegger's abstract transcendentalism.

For my part I would point to the fact that neither Vaccari nor Introna acknowledge the importance of Marx's theory of alienation for Stiegler's critique of Technics, which not only serves to distinguish his historical concerns from Heidegger's aesthetic critique, but also helps to address the deficiencies emphasized by Vaccari. For example, although inscription clearly differs from incorporation, the introduction of human labour and production as metabolism accommodates both, thus helping to moderate any overemphasis on language, while promoting notions of routines and enactment over the merely textual!

It would probably help to elaborate on this point by turning to another example of how this dialectic can be gainfully applied. In Jean Baudrillard's (1975) critique of Marxist political economy, *The Mirror of Production*, the author identifies the co-presence in Marxist thought of an *ethic of labour* (attributing an absolute value to labour and defining play as mere recuperation or absence of work), and an *aesthetic of non-he labour*. In effect, Baudrillard contends that this paradoxical duality cannot become the object of a science that has pretences to surpass political economy.

In this philosophical dialectic of means and ends, he observes that, for Marx, labour conceived as *alienation* and *externalization* can only be overcome through the liberation of productive forces, through a rational, non-repressive, and *qualitative* transformation of blind, necessary, and *quantitative* labour into a 'free objectivation' of powers, which would thus become ends in and for themselves (much like the Kantian categorical imperative that must be imposed not only over moral judgement, but also over aesthetic design).

In response, I would point out that Baudrillard's critique ignores any scope for philosophical intervention that could once again draw upon this dialectical relationship holding between use value (i.e. aesthetic value) and exchange value (i.e. expenditure of abstract human effort). To my mind it is plain to see how this dialectical conception of value, when correlated with the distinction between concrete and abstract labour, clearly explains how Marx could coherently hold to both conceptions: i.e. his ethic of labour and so-called aesthetic of non-labour.

I would also caution against a naïve acceptance of Introna's Post-Phenomenological approach given: (a) the proximity of both Husserl and Brentano to Social Constructivism (via Alfred Schutz) and to (Diltheyan) Hermeneutics; and (b) the questionable contribution made by simplistic forms of Empiricism to scientific progress, beyond the Classical period. Moreover, for would-be critics of culture and technology, an alternative is readily at hand which can trace its impetus back to Aristotle's metaphysics, albeit, one that has been re-invigorated by Schelling's notion of Positive Philosophy, and Peirce's triadic conception of ontology. Especially once it has been it is acknowledged that this Marx-cum-Schelling framework could be gainfully combined with key elements of Whitehead's thinking.[1]

In *States of Shock*, Stiegler (2015) returns to Marx to highlight the latter's prescient views about technology and machine intelligence. He first quotes from *The German Ideology* (1845), to argue that, for Marx too, materialism identifies the first 'historical act' of noetic beings with their technical capacity, despite Marx's famous riposte to Benjamin Franklin that Man is a social animal rather than a tool-making animal! Stiegler insists that for Marx, non-inhuman beings "begin to distinguish themselves from animals as soon as they begin to *produce* their means of subsistence, a step which is conditioned by their physical organisation".

> As individuals express their life, so they are. What they are, therefore, coincides with their production, both with *what* they produce and with *how* they produce. Hence what individuals are depends on the material conditions of their production.
>
> (Marx and Engels, 1976: 37)

I have reproduced the most prescient and pertinent of these quotes below as a precursor to the next section of the chapter, which provides a summary of arguments that have been made in each chapter of the text.

The science which compels the inanimate limbs of the machinery, by their construction, to act purposefully, as an automaton, does not exist in the worker's consciousness, but rather acts upon him through the machine as an alien power, as the power of the machine itself.

(Marx, 1973: 692)

The increased productive force of labour is posited rather as the increase of a force [*Kraft*] outside itself, and as labour's own debilitation [*Entkräftung*]. The hand tool makes the worker independent—posits him as proprietor. Machinery—as fixed capital—posits him as dependent, posits him as appropriated. This effect of machinery holds only in so far as it is cast into the role of fixed capital, and this it is only because the worker relates to it as wage-worker.

(Marx, 1973: 702)

The technical individual becomes at a certain point man's adversary, his competitor, because man had, when there were only tools, centralized all technical individuality within himself; the machine then takes the place of man because man grants to the machine the function of tool-bearer.

(Marx, 1973: 692–693)

A Whiteheadian response:

While technics does not help us to overcome the bifurcation of nature, a better understanding of the 'lure of the proposition' certainly would. In achieving this understanding, we must remember that Whitehead's proposition is a remarkable existent (spanning both the aesthetic and the logical) because it brings two subjects together (the logical subject as the bearer of its predicates) and the prehending subject, or rather, superject (whose concresence is a monadic manifestation of creativity whereby the many become the one and are increased by one). However, to perfect this understanding we must abandon any notion of dualism between mind and body that can only be reconciled through logic for ontology always dominates and determines logic.

One or two Aristotles?

It is conventional and simplistic to view the rivalry between followers of Plato and Aristotle as one reflecting the struggle between a fledgling idealism and a seminal logical and scientific materialism. Although this opposition seemed obvious in the thirteenth century, when it set the natural science and theology faculties of some European universities against one another, the work of Avicenna, Averroes, and Aquinas, among others, continued to work on reconciling the views of each camp, culminating in the integrative monadology of Leibniz and the expressionism of Spinoza.

From a political economy perspective, what seems to be at play in the modern era, however, are two very different and opposing Aristotelian conceptions of what is 'economic': on one hand, an Austrian version drawing on the substance-and-relation metaphysics of Brentano and Husserl (which, itself, may be more accurately viewed as a species of Platonic idealism) and the other and a (materialist) conception based on Aristotle's notion of concrete universals drawing on Schelling and Marx (see Pike, 1995; Medri, 2014; Lumsden, 2016; and Garcia, 2016)!

In a nutshell, Aristotle's notion of the universal as derivative of and secondary to the particular existent or instant which actively embodies it, can be viewed as the bridge between Marx's early work on alienation (conceived as the entailing subordination of concrete labour to abstract labour with the notion that, under capitalist relations of production, accumulation on an expanding scale has supplanted human purpose and endeavour) and his metabolic notions of production in the 1857 Introduction to the *Grundrisse* and mature analysis of the value-form in *Capital*. Terry Eagleton sides with a version of vitalist materialism that he conceives of as passing through Alfred North Whitehead. As he puts it in *Materialism* (2016: 9):

> Dialectical materialism, so some have argued, belongs to a current of vitalist materialism which passes from Democritus and Epicurus to Spinoza, Schelling, Nietzsche, Henri Bergson, Ernst Bloch, Gilles Deleuze and a range of other thinkers. One benefit of this creed is that it allows you to make room for spirit without going disreputably dualist, since spirit, in the form of life or energy, is built into matter itself. It has also, however, been rebuked as a form of irrationalism. Reality on this view is volatile, mercurial and constantly mutating, and the mind, which tends to carve up the world according to certain rather arthritic categories, finds it hard to keep abreast of this constant flux.

The contrast between abstract and concrete carries over to value theory. The importance of Marx's fundamental distinction between use value and exchange value is recognized by eco-socialists as a powerful theoretical weapon against the privatization of the commons. Critics of Environmental Economics, such as Douai (2009), discuss the famous Lauderdale paradox in these very terms. Douai (2009) observes that this two-fold conception of value is based, in turn, on a two-fold conception of labour as concrete (and thus expressive of qualitatively different ways of transforming matter and energy) and abstract (counting as so much productive expenditure of brains, muscles and nerves, with the money-form representing socially validated economic value). For Jonathon Pike, this way of using the distinction between concrete and abstract or contingent and universal is thoroughly Aristotelian.

For Marx, then, a thing can be useful without having economic value but nothing can possess economic value without being useful. This Aristotelian Marxist perspective is clearly at odds with Utilitarian conceptions of the "intersubjective creation of 'truth, beauty and utility'". As Pike (1995: 38) observes,

It is certainly true of Marx's position that it rejects a standpoint of the un-investigated, merely posited, universal category such as utility. In this manner he condemns Bentham for introducing the empty universal "principle of utility" without relating it to the sorts of objects that exist in the world such as dogs and men.

Pike (1995: 95) elucidates this point by citing the following quote from the *Grundrisse*:

> The ahistoricism of the account provided by political economy maps to the alienation of labour under capitalism—whereby labour is increasingly not of a time or place, but of a form and for a purpose, and yet that purpose is dislocated from the human needs of the social whole from which it emerges. Labour is in a profound sense, ahistoric under capital since it is not *for* or *by* any individual in any determinate situation. Aside from its importance to the working out of the labour theory of value, Marx's characterisation of labour under bourgeois social relations as *abstract* is indicative of the nature of alienated labour under such relations. It is abstract for the worker, as well as within the theoretical system. Marx comments that "labour itself is objectless, is a reality only in the immediate vitality of the worker".

And this process of abstraction applies to concrete forms of affective labour no less than it does to other forms of labour. In this light, it would be foolish, indeed, to throw this baby out with the LTV bath-water, especially at a time when new approaches to the LTV (Wright, 2013, 2014) now promise to overcome much of the earlier confusion around the transformation of labour values into prices of production!

Post Keynesian economists have also made important general contributions to the study of the digital economy. Far from viewing BlockChain as a revolutionary technology beyond State and Market that supports new, decentralized and democratic forms of 'platform co-operativism' at both a local community level and across global networks, these critiques have focused on the precariousness of digital labour and the downsides of financialization by: (i) developing more comprehensive measures of labour under-utilization (see Mitchell and Muysken, 2008); (ii) highlighting the fact that financialization has promoted short-termism and speculation (Tori and Onaren, 2017); and, in this context, (iii) recommending Schumpeterian programmes of state investment to boost rates of accumulation and achieve social objectives (Mazzucato and Penna, 2015; Mazzucato and Wray, 2015), while (iv) describing the adverse economic consequences of real wage repression, where growth in wages falls below that of productivity, leading to a decline in the wage-share of national income (Onaren and Stockhammer, 2005; Onaran and Galanis, 2012). They have also provided us with powerful critiques of Thomas Piketty's mainstream efforts to interpret what his data on growing inequality has revealed (see the October 2014 edition of the *real-world economics review*, special issue on Piketty's *Capital*, 69(7), especially Varoufakis's contribution (2014)).

Schelling and Aristotle

As Medri (2014: 809) observes, in his Berlin lectures, Schelling also drew on Aristotle in developing his revelatory conception of positive philosophy as the basis for a critique of Hegelian Idealism. Medri begins his justification of this interpretation with Aristotle's critique of the *Sophists*, who only engaged with logical relations (i.e. connections between subjects and predicates) without proceeding towards substance as the bearer of these attributions. This raises the question of how Aristotle made substance visible as causally primordial. What must be revealed are the $\alpha\pi\lambda\hat{\alpha}$, or simple, still unrelated elements that are necessarily true (because error can only arise in the judgements that connect a subject with a predicate). Although they are mere beings, each is different from the rest and does not express being in general. As such, they cannot be known rationally, but only through intuition and experience.

Medri notes that Schelling, In the sixth lesson of the Introduction of Berlin, maintains that Socratic knowing is a kind of not-knowing, not as a form of ignorance but a knowledge thanks to which we know that we do not know. This, in turn, raises the question of how the negative determination of not-knowing can be translated into a positive determination. This knowledge that does not know demands a positively determined knowledge that knows! Schelling complains that Plato and Socrates always treated this mode of positive knowledge in a prophetic and mythical guise. However, for Schelling, positive knowledge is based on the distinction between 'whatness' and 'thatness', between essentia and existentia, concept and reality (Medri, 2014: 800).

In their ontologically grounded proofs of God, both Descartes and Spinoza fall into the error of passing to the notion that God exists necessarily from the claim that God does exist (i.e. in the syllogism that a perfect Being cannot exist accidentally, thus must exist necessarily, that God is a perfect Being, and so must also exist necessarily). So too, Schelling complains that existence cannot be inferred from the concept or idea and that Spinoza's substance is a mere logical concept.

Nevertheless, Schelling insists that negative philosophy is far from being a mere logical vacuity. Rather, "it entertains a close relation with the Being, to the extent that, in the course of its development, it turns necessarily into the Empirical" (Medri, 2014: 803). As such, it contains the Being potentially, merely lacking the actualization of this potential content. However, it must first recognize its own provisional nature and incompleteness if it is to transcend itself. Crucially, this act is not a mystical one as Boehme would have it, through which "the soul would find itself united with its constitutive Principle" (Medri, 2014: 804) Schelling calls the joint between the two phases of positive and negative philosophy, 'ecstasy', but insists that it is both decided by and describable by reason. Thus, positive philosophy does not deny negative philosophy, rather, it completes or fulfils it. Because the final term of negative philosophy is a simple concept, whereas the first term of positive philosophy is a real existent, the passage between them can only be a fracture or caesura whose interface is the ecstasy.[2]

Medri (2014: 807) observes that Aristotle begins his ascendant path with absolute potency (δυνάμις) traversing through the stirring of nature, before arriving at last at the pure act (εντελεΧεια), which founds each potency. For Schelling, the pure act cannot be the last term in the series but is independent of the series as its condition of possibility and foundation. Although Aristotle recognizes the actual Existent as a fundamental principle, his real goal is the essence. However, for Schelling, Aristotle's substance (ουσία) is a transitive cause, the 'IS' in the special sense of "making-to-be". As the cause of essence it is still distinct from it, but Aristotle erroneously makes it the end point or final cause of his ontological system rather than the beginning point so that it merges with essence and becomes conflated with ειδοσ—a view which ultimately led to Aristotle's concept of the unmovable mover. Nevertheless, Aristotle showed the way to a positive philosophy even though he never arrived at it himself. And Hegel, too, remained trapped within a purely rational philosophy and its correlate—the empty concept—unable to attain to any real content. At least Aristotle then, was for Schelling the embodiment of the ecstasy of reason.

Whitehead and Aristotle's substance

Felt suspects that Whitehead's interpretation of "substance" in Aristotle had a stronger influence on the formation of his own metaphysics than is generally supposed. He conjectures that Whitehead evidently read Aristotle (or perhaps W. D. Ross's book about Aristotle) with the spectre of modern mechanistic materialism haunting his mind, thinking that he recognized in Aristotle's "substance" its remote but unmistakable ancestor. He cites some quotes from Hartshorne to back up this view:

> All genuine interests and purposes transcend the mere self. Egoism rests on a superstitious absolutizing of self-identity and consequent absolutizing of nonidentity with other persons. . . . Whitehead once humorously summed up the ethical objection to substance theories by remarking, "I sometimes think that all modern immorality is produced by Aristotle's theory of substance".
>
> (RFP 72)

The baseless metaphysical doctrine of "undifferentiated endurance" [that Whitehead discerns in Aristotle's concept of substance] is a subordinate derivative from the misapprehension of the proper character of the extensive scheme.

The stuff undergoes change in respect to accidental qualities and relations; but it is numerically self-identical in its character of one actual entity throughout its accidental adventures. The admission of this fundamental metaphysical concept has wrecked the various systems of pluralistic realism.

In other words, for Felt, Whitehead interprets Aristotle's substances:

(1) as self-contained, self-sufficient units of actuality, lacking the possibility of internal relationships to one another, and (2) as entities whose individual histories consist in acquiring or losing various accidental characteristics, while they, the subjects of these accidental changes, remain themselves unchanged.

Felt observes that the proposition that someone is sitting passes from true to false when the person stands up (i.e. changes its truth-value because of a change in something *else*, something other than itself—namely, the person who stood up). Aristotle insists that it is a distinctive mark of Entity that, while remaining numerically one and the same, it is nevertheless capable of admitting contrary qualities, for "it is by *themselves* changing that Entities admit contrary qualities" (e.g. that which was hot becomes cold, for *it enters into a different state*). There is, therefore, *no "undifferentiated endurance" for the Aristotelian Entity!* He insists, on the contrary, that there is *intrinsic development, change, becoming*. He recalls that natural things, especially animals, are examples *par excellence* of Aristotelian Entities. Yet "they not only change, they even move themselves to their own activities".

It should be apparent that this aspect of Aristotelian metaphysics has been pursued by Marx, especially when it comes to examining the displacement of one mode of production by another. For obvious reasons, it is largely ignored by the founders of Austrian economists: the obvious exception being when they focus on innovation under the auspices of entrepreneurial individuals.

So what insights into the digital economy are afforded by this foray into Post-Cognitivism apart from the paired notion that machines do not yet think and that brains are not machines? I have argued above that humans are unlikely to be replaced by machines in planning, forecasting, and learning, in the near future, despite their capacity for decentralized control due to: (i) the incremental and interactive nature of New Product Development; (ii) the crucial nature of the requirements engineering stage in this process; (iii) the incompleteness and undecideability of higher-order logics; (iv) issues of uncertainty; and (v) difficulties in developing mathematical approaches to creativity. Accordingly, there is an on-going need for *tacit* knowledge to be brought to bear in real-world problem-solving.

By way of a recapitulation, let me begin by arguing against the Social Constructivists: (i) under existing social relations of production the alienation of labour is inscribed into the very metabolism between humans and nature; (ii) computational ontologies interact with the register of the Real in both syntactical and semantic terms. This can be seen in Whitehead's notion of the proposition, which brings together two subjects. On one hand there is the logical subject functioning as a bearer of predicates and on the other hand there is the prehending subject; (iii) the relevance of the proposition depends on the extent of the isomorphism holding between former and latter such that any opportunities for both emancipation and enhanced communication must be anticipated and articulated; (iv) the distinction between use value and exchange value will continue to play a crucial epistemological role in this articulation; and (v) while semantic technologies have the potential to transform the labour process, but this will require a broader transformation in power–knowledge relations.

As I explained in Chapter 7 and elsewhere, the terrain demarcated by the work of Stell, Patterson, Metron, VA, SAP Germany, and the Categorical Informatics Group provides semantic technologies that: (1) can link database schemas and ologs to dynamic systems (via instance data for linear relations) and have contributed to the development of the IEEE's SUMO project, while helping to develop ISO standards for the Process Industries; (2) can achieve interconnection (via the compositionality of lax functors), which supports Willems' notion of viewing complexity as the result of combining simple component parts; (3) can extend Formal Concept Analysis, through the deployment of techniques derived from mathematical morphology; and (3) can link string diagram formalization (for (bi-)monoidal categories) to the formal representation of Petri nets, signal flow graphs, Existential Graphs etc., in such a way that these techniques of diagrammatic reasoning can be used to transform 'information' into 'intelligence'. However, what results from all this is ultimately one of the most important political issues for our times.

Notes

1 By the same token, in Chapter 2 I argued that certain aspects of Whitehead's ontological framework could be deployed as a corrective for the incompleteness of Merleau-Ponty's last work on a monistic metaphysics of the "flesh".
2 Spinoza's argument that the existence of Substantia follows from a clear and distinct rather than a fictitious notion grounded in the definition of an attribute could, perhaps, be salvaged if it was interpreted in terms of the third kind of knowledge which, Janus-headed, gazes towards attributes on one side and modes on the other! And Whitehead's notion of the Proposition plays a similar role in his ontology by providing a bridge between the logical and the prehending subject.

Bibliography

Barwise, Jon, and Jerry Seligman (1997). *Information Flow: The Logic of Distributed Systems*. Cambridge University Tracts in Theoretical Computer Science 44. Cambridge: Cambridge University Press.

Baudrillard, Jean (1975). *The Mirror of Production*. Trans. Mark Poster. New York, NY: Telos Press.

Borgmann, Albert (1984). *Technology and the Character of Contemporary Life: A Philosophical Inquiry*. Chicago, IL: University of Chicago Press.

Borgmann, Albert (1992). *Crossing the Postmodern Divide*. Chicago, IL: University of Chicago Press.

Bynum, Terrell (2016). Computer and Information Ethics. *The Stanford Encyclopedia of Philosophy* (Winter 2016 Edition), ed. Edward N. Zalta. https://plato.stanford.edu/archives/win2016/entries/ethics-computer/.

Clark, Andy and David Chalmers (1998). The Extended Mind. *Analysis*, 58: 10–23.

Douai, Ali (2009). Value Theory in Ecological Economics. The Contribution of a Political Economy of Wealth. *Environmental Value*, 18(3): 257–284.

Dreyfus, H. L. (1992). *What Computers Still Can't Do: A Critique of Artificial Reason*. Cambridge, MA: MIT Press.

Eagleton, Terry (2016). *Materialism*. New Haven, CT: Yale University Press.

Feenberg, Andrew (2000). From Essentialism to Constructivism: Philosophy of Technology at the Crossroads. In Eric Higgs, Andrew Light and David Strong (eds), *Technology and the Good Life?* Chicago, IL: University of Chicago Press.

Felt, James W. (1985). Whitehead's Misconception of "Substance" in Aristotle. *Process Studies*, 14(4) (Winter): 224–236. www.anthonyflood.com/feltwhiteheadsubstance.htm.

Flyvberg, Bent and Tim Richardson (2002). Planning and Foucault: In Search of the Dark Side of Planning Theory. In Philip Allmendinger and Mark Tewdwr-Jones (eds), *Planning Futures: New Directions for Planning Theory*. London and New York, NY: Routledge, 44–62.

Garcia, M. (2016). Energeia vs Entelecheia: Schelling vs Hegel on Metaphysics Lambda. *Tópicos, Revista de Filosofía*, 51: 113–137.

Heidegger, M. (1977). *The Question Concerning Technology and Other Essays*. New York, NY: Harper Torchbooks.

Huff, Toby E. (1984). *Max Weber and the Methodology of the Social Sciences*. New Brunswick, NJ: Transaction Books.

Hutchins, Edwin (1995). *Cognition in the Wild*. Cambridge, MA: MIT Press.

Ihde, L. D. (2010). *Heidegger's Technologies: Post-Phenomenological Perspectives*. New York, NY: Fordham University Press.

Introna, L. D. (1997). On Cyberspace and Being: Identity, Self and Hyperreality. *Philosophy in the Contemporary World*, 4(1 and 2): 16–25.

Introna, L. D. (2007). Maintaining the Reversibility of Foldings: Making the Ethics (Politics) of Information Technology Visible. *Ethics and Information Technology*, 9(1): 11–25.

Introna, Lucas D. (2017). Phenomenological Approaches to Ethics and Information Technology. *The Stanford Encyclopedia of Philosophy* (Fall 2017 Edition), ed. Edward N. Zalta. https://plato.stanford.edu/archives/fall2017/entries/ethics-it-phenomenology/.

Kent, Robert E. (2003). The IFF Foundation for Ontological Knowledge Organization. *Cataloguing & Classification Quarterly*, 37(1–2): 187–203.

Kent, Robert E. (2011). The Information Flow Framework: A Descriptive Category Metatheory. arXiv:1108.4133v1 [cs.NI] 20 August 2011.

Latour, Bruno (1999). *Pandora's Hope: Essays on the Reality of Science Studies*. Cambridge, MA: Harvard University Press.

Lumsden, J. M. (2016). At the Limit of the Concept: Logic and History in Hegel, Schelling and Adorno. Thesis, School of Philosophy and Art History, University of Essex.

Marx, Karl (1973). *Grundrisse: Foundations of the Critique of Political Economy (Rough Draft)*. London: Penguin.

Marx, Karl and Friedrich Engels (1976). *The German Ideology*. Moscow: Progress Press.

Mazzucato, Mariana and Caetano C. R. Penna (2015). Beyond Market Failures: The Market Creating and Shaping Roles of State Investment Banks. Levy Economics Institute of Bard College, Working Paper No. 831.

Mazzucato, Mariana and L. Randall Wray (2015). Financing the Capital Development of the Economy: A Keynes-Schumpeter-Minsky Synthesis. Levy Economics Institute of Bard College, Working Paper No. 837.

Medri, A. (2014). The Role of Aristotle in Schelling's Positive Philosophy. *Review of Metaphysics*, 67(4): 791–810.

Mitchell, William and Joan Muysken (2008). Full Employment Abandoned: Shifting Sands and Policy Failures. Cheltenham, Glos: Edward Elgar.

Onaran, Ö. and G. Galanis (2012). *Is Aggregate Demand Wage-Led or Profit-Led? National and Global Effects*. International Labour Organization Conditions of Work and Employment Series 40. Geneva: ILO.

Onaran, Özlem and Engelbert Stockhammer (2005). Do Profits Affect Investment and Employment? An Empirical Test Based on the Bhaduri-Marglin Model. Working Papers

Series "Growth and Employment in Europe: Sustainability and Competitiveness", 44. Inst. für Volkswirtschaftstheorie und -politik, WU Vienna University of Economics and Business, Vienna.

Pike, Jonathan E. (1995). Marx, Aristotle and Beyond: Aspects of Aristotelianism in Marxist Social Ontology. PhD thesis. http://theses.gla.ac.uk/3480/.

Spivak, David and Robert E. Kent (2012). Ologs: A Categorical Framework for Knowledge Representation. *PLOS One*, 7(1): e24274.

Stiegler, B. (1998). *Technics and Time, 1: The Fault of Epimetheus*. Stanford, CA: Stanford University Press.

Stiegler, B. (2009). *Technics and Time, 2: Disorientation*. Stanford, CA: Stanford University Press.

Stiegler, B. (2015). *States of Shock: Stupidity and Knowledge in the 21st Century*. Trans. D. Ross. Cambridge: Polity Press.

Stiegler, B. (n.d.). Desire and Knowledge: The Dead Seize the Living. *Ars Industrialis*. www.arsindustrialis.org/desire-and-knowledge-dead-seize-living.

Tori, D. and Ö. Onaren (2017). The Effects of Financialization and Financial Development on Investment: Evidence from Firm-level Data in Europe. Foundation for European Progressive Studies, February.

Vaccari, A. (2009). Unweaving the Program: Stiegler and the Hegemony of Technics. *Transformations*, 17: 1–30.

Varoufakis, Yannis (2014). Egalitarianism's Latest Foe: A Critical Review of Thomas Piketty's *Capital* in the Twenty-First Century. *real-world economics review*, 69(7): 18–35.

Weber, Max (1975). *Roscher and Knies: The Logical Problems of Historical Economics*. Trans. and introduction Guy Oakes. New York, NY: The Free Press.

Whitehead, Alfred North (1978). [1929]. *Process and Reality* (Corrected ed.), ed. David Ray Griffin and Donald W. Sherburne. New York, NY: The Free Press.

Wojtowicz, Ralph L. (2009). Non-Classical Markov Logic and Network Analysis. Paper presented at the 12th International Conference on Information Fusion, Seattle, Washington, July 2009. www.isif.org/fusion2009.htm.

Wright, I. (2013). Pasinetti's Hyper-integrated Labor Coefficients and the "Pure Labor Theory of Value". Accessed 28 January 2015. http://ssrn.com/abstract=2255732.

Wright, I. (2014). A Category-Mistake in the Classical Labour Theory of Value. *Erasmus Journal for Philosophy and Economics*, 7(1): 27–55.

Glossary of key concepts from category theory

What follows should provide some guidance to the specialist literature. Ologs (applied to products, pullbacks, and pushforwards) and PROPs have already been described in diagrammatic terms in the Technical Appendix to Chapter 7. In keeping with the preceding emphasis on the role of diagrammatic reasoning within semantic technology, the following concepts will be discussed in both a discursive and a diagrammatic manner: operads, opetopes, PROPs, and the respective adjunctions holding between PROPs, Operads and Opetopes, on one hand, and monoidal categories and multicategories, on the other hand. This glossary is motivated by the following observations:

1   We need to understand and influence the nature of the new digital economy (perhaps best characterized by an interweaving of information and communication technology with physical reality).
2   This requires a trans-disciplinary approach that can achieve integration across the mathematical, natural, and social sciences, with a strong focus on issues of policy, coordination, and collaboration
3   In my view, the achievement of 2, necessitates: (A) a coherent philosophical ontology and social theory; allied to (B) an equally coherent constellation of new mathematical insights into the characteristics of the interweaving described in 1; and, (C) the development of platforms to support collaborative learning.
4   In my view, the best candidate for achieving the coherence described in 3(B), is category and topos theory, but this is a highly abstract and complex branch of modern mathematics and there are many rabbit holes into which one can fall!
5   Therefore, to render the theory described in 4 more intelligible and transferable to others it should be (i) simplified, wherever this is possible; (ii) expressed in a variety of forms that exploit diagrammatic reasoning, especially given 3(C).
6   On the downside, while all this will undoubtedly restrict the artist's 'palette', the upside is that it will allow more to participate than would otherwise be the case in the act of 'painting' (moreover, diagrams deploying a wide variety of PROPs, operads, and opetopes are not terribly restrictive for most industrial and commercial applications).

Adjunctions: some category theorists consider their field of mathematics as contributing directly to the continuation of Klein's *Erlanger Programm*, with its emphasis on the pre-eminent question of invariance. Marquis (2009: 28) suggests that, from Klein's perspective, a geometry

> is given by three components: (1) an underlying space, (2) a group acting on that space, and (3) a generating element. Epistemologically, these three components correspond to: (1) a given support on which the various geometric figures can be represented, (2) a structure imposed on this support which gives it a shape, and (3) a choice of a specific "intuition", or concrete representation from which all the others are obtained via the global structure.

He goes on to argue that, in category theory, this function of identifying structures of invariance is taken on by adjunction. Adjunctions obtain in the case where we have two categories with morphisms going between them in opposite directions. More formally, given functors (Turi, 2001: 36):

$$D \underset{U}{\overset{F}{\rightleftarrows}} C$$

we say F is *left adjoint* to U (denoted $F \dashv U$) if there is a natural Isomorphism $D(FC,D) \cong C(C,UD)$

That is, there is a family of arrows $\{a_{C,D} : D(FC, D) \to C(C,UD)\}$ which determines a natural isomorphism of functors (natural in C and D),

$$\{a_{-,-} : D(F\text{-}, \text{-}) \to C(\text{-},U\text{-})\}$$

This isomorphism determines a natural bijection of arrows:

$$\frac{FC \to D \, in \, D}{C \to UD \, in \, C}$$

The *universal mapping property* (UMP) of a functor F: for each object $C \in X$, there is an object $FC \in \Delta$ and an arrow $\eta_C : C \to UFC$, such that for any arrow $f : C \to UD \in X$, there is a unique $f^* : FC \to D \in \Delta$ satisfying: $U(f^*)\eta_C = f$, i.e.

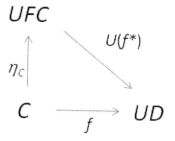

Adjunctions are responsible for some of the most important mathematical structures. The universal mapping properties associated with each of the adjoints give rise to what are called limits (or colimits). Limits (or colimits) can be thought of as mappings between a universal arrow and all the nodes of a given diagram which, as such, afford a remarkable economy. A diagram can be accessed through the universal arrow which is, itself, individually linked to each and every node within the given diagram. Morphisms between limits (and colimits), in turn, allow diagrams to be reproduced and arranged like jig-saw pieces in a much larger picture, including both recursively and hierarchically. As we shall see below, it is this aspect of diagrams that gives category theory so much of its expressive power. For example, in their 2010 paper on an "Abstract Characterization of Thompson's F-group", Marcelo Fiore and Tim Leinster prove that F is the group of automorphisms of A within a monoidal category freely generated by an object A and an isomorphism $A \oplus A \rightarrow A$ (i.e. intuitively, in this particular case the automorphism group of some object is known only to be isomorphic to a combination of two copies of itself) by exploiting the chain of adjunctions (and the inclusion of operads in multicategories) that is depicted below, with *Operad*, being the category of operads, *MonCat* representing the monoidal categories, *MonGpd*, the category of monoidal groupoids, and the asterisk denoting the respective category equipped with a distinguished object:

$$Set_N \; \rightleftharpoons \; Operad \; \hookrightarrow \; Multicat_* \; \rightleftharpoons \; MonCat_* \; \overset{\rightleftharpoons}{\underset{\rightarrow}{}} \; MonGpd_*$$

Adjunctions: (a useful philosophical interpretation). One category theorist who places enormous importance on the role of universal mappings in adjunction is David Ellerman (2006: 173) who notes that universals "construct the object" by representing all the possibilities that might be directly determined (via the UMP). Particularization only comes with the indirect factor map that selects certain possibilities from what is universally available. These two aspects of the adjunction give rise to a composite effect, reflecting the fact that the composition of the specific factor map then implements the possibilities to agree with the direct determination.

Having described the nature of universals in category theory Ellerman goes on to consider the applicability of this concept to certain developments in the Social Sciences. To this end, he distinguishes two mechanisms: instruction and selection. Instruction is applicable to relations between the environment and the organism, teacher and pupil, and antigen and the immune system. In each of these cases the first member of the pair can be conceived as actively instructing the second member about adaptive features, capabilities, or the required anti-pathogenic response.

A selectionist mechanism working within the population, amongst students, or internal to the immune system explores possibilities already generated by variation, already "imprinted" on the soul, or constructed by the immune system (Ellerman, 2006: 175–178). For example, in the process of biological evolution the DNA sequence takes on both roles, first as a determinee, then after the splitting of the double-helix, as a determiner. In linguistics, the Chomskyian notion of a generative grammar conceives of linguistic competence as an innate capacity to acquire language that unfolds according to experience of a child. Similarly, Ellerman notes that in Edelman's conception of neural Darwinism internal selection processes lead to the privileging of one neuronal group over another. In each case, a composite effect obtains whenever a process of external instruction, potential self-reproduction, and internal selection lead to the differential reproduction of selected variants.

Along these lines, Ellerman (2006: 176) summarizes the implications of recent developments in immunology by suggesting that organisms function more like juke-boxes (characterized by an internally structured repertoire of capabilities) than phonographs (which can only play records that have been chosen by some external process). Finally, Ellerman (2006: 179) turns to a telling political example in the form of (heteronomous) governance relations between employer and employee. Under his category-theoretic conception of composition these relations can be restructured (i.e. factored via the indirect form) to form a political democracy characterized by self-management. In this way, once again under the sway of chimera adjunctions, the determinee becomes a self-governing determiner.

In his concluding comments Ellerman observes that his work identifies a series of "unreasonably effective analogies" between mathematical concepts on one hand, and some central philosophical themes, on the other hand. Specifically, he observes that his chimeric conception of adjunction as both organized and self-organizing, achieves a reconciliation between the two poles of the famous Kantian antinomy between external and efficient cause or internal and final cause. At one stage Ellerman also refers to the conceptual structure of determination through universals as a "normative model".

For his part, Marquis (2009: 160) shows how general the notion of adjoint functors is, then proceeds to emphasize the crucial role played by this structural component both in pure category theory and in various direct applications. In this regard, he acknowledges the contribution of Kan who, in the 1950s, first defined the algebraic notions of limits and colimits in purely categorical terms and then revealed how these notions were related to adjoint functors. Specifically, adjoints have important preservation properties and equivalences preserve the key facts about categories: (i) a left adjoint, as a left adjoint, preserves every existing colimit of its domain category; and (ii) a right adjoint, as a right adjoint, preserves every existing limit of its domain category.

From another perspective, we can think of a functor as translating a certain property, or even a "problem", from one category into another. The existence of an adjoint then ensures that this problem has a solution and that, in fact, it is the best possible solution of a certain type.

Another important and related notion is that of an *equivalence* between two categories. An equivalence between categories C and D is given by an adjunction such that the natural transformations η and ξ are natural isomorphisms: in the case of equivalences, the pertinent functors preserve and reflect isomorphisms. Marquis (2009: 161) notes that isomorphic categories are simply isomorphic objects in the category of categories. In other words, two categories C and D are equivalent if there is an equivalence between them, that is if there are functors $F : C \rightarrow D$ and $G: D \rightarrow C$ such that $FG \rightarrow 1_D$ and $GF \rightarrow 1_C$

As an obvious and important example, Marquis considers the topology of a space X (the family $O(X)$ of opens of X) and takes the functor category $\mathbf{Set}^{O(X)}$, from the dual of $O(X)$ into the category of sets. In this category, objects are the presheaves on X; the category of sheaves on X, denoted by $Sh(X)$ being the (full) subcategory of the category of presheaves on X. Moreover, a sheaf (of sets) on X is a functor $F : O(X) \rightarrow \mathbf{Set}$ satisfying the following condition: for each open covering $U = \cup_i U_i$, $i \in I$, of an open set U of X, the following diagram is an equalizer:

$$F(U) \xrightarrow{e} \prod_i F(U_i) \underset{q}{\overset{p}{\rightrightarrows}} \prod_{i,j} F(U_i \cap U_j) \text{ where for } t \in F(U),$$

$$e(t) = \left\{ t \big|_{U_i} \big| i \in I \right\} \text{ and for } p(t_i) = \left\{ t_i \big|_{U_i \cap U_j} \right\} U_j,$$

$$q\{t_i\} = \left\{ t_j \big|_{(U_i \cap U_j)} \right\}$$

Marquis (2009: 154) examines a variety of fundamental adjoints in his text on category theory. Kan himself drew attention to the adjoints setting up a natural bijection between continuous maps and those defined by complex singular complexes, which (i) helped to clarify and prove known results that are judged significant by at least one community of mathematicians (i.e. algebraic topologists); (ii) made it possible to solve problems that were still unsolved and non-trivial; and (iii) was sufficiently due to then functorial properties of the construction (Marquis, 2009: 138). For our purposes, the most telling example is the functor Marquis labels "points of a space", represented by $\mathbf{Hom}(1, -)$: $\mathbf{Top} \rightarrow \mathbf{Set}$. In this instance, the right-adjoint G: $\mathbf{Set} \rightarrow \mathbf{Top}$ associates to a set Y the topological space $G(Y)$ with the indiscrete topology; while the left-adjoint F : $\mathbf{Set} \rightarrow \mathbf{Top}$ associates to a set Y the space $F(Y)$ with the discrete topology. Moreover, functor F itself has a left adjoint. More specific sets of so-called "triple" adjunctions pertain to homotopy type theory.

A Category: a category consists of a collection of objects and a collection of morphisms. Every morphism has a source object and a target object. If f is a morphism with x as its source and y as its target, we write $f : x \rightarrow y$, and we say that f is a morphism from x to y. In a category, we can compose a morphism $g: x \rightarrow y$ and a morphism $f: y \rightarrow z$ to get a morphism $f \circ g: x \rightarrow z$ Composition is associative and satisfies the left and right unit laws. More formally, a category X consists of (i) a collection Obj_C of objects $A, B, C, \ldots, X, Y, \ldots$; and, for each pair of objects A and B, a collection $X(A;B)$ of arrows $f: A \rightarrow B$ from A to B; where A is the domain and B is the codomain of $f: A \rightarrow B$ (this collection of all arrows $f, g, h, k, \ldots$ of X is denoted by $Arr_{<\sigma \cup \beta > X </\sigma \cup \beta>}$, and arrows are also called maps or morphisms); (iii) for each object A, an identity arrow $id_A : A \rightarrow A$; (iv) for each pair of arrows:

$$A \xrightarrow{f} B \xrightarrow{g} C \text{ a composite arrow } g \circ f: A \rightarrow C.$$

These data have to satisfy the following generalized (monoid) laws:

1   Identity: if $A \xrightarrow{f} B$, then $id_B \circ f = f = f \circ id_A$ f

2   Associativity: if $A \xrightarrow{f} B \xrightarrow{g} C \xrightarrow{h} D$, then $(h \circ g) \circ f = h \circ (f \circ g)$ (Turi, 2001: 8)

Endomorphism: An endomorphism of an object x in a category C is a morphism $f: x \rightarrow x$ An endomorphism that is also an **isomorphism** is called an automorphism.

Isomorphism: An isomorphism is an invertible morphism, hence a morphism with an inverse morphism.

A Lawvere Theory: In his 1963 doctoral dissertation, Bill Lawvere introduced a new categorical method for doing universal algebra, alternative to the usual way of presenting an algebraic concept by means of its logical signature (with generating operations satisfying equational axioms). The rough idea is to define an algebraic theory as a category with finite products and possessing a "generic algebra" (e.g. a generic group), and then define a model of that theory (e.g. a group) as a product-preserving functor out of that category. This type of category is what is nowadays called a Lawvere algebraic theory, or just Lawvere theory (Yusufzai, 2017). Formally, a Lawvere theory consists of a small category L with (necessarily strictly associative) finite products and a strict finite-product preserving identity-on-objects functor $I : \aleph_0{}^{op} \rightarrow L$. A map of Lawvere theories from L to L' is a (necessarily strict) finite-product preserving functor from L to L' that commutes with the functors I and I' (Lawvere, 1963). In 1966, Linton made the general connection between monads and Lawvere theories: every Lawvere theory gives rise to a monad on **Set** whose category of algebras is equivalent to the category of models of the Lawvere theory, and, subject to a generalization in the definition of Lawvere theory, every monad arises thus, uniquely up to coherent isomorphism (Behrisch et al., 2012)

A Monad: A monad on a category **C** (see Turi, 2001: 41): is a three-tuple (T, η, μ) where: $T: C \rightarrow C$ *is a functor*, and, η: Id $\rightarrow T$ is *unit* while μ: $T^2 \rightarrow T$ is *multiplication*. This tuple of operators satisfies the isomorphisms embodied in the commutative diagrams in Figure G.1.

Given a monad $T = (T; \eta; \mu)$ on a category C, the (Eilenberg-Moore) category T-**Alg** (or CT) of T-algebras has objects $X = \langle X, h \rangle$; given by an object X of C and a morphism $h : TX \rightarrow X$ of C satisfying the T-algebra laws in Figure G.2.

The (homo)morphisms $f : \langle X, h \rangle \rightarrow \langle X', h' \rangle$ of T-**Alg** are then given by morphisms $f : X \rightarrow X'$, such that the diagram commutes (see Figure G.3).

For example, the functor Paths: Grph→Grph, which send a graph to its paths-graph is the functor part of a monad that represents the category of graphs. The unit

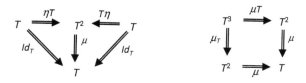

Figure G.1 Commutative Diagrams Satisfied by a Monad
Source: Turi, 2001: 41

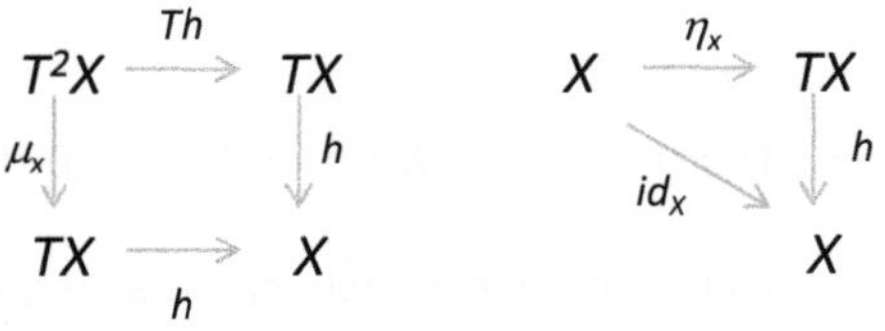

$$T^2X \xrightarrow{\;Th\;} TX$$

$$\mu_x \downarrow \qquad \downarrow h$$

$$TX \xrightarrow[\;h\;]{} X$$

$$X \xrightarrow{\;\eta_x\;} TX$$

$$\quad {}_{id_x}\searrow \quad \downarrow h$$

$$\qquad\qquad X$$

Figure G.2 T-Algebra Laws
Source: Turi, 2001, Def. 9.2.: 41

$$TX \xrightarrow{\;Tf\;} TX'$$

$$h \downarrow \qquad \downarrow h'$$

$$X \xrightarrow[\;f\;]{} X'$$

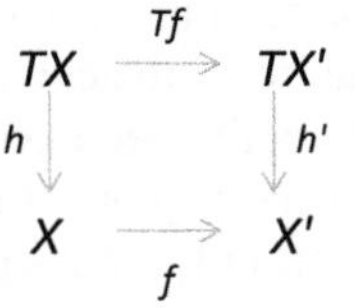

Figure G.3 Homomorphisms of a T-Algebra
Source: Turi, 2001, Def. 9.2.: 41

map η includes a graph into its paths-graph using the observation that every arrow is a path of length 1. And the multiplication map μ concatenates paths of paths.

On the basis of a preliminary discussion of monads, Spivak introduces the *Kleisli Category* associated to the monad T, denoted **Kls(T)** and defined as follows (Spivak, 2014): (i) Objects are sets: Ob(**Kls(T)**) = Ob(Set) and for any sets X, $Y \in$ Ob(**Kls(T)**) we put $\mathrm{Hom}_{\mathbf{KLS(T)}} (X, Y) = \mathrm{Hom}_{\mathrm{Set}}(X, T(Y))$; (ii) Given morphisms $f: X \to Y$ and $g: Y \to Z$ the composite $g \circ f$ is defined as follows: in the category **Set**, $f: X \to T(Y)$ and $g: Y \to T(Z)$, so take $g^*: T(Y) \to T(Z)$ which yields the composite below so that $g \circ f$ in Set becomes the composite of f and g^*:

$$T(Y) \xrightarrow{\;T(g)\;} T(T(Z)) \xrightarrow{\;\mu\;} (T(Z)$$

The following table depicts the relationship between different mathematical constructs and correlated notions of monads that come into play within the pertinent version of the Kleisli Category (Spivak, 2014: 2):

Table G.1 Versions of Kleisli Categories

Mathematical Construct	Monad T
Discrete Dynamical System	Atomic
Graph	Multiset
Markov Chain	Dist
Finite State Automaton	Inp^u
Turing Machine	$\mathrm{Tur}^{(0,1)}$ L, R, W1, W2
Jordan Canonical Form	Vect
Multigraph	Free rig

Source: Spivak (2014: 2)

Monoids: a monoid is a set X, equipped with a function:

$\times: X \times X \to X$ (monoidal multiplication)

and a distinguished element e (monoid identity) such that,

$x(yz)=(xy)z$ for all x,y,z

$xe = x = ex$ for all x

X' is a submonoid of the monoid X if X contains the identity and is closed under multiplication: if $x1,x2$ are in X then $x1,x2$ are in X'. Monoids and their homomorphisms form a category **Mon**. A monoid is a category with one object.

   A (Weak) Monoidal Category: A monoidal category consists of (Coecke and Paquette, 2011):

1 A category C
2 A **tensor product** functor $:CC \to C$
3 A **unit object** $I \in C$
4 A natural isomorphism called the **associator** assigning to each triple of objects X, Y, $Z \in C$ an isomorphism:
5 $\alpha_{X,Y,Z}: (X\,Y)Z \to X(Y\,Z)$
6 Natural isomorphisms called the **left** and **right units** assigning to each object $X \in C$ isomorphisms:
7 $l_X: IX \to X$
8 $r_X: XI \to X$

   Such that the triangle and pentagon equations hold (see Figure G.4).
Multicategory: A multicategory (depicted in Fig. G.1.) consists of:

- A class C_0, whose elements are called the objects of C for each $n \in N$ and $a1, \ldots, an$, $a \in C_0$, a class $C(a_1, \ldots, a_n; a)$, whose elements θ are called arrows or maps and depicted as $a_1, \cdots, a_n \xrightarrow{\theta} a$ satisfying the following (Leinster, 2003: 35–36; Crutwell and Shulman, 2010):

   o Identity: it possesses for each $a \in C_0$, an element $1_a \in C(a, a)$, called the identity on a satisfying for $\theta: a_1,\ldots,a_n \to a$, $\theta \circ \left(1_{a_1}\ldots 1_{a_n}\right) = \theta = 1_a \circ (\theta)$
   o Associativity:

$$\theta \circ \left(\theta_1 \circ \left(\theta_1^1,\ldots,\theta_1^{k_1}\right),\ldots,\theta_n \circ \left(\theta_n^1,\ldots,\theta_n^{k_1}\right)\right) = \left(\theta \circ \left(\theta_1,\ldots,\theta_n\right)\right) \circ$$
$$\left(\theta_1^1,\ldots,\theta_1^{k_1},\ldots,\theta_n^1,\ldots,\theta_n^{k_1}\right)$$

   o Composition:

$$C\left(a_1,\ldots,a_n;a\right) \times C\left(a_1^1,\ldots,a_1^{k_1};a_1\right) \times \cdots$$
$$\times C\left(a_n^1,\ldots,a_n^{k_n};a_n\right) \to C\left(a_1^1,\ldots,a_1^{k_1},\ldots,a_n^1,\ldots,a_n^{k_n};a\right)$$

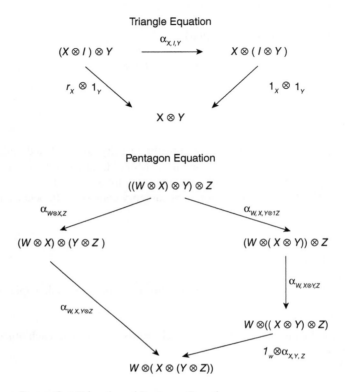

Figure G.4 Triangle and Pentagon Equations

A Natural Transformation: Natural transformations are maps between functors; one way to think of them is as a deformation of one construction (construed as a functor) into another. A sketch is a graph with imposed commutativity and other conditions; it is a way of expressing structure. Models of the structure are given by functors, and homomorphisms between them by natural transformations (Mac Lane and Moerdijk, 1992: 93).

Network Models: In their 2012 paper on the application of quantum-theoretic techniques to the analysis of network models, Baez and Biamonte discuss Stochastic Petri nets, Markov chains, Reaction Networks, Chemical Graphs, and Electrical Circuits, while reviewing a range of relevant mathematical theories and techniques, including the Anderson-Craciun-Kurtz Theorem, the Deficiency Zero Theorem, Dirichlet Forms, Renormalization groups, and Noether theorem for Markov processes.

For Baez, Moeller and Pollard (2017), a network model is a lax symmetric monoidal functor from the free symmetric monoidal category on some set to the category of categories, **Cat**. The construction of the operad corresponding to this functor proceeds via a symmetric monoidal version of the Grothendieck (functorial)

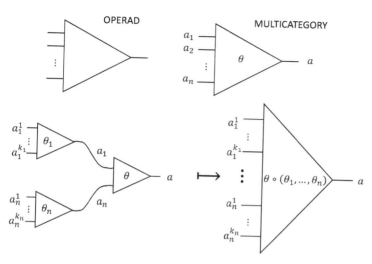

Figure G.5 Operads and Multicategories
Source: Leinster (2003: vi; and Fig. 2-B: 36)

construction, where vertices represent entities of various types (e.g. fixed or moving agents) and the edges represent relationships between these entities (e.g. that one agent is committed to take some action involving the other) including communication channels. To the above list of different network models they add open thermodynamic systems (characterized by non-equilibrium steady states, Open Dynamical Systems, Signal Flow Graphs, and Networks of Networks.

Operads: An operad is a mathematical mechanism used to describe algebraic structures in symmetric monoidal categories. It is a set of abstract operations of arbitrarily many arguments; equipped with a notion of how to compose these; and subject to evident associativity and unitality conditions. An algebra over an operad is then a concrete realization of these abstract operations. Markl, Shnider and Stasheff (2002) note:

> [T]he concept [of an operad] first arose a century ago in A. N. Whitehead's "A Treatise on Universal Algebra" [Whi98], published in 1898. Whitehead was actually describing quadratic operads in the category of vector spaces, specifically those generated by a single binary product. In sections 20–22, under the title "complete algebraic system", he fixes a product and refers to the order of higher products determined by iterated compositions thereof. In section 92 (p. 172) he defines "invariant equations of condition"; in modern language these are exactly the relations on the free operad on a single binary operation needed to produce the operad in question. He goes on in section 93 to add associativity explicitly and studies the resulting theory of symmetric and exterior algebras.

Spivak (2013) defines the Operad $\mathcal{O}$, (satisfying associativity and identity rules) in terms of objects, morphisms and functions:

- Objects: $y \in Ob(o)$, n-indexed set $x: n \rightarrow Ob(O)$
- Morphisms: $O_n(x{:}y) \in Ob(Set)$: $x \rightarrow y$
- Functions: for each $i \in n$; $s: m \rightarrow n$, with $m_i := s^{-1}(i)$; $x_i = m_i \rightarrow Ob(O)$

With composition defined as shown in Figure G.6 and illustrated by a cospan diagram:

$$\circ : \mathcal{O}_n(y;z) \times \prod_{i \in n} \mathcal{O}_{m_i}(x_i; y(i)) \rightarrow \mathcal{O}_m(x;z)$$

The process of composition using operads is probably best appreciated using a diagrammatic example, also from Spivak (2013), which reveals how a complex circuit φ' obtains when three small circuits, $\varphi_1, \varphi_2, \varphi_3$, are "plugged-in" to or composed with a larger circuit $\varphi : (X_1, X_2, X_3)$, with $X_1 = \{r,s,t\}$, $X_2 = \{u,v\}$, $X_3 = \{w,x,y,z\}$; resulting in $\varphi \circ (\varphi_1, \varphi_2, \varphi_3)$

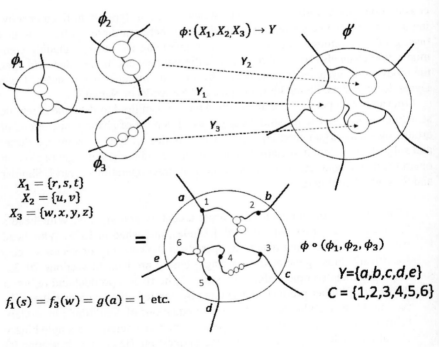

Figure G.6 Operads as "Plug-and-Play" Circuits

Source: Spivak (2003, Picture 6: 8)

To explain the importance and ubiquity of operads, Loday and Valette (2012: iii) state:

> An operad is an algebraic device which encodes a type of algebras. Instead of studying the properties of a particular algebra, we focus on the universal operations that can be performed on the elements of any algebra of a given type. The information contained in an operad consists in these operations and all the ways of composing them. The classical types of algebras, that is associative algebras, commutative algebras and Lie algebras, give the first examples of algebraic operads. Recently, there has been much interest in other types of algebras, to name a few: Poisson algebras, Gerstenhaber algebras, Jordan algebras, pre-Lie algebras, Batalin-Vilkovisky algebras, Leibniz algebras, dendriform algebras and the various types of algebras up to homotopy. The notion of operad permits us to study them conceptually and to compare them.

To motivate the structure of their research monograph, Loday and Valette (2012: iv) ask the rhetorical question, "starting with a chain complex equipped with some compatible algebraic structure, can this structure be transferred to any homotopy equivalent chain complex?" In general, they suggest, "the answer is negative". However, for associative algebras, they note that "this higher structure is encoded into the notion of associative algebra up to homotopy, alias A-infinity algebra, unearthed by Stasheff in the 1960s". Also, for Lie algebras, "it gives rise to the notion of L-infinity algebras, which was successfully used in the proof of the Kontsevich formality theorem". In fact, they insist that "It is exactly the problem of governing these higher structures that prompted the introduction of the notion of operad".

Loday and Valette (2012) establish the Koszul duality of associative algebras (in chapters 1–4 of their text); they go on to study the relationship between so-called algebraic operads and their Koszul duality (in chapters 5, 6, 7, and 8); then examine the homotopy theory of algebras over an operad (in chapters 9, 10, 11, and 12) before considering various examples of operads (in chapters 9 and 13).

For his part, Valette (2012: 17) notes that a Riemann surface, $R_{g,n,m}$, characterized by genus g, with n input holes and m output holes forms a properad, whose composition maps "are defined by sewing the Riemann surface along the holes". Furthermore, he observes that a Conformal Field Theory—as defined by Graeme Segal (2004) in, is nothing but an algebra over the properad $R_{g,n,m}$ of Riemann surfaces. He affirms that a prop is like a properad, apart from the fact that one can also compose along non-necessarily connected graphs. This is the actual operadic notion which was first introduced, by Saunders Mac Lane (1965: 17), as a symmetric monoidal category C, whose objects are the natural numbers and whose monoidal product is their sum.

Operads—Coloured: Coloured operads are a generalization of the above where the operad is allowed to possess several objects—called colours in operad theory. This models algebraic structures where elements of different types may be fed into n-ary operations. The simplest operad of all is the initial operad, I, which, in syntactic terms is the operad with only one type and only one operation, the identity and, in semantic terms, is the operad whose algebras are just sets, without any extra structure at all. Starting with I and iterating the slice operad construction ($j - 1$) times, Baez and Dolan (1997) obtain an operad whose operations they call 'j-dimensional opetopes'. A 0-dimensional opetope is just a point, whereas a 1-dimensional opetope is just an oriented interval. For $j > 1$, a j-dimensional opetope may have any number of 'infaces' but only one 'outface', thus representing a way of pasting together its infaces—certain ($j - 1$)-dimensional opetopes—to obtain its outface. In accordance with this recursive approach, they define a weak n-category an 'opetopic set' with certain extra properties.

Opetopes: are combinatorial structures parametrizing higher-dimensional many-in/one-out operations, and can be seen as higher-dimensional generalizations of trees. As Leinster (2003: 177) argues, opetopes "are something like simplices: they are a completely canonical family of polytopes, as pervasive in higher-dimensional algebra as simplices are in geometry". The term can be thought of as an abbreviation of 'OPEration polyTOPE'. Moreover, "[o]petopes were invented by Baez and Dolan [1997] so that they could frame a definition of weak n-category" (Leinster, 2003: 177). Like an operad in reverse, they arise from computads (a strict ω-category which is dimension-wise free) and higher-dimensional pasting theory which, in combination, capture the operadic notion introduced directly above, of operations with many inputs and a single output. Underpinning this mathematical construct is the famous 593-page letter Grothendieck sent to David Quillen, "Pursuing Stacks", in which he dreamt of a generalization of Galois theory,

> Underlying the connection between homotopy theory and n-category theory is a hypothesis made quite explicit by Grothendieck: to any topological space one should be able to associate an n-category having points as objects, paths between points as 1-morphisms, certain paths of paths as 2-morphisms, and so on, with certain homotopy classes of n-fold paths as n-morphisms. This should be a special sort of weak n-category called a "weak n-groupoid", in which all j-morphisms ($0 < j \le n$) are equivalences. Moreover, the process of assigning to each space its "fundamental n-groupoid", as Grothendieck called it, should set up a complete correspondence between the theory of homotopy n-types (spaces whose homotopy groups vanish above the nth) and the theory of weak n-groupoids. This hypothesis explains why all the coherence laws for weak n-groupoids should be deducible from homotopy theory. It also suggests that weak n-categories will have features not found in homotopy theory, owing to the presence of j-morphisms that are not equivalences.
>
> (Baez and Dolan, 1997: 3)

Baez and Dolan (1998) work with the so-called slice construction O^+ in their approach to higher category theory. O^+ is considered a *higher operad*, in the sense that the operations in O are now the colours in O^+, while operations in O^+ are the *reduction laws* in O, which are equations stating that the composite of certain operations is equal to some operation. Yau (2008) shows that there is an analogous slice construction for coloured PROPs, giving rise to *higher PROPs*. The algebras of the (P)-coloured PROP P^+ are exactly the C-coloured PROPs over P (where C is a non-empty set whose elements are the colours). Kock et al. (2010) give an elementary and direct combinatorial definition of opetopes in terms of (non-planar = unordered) trees, which they argue is well-suited for graphical manipulation using a representation in terms of a sequence of trees with circles (metatrees) and explicit computation. Their approach to opetopes, a modification of the original Baez and Dolan (1997) construction, is also based on the notion of 'zooming' between constellations (where a constellation is just a superposition of a tree with a nesting with a common set of dots, and such that each sphere cuts a subtree) (Kock et al., 2010: 7). A *zoom* from constellation A to constellation B, written A $\circ\!\!-\!\!\bullet$ B, is a correspondence between the underlying nesting of A and the underlying tree of B. The move from A to B is based on two bijections:

- dots(A) $\rightarrow$ leaves(B)
- spheres(A) $\rightarrow$ dots(B)

A *zoom complex* of degree $n \geq 0$ is then defined as a sequence of zooms: $X_0 \circ\!\!-\!\!\bullet X_1 \circ\!\!-\!\!\bullet X_2 \circ\!\!-\!\!\bullet \ldots \circ\!\!-\!\!\bullet X_n$. This process is probably best understood by considering a simple example. The following three figures taken from Kock et al.'s paper depict a zoom complex extending from X_0 to X_5, where X_1 is and X_0 are copies of one another. Situated below each constellation are matching network diagrams taken from a paper by Steiner (2012). This shows, at each step in the zoom complex, how a constellation can be interpreted as a network (i.e. planar tree) with appropriately labelled vertices reading from left to right (see Figure G.7b).

The final two network diagrams depicted in Figure G.7c complete the sequence of networks associated with corresponding constellations in the opetopic set.

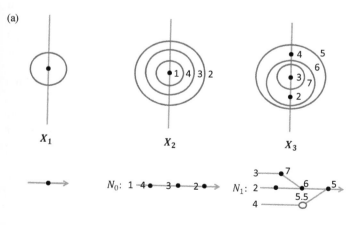

Figure G.7 (continued)

(continued)

(b)

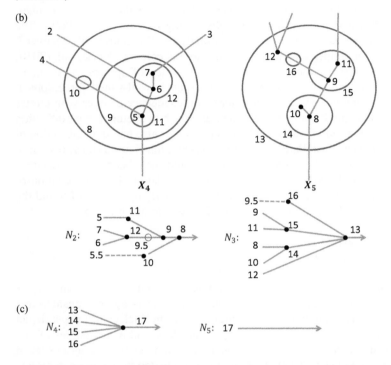

(c)

Figure G.7 An Opetope Represented as a Sequence of Trees and Networks

Source: Kock et al., 2012, Expl. 5.9.: 43-44; Steiner, 2012, Fig. 1.: 8; Fig. 2.: 9

The nested trees X_2, X_3, X_4, X_5 correspond to the networks N_0, N_1, N_2, N_3, with the empty circles 10 and 16 corresponding to the thin vertices 5.5 and 9.5 (i.e. every thin edge is an input edge and every thin vertex is the target for a unique edge, but this edge is not, itself, thin). Steiner (2012: 7, 9) notes that the trees X_0 and X_1 are redundant, because they must each have a single interior vertex and a single input edge while network N_5 is similarly redundant, because it must consist of a single edge, and the network N_4 is thus completely determined by N_3 and N_5.

Steiner (2012: 10) defines a *confluent* network as an acyclic network with a unique output edge such that each vertex is the source of exactly one edge and the target of at least one edge, before demonstrating that *every network in an opetopic sequence is confluent*. He goes on (Steiner, 2012: Th. 4.1; Th. 4.2.) to prove a general result showing that loop-free unital free augmented directed complexes generate families of networks.

Working with the CoqHTT Group at INRA, Eric Finster has developed software for diagrammatically manipulating a modified version of Baez and Dolan's (1997) opetopes for incorporation within theorem provers based on homotopy type theory (HTT).

PROPs: A 'PROP', which is an abbreviation of 'products and permutations category', is a symmetric monoidal category generated by a single object, used to describe a given sort of algebraic structure. They are more general than **operads** because they can be used to describe operations with many outputs as well as many inputs. Formally, an associative algebra is an operad, an operad is a $\frac{1}{2}$-PROP (half-PROP), a $\frac{1}{2}$-PROP is a dioperad and a dioperad induces a PROP (Johnson and Yau, 2015: Ch. 11).

For their part, Johnson and Yau (2015: xvii) demonstrate that operads, PROPs, and wheeled PROPs can all be described using collections of graphs that Markl (2008) has called 'pasting schemes'—consisting, respectively, of the level trees, the directed cycle-free graphs, and the directed graphs. In this approach, a basic graph consists of a partitioned finite set of flags equipped with an involution, so the partitions correspond to vertices, the flags correspond to half-edges, and the involution pairs two half-edges together to form edges (Johnson and Yau, 2015: xvii). Some additional structure must also be included to deal properly with exceptional graphs, which contain no vertices. A wheeled graph is then a basic graph together with three extra pieces of structure, called a direction, a colouring, and a listing. The listing is a new feature, introduced by Johnson and Yau (2015) so that the inputs or outputs of any vertex, or of the full graph, may be expressed as a (finite) ordered sequence of colours, which is vital to defining a key process they describe as graph substitution.

In principle, there should be a variant of PROPs associated to any reasonable pasting scheme: "By choosing the right pasting schemes, one can obtain colored versions of (wheeled) operads, (wheeled) properads, (wheeled) PROPs, dioperads, and half-PROPs, among others" (Johnson and Yau, 2015: xvii). Here, 'wheeled' PROP's were introduced by Sergei A. Merkulov, who deployed the construct of "wheels" to encode algebras equipped with traces.

Baez and Lauda (2006) explain that the adjunction holding between the category of PROPs and that of Algebraic Theories, say, hom(La,b) $\cong$ hom(a, Rb), is one that links Symmetric Monoidal Categories to Finite Product Categories. PROPs alone are viewed as special algebraic theories where no variable appears twice on the same side of any equation, and the same variables appear on both sides. For example, ($g \bullet h$) $\bullet k = g \bullet (h \bullet k)$ is acceptable, but $g \bullet g = g$ or $g \bullet h = g$ is not. In short, there can be no duplication or deletion of variables! The PROP for monoids C, however, can be thought of as a special algebraic theory LC in some category D with finite products. Baez and Lauda (2006: 52) note that these are the same as algebras of C in the underlying symmetric monoidal category RD of D (in fact, L and R are '2-functors' between 2-categories so the adjunction between them is a pseudo-adjunction). They further observe that L and R go between the 'classical' world of finite product categories (e.g. algebraic theories) and the 'quantum' world of symmetric monoidal categories (e.g. PROPs). Given a symmetric monoidal category C, the 'pseudo-monad' $M=RL$ throws in new morphisms, Δ_x: $x \rightarrow x \otimes x$, ε_x: $x \rightarrow I$, satisfying the conditions that make MC into a category with finite products (i.e. it is the pseudo-monad, M, that actually gives C the ability to duplicate and delete information) (Baez and Lauda, 2006: 53–54).

Johnson and Yau (2015) subsequently introduce and study a unifying object, called a generalized PROP for which the pertinent theory of pasting schemes now requires "a new definition of graph, a new description of graph substitution, a careful description of graph operations, a theory of generating sets for graph groupoids, and notions of intersections and free products of graph groupoids". In the second part of their comprehensive text, they work with an arbitrary symmetric monoidal (closed) category with enough limits and colimits to describe "the categorical properties of generalized PROPs along with their algebras and modules".

Quantum Groups: The characterization of operads, PROPs, and opetopes was given impetus by developments in quantum group theory over the last 30 years (for a very readable history of these developments see Baez and Lauda, 2009). This body of theory is grounded in efforts to achieve an integration between classical mechanics and quantum mechanics, but the title is somewhat misleading. Quantum groups arise as a certain kind of generalization of conventional groups. Downie (2012: 2) responds to the question of what this generalization means by observing that groups can be thought of as collections of transformations which act on other objects and quantum groups also possess this ability to act on structures. He also notes that groups have a strong affiliation with symmetries. Furthermore, while all transformations in a group are invertible (i.e. when a group is abelian the inverse map becomes an automorphism), this is not the case with quantum groups, which have a weaker version of an inverse mapping called an antipode and, unlike an inverse mapping, it is not required that the antipode applied to itself be the identity. Moreover, quantum groups can act on themselves in an adjoint representation and the antipode, like the inverse, provides a corresponding conjugate representation for every representation of a quantum group (Downie, 2012: 3). Representations of groups are known to admit a tensor product and this holds for representations of quantum groups as well. In addition, quantum groups are self-dual while Hopf algebras have the property that their dual linear spaces are also algebras.

> The actual name "quantum group" was coined by V. G. Drinfel'd in 1985 who, along with M. Jimbo, also did extensive work in the area of integrable systems. At first, quantum groups were understood to be associative algebras whose defining relations are expressed in terms of a matrix of constants known as a quantum R-matrix. Universal R-matrices are also attributed to Drinfel'd. In the same year, Drinfel'd and Jimbo independently observed that these algebras are really Hopf algebras.
>
> (Downie, 2012: 5)

This particular (quasi-triangular) variety of Hopf algebra results from deformations of universal enveloping algebras of Lie algebras as well as classical matrix groups (Downie, 2012: 6). In loose terms, a Lie group "is a topological group which is also a differential manifold, where the group operations respect the manifold's smooth structure". Due to the smoothness of the manifold, "one can think of the local structure as being linear" (Downie, 2012: 161). Because Lie groups are differential manifolds, there is an associated tangent space at each point of the manifold. Lie algebras can be thought of as tangent spaces of Lie groups at the identity element of the Lie group, which arises from the so-called Lie bracket. Downie (2012: 7) observes that "[t]hese deformations were originally intended to aid in the construction of solutions to the now famous Yang-Baxter equation" (which provide a starting point for the quantum inverse scattering method).

Although it is now believed that quantum groups "provide the necessary framework for solving the holy grail of physics, namely the unification of quantum mechanics with gravity", Downie (2012: 7) remarks that "they have also asserted their influence in such areas as category theory, representation theory, topology, analysis, combinatorics, non-commutative geometry, symplectic geometry and knot theory". Ross Street's 2007 text on the theory of quantum groups draws on Tannaka-Krein duality. Raedschelders (2013: 86) notes:

> Tannaka-Krein duality is the name given to a number of statements all related to reconstructing a specific type of algebraic structure from its category of representations, usually equipped with some additional data.

His thesis is one of the very few publications that explicitly examines the relationship holding between Koszul duality and Tannaka-Krein duality.

It may not always be easy to identify any direct relationship between the theory of quantum groups and pertinent industrial applications of semantic technologies (apart, that is, from the use of PROPs and operads to simplify and manipulate various network models. One pertinent example should serve as a demonstration that cases certainly do arise. Abe (1997) derives an equation for generalized entropy by applying the q-differential to the following deformation expression for the system, used in the theory of quantum groups:

$$[A]_q = \frac{q^A - q^{-A}}{q - q^{-1}}$$

Abe derives another more complex equation for generalized entropy by applying the q-differential to the above deformation expression for the system. He then shows that the resulting expression, which differs slightly from Tsallis entropy, nevertheless exhibits properties that can all be derived from those of Tsallis entropy alone. An extensive and regularly updated bibliography is available on papers relating to the theory of Tsallis entropy and a wide range of applications, including those in the fields of finance and economics. In the same way that the Gaussian distribution can be derived from Shannon entropy, the Student-t distribution (with around 4 degrees of freedom) can be derived using maximum entropy methods applied to Tsallis entropy. Significantly, the resulting asymptotic distribution is characterized by fat-tails and a narrow peak.

Representable Functors: A functor from a category C to the category of sets (a set-valued functor) is said to be representable if it is naturally isomorphic to a hom functor. A covariant functor is representable if it is naturally isomorphic to $\mathrm{Hom}(C,-)$ for some object C of C ; in this case one says that C represents the functor. A contravariant functor is representable if it is naturally isomorphic to $\mathrm{Hom}(-,C)$ for some object C (and then C represents the contravariant functor). For example the set-of-nodes functor for graphs is represented by the graph with one node and no arrows. Representable functors are a generalization of the regular representation in Group theory, and the Yoneda embedding is a generalization of Cayley's Theorem (Mac Lane and Moerdijk, 1992: 121).

The Subobject Functor: If C is an object of a category, a subobject of C is an equivalence class of monomorphisms $C_0 \rightarrowtail C$ where $f_0 : C_0 \rightarrowtail C$ is equivalent to $f_1 : C_1 \rightarrowtail C$ if and only if there are arrows necessarily isomorphisms: $g : C_0 \rightarrow C_1$ and $h : C_1 \rightarrow C_0$ such that $f_1 \circ g = f_0$ and $f_0 \circ h = f_1$ (Mac Lane and Moerdijk, 1992: 384).

A Topos: is a category which (Mac Lane and Moerdijk, 1992: 386):

1   has finite limits;
2   is Cartesian closed;
3   has a representable subobject functor.

A functor is *representable* if and only if it has a universal element.

Bibliography

Abe, S. (1997). A Note on the q-Deformation-Theoretic Aspect of the Generalized Entropies in Nonextensive Physics. *Physics Letters A*, 224: 326–330.

Baez, John C. and Jacob D. Biamonte (2012). A Course on Quantum Techniques for Stochastic Mechanics. arXiv:1209.3632v1 [quant-ph] 17 September 2012.

Baez, John C. and James Dolan (1997). Higher-dimensional Algebra III: n-Categories and the Algebra of Opetopes, e-print q-alg/9702014, 1997; also (1998). *Advances in Mathematics*, 135(2): 145–206.

Baez, J. C., J. Foley, J. Moeller, and B. Pollard (2017). Network Models. arXiv:1711.00037v1 [math.CT] 31 October 2017.

Baez, John C. and Aaron Lauda (2006). Universal Algebra and Diagrammatic Reasoning Course notes for Geometry of Computation, 30 January – 3 February. Available online at http://math.ucr.edu/home/baez/universal/.

Baez, John C. and Aaron Lauda (2009). A Prehistory of n-Categorical Physics. Accessed 5 February 2018. https://arxiv.org/abs/0908.2469.

Behrisch, M., S. Kerkhoff and J. Power (2012). Category Theoretic Understandings of Universal Algebra and Its Dual: Monads and Lawvere Theories, Comonads and What? *Electronic Notes in Theoretical Computer Science*, 286: 5–16.

Coecke, B. and E. Paquette (2011). Categories for the Practising Physicist. In B. Coecke (ed.), *New Structures for Physics*. Berlin: Springer, 173–286.

Crutwell, G. S. H. and M. A. Shulman (2010). A Unified Framework for Generalized Multicategories. arXiv:0907.2460v3 [math.CT] 9 December 2010.

Downie, R. W. (2012). An Introduction to the Theory of Quantum Groups. Master of Science in Mathematics Thesis, Eastern Washington University.

Ellerman, David (2006). A Theory of Adjoint Functors: With Some Thoughts about Their Philosophical Significance. In G. Sica (ed.), *What Is Category Theory?* Monza: Polimetrica.

Ellerman, David (unknown). Concrete Universals in Category Theory. Accessed 13 August 2010. www.ellerman.org/Davids-Stuff/Maths/Conc-Univ.pdf.

Finster, E. (n.d.). Opetopics Website. Accessed 26 January 2018. http://opetopic.net/.

Fiore, Marcelo and Tom Leinster (2010). An Abstract Characterization of Thompson's Group *F*. arXiv:math/0508617v2 [math.GR] 13 January 2010.

Johnson, Mark W. and Donald Ying Yau (2015). A Foundation for Props, Algebras, and Modules. AMS Mathematical Surveys and Monographs 203. Providence, RI: American Mathematical Society.

Kock, Joachim, André Joyal, Michael Batanin and Jean-François Mascari (2010). Polynomial Functors and Opetopes. arXiv:0706.1033v2 [math.QA] 21 February 2010.

Lawvere, William (1963). Functorial Semantics of Algebraic Theories. Ph.D. thesis, Columbia University. Published with an author's comment and a supplement in: *Reprints in Theory and Applications of Categories*, 5 (2004): 1–121.

Leinster, Tom (2003). Higher Operads, Higher Categories. arXiv:math/0305049v1 [math.CT] 2 May 2003. Pre-print version of Tom Leinster (2011). *Higher Operads, Higher Categories*. London Mathematical Society Lecture Notes Series. Cambridge: Cambridge University Press.

Loday, Jean-Louis and Bruno Valette (2012). Algebraic Operads. Version 0:999. Accessed 26 January 2018. www.math.univ-paris13.fr/~vallette/Operads.pdf.

Mac Lane, Saunders (1965). Categorical Algebra. *Bulletin of the American Mathematical Society*, 71: 40–106.

Mac Lane, S. and I. Moerdijk (1992). *Sheaves in Geometry and Logic: A First Introduction to Topos Theory*. New York, NY: Springer.

Markl, M. (2008). Operads and PROPs. *Handbook of Algebra*, 5: 87–140.

Markl, Martin, Steve Shnider and Jim Stasheff (2002). *Operads in Algebra, Topology and Physics*. Mathematical Surveys and Monographs, 96. Providence, RI: American Mathematical Society.

Marquis, Jean-Pierre (2009). *From a Geometrical Point of View: A Study of the History and Philosophy of Category Theory*. New York, NY: Springer.

Raedschelders, Theo (2013). Universal Bialgebras and Hopf Algebras Associated to Koszul Algebras. Master in Mathematics Thesis, Faculty of Science, Department of Mathematics, Vrije University, Brussels. Accessed 10 April 2018. http://we.vub.ac.be/sites/default/files/Thesis_Theo_Raedschelders.pdf.

Segal, G. (2004). The Definition of Conformal Field Theory: Topology, Geometry and Quantum Field Theory. London Mathematical Society Lecture Note Series, 308. Cambridge: Cambridge University Press, 421–577.

Spivak, D. I. (2013). The Operad of Wiring Diagrams: Formalizing a Graphical Language for Databases, Recursion, and Plug-and-Play Circuits. arXiv:1305.0297v1 [cs.DB] 1 May 2013.

Spivak, D. I. (2014). *Category Theory for the Sciences*. Cambridge, MA: MIT Press. Online (2013) *Category Theory for Scientists*. Accessed 10 April 2018. http://math.mit.edu/~dspivak/CT4S.pdf.

Steiner, Richard (2012). Opetopes and Chain Complexes. arXiv:1204.6723v2 [math.CT] 21 September 2012.

Street, Ross (2007). *Quantum Groups: A Path to Current Algebra*. Australian Mathematical Society Lecture Series, 19. Cambridge: Cambridge University Press.

Tsallis, Constantino (n.d.). Nonextensive Statistical Mechanics and Thermodynamics: Bibliography (last updated 28 January 2018). Accessed 31 January 2018. http://tsallis. cat.cbpf.br/TEMUCO.pdf.

Turi, Daniele (2001). Category Theory Lecture Notes. Accessed 10 April 2018. www.dcs. ed.ac.uk/home/dt/CT/categories.pdf.

Valette, B. (2012). Algebra + Homotopy = Operad. arXiv:1202.3245v1 [math.AT] 15 February 2012.

Yusufzai, Adeel Khan (2017). Entry on Lawvere Theories. Accessed 10 April 2018. https:// ncatlab.org/nlab/show/Lawvere+theory.

Index

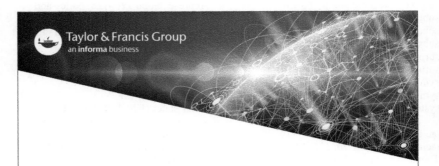

For Product Safety Concerns and Information please contact our EU
representative GPSR@taylorandfrancis.com
Taylor & Francis Verlag GmbH, Kaufingerstraße 24, 80331 München, Germany